2 Rue Big D fan

COWBOYS CHRONICLES

*A Complete History of
the Dallas Cowboys*

Marty Strasen

Merry
Merry
B-DAY
9-11-17

XXX's
and
NFTA connection

TRIUMPH
BOOKS

*To the late Carl M. Davidson, the greatest newspaper publisher,
gentleman, grandfather, and human being I have ever known*

Copyright © 2010 by Marty Strasen

No part of this publication may be reproduced, stored in a retrieval system, or transmitted in any form
by any means, electronic, mechanical, photocopying, or otherwise, without the prior written permission
of the publisher, Triumph Books, 542 South Dearborn Street, Suite 750, Chicago, Illinois 60605.

Triumph Books and colophon are registered trademarks of Random House, Inc.

Library of Congress Cataloging-in-Publication Data

Strasen, Marty.
  Cowboys chronicles / Marty Strasen.
      p. cm.
  Includes bibliographical references.
  ISBN 978-1-60078-349-4
  1. Dallas Cowboys (Football team)—History. I. Title.
  GV956.D3S765 2011
  796.332'63097642812—dc22
                    2010018726

This book is available in quantity at special discounts for your group or organization. For further infor-
mation, contact:

  Triumph Books
  542 South Dearborn Street
  Suite 750
  Chicago, Illinois 60605
  (312) 939–3330
  Fax (312) 663–3557
  www.triumphbooks.com

Printed in U.S.A.
ISBN: 978-1-60078-349-4
Design by Nick Panos
Page production by Patricia Frey

CONTENTS

FOREWORD

You love 'em. You hate 'em. But you've got to admit, you talk about them. They are the Dallas Cowboys, arguably the most successful franchise in the history of the National Football League. Unarguably, the most talked-about franchise. When any conversation hits one of those awkward lulls, just bring up the Cowboys because everyone, it seems, has an opinion.

As one who was lucky enough to play my entire career with that blue star on the side of my helmet at a position that gave me a unique and privileged view of the inner workings of the Cowboys Machine, I am honored to be a part of this book.

The Cowboys Machine was—and still is—one that is constantly changing, from owners to coaches to players to cheerleaders to front-office folks and stadiums. The only thing that doesn't change is the history. It's irrefutable, built on games and facts and feats. That's what this book is all about: No hype. No pretenses. Just facts.

I've always said that the value of playing quarterback for the Cowboys cannot be measured in dollars. It's the most visible position for the most visible team in sports. The lessons I learned during those years were invaluable. Most were not learned privately but with millions of eyewitnesses. NFL football is live television. Anyone who ever played quarterback at that level will tell you that there were many times when they would have given anything for a "take two," a "do-over," a "second chance." But that's one of the things that makes football great. There are no do-overs. As a result, the pressure to perform at a high level is extreme. That pressure can bring out the best and the worst in people. It is a valuable study in human behavior.

I benefited from one of the greatest teachers in the game and one of the greatest examples of how to be a professional on and off the field. Roger Staubach was a consummate professional on the field, just as he is in the business world and as a husband and father. I learned a lot just by watching him. Tom Landry was also an extraordinary teacher. He was a master of football, but he also taught life. One of the many famous quotes attributed to the great Vince Lombardi holds that, "Winning isn't everything; it's the only thing." Tom Landry was a Lombardi disciple, but he didn't believe that. He believed that there were far more important things than winning or football. His faith in God and love for his wife, Alicia, and their family came first. Faith. Family. Football. Those were his priorities.

As a coach, he was unsurpassed. One of his teachings was about timing as a quarterback. He would say over and over again that, as the decision-maker on the field, knowing *when* to do something was more important than knowing *what* to do or *why* to do it. I disagreed with him. I believed that if you knew *why* you did something, then you automatically knew *when* to do it, making *why* the most important of the three. I argued with him about it for years.

Then one fateful day in Texas Stadium, we were playing a big game against the Redskins (actually, every game against the Redskins was a big game). Leading by four, I called an audible on fourth-and-3 from midfield with a minute to go. Coach had told me to try to get them to jump offside with a hard snap count. If they didn't jump offside, we were to let the play clock run out, take a five-yard delay-of-game penalty, punt the ball, and let our defense win the game for us. However, I saw what I thought was an easy play to get the first down to clinch the game. So I audibled, "Green 36, Green 36." I'll never forget it. The defense stuffed the play. The Redskins took the ball, went down and scored, and we lost the game.

I told Coach Landry after the game to watch the film and that he would agree that he would have done the same thing I did. The headline in the *Dallas Morning News* the next day read, "NO DANNY NO!" I didn't know they could print letters that big! I sat in the coach's office after watching the film the next day, waiting for him. "Well, Coach," I said after he walked in. "You saw it. Wouldn't you have done the same thing I did?" I was red-faced and angry. He was calm and unruffled. He replied, "Dan, you're right. It was the perfect play to run against that defense. But I would not have done what you did because I know that the most important thing in a football game is not *what* you do or *why* you do it. It's *when* you do it."

His point was that even though that play had a 90 percent chance of success, as a quarterback, you don't take that 10 percent chance of failure with the game on the line in the final minute. It was a valuable lesson that I learned the hard way. Then, as I was leaving his office, he stopped me and said, "Dan, don't ever change the way you play football." He realized how badly I felt and also knew that there were a lot of times when that mentality had *won* games for us. Unfortunately, those didn't always make the front page of the *Dallas Morning News*, because they don't write stories about planes that land safely. He knew that one of the greatest causes of failure is the fear of failure and embarrassment, and he didn't want to destroy my confidence.

In classic Coach Landry fashion, he took me from being as low as I had ever been as a player and built me back up. *Two* lessons learned. Someone once asked me if the stoic Tom Landry ever smiled. I answered, "I don't know, I only played for him for 13 years." That's an exaggeration because he really did have a sense of humor, just a very dry one. But I will tell you something he really never did. In 13 years, I never heard him raise his voice. Think about that. It's an absolutely amazing statement to make about any coach at any level. He didn't need to. His players respected him so much that all he had to do was look at you and roll his eyes (Roger called it the "brook trout look"), and it was worse than running a million laps, paying a $1 million fine, or getting yelled at.

Those memories, those relationships, those lessons...they are the real value of my career, and they come flooding back to me as I read this book. It's a book every Cowboys fan—heck, every football fan, sports fan, or anyone related to a sports fan—should proudly display on the living-room coffee table or at least in the library or under the bed (that's you, Redskins fans).

Just imagine: your sister and her husband are over for dinner. After the dishes have been cleared, it begins...the obnoxious bragging from your brother-in-law, who claims to know everything that ever happened in any game ever played by the Cowboys. As the words, "Do you remember when Roger threw that pass to Drew in...," come out of his mouth his voice fades as you slowly get up and walk to the shelf. You return to the table, set this book down, and slide it across the table to him.

The next sound you hear is unmistakable: silence. It says it all. You have produced the most powerful know-it-all-brother-in-law-silencer ever invented for a situation like this: *Cowboys Chronicles*. The truth. The bible. "In the beginning was Clint Murchison. And he hired Tom Landry."

As his lower jaw slowly rejoins his upper, you turn his tears of embarrassment into tears of joy as you say, "That copy is yours." Euphoria. And victory. Nothing your brother-in-law can do for the rest of his life will top this. He owes you...forever.

So here it is—*Cowboys Chronicles*. Do you want to know what happened in the very first game the Cowboys ever played, or what happened the first time Landry played revolving quarterbacks with Staubach and Morton, or what happened in Tony Dorsett's first NFL game? It's in here. Care to delve into what went wrong during the most forgettable year in Cowboys history, 1989? Want to relive Troy Aikman's rise from the depths of his rookie year to the pinnacle of the game—a rise unequaled in NFL history? It's all in here, along with hundreds of other true stories and photos that comprise the great history of the Dallas Cowboys.

No Hollywood drama. No hearsay. Just facts. I hope you enjoy it as much as I have.

—Danny White

INTRODUCTION

Celebrating 50 Years of Cowboys Football

Go ahead. Debate the "America's Team" moniker all you'd like.

There are countless teams in numerous sports across this nation—hometown teams, national teams, teams with more than a century of tradition, and newer teams in fledgling markets working to make names for themselves.

The Dallas Cowboys are but one team among all those.

Over the past 50 years, though, the Cowboys have climbed to the upper echelon of professional sports franchises and set themselves apart in several ways. Their merchandise is consistently among the hottest selling at sporting goods stores across the land. Their fan base is one of the largest and most widespread on the globe. Tickets to their games, home and away, are among the most sought-after in sports, even in years when their play has fallen short of what their fans have come to expect.

America is a football-crazed country, and the Cowboys are one of the rare teams that fans either love, or love to hate. If America had an official cheerleading squad, it would be the Dallas Cowboys cheerleaders. If America invited international visitors to a sports stadium to showcase its passion for football, it might lead them to Cowboys Stadium and perhaps show highlights from five decades of Cowboys football on the world's largest HDTV.

America loves its sports heroes, and the Cowboys have provided more than their share. It doesn't get much more American than Roger Staubach, former

Navy quarterback, calling signals in a Super Bowl, or gentlemanly head coach Tom Landry patrolling the sideline wearing his trademark fedora.

Entering their 50th-anniversary season in 2010, no team in the National Football League can match the Cowboys' eight Super Bowl appearances. They have won five. The Cowboys have produced the leading rusher in NFL history in Emmitt Smith, the first defensive player to ever win the Super Bowl MVP Award in Chuck Howley, and some of the greatest legends in pro football history. The team's Ring of Honor is a shrine to American sports greatness.

So go ahead. Debate the "America's Team" thing. The fact that many fans would vehemently disagree with the nickname is, in some ways, a sign of the kind of passion—pro and con—the Dallas Cowboys can elicit.

The following pages document 50 years of Cowboys history. Fifty years of records and greats, glory and heartache. Fifty years of football for a star-helmeted team playing under a flag with 50 stars of its own. America's Team? Perhaps. To the fans, all that matters is that the Dallas Cowboys are *their* team.

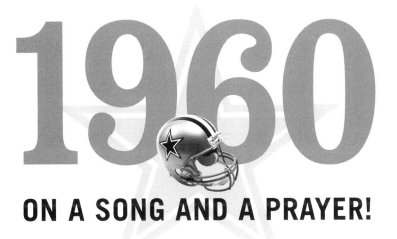

1960

ON A SONG AND A PRAYER!

Close Calls Highlight Cowboys First Season

With Washington Redskins owner George Marshall holding the cards on an NFL expansion franchise in the South and opposing a team in Dallas, Cowboys owner Clint Murchison stacked the deck. He purchased the rights to the Redskins' famous fight song and sold those rights to Marshall as a way to gain his agreement on the Cowboys. And so, a new team arrived in 1960.

The Cowboys' inaugural season featured one game against each of the 12 established teams, as Dallas was considered a "swing" club in its first year. The season also featured zero wins, but what did folks expect? They did play their first two foes and three of their first five to close games. A tie with the Giants in New York was the highlight.

GAME 1: Record Falls in Cowboys Debut

Pittsburgh 35 at Cowboys 28

September 24: Dallas made a strong bid for victory in its franchise debut before an estimated 30,000 fans on a Saturday night at the Cotton Bowl. Eddie LeBaron threw a 78-yard TD pass to Jim Doran to open the scoring as well as a seven-yard scoring strike to Fred Dugan later in the first quarter before the Steelers rallied behind a record-setting performance from QB Bobby Layne.

Layne became pro football's career passing yardage leader, overtaking Sammy Baugh, while throwing four TD passes. The veteran took his career yardage to 22,351 by game's end. LeBaron finished with three TD passes—two to Doran—and 348 aerial yards, but the Cowboys came up just short in their inaugural game. An era had begun.

GAME 2: Blocked PATs Lead to Loss

Philadelphia 27 at Cowboys 25

September 30: One of football's most routine plays, the extra-point kick, eluded the Cowboys, costing them an otherwise great chance at an initial NFL victory. The Eagles' Bobby Freeman blocked two—the margin of victory in this defensive battle.

Cowboys QB Eddie LeBaron threw for two TDs and ran for another but was intercepted five times. Chuck Weber picked off three of those passes. The visitors fared only slightly better through the air, as the Dallas defense made three interceptions. Fred Cone kicked 45- and 31-yard field goals for the Cowboys, but those PATs haunted him.

GAME 3: Road No Kinder to Cowboys

Washington 26 vs. Cowboys 14

October 9: Rain and the Redskins dampened the Cowboys' first NFL road game. It was also their first televised game, aired opposite a World Series outing. The visitors matched Washington with two TDs, but the Redskins received four field goals from Bob Khayat—no small feat at soggy Griffith Stadium—to boot Dallas to its third loss in as many games.

Eddie LeBaron was the offensive star for Dallas, passing for 275 yards, but it was his shortest completion that gave him a most historic distinction. His second scoring pass of the game, to Dick Bielski, came from the 2-inch line—half the distance of the previous NFL record for shortest TD pass, according to officials. Green Bay's Cecil Isbell had set the old mark in 1942.

GAME 4: Browns Dominate

Cleveland 48 at Cowboys 7

October 16: Bobby Mitchell, Jim Brown, and their Cleveland teammates steamrolled the Cowboys in the most lopsided loss of their inaugural season, churning out 200 rushing yards and swarming three different Dallas quarterbacks.

Paul Brown's veterans were simply too much for the NFL's newest entry. Mitchell scored three TDs, one on a 90-yard kickoff return, and the powerful Jim Brown added one score. Backup QB Don Heinrich threw a 41-yard TD toss to Billy Howton for Dallas' only points, but it came with the hosts trailing 48–0.

GAME 5: Late Kick Boots 'Boys

St. Louis 12 vs. Cowboys 10

October 23: With victory finally in their grasp, the Cowboys were heartbroken by an 18-yard field goal in the final minute. It came off the toe of 240-pounder Gerry Perry with 43 seconds on the Busch Stadium clock and gave the Cardinals the edge in a defensive scrum.

Dallas took a 3–0 lead on Fred Cone's field goal and regained the advantage 10–9 when L.G. Dupre reached the end zone from the 3-yard line in the final quarter. It was Dupre's subsequent fumble, however, that set up the winning kick for St. Louis and sent the run-deficient Cowboys to their fifth straight loss.

GAME 6: Champs Roll to Easy Win

Baltimore 45 at Cowboys 7

October 30: The two-time defending NFL champs were relentless and efficient in dismantling the Cowboys at the Cotton Bowl. The Colts limited Dallas to 147 offensive yards, racked up 493 of their own, intercepted two passes, and pounced on two fumbles in a game

that was delayed briefly as the teams scuffled near the stands in the final quarter.

It was a happy homecoming for former SMU receiver Raymond Berry, who caught TD passes of 58, 52, and 70 yards from the great Johnny Unitas. For the second time in three weeks, backup QB Don Heinrich's TD pass kept the Cowboys from being shut out.

GAME 7: Meredith Starts; Outcome Familiar

Los Angeles 38 at Cowboys 13

November 6: Don Meredith used to pack 'em in as a Southern Methodist star, but his initial start for Dallas was witnessed by only 16,000 fans at the Cotton Bowl, the smallest home crowd of the Cowboys' debut season. Meredith got rare support from a previously anemic running attack, as rookie fullback Walt Kowalczyk carried nine times for 91 yards and a score, but it was not enough to keep the Rams from their second win.

Meredith was 9-of-28 against a defense that blanketed his receivers and challenged the Cowboys to run.

GAME 8: Another Lopsided Loss

Green Bay 41 vs. Cowboys 7

November 13: Proving again that they were not yet ready to compete with the NFL's elite, the Cowboys made several errors in their first trip to Green Bay and succumbed to the Packers

Gene "Big Daddy" Lipscomb, defensive tackle for the Pittsburgh Steelers, goes after Dallas Cowboys quarterback Eddie LeBaron. (Photo by Robert Riger/Getty Images)

without drama. Dallas had two punts blocked and could not stop Jim Taylor from reaching the end zone three times for the NFL championship hopefuls.

Don Heinrich made his first start at QB for the Cowboys but went just 5-of-13 through the air against Ray Nitschke and the Packers defense. Don Meredith relieved Heinrich and threw a scoring pass to keep the visitors from being blanked before 32,294 fans, the largest crowd ever to witness a game in Green Bay.

GAME 9: Dallas Yields in Final Frame

San Francisco 26 at Cowboys 14

November 20: The Cowboys kept the 49ers out of the Cotton Bowl end zone until the fourth quarter in a strong bid for their first NFL victory, but the team fell short with the game on the line. Two fumbled kickoffs by the Cowboys in the final six minutes helped San Francisco erase a 14–9 deficit with 17 late points as Dallas lost its ninth in a row.

Coach Tom Landry decided to alternate quarterbacks for the first time, giving plays directly to Eddie LeBaron and Don Meredith and having them run into the huddle with them. Each threw a touchdown pass. However, LeBaron was also intercepted three times and Meredith once on a rainy afternoon.

GAME 10: Dallas Slump Reaches 10

Chicago 17 vs. Cowboys 7

November 27: The Cowboys matched a single-season NFL record by losing their 10th consecutive game—the 10th in their existence—but not before giving the Bears a battle at Wrigley Field in Chicago. In fact, Bears QB Ed Brown called the Dallas pass defense the best he had ever faced.

Still, that defense was not enough in a game in which Cowboys QB Eddie LeBaron suffered a rib injury that put Don Heinrich under center for most of the foggy afternoon. Heinrich completed a 64-yard TD pass to Don McIlhenny in the third quarter to make it a 14–7 game, but a late Bears field goal put the game out of reach. Dallas missed three field-goal attempts, two of which were blocked.

GAME 11: Tie Ends Losing Streak

Cowboys 31 at N.Y. Giants 31 (tie)

December 4: Tom Landry was cheered upon his return to New York, where he had served as a successful assistant coach for the Giants, and the Dallas coach then coaxed the best game yet from his new charges. It was not enough for a victory, but a dramatic tie against heavily favored New York sure felt like a win to a Dallas team that had lost the first 10 games of its existence.

A Yankee Stadium crowd of 55,033 saw the Cowboys rally from 14 points down and reach the 30-point mark for the first time. Eddie

A Star Is Born

Ladies and Gentlemen, the Dallas Cowboys

Arising star shone over the National Football League in 1960, and professional football has never been the same. It started routinely enough. For $600,000—66 times less than the cost of the giant scoreboard in Cowboys Stadium—oil mogul Clint Murchison Jr. purchased a 1960 expansion franchise that would rise to dominate pro football and become one of the most valuable and beloved sports teams on the planet. Who knew?

Murchison, investment partner Bedford Wynne, general manager Tex Schramm, and player personnel mastermind Gil Brandt made some shrewd decisions to nudge the NFL's 13th franchise toward success. They hired Giants assistant Tom Landry as the Cowboys' first head coach, a move that paid dividends for 20 years. They arranged to play their home games in the Cotton Bowl until they could build their own stadium, an arrangement that allowed them to focus more immediately on building a bevy of talented young players. And they promoted the team aggressively to a football-crazed fan base, one that grew from local to national as the Cowboys became successful.

Murchison loved football, and he also knew how to win on Wall Street. "Dad once gave me a great piece of advice," he told *Time* magazine of Clint Sr. in 1961. "He said, 'Money is like manure. If you spread it around, it does a lot of good. But if you pile it up in one place, it stinks like hell.'"[1]

The Cowboys were born to win football games, but they were also born to be profitable, or they would not have been in Murchison's portfolio. When they missed the chance to select top college players in their first

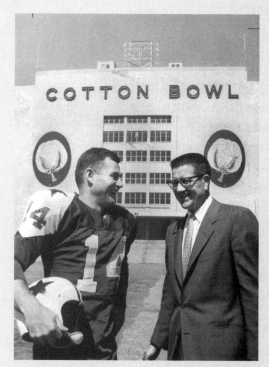

At the entrance to the Cotton Bowl are Dallas Cowboys quarterback Eddie LeBaron (left) with Clint Murchison Jr. (right) in 1961. (Photo by Ralph Crane/Time Life Pictures/Getty Images)

season because they were purchased after the NFL Draft and failed to win a game in their first year, the front office kept the faith. When they earned their first victory in 1961, they toasted success. And by the time they made the playoffs in 1966 with a winning season at 10–3–1, they were poised to remain contenders for a long, long time.

The Cotton Bowl served its purpose, but in 1971 the team moved into Texas Stadium in Irving, another Murchison success story. "One of his greatest satisfactions besides the Cowboys was Texas Stadium," said longtime friend and associate John D. O'Connell.[2]

By the time Murchison sold the Cowboys in 1984, they were worth $60 million. He had presided, in a largely hands-off manner that allowed his talented employees to utilize their skills, over five Super Bowl appearances, two championships, and a victory rate well over 60 percent.

A star was born in 1960—a blue one on a silver helmet. And it would become one of the most followed stars in sports.

LeBaron threw three TD passes—two to L.G. Dupre—and Dupre also ran for a score. LeBaron's final scoring strike found Billy Howton with 2:37 on the game clock, and Fred Cone's fourth extra-point kick of the game secured the deadlock.

Giants fans booed their team as it left the field, while the Cowboys left with their heads held high, still in search of their first NFL triumph.

GAME 12: Winless Season Ends in Detroit

Detroit 23 vs. Cowboys 14

December 11: Dallas closed its first NFL season on a frigid day in Detroit, its hopes for a victory remaining on ice. The Cowboys completed a winless initial campaign when Lions running back Nick Pietrosante ran for two long second-quarter TDs, essentially putting the game out of reach.

Dallas QB Eddie LeBaron, doubling as the punter because Dave Sherer was called to train with his National Guard unit, kept a TD drive alive when he picked up a first down on a fake boot. A hard hit on LeBaron in the fourth quarter sent mild-mannered Coach Tom Landry racing onto the field in protest, earning the Cowboys a 15-yard penalty. LeBaron threw his 12th TD pass of the season, and L.G. Dupre ran for a score.

1961
WINNER'S CIRCLE

Second Season Starts with Back-to-Back Wins

Fifty-six seconds to respectability. Okay, perhaps it took a bit longer than that for the Cowboys to truly become a factor in the NFL. But by scoring 10 points in the final 54 ticks of the clock in a season opener against Pittsburgh, Dallas got one in the win column for the first of what would become several hundred...and counting.

A pair of Dons emerged in 1961—Meredith and Perkins. The former started at QB for half the season, threw nine TD passes, and also ran for a score, while the latter rushed for 815 yards. Three more victories followed the opener, as Dallas became a team the NFL could no longer take lightly.

GAME 1: Miracle Finish Provides First NFL Win

Cowboys 27 vs. Pittsburgh 24

September 17: Dallas' first victory was the stuff of happy-ending, hold-your-breath Hollywood scripts. The Cowboys scored 10 points in the final minute of the game to stun the Steelers and send a Cotton Bowl crowd of 23,500 celebrating the first win in franchise history. If the game itself was a thriller—and it was—the last minute was legendary.

Eddie LeBaron, who took over at QB for Don Meredith, passed the Cowboys to a game-tying, 75-yard drive that culminated with a 17-yard TD pass to Dick Bielski with 54 seconds remaining. If Dallas could hold off record-setting passer Bobby Layne—a daunting task—for less than a minute, it could secure a satisfying tie.

The Cowboys fared even better, thanks to Jerry Tubbs' interception of Layne at the Cowboys' 38-yard line with five seconds left. LeBaron then heaved one to Bill Howton, who stepped out of bounds at the Pittsburgh 22. To the chagrin of the Steelers, one second remained on the clock. That was enough time for rookie Allen Green, who had missed two field goals and had a punt blocked earlier in the game, to connect on the winning field goal from the 27.

The Cowboys, at last, had a mark in the victory column.

GAME 2: From Win to Winning Streak

Cowboys 21 vs. Minnesota 7

September 24: Fresh off their first-ever victory, the Cowboys hosted the expansion Vikings and played the role of favorites for once. It suited them nicely, thanks to the legs of Don Perkins.

The Dallas halfback set club records with a 47-yard gallop and 108 total rushing yards amassed on 17 totes. He also caught a team-high five passes for 61 yards as the hosts put up the first 14 points and were never headed. While Perkins gobbled up the yardage in a balanced attack, rookie fullback Amos Marsh scored a pair of touchdowns. The Cowboys' 208 rushing yards broke the previous team record by 44 yards.

GAME 3: Back to Reality

Cleveland 25 vs. Cowboys 7

October 1: The big, bad Browns were tough enough to beat without fumbles, interceptions, penalties, and botched field goals. The Cowboys participated liberally in each of those miscues, and the result was a lopsided loss on a rainy day in Northern Ohio.

Jim Brown and Cleveland rumbled to a 15–0 halftime lead and kept the Cowboys off the scoreboard until the fourth quarter. Don Meredith's seven-yard pass to Don Perkins provided the lone Dallas TD.

A preseason photo of Bill Howton in the summer of 1961. (AP Images)

GAME 4: First Place After Four Games

Cowboys 28 at Minnesota 0

October 8: If anything was clear after four games of the Cowboys' second campaign, it's that the team had found its comfort zone. It came every time Dallas played first-year Minnesota.

The first shutout in Dallas history started when Minnesota fumbled the opening kickoff, setting up a TD pass from Don Meredith to Bill Howton. The rout was on. Meredith and Eddie LeBaron shuffled plays in at the QB position for most of the day, producing one TD in each quarter—all on drives between 50 and 60 yards.

Dallas finished the afternoon at Metropolitan Stadium 3–1 and in a four-way tie for first place in the East. If only the Vikings could appear more regularly on the schedule.

GAME 5: No Repeat of Giants Magic

N.Y. Giants 31 at Cowboys 10

October 15: The highlight of their inaugural season came when the Cowboys matched the Giants' 31 points in New York, producing a thrilling tie. Before the rematch, New York vowed the result would be different, then made sure its 31 points were more than enough to make good on that prediction.

In a game that featured six turnovers by each team, it was the Giants who made the most of their big plays. Dallas, trailing 17–10, was threatening to score a tying TD when New York's Erich Barnes intercepted an Eddie LeBaron pass in the end zone and raced the length of the field for the TD that turned a tight game into a comfortable win.

More than 42,000 fans turned out at the Cotton Bowl, the largest home crowd to witness a Cowboys game.

GAME 6: Beasts of the East Rise Up

Philadelphia 43 at Cowboys 7

October 22: Having spent the early weeks of the season tied for first place with the Cowboys, among others, the defending NFL champion Eagles spread their wings and soared to an easy win at the Cotton Bowl. Philly QB Sonny Jurgensen was 10-of-15 for 154 yards passing and watched his impressive fleet of running backs rip through the Cowboys for 289 yards on the ground before 25,000 patrons.

J.W. Lockett caught Don Meredith's five-yard TD pass for the only Dallas score of the day. By then, the visitors had scored 22 points and secured their place atop the Eastern standings.

GAME 7: Vengeance is Sweet in Big Apple

Cowboys 17 at N.Y. Giants 16

October 29: Two weeks after falling to the Giants by 21 points, the Cowboys—two-touchdown underdogs—raced to a big lead,

Bigger Than Texas
Tex Schramm Built America's Team and Changed the NFL

If any man was destined to head the expansion Dallas Cowboys, it was Tex Schramm—despite the fact he was raised in California. Named after his father, Texas Sr., and a graduate of the University of Texas, Schramm served as the Los Angeles Rams' general manager from 1947 to '56. Three years later, he hungered to oversee the Dallas franchise.

"I'd always wanted, as far back as I can remember, to take a team from scratch and build it," he said. "This was an opportunity I couldn't pass up—even though we didn't have a team at the time I was hired."[1]

That's right. Clint Murchison hired Schramm as GM in 1959 before Dallas was even awarded a franchise. Once the team was a go, Tex hired the two men who would mastermind the Cowboys' dynasty—Gil Brandt as personnel director and Tom Landry as head coach.

While Brandt and Landry built a winner, Schramm infused excitement into the team. He brought Cowboys games to Thanksgiving Day, launched the first club-owned weekly newspaper, unveiled the Dallas Cowboys Cheerleaders, and created the Cowboys Ring of Honor. By taking advantage of computer technology, he improved the Cowboys' scouting system.

Moreover, many of Schramm's Draft Day trades turned out to be bonanzas, such as those for Bob Lilly, Ed "Too Tall" Jones, and Randy White. And he was the guy who plucked Chuck Howley out of the gas station business and resurrected his career.

Schramm, who as Rams GM had hired Pete Rozelle as the team's public relations director, wielded enormous league power once Rozelle became commissioner. Schramm helped coordinate the NFL-AFL merger, and he chaired the NFL Competition Committee for 23 years. Tex was a driving force behind the following innovations:

A portrait of Dallas Cowboys General Manager Tex Schramm in 1981. Schramm was the Cowboys president and general manager from 1960 to 1989. (Photo by J. Kamin-Oncea/Getty Images)

- sudden-death overtime
- the 30-second clock
- a microphone for the head referee during penalty announcements

> • moving the hash marks closer to the middle of the field to stimulate more offense
> • a six-division, wild-card playoff system
> • the NFL Scouting Combine
> • instant replay
>
> Most of all, fans will remember Schramm for overseeing a generation of exciting Cowboys football. From 1966–85, his team finished with a winning record every season, made the play-offs 18 times, and played in five Super Bowls. Schramm resigned as GM in 1989 shortly after Tom Landry was let go. Two years later, he was inducted into the Pro Football Hall of Fame.

surrendered it, then stunned the New Yorkers on a 32-yard field goal by Allen Green with slightly more than one minute to play. A hot rivalry was burgeoning between Dallas coach Tom Landry's former and current teams.

More than 60,000 New York fans turned out to celebrate Kyle Rote Day, but it was the visitors who raced to a 14–0 lead on two Eddie LeBaron TD passes. Rote played a strong game for the Giants, who scored the next 16 points to take a late advantage, but Green overcame an earlier blocked field goal to boot the winner and propel the surprising Cowboys to their fourth win in seven starts.

GAME 8: Miscues Lead to Defeat

St. Louis 31 at Cowboys 17

November 5: Dallas was learning the hard way that giving up the football also relinquishes a team's chance to win. The Cowboys threw five interceptions, two of which were returned for scores by the speedy Billy Stacy within a three-minute stretch of the second quarter. Those runbacks gave the visitors a three-TD lead that rendered the remainder of the game a battle to set the final score of the Cowboys' fourth loss.

Eddie LeBaron hit Frank Clarke for two second-half TDs, but they were not enough to overcome his earlier misfires. Both teams finished the game with 4–4 records.

GAME 9: Steelers Bite Back

Pittsburgh 37 vs. Cowboys 7

November 12: Victims of the Cowboys' milestone first victory in the season opener, the Pittsburgh Steelers were not about to let lightning strike twice. Looking like a different team at Forbes Field, the Steelers made sure the rematch would not hinge on any late-game heroics, taking control early and never relenting.

Pittsburgh totaled 371 yards of offense and added another 112 on two interception returns. Neither Don Meredith nor Eddie LeBaron could solve the Steelers' defense for a Dallas team that managed just 122 offensive yards. Don Perkins ran for the lone Cowboys score.

GAME 10: Wild Day Ends in Deadlock

Cowboys 28 vs. Washington 28 (tie)

November 19: The Cowboys rallied from a two-touchdown deficit and had a chance to win in the final minute before settling for a home tie against the struggling Redskins. It was not nearly as satisfying as Dallas' first tie—a 31-all split with the Giants late the previous season—but given that the Cowboys had once trailed 21–7, they couldn't be too disappointed.

QBs Don Meredith and Eddie LeBaron each led long Dallas TD drives, but Redskins rookie Norman Snead was even better, completing 16-of-23 passes for 234 yards and a TD. Dallas marched into Washington territory in search of the winning points in the final minute. With regular kicker Allen Green injured, however, the Cowboys tried to move closer to the goal line for end Dick Bielski's foot, but they lost the ball on downs.

GAME 11: Eagles Fly Again

Philadelphia 35 vs. Cowboys 13

November 26: Backup kicker Dick Bielski opened the scoring at Franklin Field with a 42-yard field goal, and it looked like the Cowboys might just give the defending champs a battle before 60,000-plus fans. It was a fleeting feeling, to be sure.

The next four scores came on Sonny Jurgensen TD passes—two to Tommy McDonald—and there was no further doubt about the outcome. The Eagles racked up 337 aerial yards to the Cowboys' 240. Amos Marsh scored the only Dallas TD late in the contest.

GAME 12: Browns Too Much

Cleveland 38 at Cowboys 17

December 3: The Cowboys' Don Perkins outrushed the great Jim Brown, but Brown's Cleveland team was much stronger as Dallas closed the home portion of its season with a loss before a light Cotton Bowl crowd. Perkins rushed 20 times for 123 yards—37 more than Brown managed. However, the Browns' Bobby Mitchell sprinted for 140 yards on just 12 carries as the visitors took an early lead and never looked back.

Cleveland scored TDs on two fumble returns in the opening six minutes to take command of the game before ever taking an offensive snap. Eddie LeBaron passed for 202 yards and two TDs for the Cowboys, but he was also intercepted three times.

GAME 13: Cardinals' Magic Number: 31

St. Louis 31 vs. Cowboys 13

December 10: For the second time in as many meetings, St. Louis scored 31 points against Dallas. This time, the Cardinals scored those points consecutively, overcoming a 13–0 deficit on a cold day at Busch Stadium.

Dick Bielski kicked two first-quarter field goals and Don Perkins scored on a two-yard run to give the Cowboys the early advantage. Despite Perkins' 110 rushing yards in the game, however, Dallas did not have enough defense to keep the Cardinals from responding or enough offense to keep up with the onslaught. St. Louis QB Sam Etcheverry, the Canadian League import, threw for 260 yards to ignite the comeback.

GAME 14: Redskins Find Team They Can Beat

Washington 34 vs. Cowboys 24

December 17: After 23 games without a regular-season victory—a skid that began after a win over the Cowboys 14 months earlier—Washington upended Dallas again to end its embarrassing run. It did so behind Dick James' club-record four TDs and 146 rushing yards.

And so a season that began with such promise ended with a seven-game winless streak for the Cowboys. They failed to reach the end zone until the third quarter against the Redskins, who took a 14–3 lead. Eddie LeBaron hit Frank Clarke with two long TD passes in the third quarter to spark the Dallas attack.

1962

OFFENSE EMERGES

Cowboys Become Potent in a Hurry

How explosive had Dallas become in just its third season? When Amos Marsh raced 101 yards with a kickoff and Mike Gaechter returned an interception 100 yards for TDs in a win over the Eagles, it marked the first time in NFL history a team made two 100-yard plays in the same game...and the Cowboys did it in one quarter!

On offense, Dallas was even better. It fielded the second-ranked scoring attack and second-ranked yardage offense in the NFL. Don Meredith and Eddie LeBaron again split QB duties, and Frank Clarke became the first 1,000-yard receiver in team history. The defense would need some time to catch up, but the Cowboys were establishing their identity in a 5–8–1 campaign.

GAME 1: High Hopes Shot Down Early

Cowboys 35 vs. Washington 35 (tie)

September 16: Failing to beat the Redskins for the fourth time in as many meetings proved to be a frustrating start for the Cowboys. They outgained Washington and had a chance to win on a last-second field goal that sailed just wide. In the end, a sparse Cotton Bowl crowd returned home with no victor having been crowned.

However, the fans did witness a dazzling performance by Frank Clarke. The Dallas wingback caught 10 passes for 241 yards and three TDs on a sweltering afternoon that saw the Cowboys' alternating QBs Don Meredith and Eddie LeBaron pass for 341 yards. LeBaron led Dallas toward a potential winning boot, but Sam Baker missed from 35 yards.

GAME 2: Controversial Safety Makes the Difference

Pittsburgh 30 at Cowboys 28

September 23: Coach Tom Landry was not aware of the rule, nor, it seemed, was anyone in the Cotton Bowl stands. A safety is awarded when a team commits a penalty in its own end zone and the spotting of the ball would place it behind the goal line. Dallas gave up two points in that manner in the third quarter, and those points proved to be the final margin of defeat against the Steelers.

Landry argued and 19,000-plus fans booed lustily, having seen the penalty nullify an apparent 99-yard TD pass from Eddie LeBaron to Frank Clarke. The rulebook supported the call, however, and Pittsburgh made it a memorable afternoon in the record books, as well. On a day that saw each team produce four converted TDs, Steelers QB Bobby Layne threw his 188th career TD pass, setting an NFL record.

GAME 3: Dallas Pulls Off Western Upset

Cowboys 27 at Los Angeles 17

September 30: After two close calls, the Cowboys secured their first victory of the season in unlikely fashion—as 11-point underdogs against the Rams at Los Angeles Memorial Coliseum. The convincing triumph ended a nine-game winless streak dating to the previous season.

Don Perkins, Amos Marsh, and Frank Clarke scored TDs for Dallas, which raced to leads of 17–3 and 24–10 and played superior defense against QBs Zeke Bratkowski and Roman Gabriel. Clarke's score came on an 85-yard reception from Eddie LeBaron.

GAME 4: Still No Answer for Browns

Cleveland 19 vs. Cowboys 10

October 7: After suffering blowout losses to the Browns in each of their previous meetings, the Cowboys were getting closer to the Eastern power. Still, Cleveland found a way to prevail. On Lou Groza Day along the shores of Lake

Erie, the legendary Browns kicker booted 35- and 42-yard field goals, and Jim Brown broke a 10–10 fourth-quarter tie on a 50-yard TD catch and run.

For the Cowboys, Don Meredith replaced Eddie LeBaron at QB after halftime and directed the team's only TD drive. His 43-yard pass to Frank Clarke in the third quarter tied the score, but Cleveland's defense shut out the visitors the rest of the way.

GAME 5: Dallas Breaks Out

Cowboys 41 vs. Philadelphia 19

October 14: Whether or not turnabout is fair play, it sure felt good to the Cowboys on this October day in the Cotton Bowl. The last time the Eagles visited, they routed Dallas 43–7. This time, it was Philadelphia tasting humiliation.

Amos Marsh returned a kickoff 101 yards and Mike Gaechter ran back an interception 100 yards for the longest TDs of the day. Dallas also dominated from more conventional scoring range, as Frank Clarke caught four passes for 118 yards and two TDs. Eddie LeBaron alternated with Don Meredith at QB and was a perfect 7-for-7 passing.

GAME 6: Offense Catches Fire

Cowboys 42 at Pittsburgh 27

October 21: One week after topping 40 points for the first time in franchise history, Dallas did it again. It wasn't just the offense, either. The Cowboys got big plays from their defense and did the better job of capitalizing on miscues to attain their highest-ever point total, thereby winning back-to-back games.

Eddie LeBaron led the attack with five TD passes, including three in the second half. Though Dallas never trailed after breaking a 7–7 tie early in the game, the Steelers clawed within 28–27 in the second half before LeBaron and the Cowboys took control. Don Bishop led the Dallas "D" with two interceptions and a blocked field-goal attempt.

GAME 7: Cardinals Strike Early, Hold On

St. Louis 28 at Cowboys 24

October 28: On their first snap from scrimmage, the visiting Cardinals produced an 86-yard TD pass from Charlie Johnson to Sonny Randle. If a cold rain didn't dampen the spirits of 16,027 Cotton Bowl patrons, that play surely did, as St. Louis maintained its mastery of the Cowboys.

After scoring 83 points in its previous two games, Dallas was not nearly as sharp in a contest plagued by turnovers, miscues, and dreary weather. The Cowboys led 10–7 in the second quarter but found themselves trying to rally from a 28–17 hole late in the game. They reached the St. Louis 9-yard line with 31 seconds to play, but QBs Eddie LeBaron and Don Meredith were thrown for losses on back-to-back plays and the clock expired.

The New York Giants defeated the Cowboys twice in 1962. (Photo by Ralph Morse/Time Life Pictures/Getty Images)

GAME 8: Breakthrough Against 'Skins

Cowboys 38 at Washington 10

November 4: On four previous occasions, the Cowboys had faced the struggling Redskins without a victory. With nearly 50,000 people packing D.C. Stadium—the largest crowd ever to witness a Washington sporting event—that slump came to a convincing halt.

It was the defense that did the job. The Cowboys chased QB Norm Snead from the game, causing the Redskins to turn to backup Galen Hall. Dallas broke open a 3–3 game with 35 straight points while keeping Washington out of the end zone until 11 seconds remained. Don Meredith threw two Cowboys TD passes, and Amos Marsh rushed for 109 yards on just 10 carries.

GAME 9: Cowboys Humiliated at Home

N.Y. Giants 41 at Cowboys 10

November 11: The Cowboys attracted their largest crowd by far—more than 45,000 strong—to the Cotton Bowl for this much-

"Chiseled from Granite"
The Stoic Tom Landry Led Dallas to Three Decades of Glory

Don Rickles, the cut-up comedian, once took aim at Tom Landry. "There's 70,000 people going bananas, and there's Tom Landry on the sideline trying to keep his hat on straight," Rickles snipped. "Once, he got into a grinning contest with Mt. Rushmore, and Mt. Rushmore won!"

His joke might have elicited big laughs in New York and L.A., but in Texas Rickles would have faced stone silence. In the Lone Star State, Tom Landry was the most revered figure since Sam Houston. For 29 years, Landry walked stoically along the sidelines in his suit and trademark fedora. He hardly ever cracked a smile or lost his cool. He was in charge and in control, and the players on both teams knew it.

"He looked like he was chiseled from granite," said longtime NFL head coach Mike Holmgren. "He had the hat, he was always dapper, and had a very impressive demeanor.... I think the ability to think analytically and calmly on the sideline is hugely important. It showed me tremendous self-discipline."[1]

Born in Mission, Texas, Landry served as a bomber pilot during World War II. He flew 30 missions and was lucky to survive—he crash-landed in Belgium and lived to tell the tale.

With his military experience, keen intelligence (he holds a degree in industrial engineering), and All-Pro career as an NFL defensive back, Landry had just the right résumé to become an NFL coach. He shined as an assistant with the New York Giants before the Cowboys tapped him to be their first-ever head coach in 1960. He held the position for 29 years, posting a career record of 280–178–6, including playoffs. Landry won 13 division titles, coached five Super Bowl teams, and ran off 20 consecutive winning seasons (1966–85)—still the best mark in NFL history.

Landry was an innovative genius on both sides of the ball. He created the flex defense

Cowboys head coach Tom Landry during a game against the Washington Redskins on December 13, 1987, in Washington, D.C. (Photo by Ronald C. Modra/Sports Imagery/Getty Images)

and brought the shotgun formation into vogue. When other teams began to mimic the flex defense, he thought up ways for his offense to exploit their flex.

Devoutly religious and a man of unquestioned character, Landry commanded unparalleled respect. He was such a stickler for discipline that he once gave Cowboys running back Dan Reeves a tongue-lashing because he had dared to speak in the huddle. When Landry oversaw practice from the top of his 30-foot tower, players looked up to him and saw a man larger than life. It was a fitting image.

hyped game against the Giants. But most fans left scratching their heads, wondering how they could have better spent their hard-earned cash. They did get to see a terrific performance, but it came from 36-year-old Giants QB Y.A. Tittle, a future Hall of Famer who went 20-of-29, passing for 315 yards and three scores.

Dallas had no answer in a game in which Eddie LeBaron and Frank Clarke suffered injuries. Don Meredith's six-yard TD pass to Bill Howton into the teeth of a 30-mph wind was one of the rare bright spots for the home team.

A missed extra point—the Cowboys' first PAT miss since their inaugural 1960 season— proved to be the difference. It came after the first Dallas TD early in the second quarter. Johnny Morris caught 10 passes for 207 yards to lead the Bears, while Mike Ditka collected seven aerials for 133. Don Meredith threw three TD passes to spark the Cowboys, while Amos Bullocks dashed 73 yards for a score that handed Dallas a seemingly commanding 33–24 lead with nine minutes remaining before LeClerk's field goal.

GAME 10: Bears Win Wild One

Chicago 34 at Cowboys 33

November 18: One week after a record crowd saw the Cowboys lay an egg against the Giants, a mere 12,692 showed up at the Cotton Bowl for a downright wacky tussle with the Bears. Despite a gaudy 466 passing yards from veteran QB Bill Wade, Chicago needed Roger LeClerc's 15-yard field goal with 31 seconds remaining to earn the conquest.

GAME 11: Dallas Limps to Third Straight Loss

Philadelphia 28 vs. Cowboys 14

November 25: Without injured stars Eddie LeBaron and Frank Clarke, the Cowboys allowed the Eagles to right themselves before more than 58,000 fans in Philadelphia. Sonny Jurgensen and Tommy McDonald sparked Philadelphia to a 17–0 lead, and from there the hosts cruised to their first victory since September.

Amos Marsh rushed for both Dallas TDs. QB Don Meredith, filling in for the injured LeBaron, got off to a shaky start but settled in to coax the Cowboys within 21–14 in the third quarter. It was not enough as Dallas dropped its third straight game.

GAME 12: Finally the Browns Go Down

Cowboys 45 vs. Cleveland 21

December 2: Paul Brown. Jim Brown. Cleveland Browns. Any and all of them. Ohio's NFL franchise continually left the Cowboys feeling blue by winning the first four meetings between the clubs by a combined 89 points. In this final home game of the 1962 season, the roles reversed.

Playing perhaps the best all-around game in their history, the Cowboys dominated from start to finish. Don Meredith attempted just five passes in the first half and completed all of them, including scoring strikes to Frank Clarke and Lee Folkins. Eddie LeBaron returned under center from an injury, Don Perkins and Amos Marsh provided strong running, and the Dallas defense clamped down on an offense that had caused fits in previous matchups.

GAME 13: Letdown in Missouri

St. Louis 52 vs. Cowboys 20

December 9: One week after perhaps their most impressive victory, the Cowboys froze in St. Louis. Dallas took a 20–14 halftime lead, before a mere 14,000 brave Missourians huddled together in the stands on a bitter day, only to surrender 38 unanswered points in a humiliating second half.

Charley Johnson threw five TD passes for the Cardinals, including two covering more than 70 yards, on a 302-yard passing day. Defensive back Jerry Norton got Dallas on the scoreboard when he caught a short field-goal attempt and returned it 94 yards for a TD. After building the halftime cushion, however, the Cowboys managed just 13 offensive yards in the second half.

GAME 14: Outscored in New York

N.Y. Giants 41 vs. Cowboys 31

December 16: Though they stood much taller in Yankee Stadium than they did against these same Giants one month earlier in Dallas, the Cowboys still failed to solve the problem of quarterback Y.A. Tittle. The veteran fired six TD passes, helping the Giants set an NFL season record. It was an impressive offensive tune-up for New York's NFL championship game clash with Green Bay.

Dallas, meanwhile, put up a fight this time. The visitors had two late scoring opportunities after pulling within 35–31, but the team failed to convert them. Don Meredith connected with Bill Howton twice for TDs for the Cowboys, who finished their third NFL season one game better than they did their second.

1963

THE ONLY TEAM IN TOWN

Texans' Departure Gives Cowboys Key to the City

Truth be told, no one in the NFL gave AFL franchises much respect before Joe Namath and the Jets changed the course of history in Super Bowl III. In 1963, years before the Super Bowl was a thought in anyone's head, the Cowboys took a monopoly hold on Dallas pro football fans when the AFL's Dallas Texans moved to Kansas City.

To celebrate, the Cowboys went out and lost four in a row to open the season. It was the start of a disappointing 4–10 slate in which the club struggled on both sides of scrimmage. Coach Tom Landry installed Don Meredith as his full-time starting QB, setting the stage for future success.

One Cowboy also set an NFL record in 1963. In the third game, Billy Howton broke Don Huston's career record for receiving yardage, becoming the first player in history to reach the 8,000-yard plateau.

GAME 1: Big Crowd, Little Reason to Cheer

St. Louis 34 at Cowboys 7

September 14: The largest crowd to witness a Dallas home opener—more than 36,000—remained largely silent as the Cowboys succumbed to the Cardinals. Jimmy Hill returned an interception 58 yards for a St. Louis TD with less than a minute left in the first half. The Cardinals added a field goal before the break, taking a 20–7 lead and all the momentum.

Don Meredith's 15-yard TD pass to Pettis Norman opened the game's scoring, but the Cowboys were blanked the rest of the way.

GAME 2: Brown, Browns Run Wild

Cleveland 41 at Cowboys 24

September 22: The great Jim Brown enjoyed the third-most productive rushing day of his seven-year career on a warm afternoon at the Cotton Bowl, flattening Dallas defenders on his way to 232 rushing yards. The strong, swift back burst for scores of 71 and 62 yards, the former giving the Browns a comfortable second-quarter cushion from which Dallas never recovered.

Brown needed just 20 carries to amass his yardage total, averaging more than 11.5 yards per carry. The Cowboys, meanwhile, spent the day playing catch-up. Don Perkins carried 22 times for 59 yards and two of Dallas' three TDs.

GAME 3: Howton's NFL Record Can't Save Dallas

Washington 21 vs. Cowboys 17

September 29: Even in a loss, it was a big day for Dallas at D.C. Stadium. Billy Howton broke Don Huston's NFL record for career reception yardage and became the first player to top the 8,000-yard mark. His 43-yard TD catch in the third quarter gave the Cowboys a 17–14 lead, but from there the Redskins took control.

Washington drove 80 yards for the winning TD in the fourth quarter, with Jim Cunningham leaping over the line on fourth down from the 1-yard line for the deciding score. The Cowboys saw their final hopes intercepted when Jim Steffan picked off his third pass of the game in the closing minutes.

GAME 4: Dallas Drops Fourth Straight

Philadelphia 24 vs. Cowboys 21

October 6: All those promising preseason predictions of a few weeks earlier seemed light-years away after Dallas lost its fourth straight game to open the year. This time it was Tim Brown—not Cleveland's Jim Brown—who served as a one-man wrecking crew. Philadelphia's quick halfback carried 19 times for 91 yards and a TD and caught an 80-yard strike that opened the scoring and sent the Eagles to their first victory.

Dallas, plagued by penalties and assorted other miscues, fell into a 14–0 hole and never

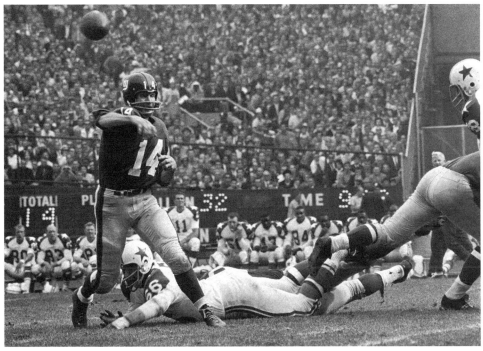

The Cowboys lost both encounters with the New York Giants in 1963 thanks to the crafty play of Giants quarterback Y.A. Tittle. (AP Photo/Ruben Goldberg)

quite recovered. Top runner Don Perkins left the game late in the first quarter with a knee injury.

GAME 5: Defense Delivers Long-Awaited Win

Cowboys 17 vs. Detroit 14

October 13: Linebacker Chuck Howley and the Dallas defense took it upon themselves to change the momentum of their season. Howley set up two scores with interceptions, and the Cowboys kept the Lions off the Cotton Bowl scoreboard until midway through the fourth quarter to win their first game of the year.

Howley had been knocked out of the previous week's game at Philadelphia, but on this day he delivered the knockout blows. His thefts set up a TD and a field goal, and he was all over the field as Dallas took a 10–0 lead into the final frame. End Gail Cogdill's fourth-quarter heroics nearly revived the Lions, but the Cowboys held on.

GAME 6: Tittle Revives Giants

N.Y. Giants 37 vs. Cowboys 21

October 20: Dallas had New York reeling, having grabbed a 21–14 second-quarter lead before more than 62,000 fans at Yankee Stadium. With more than half the game to go, though, Y.A. Tittle never flinched.

Instead, the Giants QB took his team to 23 unanswered points the rest of the way to lift them to victory, passing for 279 yards and four TDs. Eddie LeBaron threw two TD passes for New York, including a 75-yarder to Frank Clarke.

GAME 7: Meredith, Howton Shine in Loss

Pittsburgh 27 vs. Cowboys 21

October 27: Don Meredith made a solid debut as starting quarterback and Bill Howton broke Don Huston's NFL record for career receptions, but neither could keep Dallas from falling to 1–6 on a soggy day in Pittsburgh. Meredith marched the Cowboys to leads of 14–0 in the first half and 21–6 in the third quarter, throwing three TD passes. The last one was Howton's record-tying 488th reception, and he added two more catches for sole possession of the mark.

However, Pittsburgh QB Ed Brown put on a late aerial display in the rain, connecting with Buddy Dial and Red Mack as the Steelers scored the game's final three TDs at Forbes Field. Jim Bradshaw made two big defensive plays late—the clincher was an interception of Meredith in the end zone.

GAME 8: "Dandy Don," Defense Do It for Dallas

Cowboys 35 vs. Washington 20

November 3: Don Meredith threw four TD passes and the Cowboys' defense produced seven turnovers as Dallas drubbed Washington for its second win of the season. Safety Mike Gaechter snared two of the team's four interceptions and returned them for a Cowboys record 121 yards. Dallas also recovered three fumbles.

Offensively, Meredith shone in his second straight start. He directed an offense that gained only 221 total yards—less than half of what the visiting Redskins totaled—but made the most of his chances in his most productive day of TD tosses as a pro. Fewer than 19,000 fans were in the Cotton Bowl stands on that gloomy afternoon.

GAME 9: Record Passing Attack Comes Up Short

San Francisco 31 vs. Cowboys 24

November 10: Don Meredith threw 48 passes, completing 30 for 460 yards—all Cowboys records. However, the only record of concern on the flight back from Northern California was 2–7, the team's listless mark in the standings. Dallas' defense was nowhere to be found on Meredith's big passing day, surpassed only by Norm Van Brocklin (554 yards), Y.A. Tittle (505), and Johnny Lujack (468) in NFL history.

Frank Clarke (190 yards, two TDs), Bill Howton (107 yards, one TD), and Lee Folkins

(112 yards) all had big receiving days, but none could do a thing to keep the 49ers from overcoming a 21–10 deficit with relative ease. Two third-quarter TDs put San Francisco ahead for keeps en route to its second win of the season.

GAME 10: Finally, Dallas Hangs On

Cowboys 27 vs. Philadelphia 20

November 17: Having made a habit of squandering halftime leads, the Cowboys surely felt a sinking sensation when their 24–6 advantage nearly disappeared at the Cotton Bowl. However, Warren Livingston intercepted King Hill's desperation pass at the final gun to preserve victory this time.

The win was constructed on the foundation of another big passing day by Don Meredith. The QB was 25-of-33 for 302 yards and two TDs without throwing an interception. Don Perkins carried 16 times for 92 yards and a score in the winning effort.

GAME 11: Dallas No Match for Browns

Cleveland 27 vs. Cowboys 17

November 24: Two days after President John F. Kennedy's assassination in Dallas, the Cowboys left the scene of world tragedy to play in Cleveland where they made their own misery against a superior foe. Don Meredith, after racking up yardage and points against lesser defenses, threw two interceptions and lost a fumble, managing only 93 passing yards against the Browns.

Dallas did a commendable job containing Jim Brown, holding the All-Pro to 51 yards on 17 carries. But Ernie Green rushed for 97 yards, and Cleveland QB Frank Ryan threw for two scores as the Browns moved into a first-place tie in the standings.

GAME 12: Another Halftime Lead Evaporates

N.Y. Giants 34 at Cowboys 27

December 1: No Cowboys halftime lead was insurmountable, and that was again the case when the Giants visited the Cotton Bowl on this crisp December day. Dallas rode the legs of Don Perkins and Amos Marsh to a 27–14 halftime lead, but that lead vanished against the Y.A. Tittle–led Giants after the intermission. It was the Cowboys' sixth blown halftime lead of the season.

While Cowboys QB Don Meredith struggled (6-of-16 for 86 yards passing), Tittle rallied the Giants for 20 unanswered points after unleashing three interceptions in the first half. He ran for a score that made it 27–21, set up two field goals—including Don Chandler's club-record 53-yarder—and broke Bobby Layne's career record for TD passes with the winning strike in the final five minutes.

Mr. Cowboy

Bob Lilly Carried the Doomsday Defense on His Broad Shoulders

When Miami Dolphins quarterback Bob Griese saw Bob Lilly charging toward him, he ran for his life.

It was late in the first half of Super Bowl VI, and the Cowboys sensed that the next play would be a pass. With Dallas running a double stunt, Lilly—a defensive tackle—squeezed through two offensive linemen and zeroed in on the quarterback. Griese bailed out of the pocket by running right, as defensive tackle Larry Cole closed in.

In desperate straits, Griese retreated backward to escape a sack, only to be dumped to the turf by Lilly 29 yards behind the line of scrimmage.

There was no escaping the wrath of Lilly, "Mr. Cowboy." The 6'5", 260-pound lineman (massive for his day) was also amazingly quick and agile. He could bull past guards and tackles and then pounce on quarterbacks and halfbacks like a cat on mice.

In a way, the Cowboys' foundation was built on Lilly's broad shoulders. In 1961, the 'Boys selected him as their first-ever draft pick. Not only would he become the heart of the Doomsday Defense, but—as a west Texas man—he helped fans identify with the fledgling team.

Born in Olney, Texas, Lilly tore up the Southwest Conference as a consensus All-American at Texas Christian. Though Lilly was the NFL Rookie of the Year as a defensive end in 1961, coach Tom Landry determined he would be even more effective on the line's interior. So he moved Lilly to tackle, where he earned seven first-team All-Pro selections. Eleven times he was named to the Pro Bowl.

"Mr. Cowboy" Bob Lilly (No. 74) of the Dallas Cowboys tackles Charley Harraway of the Washington Redskins during a game on November 21, 1971, at RFK Stadium in Washington, D.C. The Cowboys defeated the Redskins 13–0. (Photo by Russ Russell/NFL Photos/Getty Images)

Blessed with incredible instincts in addition to his physical gifts, Lilly was a tenacious pass rusher as well as a lane clogger on running plays. Moreover, nothing could keep him out of the lineup. He played in 196 consecutive regular-season games and missed only one contest in his 14-year NFL career, which he played entirely with the Cowboys.

"A man like this comes along once in a generation," Landry said. "I don't think Bob ever was aware of how good a player he was or how valuable he was to his team."[1]

Lilly was so good for so long that he made the NFL All-Decade Team for the 1960s and the 1970s. A member of the Cowboys Ring of Honor, he was elected to the Pro Football Hall of Fame in 1980, which was, fittingly, another first for a Dallas player.

GAME 13: Again, A Dramatic Loss

Pittsburgh 24 at Cowboys 19

December 8: Trailing 19–17 and facing fourth-and-14 from their own 16, the Steelers gained 42 yards on a fake punt with less than five minutes to play and marched 80 yards for the winning score at the Cotton Bowl. It was the most recent in a humiliating succession of squandered leads for the Cowboys.

Ed Brown's pass to Red Mack from punt formation kept the winning drive alive. It ended in the final two minutes when Theron Sapp capped a 119-yard rushing day with a 24-yarder for the winning TD. Dallas scored on two Don Meredith carries and two Sam Baker field goals, including a 53-yarder.

GAME 14: Long Season Ends on High Note

Cowboys 28 at St. Louis 24

December 15: The Dallas season of giving ended with a rare takeaway. The Cowboys snatched their first-ever victory over the Cardinals by coming from behind in the waning moments, dramatically and decisively. Trailing 24–21 on a frigid day in St. Louis, the team got 39- and 24-yard hookups from Don Meredith to Frank Clarke to pull out the win.

This time, it was their opponent who self-destructed. Dallas turned two second-quarter fumble recoveries into TDs, the first on a Meredith run and the second when defensive tackle Bob Lilly rumbled 42 yards over an icy pitch with a recovered fumble for his first pro TD. The Cowboys won despite not gaining a first down in the first or third quarters.

1964

LANDRY IN FOR LONG HAUL

Eleven-Year Contract Sets New Standard

Pleased with the progress their young team was making, the Cowboys signed the only coach they had ever had, Tom Landry, to a 10-year extension before the 1964 season. He had one year remaining on his old deal, giving the man in the fedora a guaranteed salary for 11 more years, an unheard-of commitment in the world of professional sports.

In return, Landry gave the Cowboys hope of soon climbing into contention. His team went an improved 5–8–1 by playing some of the best defense in its young history. The Cowboys gave up only six rushing TDs all year, the best mark in the NFL.

GAME 1: Dallas Stymied in Opening Bid

St. Louis 16 at Cowboys 6

September 12: A failed fourth-down try in the final quarter kept Dallas from an opening win, or tie, at the Cotton Bowl. Trailing 13–6 late, Coach Tom Landry decided to go for it twice on fourth down. The first time, the Cowboys were bailed out by a pass-interference call. The second, an Amos Marsh plunge up the middle, was stuffed.

Frank Clarke caught 10 passes for 145 yards and the Cowboys' only score.

GAME 2: Marsh, Perkins Carry 'Pokes

Cowboys 24 vs. Washington 18

September 20: Led by the running of Amos Marsh (96 yards) and Don Perkins (73), Dallas controlled the first three quarters at the Cotton Bowl. When rookie Mel Renfro returned an interception 39 yards for a TD in the fourth quarter, the Cowboys led 24–9 and were on their way to a seemingly easy win.

However, when Dallas linebacker Dave Edwards intercepted a pass and then fumbled it into the end zone for a Washington safety, the tide turned and the Cowboys were forced to weather a wild finish.

GAME 3: Steelers Put Up a Wall

Pittsburgh 23 vs. Cowboys 17

September 27: The Steelers put up a defensive wall that prevented Dallas from scoring despite nine tries from inside the 10-yard line in the final minutes. The Cowboys stormed back from a 23–10 deficit and had the ball first-and-goal from the 7 with a chance to win. A Pittsburgh pass-interference penalty gave them nine snaps to do so, but each time the Steelers denied them.

Frank Clarke led Dallas with seven receptions for 110 yards and a touchdown from Don Meredith.

GAME 4: Big Crowd Backs Dominant Browns

Cleveland 27 vs. Cowboys 6

October 4: More than 72,000 fans—the largest crowd that had ever witnessed a Cowboys game—cheered their Browns to a one-sided victory on the shores of Lake Erie. Despite keeping Jim Brown to 89 yards on 23 totes, Dallas was no match for QB Frank Ryan (two TD passes) and Cleveland.

John Roach quarterbacked the Cowboys in place of an injured Don Meredith, while Don Perkins led Dallas with 80 yards on 18 carries.

Philadelphia Eagles linebacker Maxie Baughan (No. 55) tackles Cowboys running back Perry Lee Dunn (No. 37) in a 24–14 Eagles win over the Dallas Cowboys on December 6, 1964, at Franklin Field in Philadelphia, Pennsylvania. (AP Photo/NFL Photos)

GAME 5: Somehow Giants Salvage Tie

Cowboys 13 vs. N.Y. Giants 13 (tie)

October 11: Sometimes the numbers don't add up. Dallas outgained New York by nearly a 4-to-1 margin (473–128) and held Y.A. Tittle to a career-worst 33 passing yards. On the opposite side, Don Meredith threw for a career-high 296 yards. Still, the Cowboys failed to earn a victory for their efforts.

That's because Dallas hurt its own cause with two missed field goals in the final two minutes, key penalties, three interceptions, and two lost fumbles. Rookie kicker Dick Van Raaphorst had a chance to redeem his earlier missed boot with three seconds remaining, but he failed again from the 35.

GAME 6: Mistakes Keep Dallas from Upset

Cleveland 20 at Cowboys 16

October 18: Jim Brown ran 71 yards on the game's first play from scrimmage, and the Dallas offense hurt itself with miscues all day at the Cotton Bowl. The Cowboys' defense clamped down after giving up Brown's big run, but the team could not overcome two interceptions and key penalties by the offense, along with a fumbled kickoff return.

Don Perkins rushed for 96 yards and Dick Van Raaphorst booted three field goals for the Cowboys, who never led and were penalized 10 times for 105 yards.

GAME 7: Dallas Finally Gets Offense Untracked

Cowboys 31 at St. Louis 13

October 25: The tables turned for two teams on a warm Midwestern afternoon. The Cardinals' offense, tops in the NFL entering the game, failed to reach the end zone until the final minute. And a Cowboys attack that had scored just nine TDs all year erupted, knocking St. Louis out of first place.

Don Meredith completed 12-of-19 passes for 192 yards. His favorite target, Frank Clarke, caught seven balls, scoring one TD and setting up another. And the Dallas rushing attack saw three backs gain at least 45 yards before a stunned St. Louis crowd.

GAME 8: Dallas Knocks Off NFL Champs

Cowboys 24 at Chicago 10

November 1: The Cowboys earned their first-ever win over the Chicago Bears, the defending NFL champions, in impressive fashion at Wrigley Field. After giving up a field goal to open the scoring, Dallas scored 24 consecutive points to score its second straight decisive victory over a quality opponent.

Bob Lilly recovered a fumble and led another inspired Dallas defensive effort. On offense, Don Meredith hit 10-of-19 passes for 158 yards, throwing for one score and running for another. The win spoiled the Bears' Bill George Day before a packed house of 47,522 fans.

GAME 9: Win Streak Reaches Three

Cowboys 31 at N.Y. Giants 21

November 8: Though some people—New Yorkers, in particular—contended the Cowboys didn't deserve it, Dallas won their third straight game for the first time in their history. They did it by turning two interceptions and two fumble recoveries into all four of their TDs before a hostile Yankee Stadium crowd.

The Giants were their own worst enemy, but credit the Cowboys for taking advantage of virtually every miscue. Dallas needed to run just three plays for its first 14 points, thanks to an opportunistic defense that hounded Y.A. Tittle all afternoon. The Cowboys blitzed to a 21–0 lead and were never threatened thereafter.

Dandy Don
Brash, Homegrown Meredith Leads Big D to Glory

When writer Gary Cartwright spoke to Don Meredith in 2008, he told Don that Dallas fans look at Tony Romo and see a young Meredith.

"You mean he's that good-looking?" Meredith quipped.[1]

Ah, Dandy Don. Even in old age, he still had the sharp wit and Texas charm that football fans had adored for decades. Born and raised in Mount Vernon, Texas, an hour east of Big D, Meredith starred at Dallas' Southern Methodist University. He was so popular at SMU—earning All-America honors in 1958 and 1959—that some fans referred to the school as Southern Meredith University.

Although the Chicago Bears drafted Dandy Don (a nickname he picked up from his brother Billy Jack) in the third round in 1960, the Cowboys coveted him for his seat-packing charisma and the swagger that could one day lead the team to glory. A trade for draft picks brought Meredith back home.

As a starter from 1962–65, the brash, wisecracking quarterback found himself in trouble on Sunday afternoons due to the Cowboys' subpar offensive line and a less-than-stellar corps of receivers. But the talent improved in 1966, and Meredith maximized the team's potential. He fired 24 touchdown passes that year, including a 95-yarder to "Bullet" Bob Hayes, en route to a 10–3–1 record and the NFL Player of the Year award.

From 1966–68 (when he abruptly retired at age 30), Meredith made the playoffs and the Pro Bowl each year. He didn't lead the NFL in any major statistical categories, but he finished second in passing yards per game in 1966 (216) and second in passer rating in 1968 (88.4).

Meredith's biggest disappointments came in the postseason, where he went 1–3 from 1966–68. His 68-yard touchdown pass to Frank

Quarterback Don Meredith (No. 17) of the Dallas Cowboys scrambles with the ball during a game on September 17, 1967, against the Cleveland Browns at Municipal Stadium in Cleveland, Ohio. (Photo by Tony Tomsic/Getty Images)

Clarke highlighted a solid performance in the 1966 NFL Championship Game loss against Green Bay. He was brilliant in a 52–14 rout of Cleveland in the 1967 playoffs (11-of-13, 212 yards, 2 TDs, 0 INTs), but he couldn't throw the frozen leather the next week in the infamous "Ice Bowl" (25 attempts, 59 yards).

From 1970–73 and 1977–85, Meredith charmed America as a colorful color man for *Monday Night Football*. "Turn out the lights," he would sing once a team was hopelessly behind, "the party's over."

A Ring of Honor member, Meredith ranks with Roger Staubach and Troy Aikman among the most popular Cowboys quarterbacks of all time.

GAME 10: Big Crowd Witnesses Stunning Loss

Philadelphia 17 at Cowboys 14

November 15: Three straight wins attracted 56,000 to the Cotton Bowl, the largest regular-season crowd in Cowboys history. And they let out a collective groan when an Eagles team that had not managed a first down in the second half drove 96 yards in the closing minutes, winning the game on a 38-yard TD pass from King Hill to Pete Retzlaff on fourth-and-15. It was the shocker of the week in the NFL.

Dallas had rebounded from a 10–0 halftime deficit thanks to its defense. Lee Roy Jordan swiped the ball from Hill at the Eagles' 3-yard line in the third frame, and Don Meredith ran in on the next play to get the Cowboys on the board. They took a 14–10 edge on a Don Perkins run and had pinned the Eagles deep in their own territory late when the Dallas defense yielded a drive that would send the season spiraling the wrong way.

GAME 11: Dallas Coughs Up Football in Loss

Washington 28 vs. Cowboys 16

November 22: Dallas' offense continued to pummel itself, and this time the results showed directly on the D.C. Stadium scoreboard. The Redskins ran two interceptions back for TDs and sent the mistake-prone Cowboys home with a loss. Dallas suffered two apparent TDs erased by penalties, botched two easy field goals, and threw four interceptions.

Mel Renfro's 168 yards on four kickoff returns provided most of the Cowboys highlights. He also intercepted a pass in the losing effort.

GAME 12: Packers Overwhelming in First Trip to Big D

Green Bay 45 at Cowboys 21

November 29: A normally stingy Cowboys defense collapsed in the powerful Packers' first visit to the Cotton Bowl. Green Bay's 45 points were the most yielded by the 'Pokes in 28 starts. The Packers led just 17–14 at halftime but pulled away for an easy win against a banged-up Dallas club.

The Cowboys scored only one offensive TD. The others came on a 69-yard Mel Renfro punt return—the first punt-return score in franchise history—and a 17-yard fumble return from Warren Livingston.

GAME 13: Dallas Drops Fourth Straight

Philadelphia 24 vs. Cowboys 14

December 6: The nemesis that snapped Dallas' three-game winning streak less than one month earlier prolonged the misery, handing the Cowboys their fourth straight loss on the strength of a defense that surrendered just 133 total yards.

Jim Ridlon returned a fumble recovery 63 yards for a Dallas score, but the Cowboys'

offense managed just one TD in the game. Eagles QB Jack Concannon passed for 134 yards and ran for 90—more rushing yards than Dallas managed as a team.

GAME 14: Dallas Closes With Win

Cowboys 17 vs. Pittsburgh 14

December 13: The Cowboys halted a four-game losing streak in the season finale, securing a win over the Steelers when Warren Livingston intercepted a Pittsburgh pass on the game's last play. A limping Don Meredith passed for one TD and set up a Perry Lee Dunn scoring scamper with more gutsy passing as the Cowboys built leads of 10–0 and 17–7 and then held on for the victory.

Buddy Dial caught five passes for 100 yards in his best day with the Cowboys. Meredith completed half of his 28 passes for 223 yards.

1965

.500, WITH A BULLET

Hayes Races onto Scene as Dallas Climbs to 7–7

The fastest man in the world, a rookie named "Bullet" Bob Hayes, joined the Cowboys in 1965 and helped speed their run toward contention. Hayes tied for the NFL lead with 12 TD receptions as Dallas became a threat to score from anywhere on the field.

The Cowboys finished 7–7, their first non-losing season. They also drew their first sellout home crowd, as more than 76,000 jammed the Cotton Bowl to witness a November loss to Cleveland. With Hayes racing downfield, QB Don Meredith threw for 22 TDs this season. The Cowboys also outscored their opponents for the first time in their history, and a winning season was right around the corner.

GAME 1: Dallas Defense Dominates

Cowboys 31 vs. N.Y. Giants 2

September 19: A regular-season record Cotton Bowl crowd of 59,366 cheered the "Doomsday Defense" to one of its most impressive outings. New York's only points came on a high snap that sailed into the end zone for a Giants safety. All other scoring threats were stamped out by a Dallas "D" that set up two TDs with fumble recoveries and stopped two Giants drives with key interceptions. New York failed to make a first down until the third quarter and had minus-4 net yards in the first half.

Not that the Cowboys needed much offense, but Perry Lee Dunn scored two TDs and rookie Bob Hayes brought the big crowd to its feet with a dazzling 45-yard scoring scamper in the final quarter.

GAME 2: Stop Troops Keep Rolling

Cowboys 27 vs. Washington 7

September 26: The Cowboys' defense extended its shutout streak to the first seven quarters of the season before yielding its first points with 4:13 left in the game. By then, a 27–0 lead assured the Texas team a victory before another record crowd of more than 60,000 at the Cotton Bowl.

Rookie Bob Hayes, the 1964 Olympic champion, touched the ball three times and scored three apparent TDs. One was called back by a penalty, but that was nothing to cry over for a team with a defense like that of the Cowboys. At the time Dallas took a 20–0

cushion in the first half, Washington had mustered just 75 offensive yards.

GAME 3: Hot Start Cooled in Missouri

St. Louis 20 vs. Cowboys 13

October 4: The Cardinals overwhelmed the Cowboys early, just as Dallas had against its two previous opponents. St. Louis scored two TDs in the first quarter against a defense that had allowed just one previously, and the Cardinals amassed a 271–47 yardage advantage in the opening half.

Just when it appeared the Cardinals were about to take a three-TD lead at halftime, Mel Renfro returned an interception 90 yards for the only Cowboys TD, making the halftime score a mere 14–7. But the Dallas offense managed just two field goals, and the Cardinals matched them in the second half to send the Cowboys to their first loss.

GAME 4: Rookie Can't Carry Dallas to Win

Philadelphia 35 at Cowboys 24

October 10: Bob Hayes enjoyed a game most rookies can only dream of, catching eight passes for 177 yards and two TDs for the Cowboys. However, the Eagles swarmed his teammates, caused several Dallas mistakes, and made a defense that opened the year dominating its opponents look inept.

Bob Hayes had an excellent rookie season with the Cowboys in 1965. (Photo by Donald Uhrbrock/Time Life Pictures/Getty Images)

Starting QB Don Meredith was benched by Coach Tom Landry for the rookie duo of Craig Morton and Jerry Rhome, but neither of those QBs could approach the impact of first-year man Hayes. Who could? While the three signal-callers did combine for a healthy completion percentage (15-of-26), it was the defense that abandoned the Cowboys.

GAME 5: Slump Continues in Cleveland

Cleveland 23 vs. Cowboys 17

October 17: The Browns maintained their mastery of Dallas, relying on the passing of Frank Ryan (14-of-27, 247 yards, two TDs), the running of Jim Brown (85 yards and a score), and the toe of Lou Groza (three field goals, including a 48-yarder) before 80,000-plus—the largest crowd ever to witness a Cowboys game.

Don Meredith passed for 185 yards and two TDs, but his Dallas team seemed to be a step behind all day. The Browns improved to 10–1 against the Cowboys despite having two apparent TDs nullified by penalties.

GAME 6: Mistakes Doom Dallas in Milwaukee

Green Bay 13 vs. Cowboys 3

October 24: The Cowboys did everything but win, squandering an otherwise dominant effort with three fumbles and two interceptions against the mighty Packers in Milwaukee. So stout were the defenses that the teams combined for an NFL record 18 punts. The Cowboys continually swarmed top-ranked QB Bart Starr, forcing 23 incompletions. Dallas outgained Green Bay by a staggering 193–62 yardage margin.

But the miscues were costly. Rookie QB Craig Morton, in his first start, was intercepted twice by the Packers. And although Don Perkins ran 22 times for 133 yards against the Green Bay defense, mistakes kept Dallas out of the end zone.

GAME 7: Losing Streak Reaches Five

Pittsburgh 22 vs. Cowboys 13

October 31: A year that started with such promise became officially nightmarish, fittingly, on Halloween. Four fumbles—two lost, an interception, and 22 incomplete passes in 34 attempts sent the Cowboys to their fifth consecutive loss and into last place in the standings.

Run-of-the-mill QB Bill Nelsen threw for 272 yards and three TDs against a Dallas defense that had begun the season looking dominant in back-to-back wins. The Cowboys opened the scoring on a short toss from Don Meredith to J.D. Smith, but Nelsen fired all three of his TD passes in the second quarter as the Steelers took command at Pitt Stadium.

GAME 8: Big Plays Halt Dallas Slump

Cowboys 39 vs. San Francisco 31

November 7: Mel Renfro returned the opening kickoff the full length of the field for a score and the Dallas defense added two second-quarter TDs as the Cowboys snapped a five-game losing streak despite yielding 411 total yards to the high-powered visitors from San Francisco. George Andrie recovered a fumble for a score, and Bob Lilly returned an interception 17 yards for another as the Cowboys took a 27–10 half-time lead.

The 49ers charged back in the second half, grabbing a 31–30 edge early in the fourth frame. But Don Meredith and rookie sensation Bob Hayes hooked up on their second TD pass of the game to give Dallas the lead with 4:18 to play, and Danny Villanueva booted his second field goal to seal the win.

GAME 9: Barrage of Interceptions Picks Up Dallas

Cowboys 24 vs. Pittsburgh 17

November 14: Trailing 17–10 in the fourth quarter, the Cowboys intercepted a club-record five Pittsburgh passes in the game's final 14 minutes to snare an improbable win. Cornell Green's interception early in the fourth led to the tying TD, a short run by Dan Reeves.

Late in the game, a diving interception by Dave Edwards on Pittsburgh's 31-yard line set up the winning score. Bob Hayes, whose earlier fumble had led to the Steelers' go-ahead TD, scored on a 28-yard pass from Don Meredith in the game's final two minutes. Meredith passed for 245 yards and two scores.

GAME 10: Fans, Cowboys Turned Away

Cleveland 24 at Cowboys 17

November 21: A record crowd of more than 76,000 stretched the Cotton Bowl to its limits, and several others wanting to get in were turned down at the gates. Don Meredith was treated just as rudely by the Browns, who intercepted the Cowboys QB three times to escape with a win.

For much of the day, the Cowboys outplayed the defending NFL champs, outgaining Cleveland 293–200 in total yardage. Meredith connected on TD passes to Bob Hayes and Pettis Norman, but he was intercepted twice in Browns territory late in the game after having pulled the Cowboys within seven points. Jim Brown powered Cleveland, rushing for 99 yards and a score.

GAME 11: Redskins Rally in Final Minutes

Washington 34 vs. Cowboys 31

November 28: Dallas got TDs from its offense, defense, and special teams to take a 21–0 cushion at D.C. Stadium, only to watch Sonny Jurgensen quarterback the Redskins to

Doomsday 'Backer

Chuck Howley Rose from a Gas Pumper to an All-Pro Linebacker

Chuck Howley was in the shower, washing off the filth of the horribly played Super Bowl V, when someone told him the news, "Hey, Chuck, you were named the game's Most Valuable Player."

Howley remains the only player from a losing team to win the Super Bowl MVP Award—or in the case of a game marred by 11 turnovers, the "Blooper Bowl" MVP Award. In the first quarter, the Cowboys linebacker made a diving, juggling catch of a Johnny Unitas throw and returned it to Baltimore territory. In addition to a fumble recovery, he also picked off a fourth-quarter pass in the end zone to kill a Colts drive. Nevertheless, Baltimore prevailed 16–13 on a last-second field goal.

"I think it was an odd experience, to put it mildly," Howley recalled. "When you lose a ballgame and end up the MVP, it's hard to take any satisfaction out of it because we went there as a team and lost there as a team."[1]

Nevertheless, it was an extraordinary milestone for a player who had been forced to retire from the Chicago Bears due to a knee injury he suffered in 1959. More than a year later, Howley was running a gas station in West Virginia when Cowboys president Tex Schramm gave him a call. The woeful expansion team needed a good linebacker, and with Howley's knee much improved, they acquired his rights from the Bears and signed him to a contract.

Howley helped anchor the Doomsday Defense from 1961–73, earning six trips to the Pro Bowl. Exceptionally athletic (he had lettered in football, wrestling, diving, track, and gymnastics at West Virginia University), Howley

Dallas Cowboys linebacker Chuck Howley played 15 seasons in the NFL, 13 of which were with the Dallas Cowboys. From 1961 to 1973, he recorded 24 interceptions in 168 games. (Photo by NFL/NFL)

wreaked havoc all over the field. He intercepted 25 passes and recorded 25.5 sacks in his NFL career—big numbers for a linebacker.

"Sometimes we allow certain people like Chuck or Bob Lilly to vary from our defensive pattern," said Tom Landry. "People like Chuck can often do this and get away with it because of their outstanding athletic ability."[2]

Howley was so intense on game day that teammate Charlie Waters deliberately kept his distance from him. Chuck's bad knee not only held up, but he got better with age. He earned AP first-team All-Pro honors each year from 1966–70.

In 1977, Howley was enshrined in the Cowboys Ring of Honor. To this day, many fans insist he was the greatest linebacker ever to wear the silver star.

a last-minute conquest of the Cowboys. It prevented Dallas, which drew 13 penalties for 135 yards, from climbing into second place in the standings.

Cornell Green returned a fumble five yards for a score, Mike Gaechter raced 60 yards to the end zone after a blocked field goal, and the Dallas defense also set up its offensive mates for a short score in the early going. However, Jurgensen passed for 411 yards and three scores, directing three long fourth-quarter TD drives. His five-yard toss to Angelo Coia posted the winning points on the board with 1:16 remaining.

Logan intercepted a Sam Snead pass at the goal line, giving Dallas its first-ever victory at Franklin Field. It was the biggest defensive play in a game filled with them, particularly from the Cowboys.

After fullback Earl Gros hit Ray Poage for a 63-yard TD on a trick play to start the game, Dallas kept the Eagles out of the end zone. Philadelphia kicked four field goals, but the Cowboys blocked two others. Don Meredith threw for two scores and ran for another, then thanked Logan and the defense for lifting Dallas after back-to-back losses.

GAME 12: Dallas Posts First Win at Franklin Field

Cowboys 21 at Philadelphia 19

December 5: The Eagles scored on their first play from scrimmage and seemed destined to reach the end zone for a late victory when Obert

GAME 13: Dallas Ensures Top Win Total

Cowboys 27 vs. St. Louis 13

December 11: Don Meredith threw for 326 yards and three TDs to lift the Cowboys to their sixth win—a high-water mark in franchise history. The Cardinals gained 339 yards of total offense but could not slow Meredith and a suddenly potent Dallas offense that racked up 403.

The game was tied at 13 entering the final quarter, but Meredith connected with Dan Reeves and Pettis Norman to seize control. Bob Hayes caught an earlier scoring pass and again topped 100 receiving yards.

GAME 14: Dallas Evens Record in Finale

Cowboys 38 at N.Y. Giants 20

December 19: An unlikely win at Yankee Stadium gave the Cowboys their first .500 season. Don Meredith threw three TD passes for the second straight week, and this time the team did not cough up an interception. The result was a game in which Dallas never trailed.

Bob Hayes finished a brilliant rookie season with two more TD receptions. Three Dallas runners—Meredith, Don Perkins, and J.D. Smith—each topped 50 yards. There were still 16 seconds on the clock and the Cowboys were threatening to score again when the game was put to rest, thanks to an uprising of fans on the field that started when a young boy swiped the hat of a police officer and ran behind the Dallas huddle.

1966

JUST DANDY!

Cowboys Romp to First Winning Season as Meredith Wins Maxwell

The Cowboys had never enjoyed a winning season prior to 1966. Nevertheless, they had set a foundation over their previous six years on which to build a perennial NFL title contender. Consider 1966 the ribbon-cutting ceremony.

Dallas reeled off four straight wins to start the year and played the powerful Cardinals to a 10–10 draw, establishing itself as an Eastern Conference title contender. All three losses during their 10–3–1 regular season were against rivals the Cowboys also defeated. The result was their first trip to the NFL Championship Game.

Although the title game against Green Bay did not go their way, coach Tom Landry understood the significance of the huge strides the young franchise had taken.

"The world doesn't stop when you lose," Landry said. "You must think about the good things that happened to you. You must look ahead."

With Landry switching formations at the line of scrimmage and frequently burning defenses by sending "Bullet" Bob Hayes on deep routes, the Cowboys fielded the most explosive attack in the NFL. They led the league in total offense, scoring offense, and passing offense, and they were second in rushing offense.

The brightest star was QB Don Meredith, who won the Maxwell Award as Player of the Year in the NFL. Meredith passed for 2,805 yards and 24 scores against 12 interceptions. "Dandy Don" also ran for five TDs.

GAME 1: Meredith Connects for Five TDs

Cowboys 52 vs. N.Y. Giants 7

September 18: The Cowboys handed the visiting Giants the third-worst loss in their history, scoring on seven of their first eight possessions. Five of those tallies were TD tosses from Don Meredith, who was 14-of-24 for 358 yards in

less than three quarters of work. His five scoring strikes set a team record.

"Bullet" Bob Hayes burned New York for six receptions, covering 195 yards and two TDs. Running back Dan Reeves also caught six balls—three for scores—as Dallas gained a club-record 518 yards from scrimmage. Cornell Green returned one of the Cowboys' four interceptions for a TD.

GAME 2: Late Comeback Topples Vikings

Cowboys 28 vs. Minnesota 17

September 25: Overcoming a 10–0 deficit, the Cowboys charged past visiting Minnesota on the strength of three 80-yard touchdown drives. Don Meredith found Bob Hayes for a 37-yard TD pass that cut Dallas' halftime deficit to 10–7.

Meredith, under pressure from Minnesota's defensive line for much of the day, completed only eight throws. But he ran for a four-yard score in the third quarter that gave the Cowboys their first lead, and his eight-yard TD pass to Buddy Dial in the fourth put Dallas on top for keeps, 21–17. Don Meredith's 11-yard run rounded out the scoring.

GAME 3: Falcons No Match

Cowboys 47 at Atlanta 14

October 2: Dan Reeves' running and Don Meredith's passing continued to carry the

Cowboys in their first road game of the season. Reeves ran for one score and caught a Meredith pass for another, bringing his total to six TDs in three games—all victories.

Both Reeves scores came in the second quarter, turning a 7–3 Dallas deficit into a 17–7 lead. The Falcons got within 17–14 early in the third quarter, but Meredith hit Bob Hayes on a 49-yard TD bomb, and the rout was on. The Cowboys also scored on a safety and a 97-yard fumble return by Chuck Howley.

GAME 4: Another Five-TD Day for Meredith

Cowboys 56 vs. Philadelphia 7

October 9: For the second time in four weeks, Don Meredith threw for five TDs, tying the team record he had set in the season opener against the Giants. The Cowboys also broke their franchise record for points in a game.

Meredith completed 19-of-26 passes for 394 yards and did not throw an interception for the

Dallas quarterback Don Meredith turns to hand off to running back Don Perkins as Green Bay defensive tackle Ron Kostelnik breaks through the line in the Packers' 34–27 win over the Cowboys in the 1966 NFL Championship Game on January 1, 1967, at the Cotton Bowl. (Photo by Vernon Biever/NFL)

fourth consecutive game. In three quarters, he hit "Bullet" Bob Hayes for three scoring strikes and connected with Dan Reeves and Frank Clarke once each for TDs.

GAME 5: Cardinals, Cowboys Battle to Draw

Cowboys 10 at St. Louis 10 (tie)

October 16: One of the greatest defensive tussles in years ended without a victor before 50,673 fans—at the time, the largest crowd to ever watch a sporting event in St. Louis—and a national television audience. The tie kept both teams undefeated.

Don Meredith had a string of 156 straight passes without an interception, but the string was snapped as the Cardinals' defense picked off three of his throws. Bob Hayes failed to catch a scoring pass for the first time in eight games. Dan Reeves' four-yard TD run gave Dallas a 10–7 lead in the fourth quarter, but Hayes later fumbled an attempted fair catch in his own territory and the Cardinals capitalized, kicking the tying field goal from the 27.

GAME 6: Browns Reward Record Crowd

Cleveland 30 vs. Cowboys 21

October 23: Despite outgaining the Browns 416 yards to 264, the Cowboys fell behind the defending Eastern champs 30–7 and ultimately suffered their first loss. Don Meredith threw four interceptions in front of 84,721 fans, at that point the largest crowd to witness a Cleveland home game.

Mistakes crippled the Cowboys. Ross Fichtner intercepted three Meredith passes, and Mike Howell snared one. Two of the picks set up Browns touchdowns, and the other two stopped Dallas drives deep in Cleveland territory. Browns kicking legend Lou Groza, 42, had missed six straight field goal tries entering the game, but he split the uprights on three straight attempts.

GAME 7: Dallas Bounces Back

Cowboys 52 vs. Pittsburgh 21

October 30: Don Meredith recovered from a four-interception game by completing four TD passes, including a bomb to Pete Gent that covered more ground—84 yards—than any pass play in Meredith's career.

The Cowboys also scored once on defense and once on special teams. Lee Roy Jordan returned an interception 49 yards for a TD, and Mel Renfro found the end zone on an 87-yard kickoff return. The Dallas defense held Pittsburgh to just one first down in the opening half.

GAME 8: Kick Returns Burn Cowboys

Philadelphia 24 vs. Cowboys 23

November 6: Dallas dominated the game from scrimmage, but its coverage teams handed the game to the Eagles. Philadelphia's Tim Brown returned kickoffs 93 and 90 yards for scores, and Aaron Martin reached the end zone on a 67-yard punt return to leave the Cowboys scratching their heads after their second loss of the season.

The Eagles scored all their points during a first half in which they gained just six yards of offense. Dan Reeves caught a Don Meredith pass in the final minute deep in Philadelphia territory but lost the ball to Joe Scarpati, ending the Cowboys' bid for a comeback win.

GAME 9: Villanueva Boots Dallas to Late Win

Cowboys 31 at Washington 30

November 13: Don Meredith directed an 86-yard drive in the closing minutes, and Danny Villanueva capped it with a 20-yard field goal with 15 seconds remaining as the Cowboys edged the Redskins. Washington had taken a 30–28 lead on Sonny Jurgensen's third TD pass and had backed up the Cowboys to their own 1-yard line on a late punt.

But Meredith was up to the task. The Dallas QB had earlier run for a score and found Bob Hayes for two others. His 95-yard TD connection with Hayes was the longest in club history.

GAME 10: Ten is Not Enough to Stop Cowboys

Cowboys 20 at Pittsburgh 7

November 20: The Steelers lined up with 10 men on two key plays but were no match for Dallas. One of the miscues came on Don Meredith's touchdown run that opened the scoring, and another resulted in a Steelers fumble when an 11th man raced into the game and had a snap bounce off his leg.

The Cowboys' defense dropped Pittsburgh quarterbacks 12 times for 77 lost yards. Bob Hayes caught a Meredith pass for a score—his 10th TD reception of the season.

GAME 11: Villanueva's Foot Carries Dallas to Key Win

Cowboys 26 vs. Cleveland 14

November 24: Coach Tom Landry called it the most important game in the seven-year history of the Cowboys, and his team used four Danny Villanueva field goals and a stout defense to win it before a record Cotton Bowl crowd of 80,259.

The win avenged an earlier loss to the Browns and gave Dallas a half-game lead over the Cardinals. Don Perkins rushed for 111 yards and the game's final touchdown. Villanueva kicked two field goals in each half, with his second-half boots erasing a 14–13 Cowboys halftime deficit.

The Two-Year Miler

Don Perkins Saved His Best Running for Sunday Afternoons

It really ticked off Tom Landry that Don Perkins couldn't run a mile in six minutes. The coach expected each of his running backs to achieve that modest feat, but Perkins was always chugging toward the finish line, gasping for breath, when the six minutes expired.

Yet on the football field, Perkins made it up to the coach. In his first two seasons as a Cowboy, he rushed for a mile—exactly. His 815 yards in 1961 plus 945 in 1962 equals 1,760 yards, or 5,280 feet, which equates to precisely one mile. Landry would be intrigued by the irony—although he still would have wanted him to complete that darned race.

Perkins wasn't exactly a workhorse running back (14 carries per game average for his career), and Bullet Bob Hayes could have left him in the dust in a footrace. But Perkins was quick and agile, with an extraordinary ability to cut through a hole and maintain his balance. Moreover, he was remarkably consistent and reliable, missing only five games during his NFL career (1961–68, all with the Cowboys) and averaging between 3.9 and 4.4 yards per carry each season. The result was some of the great career rushing numbers in Cowboys history.

Green Bay Packers future Hall of Fame cornerback Herb Adderley prepares to drill Dallas Cowboys running back Don Perkins in the Packers' 34–27 win over the Cowboys in the 1966 NFL Championship Game on January 1, 1967, at the Cotton Bowl in Dallas, Texas. (Photo by Vernon Biever/NFL)

President of the student body as a senior at Iowa's Waterloo West High School, Perkins starred at the University of New Mexico, which would one day retire his number. Had he not broken his foot in training camp, he would have played for the original 1960 Cowboys. As it was, his 815 yards rushing and 298 yards receiving in 1961 earned him NFL Rookie of the Year honors, and he was selected to the first of six Pro Bowls.

In 1962, Perkins earned first-team All-Pro honors en route to his greatest rushing season of all (including a career-high 137 yards against St. Louis). During every season of his career, he finished in the NFL's Top 10 in rushing. Even during his last two seasons, when he was noted as a hard-blocking fullback, he topped 800 yards each year.

When he left the game, Perkins ranked fifth in NFL history with 6,217 rushing yards—a total that through 2009 ranked third in Cowboys annals behind those of Emmitt Smith and Tony Dorsett. Fittingly, these three legends are the only running backs in the Cowboys Ring of Honor.

GAME 12: Dallas Defense Breaks First-Place Deadlock

Cowboys 31 vs. St. Louis 17

December 4: The Cowboys emerged from a fog that blanketed the Cotton Bowl and a first-place tie with the Cardinals by shutting out the visitors in the middle quarters. The teams played to a 10–10 draw in their first matchup. This time, St. Louis matched that total with 10 points in the first quarter.

However, that was all the Dallas defense would allow until the Cowboys had amassed a 24–10 lead in the fourth. Dan Reeves got the Cowboys started with a 45-yard touchdown run, and Don Perkins rushed for a pair of Dallas scores.

GAME 13: Redskins Kick Cowboys, But Not Out of First

Washington 34 at Cowboys 31

December 11: Charlie Gogolak's 29-yard field goal with eight seconds remaining lifted the Redskins to victory, but the Cowboys held onto their one-game Eastern Division lead thanks to the Cardinals' loss to the Falcons.

Dan Reeves appeared to have Dallas headed toward victory when he raced 67 yards for a fourth-quarter score, but Washington twice tied the score in the final frame on Sonny Jurgensen (295 passing yards) TD passes. Cowboys quarterback Don Meredith was knocked out on a second-period hit by Sam Huff and did not return to the game.

GAME 14: After Clinching Title, Dallas Subs Win

Cowboys 17 at N.Y. Giants 7

December 18: Having clinched the Eastern Conference title on a Cardinals loss the previous day, Dallas knew it wouldn't matter that QB Don Meredith and DT Ted Lilly had to sit out the season finale due to injuries. Even a lackluster effort from the reserve-laden Cowboys was enough to get past a Giants team whose fans were singing and screaming not-so-fond farewells to their coach, Ali Sherman.

Craig Morton's 41-yard TD pass to Bob Hayes broke a 7–7 tie in the fourth quarter and gave the Cowboys a victory that did not thrill coach Tom Landry, despite the fact his team was about to play in the NFL Championship Game for the first time.

GAME 15: Packers Hold Off Cowboys for NFL Title

Green Bay 34 at Cowboys 27

January 1, 1967: The upstart Cowboys had their chances against the veteran Packers in the NFL Championship Game, but two dropped passes and an illegal procedure penalty near the goal line in the final two minutes prevented them from a chance to advance to the inaugural Super Bowl.

Bart Starr, playing in his fifth NFL Championship Game, quarterbacked the Packers brilliantly, throwing for 304 yards and four scores. Dallas never led, but first-half TD runs by Dan Reeves and Don Perkins erased a 14–0 Green Bay lead.

The Packers regained a 14-point cushion in the second half, but Don Meredith hit Frank Clarke on a 68-yard touchdown pass that brought Dallas within 34–27, and the Cowboys had a chance to tie the score down the stretch with first-and-goal from the 2-yard line. However, Dallas dropped two passes, drew a penalty and, on fourth down, had a desperation pass from Meredith intercepted by Tom Brown.

1967

ICY ENDING

Second Straight Title Bid Ends in NFL Classic

The Cowboys had officially arrived. Now all they had to do was scrape the ice off their championship hopes going forward.

A second straight trip to the NFL title game produced a second straight loss to the Packers. This time, it came in one of the most frigid and famous settings in the history of the league—the Ice Bowl at Lambeau Field. Getting there, however, was another warm tale for Dallas fans.

Though a 9–5 record marked a drop-off from the previous year, both Dan Reeves and Don Perkins rushed for more than 600 yards, and Dallas out-gained its foes on the ground by more than 800 yards on the season. A 5–1 start sent the Cowboys on their way to a first-place finish in the new Capital Division.

GAME 1: Cowboys Finally Win at Cleveland

Cowboys 21 at Cleveland 14

September 17: Dallas defended its Eastern title by doing something it had never managed before—gaining a win at Cleveland's Municipal Stadium. And in typical Cowboys fashion, it was the defense that settled it, limiting the Browns to 221 yards of offense and notching what became the winning TD on Chuck Howley's 28-yard interception return in the third quarter.

Don Meredith accounted for the other two Dallas TDs through the air, hitting Bob Hayes and Dan Reeves in the first half. Reeves helped the Cowboys control the game on the ground, carrying 18 times for 114 yards.

GAME 2: Dallas Prevails in Home Opener

Cowboys 38 vs. N.Y. Giants 24

September 24: The Giants put up the first 10 points before 66,000-plus at the Cotton Bowl, but it didn't take long for the Cowboys to treat the home folks to a convincing win over their rivals. Don Meredith overcame a shaky start to complete 16-of-28 throws for 243 yards and four TDs—two to favorite big-play target Bob Hayes.

Dallas outscored New York 38–7 between the Giants' quick start and their meaningless TD near the finish. Dan Reeves caught a TD pass and rushed for a game-high 69 yards.

GAME 3: First Loss a Convincing One

Los Angeles 35 at Cowboys 13

October 1: Against a Rams team that had not lost a game—including the preseason—Dallas made numerous mistakes and paid the price. Three interceptions, a lost fumble, and 65 yards in penalties contributed to a day on which the Cowboys never held a lead before a stunned Cotton Bowl gathering of more than 75,000 fans.

Rams QB Roman Gabriel ran for two TDs and operated an efficient offense that racked up 356 yards. Don Meredith was intercepted twice and Craig Morton once for the Cowboys, who got nine receptions for 102 yards from Lance Rentzel.

GAME 4: Fantastic Finish Saves Dallas

Cowboys 17 at Washington 14

October 8: A Cowboys offense that stood paralyzed all day broke into a game-deciding sprint in the final minutes, somehow snaring victory when Don Meredith hit Dan Reeves on a 36-yard TD pass with 10 seconds to play. The dramatic play capped an improbable 71-yard drive after Washington had taken the lead with 70 seconds on the clock thanks to Sonny Jurgensen's eight-yard pass to Charley Taylor.

Meredith, who had been bottled up much of the game, made the winning throw on a fourth-and-4 play. Reeves ran from the backfield down the sideline and was wide open, catching Meredith's lob on the 10 and running it in to the chagrin of the Redskins, their home crowd, and coach Otto Graham, who launched his clipboard high in the air at the turn of events.

GAME 5: Expansion Saints Nearly Score Upset

Cowboys 14 vs. New Orleans 10

October 15: If weather is the great equalizer, a downpour of rain throughout the morning and afternoon nearly had the expansion Saints on equal, albeit sloppy, footing with the defending Eastern champs. The Cowboys needed two defensive stops deep in their own territory in the final four minutes to hold off visiting New Orleans.

Neither team managed even 250 yards of offense, and each committed three turnovers in the mud. Dallas took two seven-point leads, first on a Don Perkins run and next on a 20-yard pass from Craig Morton to Lance Rentzel. Charlie Durkee kicked a remarkable 47-yard field goal for the Saints in horrendous conditions, but two late chances for New Orleans to pull an upset ended with a turnover on downs and a fumble inside the 10.

GAME 6: Dallas Dynamite Late

Cowboys 24 at Pittsburgh 21

October 22: For the second time in three weeks, a Dallas team left for dead sprang to life in a last-second resurrection. This time it was a five-yard pass from Craig Morton to Pettis Norman with 24 seconds on the clock, stunning a Steelers team that seemed to have victory locked away.

Morton was the main reason for the turn-around. He completed 12-of-16 passes for 256 yards and three scores. His first two TD passes went to Bob Hayes, who totaled 170 yards on seven receptions. Rookie QB Kent Nix (313 passing yards) led the Steelers on two TD drives of 90-plus yards in the second half, lifting Pittsburgh to its first lead at 21–17 in the fourth quarter. But Dallas answered once again.

GAME 7: Slow Start Costs Dallas

Philadelphia 21 vs. Cowboys 14

October 29: This time, the fast-finishing Cowboys dug themselves too deep of a hole. The Eagles soared to a 21–0 second-quarter lead that could have been greater and held off the visitors in a mistake-filled game that included 11 turnovers.

Despite countless miscues, the Cowboys had a chance to ride fourth-quarter heroics to victory for the fourth straight game. However, Craig Morton had his last pass intercepted at Philadelphia's 37-yard line. Bob Hayes led Dallas with six catches for 131 yards and a score. Tom Woodeshick ran for 101 yards and an Eagles TD.

GAME 8: Meredith, Victory Return

Cowboys 37 vs. Atlanta 7

November 5: After missing three weeks with injured ribs and illness, Don Meredith was back under center and steered the Cowboys to an easy win over Atlanta. His numbers were nondescript—two TD passes, two interceptions— but his presence sparked a Cowboys team coming off its second loss of the year.

Dan Reeves scored four TDs—two on receptions and two on rushes. He caught six balls for 114 yards and ran for 42 yards. Don Perkins carried 21 times for 111 yards for the victors.

Boyd Dowler (No. 86) of the Green Bay Packers grabs a Bart Starr touchdown pass against Mel Renfro of the Dallas Cowboys in the NFL Championship Game at Green Bay, Wisconsin, on December 31, 1967. The "Ice Bowl," played in frigid temperatures, was won by the Packers 21–17. (AP Photo)

GAME 9: Bourbon Street Kind to Dallas

Cowboys 27 at New Orleans 10

November 12: After a close call against the lowly Saints at home, Dallas visited New Orleans for the first time and impressed the largest crowd ever to witness an NFL game in the South at 83,437 strong. Bob Lilly and the Cowboys' defense spent much of the game in the Saints backfield after New Orleans struck for a 7–0 lead. The Saints failed to reach the end zone the rest of the way, while Dallas launched a balanced attack.

Frank Clarke ran 56 yards for a score on his only carry of the game, while Dan Reeves and Don Perkins also rushed for TDs. The Cowboys held the hosts to 43 net rushing yards on 18 carries.

GAME 10: Redskins Exact Revenge

Washington 27 at Cowboys 20

November 19: Eager to spit out the bitter taste of a last-second loss to Dallas in their last meeting, the Redskins raced to a 27–6 cushion and this time held on. Sonny Jurgensen was almost unstoppable, hitting 23-of-33 passes for 265 yards and four TDs against a Dallas defense that was out of sorts until late.

As usual, the Cowboys mounted a comeback. It came after Craig Morton replaced Don Meredith at quarterback. However, the visitors came up short despite a mammoth pass-catching day by Lance Rentzel, who caught 13 balls

for 223 yards and a TD. Bob Hayes added nine receptions for 135 yards in the losing effort.

GAME 11: Dallas Gives Thanks for Big Win

Cowboys 46 vs. St. Louis 21

November 23: Dallas feasted on an attacking Cardinals defense on Thanksgiving Day at the Cotton Bowl, putting up its biggest point total in 18 games and strengthening their hold on the Capital Division lead. Bob Hayes tied his career high with three TDs, one on a 69-yard punt return and two on long passes from Don Meredith.

It was a big day for several on the Dallas offense. Meredith threw for three TDs, and running back Dan Reeves tossed a 74-yard scoring strike. Lance Rentzel caught that one, along with another TD pass among his five catches for 145 yards. And Don Perkins ran 21 times for 84 yards and a score.

GAME 12: Moore Delivers Colts in Thriller

Baltimore 23 vs. Cowboys 17

December 3: For all their accomplishments, a defeat of the Colts remained out of reach for the Cowboys. Baltimore prevailed for the third time in as many meetings, seizing victory on a two-yard Lenny Moore TD run with 1:35 remaining.

It was a bitter finish in snowy Baltimore for Dallas, which had rallied from a 10–0 deficit to

Bad, Bad Lee Roy Jordan

"Undersized" Linebacker Set Team Record for Tackles

Who's that guy? President Kennedy must have wondered when he attended the 1963 Orange Bowl. *Who's making the tackle on every play?*

Gil Brandt, the Cowboys vice president of player personnel, knew who that guy was. It was Alabama linebacker Lee Roy Jordan, who recorded a phenomenal 31 tackles that day in a shutout of Oklahoma. Both Kennedy and Jordan would arrive in Dallas later that year. The President would be assassinated, while Jordan's NFL career would bloom with the Cowboys.

In the 1963 NFL Draft, five other teams passed on Jordan because of his small frame (6'1" and 215 pounds). But Brandt believed that Jordan's aggressiveness and nose for the ball carrier would compensate for his lack of size. Boy, was he right. In 14 years with the Doomsday Defense, Jordan recorded 1,236 career tackles, which remains a Cowboys record. His 743 solo tackles, another team record, proves he was plenty big enough to get the job done.

Jordan played for two of football's greatest coaches, Bear Bryant at Alabama and, of course, Tom Landry, and each raved about Jordan's competitive nature and ability to patrol the whole field. During the week, Jordan absorbed game films like Roger Ebert takes in movies. On Sundays, he played with such ferocious intensity that his teammates called him "Killer."

Said teammate Obert Logan, "He would rack up his own brother if his brother was wearing the wrong-colored jersey."[1]

Jordan is one of the few defensive players who can be measured by statistics. In 1975, he

Linebacker Lee Roy Jordan (No. 55) of the Dallas Cowboys follows the play during a game on September 19, 1971, against the Buffalo Bills at War Memorial Stadium in Buffalo, New York. (Photo by Tony Tomsic/Getty Images)

recorded the rare feat of 100 tackles in a single season, and his 32 career interceptions rank third in NFL history among linebackers. In some games, he was a raving maniac. Against the Philadelphia Eagles on September 26, 1971, he set a Cowboys record with 21 tackles. In a game two years later, he hauled 14 Eagles to the ground all by himself.

On November 4, 1973, Jordan haunted Kenny Anderson like a poltergeist. In the first quarter, he intercepted the Cincinnati quarterback three times in a span of five minutes. He returned one of the interceptions 31 yards for a touchdown.

Jordan played in five Super Bowls, was selected to five Pro Bowls, and was inducted into the Cowboys Ring of Honor in 1989.

claim a 17–10 lead entering the fourth quarter. However, two Lou Michaels field goals—one from 53 yards—brought the Colts to within 17–16 and set the stage for the short winning drive that followed a Cowboys punt into the wind. Each team gave up four turnovers, and Dallas managed only 223 total yards.

GAME 13: Dallas Bounces Back

Cowboys 38 vs. Philadelphia 17

December 10: Continuing a season-long trend, Dallas refused to drop back-to-back games. The Cowboys rebounded from a loss in Baltimore with an impressive win over the rival Eagles. There was no doubt about this one, as the margin was 31–3 before the end of the third quarter and Philadelphia managed a mere 23 net rushing yards.

QB Don Meredith was knocked out of the game early with a broken nose, but backup QB Craig Morton ably filled in. Amazingly, running

back Dan Reeves scored TDs passing, rushing, and receiving for the victors.

GAME 14: Dallas Drops Meaningless Finale

San Francisco 24 vs. Cowboys 16

December 16: The regular-season finale meant nothing to Dallas, which had wrapped up a division title weeks before. And that's exactly how the Cowboys played it. The 49ers shot to a 24–3 lead before two fourth-quarter Dallas scores made the final margin look closer than the game actually was.

GAME 15: Dallas Romps in Divisional Playoff

Cowboys 52 vs. Cleveland 14

December 24: Capital Division champion Dallas and Century Division winner Cleveland finished with identical 9–5 records, but the gap between the teams was enormous on Christmas Eve at the Cotton Bowl.

The Cowboys pummeled the Browns with 24 consecutive points to open the game and never looked back. Cleveland finally got on the board before halftime, but four straight Dallas TDs—one on a 60-yard Cornell Green interception return—stretched the advantage to a jaw-dropping 52–7.

Don Meredith threw two TD passes, Bob Hayes caught five balls for 144 yards and a score, and Craig Baynham totaled three TDs— two rushing and one receiving—to assure the Cowboys a rematch with the Packers in the NFL title game.

GAME 16: Ice Bowl Leaves Dallas Out in Cold

Green Bay 21 vs. Cowboys 17

December 31: The "frozen tundra" of Lambeau Field was indeed frozen solid on this day for one of the greatest games in NFL history. With temperatures double-digits below zero and everyone in the stadium doing all they could to retain circulation, the Packers iced a return trip to the Super Bowl with a second-straight stunning finish to beat the Cowboys in the NFL title game.

This time, it was Bart Starr sneaking over the goal line from inside the 1-yard line on third down with 16 seconds on the clock. The run was a surprising call since the Packers might not have had time to run another play had the attempt failed. Green Bay, however, knew how to win championships, and the Packers left the Cowboys empty in the closing seconds.

Dallas battled bravely in the most miserable of conditions, rallying from an early 14–0 deficit. George Andrie scored on a seven-yard fumble return in the second quarter, and Danny Villanueva added a short field goal before halftime. The Cowboys then took the lead on a dramatic 50-yard halfback pass from Dan Reeves to Lance Rentzel in the fourth quarter, leaving Green Bay in position to break their hearts again.

1968

DOMINANT YET DISAPPOINTING

Impressive Run Ends Far Short of Goal

The Cowboys looked unstoppable for much of 1968. They led the NFL in scoring. They finished second in the league in defense. They took 12 games while dropping only two, taking the Capital Division with the best record in franchise history. They pounded opponents by an average of 17.5 points per game.

Then came the playoffs, where an upset loss to Cleveland denied them a third straight trip to the NFL title game.

The Cowboys were the only team in the NFL to pass for more than 3,000 yards. Don Meredith was responsible for 2,500 of that total. They also finished second in the NFL in rushing, with Don Perkins going for 836. Dallas avenged one of its regular-season losses, to the Giants, and was hoping for a shot to avenge the other against the Packers. This year, it was not to be.

GAME 1: For Openers, Cowboys Set a Scoring Record

Cowboys 59 vs. Detroit 13

September 15: The Cowboys shredded Detroit's highly touted defense in setting a club scoring record. Their previous single-game high was 56 points in a 1966 game against the Eagles. Dallas racked up 542 total yards—an average of 7.2 yards per play—in the one-sided season opener.

Don Meredith misfired just three times in 19 pass attempts, racking up 228 of the Cowboys' 381 aerial yards and throwing two TD passes before calling it a day. The Dallas defense sacked rookie QB Greg Landry five times.

GAME 2: Browns Ground Game Grounded

Cowboys 28 vs. Cleveland 7

September 22: The NFL's top rushing team in each of the two previous seasons was no match for the Doomsday Defense on this day. Cleveland managed just 87 rushing yards at the Cotton Bowl, while the Cowboys ran for 203 in a thorough and impressive win.

Dan Reeves carried 17 times for 98 yards and two touchdowns, and the Dallas defense even got in on the scoring for the second straight week. Willie Townes returned a fumble 20 yards for a second-quarter TD that gave the Cowboys a 14–0 advantage.

GAME 3: Bumbling Birds Overmatched

Cowboys 45 at Philadelphia 13

September 29: With their fans chanting "Joe's Gotta Go!" in an effort to run coach Joe Kuharich out of town, the Eagles coughed up seven turnovers against the Cowboys. Five of those came on interceptions. Dallas led just 14–13 at halftime but scored 31 unanswered points in the second half.

Don Meredith was 15-of-22 for 231 yards and five TDs, hitting four different receivers in the end zone and matching his career high for scoring strikes in a game.

GAME 4: Shy Not Bashful in Breakout Game

Cowboys 27 at St. Louis 10

October 6: Les Shy stepped in for an injured Dan Reeves and rushed for 89 yards on 16 carries to lift the Cowboys to their fourth straight win to open the season. Reeves was hit on the knee early in the game and was carried off the field with an injury that required immediate surgery. In his absence, the Cowboys were methodical if not always impressive.

The game was tied 10–10 in the third quarter when Mike Clark booted a 50-yard field goal that turned the tide in Dallas' favor. Shy and QB Don Meredith added fourth-quarter TD runs to stretch the final margin.

Defensive back Karl Kassulke (No. 29) and defensive tackle Alan Page (No. 88) of the Minnesota Vikings stop running back Don Perkins (No. 43) of the Dallas Cowboys on October 20, 1968, at Metropolitan Stadium in Bloomington, Minnesota. The Cowboys defeated the Vikings 20–7. (Photo by Vernon Biever/NFL)

GAME 5: Philly Still Winless After Trip to "Big D"

Cowboys 34 vs. Philadelphia 14

October 13: More than 72,000 fans at the Cotton Bowl enjoyed a lopsided contest between the winless Eagles and their undefeated Cowboys. The outcome was never in doubt, as Dallas outgained Philadelphia 414–164, and almost half the visitors' yards came on a meaningless late drive.

Don Meredith passed for 306 yards and two scores. Lance Rentzel caught 10 passes for 152 yards, and Don Perkins led the ground attack with 79 yards and a TD on 16 totes.

GAME 6: Record Start Reaches Six Straight

Cowboys 20 at Minnesota 7

October 20: Dallas ran its club-record winning streak to six in a row, narrowly escaping Metropolitan Stadium with a win over the Vikings. Though Minnesota managed just one score against the Doomsday Defense, the outcome was up for grabs until Cornell Green intercepted a Joe Kapp pass and returned it 55 yards for a TD midway through the final quarter.

The score capped a day on which the defenses dominated. Dallas picked off two Kapp passes and won despite gaining just 177 yards on offense. Minnesota totaled 274 yards but had three turnovers to the Cowboys' two.

GAME 7: First Loss Comes at Familiar Hands

Green Bay 28 at Cowboys 17

October 28: The Cowboys had won six straight games to open the season. After this one, they had lost six without a victory—the history of their series with the Packers. Green Bay maintained its mastery over Dallas by intercepting Don Meredith three times and parlaying four Bart Starr TD passes into a come-from-behind win.

The Cowboys took a 10–0 lead on a scoring pass from Meredith to Bob Hayes and a short Mike Clark field goal. However, Starr threw three straight TD passes in the second and third quarters to send Dallas to its first loss in seven games. While Starr was 17-for-25 for 260 yards, Meredith completed just 13-of-30 passes for two scores.

GAME 8: Dallas Wins Ugly

Cowboys 17 at New Orleans 3

November 3: Good thing for the Cowboys that the New Orleans Saints were hospitable. Otherwise, they might not have won a game while committing seven turnovers, as they did before close to 85,000 fans at the Sugar Bowl. Dallas lost five fumbles and threw two interceptions, but the team still bounced back victoriously from its first loss.

Part of the reason New Orleans failed to capitalize on the Cowboys' generosity was due to the Saints' own four interceptions. There was also the fact that the Saints managed just 243 yards, while Dallas got 405. Bob Hayes caught six passes for 108 yards and two TDs—one that opened the scoring in the second quarter and another that closed it in the fourth.

GAME 9: Turnovers Cost Dallas

N.Y. Giants 27 at Cowboys 21

November 10: Five turnovers were too much for the Cowboys to overcome against the rival Giants, who got two Pete Gogolak field goals in the fourth quarter to pull away from a 21–21 tie and move within one game of Dallas in the standings. Don Meredith threw three interceptions and the Cowboys lost two fumbles, while New York committed a single turnover in the game. That's how Dallas tumbled despite getting 256 passing yards and two TDs from Meredith. Bob Hayes caught six passes for 85 yards and a score, but the Cowboys' ground game failed to generate 100 yards.

GAME 10: Second-Half Surge Sinks 'Skins

Cowboys 44 at Washington 24

November 17: The Redskins seemed on the verge of an upset, having taken a 17–14 lead in the third quarter against a Cowboys team that had lost two of its last three games. Then lightning struck. Dallas scored on four straight possessions to not only weather a D.C. Stadium scare but to right its season.

Despite losing QB Don Meredith to a third-quarter knee injury, the Cowboys amassed 515 offensive yards—220 on the ground and 295 through the air. Meredith threw two TD passes before leaving the game. Lance Rentzel caught two scores. Don Perkins ran for 105 yards on just 13 carries, while Craig Baynham gained 90 on 14. Dallas also got a defensive score on Larry Cole's 21-yard fumble return.

GAME 11: Bears' Only Fight Comes Late

Cowboys 34 at Chicago 3

November 24: In a game that was stopped with 42 seconds still on the clock because players from both teams seemed more intent on fighting than running plays, the Cowboys used dominant defense to post an easy win at Wrigley Field. QB Don Meredith rested a sore knee, but backup Craig Morton filled in with a 240-yard passing day and hit Bob Hayes for a score.

Walt Garrison added two rushing TDs, which was plenty of offense against the Bears. Chicago managed just 147 total yards against the Doomsday D.

GAME 12: Rematch Yields Same Outcome

Cowboys 29 vs. Washington 20

November 28: Just 11 days after meeting in Washington, these rivals squared off on Thanksgiving Day at the Cotton Bowl. It was

Teacher Had a Vision
Mrs. Honeywell Was Right When She Predicted Greatness for Mel Renfro

When Mel Renfro was in fifth grade, his teacher, Mrs. Honeywell, pulled him aside. "I see something special in you, Melvin," she said. "One day, you're going to be someone."[1]

These were pretty heady words for a 10-year-old athlete, especially a black child in Portland, Oregon, in 1952. At the time, only a smattering of African Americans played professional sports. "But she saw in me a vision," Renfro said, "a vision of a professional athlete. She encouraged me to stay on the right path."[2]

Renfro stayed on that path, one that led all the way to Dallas, Texas, and Canton, Ohio.

A speed demon at the University of Oregon, Renfro was part of the 1962 Ducks track team that set a world record in the 440-yard relay. He earned All-America honors as a halfback and defensive back, dazzling fans with his game-breaking runs and spectacular interceptions. Despite a serious hand injury that he suffered before the 1964 NFL Draft, the Cowboys took him in the second round after praying that he would still be available. They envisioned Renfro, who had run the 120-yard high hurdles in a superhuman 13.8 seconds, to be the "Bullet" Bob Hayes of the defense and special teams.

Renfro made an immediate impact as a Dallas rookie. He picked off seven passes as a safety, led the NFL in both kickoff and punt return yardage, and was invited to the Pro Bowl. In his first 10 seasons in the league, he earned Pro Bowl invitations every single year and was selected All-Pro five times.

With his blazing speed, Renfro averaged 26.4 yards per kickoff return in his career,

Dallas Cowboys Hall of Fame defensive back Mel Renfro in pass coverage during a game against the Philadelphia Eagles at Veterans Stadium.
(Photo by NFL/NFL)

twice going all the way. Meanwhile, his skills in the defensive backfield earned him legendary status. Renfro starred at safety before switching to cornerback in his fifth season. The following year, 1969, he led the NFL with 10 interceptions—among the 52 picks that he amassed during his career.

In the 1970 NFC Championship Game, he returned a San Francisco interception 19 yards in the second half to set up a key Cowboys touchdown. They prevailed 17–10 to earn their first trip to the Super Bowl. Renfro helped the 'Boys to four Super Bowls and was inducted into the Ring of Honor—as well as both the College Football Hall of Fame and Pro Football Hall of Fame.

He was indeed "something special."

Larry Cole who was most grateful. The Cowboys' rookie tackle scored a defensive TD for the second time in as many meetings with the Redskins, this time returning an interception for a five-yard score that sealed an otherwise sloppy victory.

Neither team cracked 300 yards of offense, and the teams combined for 221 yards in penalties. Washington took a 20–19 lead in the fourth quarter, but Dallas responded with Mike Clark's field goal and Cole's late play to hold off the visitors. Don Perkins was their offensive workhorse with 22 carries for 97 yards and a score.

GAME 13: 'Boys Ride Big Plays

Cowboys 28 vs. Pittsburgh 7

December 8: Dallas showed how explosive it could be in this one-sided win. Bob Hayes scored on a team-record 90-yard punt return and a 53-yard pass play, and Lance Rentzel

added a 65-yard scoring reception. Don Meredith, in his best game since injuring his knee a few weeks earlier, completed half of his 24 throws for 248 yards and three TDs.

The Cowboys raced to a 21–0 lead, while Pittsburgh failed to score until late in the third quarter.

GAME 14: Dallas Wins a Dozen

Cowboys 28 at N.Y. Giants 10

December 15: Giants fans sang "Goodbye, Allie!" one final time to beleaguered coach Allie Sherman on a cold and snowy day in New York, while the visiting Cowboys completed the best regular season in their history. Dallas' 12th victory in 14 games was sparked by backup QB Craig Morton, who relieved Don Meredith, ran for one TD, and threw for another.

It was not a pretty win, but it avenged an earlier loss to New York. The Cowboys threw three interceptions and gained just one more yard than the Giants. By game's end, fans in the half-filled stadium were throwing snowballs at police officers and players from both teams.

GAME 15: A Bitter End, Thanks to the Browns

Cleveland 31 vs. Cowboys 20

December 21: The Cowboys lost their two-year hold on the East against a Browns team intent on making up for its embarrassing playoff loss to Dallas one year earlier. The game was tied at 10 at halftime, but Cleveland delighted the Municipal Stadium crowd of 81,000-plus by scoring two quick third-quarter TDs to earn a chance to play for the NFL title.

It was defense that turned the tide. Dale Lindsey intercepted a Don Meredith pass and raced 27 yards for the TD that put the Browns on top for good. Meredith was then picked off again, and Leroy Kelly quickly rushed for a 35-yard score that put Dallas in a huge hole.

Meredith completed just three passes to his teammates—the same number he threw to Browns defenders. Backup Craig Morton threw another pick and was just 9-of-23 through the air on a day when Dallas did little right.

1969

NEW ERA DAWNS

"Dons" Meredith and Perkins Make Way for Newcomers

Dallas lost much of its all-time offense when Don Meredith and Don Perkins hung up their cleats before the 1969 season. In their place, however, new talent did more than pick up the slack. Rookie running back Calvin Hill began his assault on the franchise record book, running for 942 yards and eight scores and winning the NFL Offensive Rookie of the Year Award.

At QB, Craig Morton stepped in for Meredith, threw 21 TD passes, and led the Cowboys to a third-straight Capital Division championship. They outscored opponents by a double-digit average while finishing 11–2–1.

For the second straight year, however, Cleveland prevented the Cowboys from attaining their ultimate goal. The Browns' blowout of Dallas in the Cotton Bowl put an end to a decade in which the Cowboys were born, grew up, and reached the cusp of a championship.

GAME 1: Defense Dominates in Opener

Cowboys 24 vs. St. Louis 3

September 21: Dallas held St. Louis to 58 rushing yards and kept the Cardinals out of the end zone to kick off the 1969 season convincingly. It made Roger Staubach's NFL debut a routine one. The former Navy QB, starting for the injured Craig Morton, threw just 15 times, completing seven for 220 yards and a score. He also ran for a TD.

Lance Rentzel caught Staubach's TD strike of 75 yards to open the scoring and also caught a 53-yard score on a halfback pass from rookie Calvin Hill, who led all rushers with 70 yards on 18 carries.

GAME 2: Hill Dazzles in the Big Easy

Cowboys 21 at New Orleans 17

September 28: Calvin Hill made Cowboys history in just his second NFL game. The Yale rookie matched a club single-game rushing record with 138 yards on 23 carries, and his second TD of the day gave Dallas a fourth-quarter win.

New Orleans led twice—7–0 early in the game and 17–14 entering the final frame. Dallas had just enough firepower to prevail. QB Craig Morton, returning from a finger injury on his throwing hand, missed his first five pass attempts but was 8-of-9 thereafter. He threw a 49-yard TD pass to Les Shy and also ran for a TD, but it was Hill who stole the show.

GAME 3: 'Boys Blitz Birds

Cowboys 38 at Philadelphia 7

October 5: Craig Morton's sore finger was definitely not evident on this day. The Dallas QB completed 14-of-18 passes—and one of the incompletions was a drop—for 261 yards and three TDs on a day when the Cowboys could have named their score. Rookie Calvin Hill amassed 206 total yards in the first half before taking a seat, along with several other starters, in the second.

The Cowboys totaled 526 yards of offense, more than twice the Eagles' total, on the new artificial turf of Franklin Field. Philadelphia scored first before Dallas reeled off 38 unanswered points.

GAME 4: Dallas Keeps Rolling on Road

Cowboys 24 at Atlanta 17

October 12: Three straight road games, three straight wins. In a game that was not as close as the final score, Craig Morton went 15-of-20 for 239 yards and a TD to lead the Cowboys to their fourth consecutive victory and third win in a row away from home. Morton injured his shoulder late in the game after taking his team to a commanding 24–10 lead.

Walt Garrison, despite being knocked out of the game twice in the first half, ran for 68 yards and a score for a Cowboys team that outgained the Falcons 397–213.

GAME 5: Morton Passes Eagles Silly
Cowboys 49 vs. Philadelphia 14

October 19: On State Fair Day at the Cotton Bowl, Craig Morton turned rival Philadelphia into a less-than-prized pig. The Dallas QB threw a team record-tying five TD passes and set another club mark with 10 straight completions before 71,509 fans at the Cotton Bowl.

Morton, who had suffered a shoulder injury a week earlier and had been limited in practice, dissected the Eagles on 13-of-19 passing for 247 yards. Lance Rentzel caught six balls for 97 yards and three scores in a game that was never close.

GAME 6: Clark, Dallas Boot Giants
Cowboys 25 vs. N.Y. Giants 3

October 27: Dallas started the season 6–0 for the second straight year, keeping the visiting Giants out of the end zone on a windy, 41-degree afternoon at the Cotton Bowl. Despite the Doomsday Defense being on top of its game, this was no easy win. The Cowboys needed three Mike Clark field goals to overcome an early 3–0 deficit, and Dallas did not penetrate the end zone until the fourth quarter.

Clark split the uprights from 47, 35, and 15 yards. Craig Morton and Calvin Hill each threw fourth-quarter TD passes, and Dallas also added a fourth-quarter safety for tackling scrambling QB Fran Tarkenton in the end zone. New York gained just 40 rushing yards.

GAME 7: Browns Leave Dallas Blue
Cleveland 42 vs. Cowboys 10

November 2: The Cowboys' 6–0 start to the season came crashing down in a hurry at Municipal Stadium against the Browns team that had been their playoff nemesis, too. Wrote Bob St. John in the *Dallas Morning News*, "Women and children were evacuated after the first period, and nobody under 18 was allowed to stay."

Cleveland scored two TDs in each of the first two quarters for a 28–3 halftime lead that held up into the fourth quarter when things got even uglier for Dallas. Though outgained by just two yards, the Cowboys turned the ball over six times and watched Browns QB Bill Nelsen complete 18-of-25 throws for 255 yards and five scores.

GAME 7: Dallas Pulls Away Late
Cowboys 33 vs. New Orleans 17

November 9: Shaking the sour taste of a lopsided loss in Cleveland was not as easy as the Cowboys hoped. The pesky Saints hung around, erasing a 17–3 deficit at the Cotton Bowl before the Cowboys pulled away from a 17–17 tie in the final quarter.

Craig Morton threw for 292 yards and two TDs, while Calvin Hill rushed 13 times for 109 yards and a score. Dan Reeves scored what became the winning TD on a seven-yard run in the fourth period.

GAME 9: Record-Setting Rookie Lifts Dallas

Cowboys 41 at Washington 28

November 16: President Richard Nixon left Capitol Hill to witness Calvin Hill. The rookie running back broke the Cowboys' single-game rushing record he shared with Don Perkins, chewing up 150 yards on 27 carries—another team record. He also scored twice, returned three kickoffs for 100 yards, and caught two passes for 35.

QB Sonny Jurgensen was Mr. Everything for Washington—both good and bad. He completed 24-of-35 passes for 338 yards and a personal-best four TDs. However, he also threw four interceptions, including two to Mel Renfro.

GAME 10: Rams a Perfect 10

Los Angeles 24 vs. Cowboys 23

November 23: More than 70,000 fans in the L.A. Coliseum cheered their Rams to a 10th

Quarterback Bill Nelsen (No. 16) of the Cleveland Browns calls signals in the divisional playoff game against the Dallas Cowboys on December 28, 1969, in Dallas, Texas. (Photo by Herb Scharfman/Sports Imagery/Getty Images)

consecutive victory to start the season—a first in the NFL since the Packers in 1962. Ed Meador's interception in the closing moments sealed the win for the Rams against a Dallas team playing without several of its regulars, including rookie RB Calvin Hill.

The Rams led most of the way, but Craig Morton engineered a 99-yard drive in the fourth quarter to pull Dallas within 24–23. Then, nearing field goal range down the stretch, he threw one of his two interceptions to go along with 204 passing yards and two TDs. Roman Gabriel threw for two Rams scores and ran for another.

GAME 11: Dallas Settles for Turkey Day Tie

Cowboys 24 vs. San Francisco 24 (tie)

November 27: Dallas spotted the 49ers a 14–0 lead, then rallied for a tie and missed a late chance to win on Thanksgiving at the Cotton Bowl. San Francisco blocked Mike Clark's late field-goal attempt from 37 yards to preserve the draw.

A toe injury that sidelined rookie sensation Calvin Hill limited him to four totes in this one. Walt Garrison ran 12 times for 85 yards in his absence, and Craig Morton threw for 206 yards and two TDs. However, Morton also threw three interceptions, and 21 of his 37 throws were incomplete.

GAME 12: Dallas Slops to Victory

Cowboys 10 at Pittsburgh 7

December 7: Winning for the first time in three weeks felt good to Dallas, even if the victory was an ugly, mud-caked, rain-soaked one at Pitt Stadium against a Steelers team that lost its 11th straight. Mike Clark's first-quarter field goal and Craig Morton's second-quarter TD run provided all the points the Cowboys needed to clinch the division title.

The teams combined for just 419 yards of offense in the miserable conditions. The game's top rusher, Pittsburgh's Dick Hoak, went for just 36 yards. Calvin Hill returned from a toe injury and carried 15 times for Dallas, but he covered just 23 yards.

GAME 13: Dallas Dumps Traditional Power

Cowboys 27 vs. Baltimore 10

December 13: Though the game meant nothing in the standings, there was satisfaction to be gained in turning back one of the teams that had dominated pro football for years. The Cowboys did just that by outscoring the Colts 17–0 in the second half at the Cotton Bowl.

Craig Morton broke a 10–10 tie with a 19-yard TD pass to Pettis Norman. After a short Mike Clark field goal completed the third-quarter scoring, Walt Garrison ran in from the 1-yard line to keep Baltimore at bay. Morton also threw a first-half TD to Lance Rentzel for a Cowboys team that amassed a 408–224 yardage cushion.

World's Fastest Human
"Bullet" Bob Hayes Went Deep and Changed the Game

During a game against the Cowboys, Washington Redskins linebacker Sam Huff called for a blitz. Cornerback Jim Shorter, however, vociferously objected. The reason? "Because that means I'm covering Bob Hayes," Shorter told Huff, "and I can't cover Bob Hayes."[1]

Shorter had a point. After all, Bob Hayes was the "World's Fastest Human"—ever.

As a sprinter at Florida A&M, Hayes had set world records in the 60-yard dash (5.9 seconds) and 100-yard dash (9.1 seconds). The Cowboys drafted him in the seventh round in 1964 knowing he would miss that season because of his participation in the Summer Olympics, held in Tokyo in October. After winning two gold medals (the 100 meters in world-record time and the 4 x 100-meter relay), Hayes joined the Cowboys in 1965.

Immediately, "Bullet" Bob Hayes struck fear into the hearts of defensive coordinators. Though he caught only two passes in his first game, they were for a combined 81 yards and a touchdown. When he caught eight balls for 177 yards in Week 4, he began to alter the mindset of the league. Coaches would begin to create zone defenses to contain him, and teams would eventually draft their own speed-burner receivers.

Hayes amassed 1,003 receiving yards and a league-high 12 touchdown receptions in 1965 while helping Dallas improve from 12th in the NFL in points scored to seventh. A year later, during the

"Bullet" Bob Hayes (No. 22) of the Dallas Cowboys carries the ball during Super Bowl VI against the Miami Dolphins on January 16, 1971, in New Orleans, Louisiana. (Photo by Herb Scharfman/Sports Imagery/Getty Images)

Cowboys' breakout 10–3–1 campaign, they topped the league in scoring. Hayes helped lead the way with a career-high 1,232 receiving yards, including 246 yards in a game against the Redskins.

Bullet Bob earned Pro Bowl invitations his first three seasons. And although his numbers dwindled as his career progressed, he still finished his 11-year career (including 10 seasons with Dallas) with 7,414 receiving yards and 76 touchdowns—including three scores on punt returns.

Hayes still holds numerous Cowboys receiving records, but he will always be remembered as one of the game's greatest deep threats. He averaged a league-best 26.1 yards per catch in 1970, and he averaged 20.0 yards per reception for his career.

A Ring of Honor member, Hayes died of kidney failure at age 59 in 2002. Seven years later, he was inducted into the Pro Football Hall of Fame. Roger Staubach and Bob Hayes Jr. were on hand to unveil his bust.

GAME 14: Redskins Fall in Finale

Cowboys 20 vs. Washington 10

December 21: Dallas never trailed in its 11th victory of the season, but it wasn't easy. The Cowboys had to overcome nine penalties for 73 yards and a Washington team that stayed close throughout. Calvin Hill capped a 73-yard rushing game with a fourth-quarter TD scamper that finally sealed the outcome.

The Cowboys held Washington QB Sonny Jurgensen without a TD pass, a rare feat, and intercepted him once. Mike Clark booted two Dallas field goals in the regular-season finale.

GAME 15: Old Nemesis Bites Dallas Again

Cleveland 38 at Cowboys 14

December 28: One thing seemed certain as the Cowboys played their final game of the 1960s— the Browns were destined to be their thorn. For the second straight December, a playoff meeting with Cleveland was a one-sided affair. Dallas fell behind 24–0 before nearly 70,000 Cotton Bowl patrons knew whether to boo, cheer, or go home.

Craig Morton drove the Cowboys 72 yards and scored their first points on a broken play with 3½ minutes to play in the third quarter, but it was far too late to rescue an effort that produced just 217 total yards on the day. The Browns compiled 344. Morton was intercepted twice and passed for just 92 yards before he was replaced late by Roger Staubach.

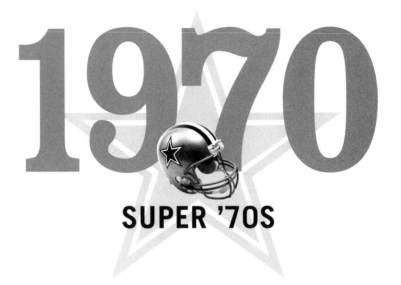

1970

SUPER '70S

Cowboys Gain Super Status

It was not the most dominant team Dallas had fielded in its 11-year history. Its 10–4 record was matched or bettered by five other NFL teams, and its average winning margin was less than six points per game. However, one important thing could be said about the 1970 Cowboys that could not be claimed about its predecessors.

This team was Super.

Dallas took a giant step toward vanquishing its playoff demons and reached Super Bowl V by shutting out Detroit and upsetting San Francisco in the NFC title game. Though the Colts won the big game, it marked the arrival of the Cowboys on football's grand stage—a stage on which they would become accustomed to performing.

With Walt Garrison, Calvin Hill, and Duane Thomas all running for more than 500 yards, the Cowboys fielded the No. 1 rushing offense in the NFL. Throw in the fourth-stingiest defense in the league, and Dallas had a formula that gave it a chance in every ballgame.

That was particularly true down the stretch when the Cowboys won five straight games to win the NFC East and then rode the momentum all the way to Miami.

GAME 1: Dallas Churns Out Opening Win

Cowboys 17 at Philadelphia 7

September 20: Abandoning the big-play pattern that had carried them in previous years, the Cowboys became grinders in a season-opening victory at Franklin Field. Calvin Hill ran for 117 yards on 25 carries, and Roger Staubach, starting in place of QB Craig Morton, went 11-of-15 for 115 yards and a TD and added 51 rushing yards.

The Eagles went up 7–0 in the first quarter, but Walt Garrison tied it on a second-quarter score and Lance Rentzel tallied the winner on a 31-yard toss from Staubach in the third. Three different Cowboys intercepted Philadelphia's Norm Snead.

GAME 2: Second-Half Surge Revives Dallas

Cowboys 28 vs. N.Y. Giants 10

September 27: It wasn't a halftime speech that inspired a listless Dallas team that trailed 10–0 at the break. It was an interception by rookie Cliff Harris on the Giants' first play of the second half. Harris returned the pick 60 yards to set up the Cowboys' first score, and three more TDs followed in a Jekyll-and-Hyde home opener.

Harris finished with two interceptions of Fran Tarkenton and a fumble recovery. Offensively, Roger Staubach and receiver Lance Rentzel—on a trick play—each fired a TD pass to Bob Hayes, who caught five balls for 112 yards.

GAME 3: Shutout Averted—Barely

St. Louis 20 vs. Cowboys 7

October 4: Dallas was nearly shut out for the first time in franchise history, but Calvin Hill's otherwise meaningless TD with 3:06 remaining salvaged at least something from an otherwise dreary performance. The Cardinals put up a wall, chasing Cowboys QB Roger Staubach from the game. Neither Staubach nor Craig Morton could get much going in a defensive battle at Busch Stadium.

Jim Hart threw two TD passes for the Cardinals. Dallas totaled just 269 yards.

GAME 4: Falcons Drenched by Dallas D

Cowboys 13 vs. Atlanta 0

October 11: Heavy rain and an even heavier dose of Doomsday Defense left Atlanta mired at the Cotton Bowl. The Cowboys pitched their second shutout in history, holding the Falcons to 128 yards—an average of 2.6 yards per play. The visitors never drove inside the Dallas 40, and when an interception return got them closer, they twice missed field goals, the second chance resulting from a Cowboys penalty on the first.

Dallas failed to slosh its way to the end zone until the fourth quarter, but two short Mike Clark field goals proved to be plenty of offense on this day. Calvin Hill accounted for nearly half the Cowboys' offense, carrying 29 times for 117 yards.

GAME 5: Vikings Hand Dallas Most Lopsided Loss

Minnesota 54 vs. Cowboys 13

October 18: When the Vikings weren't dominating, the Cowboys were beating themselves. The result was the biggest loss in franchise history. After Dallas took a 3–0 lead, Minnesota scored 54 of the next 57 points. The Cowboys committed four turnovers, while the Vikings took care of the ball and committed just one penalty.

QB Craig Morton left the game with a knee injury in the second quarter, and Roger Staubach replaced him. They combined for four interceptions and had no luck moving the offense. Ed Sharockman returned one of the picks for a Vikings TD.

GAME 6: Dallas Bounces Back

Cowboys 27 at Kansas City 16

October 25: Mel Renfro intercepted two Len Dawson passes and rookie Duane Thomas rushed for 134 yards and two TDs as Dallas shook off the sting of the worst loss in team history with a win over the defending Super Bowl champs. The Cowboys carried owner Clint Murchison off the field after the game.

Dallas ran for 195 yards against one of the top defenses in the NFL. Thomas' 47-yard scamper opened the second-half scoring, giving the Cowboys a 20–10 lead, and they broke it open on an 89-yard TD pass from Craig Morton to Bob Hayes later in the third quarter.

GAME 7: Bombs Carry Dallas Past Birds

Cowboys 21 vs. Philadelphia 17

November 1: Three long TD passes and four interceptions rescued the Cowboys on a day when they failed to mount any sustained offense. It was an old formula, but it worked. Craig Morton hit Lance Rentzel from 86 yards and 56 yards and Bob Hayes from 40 before a chilly Cotton Bowl crowd.

Take away the three long pass plays, and Dallas managed less than 100 yards of total

Defensive lineman "Turkey Joe" Jones of the Cleveland Browns tries to shed the block of offensive lineman Rayfield Wright (No. 70) of the Dallas Cowboys during a game on December 12, 1970, at Municipal Stadium in Cleveland, Ohio. (Photo by Tony Tomsic/Getty Images)

offense. Take away any of Norm Snead's four interceptions, and the Eagles probably win the game despite trailing 14–0 at halftime and 21–10 after Rentzel's second scoring reception.

GAME 8: Fran's the Man in Final Minutes

N.Y. Giants 23 vs. Cowboys 20

November 8: Fran Tarkenton fired a 13-yard TD pass to Ron Johnson with 3:03 remaining, giving New York its first lead of the day and a dramatic win over visiting Dallas. The Cowboys led 20–9 when Johnson ran for a third-quarter score to pull the Giants within striking distance. And with the game on the line, Tarkenton took over.

For Dallas, Craig Morton threw two long TD passes to Bob Hayes in the first half. He looked to be driving the Cowboys toward a winning or tying score in the final seconds, but key penalties erased some big gains and the visitors slipped into a second-place tie with a Giants team whose fans stormed the Yankee Stadium field to celebrate the win.

GAME 9: Dallas Flops on National TV

St. Louis 38 at Cowboys 0

November 16: On ABC's *Monday Night Football*, it was obvious which team was ready for prime time. The first-place Cardinals steamrolled the Cowboys at the Cotton Bowl, rushing for 242 yards and four TDs and handing Dallas its first-ever shutout loss.

Johnny Roland ran for 78 yards and two TDs and MacArthur Lane added 70 yards on the ground, each carrying 16 times. The St. Louis defense intercepted Craig Morton four times and Roger Staubach once. In all, the Cowboys committed six turnovers.

GAME 10: Rebounding Club Nearly Flawless

Cowboys 45 at Washington 21

November 22: Dallas did everything it had failed to do the previous week—running well, passing well, blocking well, and taking care of the football in a rout of the Redskins in the nation's capital. Duane Thomas, replacing an injured Calvin Hill at halfback, ran for 104 yards and three TDs, while Craig Morton was a sizzling 12-of-15 passing for 176 yards and two scores.

The game's biggest play came on special teams. After Washington pulled within 24–14 in the third quarter, Cowboys rookie Mark Washington returned the ensuing kickoff the length of the field—100 yards—for a score.

GAME 11: A Milestone First: Packers Fall

Cowboys 16 vs. Green Bay 3

November 26: For the first time in a game that counted, Dallas knocked off the Packers. The Cowboys had never done so in a regular-season or playoff contest, but under perfect Thanksgiving Day sunshine at the Cotton Bowl, the Doomsday Defense dominated.

The Cowboys held Green Bay to 78 rushing yards and hounded Bart Starr into 9-of-21 passing. As a result, the visitors never crossed the goal line. Meanwhile, Craig Morton hit 12-of-20 passes for 201 yards, Bob Hayes clinched the Dallas victory with a 13-yard TD run, and Mike Clark booted three short field goals after Green Bay grabbed an early 3–0 edge.

GAME 12: Redskins Routed

Cowboys 34 vs. Washington 0

December 6: The NFL schedule-maker did not do Washington any favors, with two late-season games in three weeks against the Cowboys. This time, Dallas pounced on four turnovers and outgained the Redskins 424–166 in a shellacking at the Cotton Bowl.

Duane Thomas carried 19 times for 123 yards but left the scoring to others. Dan Reeves ran for two TDs, and Walt Garrison reached the end zone on a rush and a pass reception.

GAME 13: Defense Scores Huge Win

Cowboys 6 at Cleveland 2

December 12: Dallas extended its string of keeping opponents out of the end zone to 13 consecutive quarters, and on this day its defense was strong enough to secure one of the biggest victories in franchise history. By upending

mighty Cleveland in the Municipal Stadium muck, the Cowboys boosted their playoff hopes and proved they could overcome not only a strong foe but also the elements.

The Browns caught Bob Hayes in the end zone on a punt return for a safety that produced a 2–0 halftime lead. However, the second half belonged to the visitors. Dallas got 39- and 31-yard field goals from Mike Clark, and Dave Edwards made the second of his two interceptions with a little more than two minutes remaining to seal the win. Four turnovers led to Cleveland's demise.

GAME 14: Playoff Berth Secured

Cowboys 52 vs. Houston 10

December 20: Dallas ended the regular season with its fifth straight triumph to claim the NFC Eastern Division championship. By game's end, the only drama was whether Dallas would finally surrender a TD. After 16 consecutive quarters keeping foes out of the end zone, Houston scored on a fumble return. The Cowboys defense, however, extended its string of TD-less quarters to 17.

Craig Morton and Bob Hayes treated the finale like a game of pitch-and-catch. Morton completed 13-of-17 passes for 349 yards and five TDs, hitting Hayes for four of those scores. Hayes caught six balls for 187 yards.

Super Bowl V: The Blooper Bowl

Miscues, Last-Second Colts Kick Boot Cowboys in Super Bowl Debut

The Dallas Cowboys reached their first Super Bowl before the game was, well, the game it is today. A ticket for the January 17, 1971, game at Miami's Orange Bowl cost $15. The halftime entertainment was provided not by a 1970s supergroup (KISS or ABBA, anyone?) but by the Florida A&M University marching band. While the event has changed exponentially since Super Bowl V, one thing remains constant. Mistakes spell doom in a big game.

The Cowboys learned as much in a championship some call the "Blooper Bowl" or "Blunder Bowl," a game plagued by turnovers, penalties, and erratic officiating. The Baltimore Colts committed seven turnovers. The Cowboys coughed up three interceptions and a fumble and committed 10 penalties for 133 yards. Baltimore was flagged just four times for 31.

A thrilling finish kept fans on the edge of their seats, as Jim O'Brien's 32-yard field goal with five seconds remaining lifted the Colts to a 16–13 victory in the first Super Bowl since the AFL-NFL merger. Dallas held a 13–6 halftime lead, but Cowboys QB Craig Morton threw second-half interceptions that set up both the tying TD and winning field goal.

"I just didn't do it," a despondent Morton said after the game.[1]

Dallas Cowboys running back Duane Thomas (No. 33) follows guard Blaine Nye (No. 61) during Super Bowl V, a 16–13 loss to the Baltimore Colts on January 17, 1971, at the Orange Bowl in Miami, Florida.
(Photo by NFL/NFL)

For some time, it looked as though Baltimore's miscues would prove more costly. A lost fumble and a penalty for roughing Morton put the Colts' defensive backs to the wall twice early, but the Cowboys managed only a pair of field goals thanks to their own mistakes. Then Johnny Unitas overthrew Colts receiver Eddie Hinton, but Hinton jumped to tip the pass, which also seemed to graze the fingertips of Dallas' Mel Renfro before settling into the hands of John Mackey for a 75-yard catch-and-run for a score.

NFL rules of the day would have disallowed the play had Renfro not touched the ball, as passes were not allowed to be deflected from one offensive player directly to another. Renfro claimed he did not touch it. Officials ruled otherwise.

Dallas blocked the PAT and scored on a Morton-to-Duane Thomas pass to regain the lead at 13–6, a cushion that normally would have held up against a team that turned the ball over seven times. But this was no ordinary game.

As the Colts celebrated their dramatic victory and Tom Landry's Cowboys were left to ponder what might have been, it was announced that Dallas linebacker Chuck Howley had been named the game's MVP. It was the first time in Super Bowl history that a defensive player and a representative of the losing team earned the award. Howley intercepted two Unitas passes and recovered a fumble.

GAME 15: Detroit Doomed in Playoff Opener

Cowboys 5 vs. Detroit 0

December 26: The Cowboys' Doomsday Defense stretched its string to 21 consecutive quarters without allowing a TD, and it did so against a talented playoff foe at the Cotton Bowl, vaulting Dallas into the NFC title game.

The Cowboys held Detroit to 156 yards and took advantage of three turnovers. While their own offense struggled for much of the day, Duane Thomas did ramble for 135 yards on 30 carries as Dallas controlled the pace. Mike

Clark's 26-yard field goal in the first quarter provided the only offensive points of the day. The Cowboys also hauled down Greg Landry in the end zone in the fourth quarter for a safety to close the scoring.

GAME 16: Dallas Earns Super Bowl Trip

Cowboys 17 at San Francisco 10

January 3, 1971: Left for dead after back-to-back losses in November, Dallas earned its first trip to the Super Bowl with another strong defensive effort in the NFC Championship Game in San Francisco. It was the last pro football game played at Kezar Stadium.

Workhorse rookie Duane Thomas was too much for the 49ers. He carried 27 times for 143 yards and the game's first TD, a 13-yard scamper that broke a 3–3 halftime tie. Later in the third quarter, Walt Garrison caught a short scoring toss from Craig Morton to give Dallas a 17–3 cushion. John Brodie's passing (262 yards) kept the 49ers within striking distance, but San Francisco's high-powered offense was largely grounded by a defense that finally surrendered a TD after 23 consecutive quarters keeping foes out of the end zone.

GAME 17: Super Bowl a Classic

Baltimore 16 vs. Cowboys 13

January 17, 1971: A championship was there for the taking, but Dallas could not quite wrap its fingers around it. The Colts came roaring back from a 13–6 deficit by scoring the last 10 points, including Jim O'Brien's winning 32-yard field goal in the closing seconds.

The contest capped another heartbreaking title-game loss for the Cowboys, who had dropped late decisions to the Packers in two NFL Championship Games. It seemed for most of the day in Miami that their fortunes were about to change. Mike Clark's two early field goals and Craig Morton's seven-yard TD pass to Duane Thomas had given Dallas' dominant defense a cushion.

However, the Colts overcame a seven-turnover day when it mattered most. After tying the score on a TD plunge by Tom Nowatzke, the Colts got a late interception from Mike Curtis on a Morton pass that bounced off the hands of Dan Reeves. Curtis returned the pick to the Dallas 27 with 1:09 remaining, setting up an historic boot by a kicker who earlier in the game had missed a PAT.

Dallas linebacker Chuck Howley, who intercepted two passes and was all over the field, was voted the game's Most Valuable Player.

1971

CHAMPIONSHIP WELCOME TO TEXAS STADIUM

Move to New Home Coincides with Super Bowl Title

A midseason move into their new Texas Stadium home provided ample comfort to the Cowboys. The team went 11–3, again topped its division, and won its last 10 regular-season and playoff games, including a 24–3 smashing of Miami in Super Bowl VI.

It was the season Cowboys fans had been waiting for since the team joined the NFL in 1960. Dallas fielded the top-ranked offense in the league, its 406 points a whopping 62 more than its closest competitor. The Cowboys could run or throw, and they had a defense capable of winning games on its own.

Roger Staubach was the catalyst, though he started just 10-of-14 regular-season games while sharing the spotlight with Craig Morton. His 104.8 passer rating was easily the best in the NFL, and he was rewarded with the Bert Bell Award as Player of the Year.

The Cowboys, playoff regulars and division winners for the past six years, could now add one more title to their résumé—world champions.

GAME 1: Opening Shootout
Cowboys 49 at Buffalo 37

September 19: The first-ever meeting between Dallas and Buffalo was not the blowout some expected. The Bills stayed close until the final quarter in a game that set a Cowboys record for combined points.

Big plays on a rain-soaked, muddy War Memorial Stadium field were the stories of the game. Craig Morton needed just 14 pass attempts for 10 completions, 221 yards, and two TDs. Buffalo's Dennis Shaw passed for 353 yards and four scores, but his three interceptions were costly.

GAME 2: Eagles Still No Match
Cowboys 42 at Philadelphia 7

September 26: Dallas defeated the Eagles for the eighth consecutive time in a one-sided, rain-soaked blowout. It was a mismatch from the start. The Cowboys held the hosts to 32 rushing yards and took advantage of eight turnovers, including three interceptions from Herb Adderley. Pete Liske threw an Eagles record six picks.

Craig Morton led the Dallas offense on 15-of-22 passing for 188 yards and two TDs. He also ran for a score.

GAME 3: Redskins Re-Emerge
Washington 20 at Cowboys 16

October 3: Washington knocked Dallas out of first place and started a season 3–0 for the first time since 1943 against a Cowboys team playing in pouring rain for the third straight week. The Redskins challenged Dallas to stop the run, but the Doomsday Defense failed to do so, allowing 200 yards on the ground. Charlie Harraway carried 18 times for 111 yards and a TD.

The Cowboys settled for three short field goals in the first half, struggled to move the ball on the ground, and did not reach the end zone until the fourth quarter. Roger Staubach took over at QB for Craig Morton in the second half and went 6-for-9 for 103 yards.

GAME 4: Dallas Overcomes Monday Night Miscues
Cowboys 20 vs. N.Y. Giants 13

October 11: The Cowboys and Giants combined to lose 10 fumbles in a sloppy *Monday Night Football* performance. Dallas won despite putting the ball on the ground seven times, losing five, and throwing an interception.

The Cowboys never trailed, but it was far from smooth sailing at the Cotton Bowl. Mike

Running back Preston Pearson (No. 26) of the Dallas Cowboys tries to shake the tackle of Doug Sutherland (No. 69) and avoid linebacker Jeff Siemon (No. 50) of the Minnesota Vikings during the NFC divisional playoff game on December 25, 1971, at Metropolitan Stadium in Bloomington, Minnesota. (Photo by Tony Tomsic/Getty Images)

Clark kicked 42- and 41-yard field goals before starter Roger Staubach and backup Craig Morton each threw a TD pass. The difference came on the ground. Dallas revived its rushing game, churning out 222 yards on 45 attempts.

GAME 5: Saints Get Historic Win

New Orleans 24 vs. Cowboys 14

October 17: The Saints beat the Cowboys for the first time in history. However, Dallas had at least as much to do with its own demise as New Orleans did. Despite outgaining the Saints almost two-to-one (300–157), the Cowboys gave up any chance to win by losing six turnovers for the second straight week.

Craig Morton started at QB for the Cowboys but, trailing 17–0, was replaced by Roger Staubach. Staubach was sharp, going 7-for-10 for 117 yards and two TDs, but his team was simply too generous with the ball.

GAME 6: Texas Stadium Springs to Life

Cowboys 44 vs. New England 21

October 24: After committing 12 turnovers the two previous weeks, the Cowboys took care of the ball in an impressive rout of the Patriots in the first game at Texas Stadium. Roger Staubach directed a turnover-free attack at the sparkling new venue in Irvin, hitting 13-of-21 passes for 197 yards and two TDs to Bob Hayes. Dallas also ran for three scores.

The Cowboys raced to a 34–7 halftime lead, scoring on six of eight first-half possessions, and they were never really challenged before 65,708 fans.

GAME 7: Bears Boot Mistake-Prone Dallas

Chicago 23 vs. Cowboys 19

October 31: Mac Percival, released by the Cowboys in 1967, kicked three field goals through the howling winds of Soldier Field while Dallas kicker Mike Clark missed three. Those stats—not counting seven turnovers and terrible special-teams coverage by the visitors—made the difference in the Windy City.

Despite outgaining the Bears in total yardage by a whopping 481–194 margin, the Cowboys fell to 4–3. Their rotating system of QBs, with Roger Staubach and Craig Morton, accounted for 344 aerial yards. However, Morton's three interceptions were costly on a day when Chicago made the most of its chances. Percival make kicks of 44, 38, and 35 yards.

GAME 8: Fritsch Kicks Cardinals

Cowboys 16 at St. Louis 13

November 7: Toni Fritsch kicked a 26-yard field goal with 1:53 remaining as the Cowboys rallied from a 10–3 halftime deficit to topple the Cardinals. Roger Staubach lasted from start to finish at QB, going 20-of-31 for 199 yards and a TD. But the game hinged on the foot of

Fritsch, and the Viennese soccer kicker connected three times.

Duane Thomas rushed for 101 yards, and Mike Ditka caught a key fourth-quarter TD pass from Staubach to give the Cowboys a 13–10 lead. St. Louis tied it on Jim Bakken's 36-yard field goal, but Fritsch came through in the clutch.

GAME 9: Dallas Handles Eagles Yet Again

Cowboys 20 vs. Philadelphia 7

November 14: Dallas' ninth consecutive win against Philadelphia was built on a defense that registered five takeaways and kept the Eagles off the scoreboard until late in the final quarter. By then, two Duane Thomas TD runs and two Toni Fritsch field goals had produced a 20–0 cushion for the surging visitors.

QB Roger Staubach threw for 176 yards and ran for 90 more while solidifying his position as No. 1. Dallas limited Philadelphia to 44 rushing yards.

GAME 10: Dallas Claims First-Place Battle

Cowboys 13 at Washington 0

November 21: With the NFC East lead at stake, the Doomsday Defense pitched a wind-aided shutout at RFK Stadium as Dallas began resembling the team that made the Super Bowl the previous season. Roger Staubach scrambled for a 29-yard TD on the Cowboys' first possession, and his defensive mates made it stand up, knocking the Redskins from their perch atop the division.

Neither team gained 300 yards in this defensive struggle. However, Mike Clark added two second-half field goals to help the Cowboys distance themselves.

GAME 11: Thanksgiving Nail-Biter Goes to Dallas

Cowboys 28 vs. Los Angeles 21

November 25: It wasn't pretty, but Dallas put another Thanksgiving Day win in the books. QB Roger Staubach fought off a sore neck and shoulder that affected his throwing motion by firing two TD passes, and the Cowboys held off a feisty Rams team to prevail.

The Rams outgained the Cowboys and led 14–7 in the first half. But Dallas, whose first score came on an 89-yard Ike Thomas kickoff return, got TD catches from Bob Hayes and Lance Alworth and a tie-breaking, fourth-quarter TD run from Duane Thomas to survive. Three L.A. turnovers helped the cause.

GAME 11: Dallas Dazzling from the Start

Cowboys 52 vs. N.Y. Jets 10

December 4: Ike Thomas returned the opening kickoff for a TD for the second straight week, and Dallas rode the momentum to an easy romp

Super Bowl VI: Champs at Last
Cowboys Rout Miami, Climb to Football's Pinnacle

Tom Landry stood in front of a microphone showing about as much emotion as the poised and stoic head coach was capable in a public setting. He praised his longtime defensive leaders, Bob Lilly and Chuck Howley, saying he was thrilled that those who had been with the club since its early-'60s growing pains could finally taste the thrill of a championship.

"I'm delighted that we're all still here after starting the franchise," Landry told NFL commissioner Pete Rozelle after accepting the Vince Lombardi trophy for the first time in the club's 12-year existence. "The way I feel right now is hard to describe. We've fought so long and been close so many times."[1]

It was the first Super Bowl ever held in New Orleans, "The Big Easy." And for the Cowboys, it was precisely that.

Miami entered Tulane Stadium having dominated the defending Super Bowl champion Colts 21–0 in the AFC title game. The Dolphins had gone 10–3–1 during the regular season. And though they were not aware of it at the time, they were one off-season away from becoming the only team in NFL history to win every game in the regular season and postseason.

Dallas head coach Tom Landry is carried off the field by his players after the Cowboys' 24–3 win over the Miami Dolphins in Super Bowl VI on January 16, 1972, at Tulane Stadium in New Orleans, Louisiana. (Photo by Vernon Biever/NFL)

On January 16, 1972, however, Dallas was through being a bridesmaid. Roger Staubach, who took over for Craig Morton as the starting QB midway through the season, completed a run of 10 straight victories to end the season with an MVP performance against the Dolphins.

Staubach completed 12-of-19 passes for 119 yards and fired seven-yard TD strikes to Lance Alworth and Mike Ditka. Duane Thomas ran for a three-yard score on his 95-yard rushing day, giving Dallas all the offense it needed on a day when its defense was a brick wall.

Howley, the MVP of the previous Super Bowl in a losing cause, and Lilly sparked a defensive effort that limited Miami to 10 first downs and kept Bob Griese, Larry Csonka, Paul Warfield, and a high-powered offensive attack out of the end zone. Howley intercepted a pass and returned it to the Miami 9-yard line, one of three Cowboy takeaways. The Dolphins gained just 185 yards from scrimmage, while Staubach directed Dallas to 352 yards.

"When the Cowboys are running the football," said Staubach, directing praise toward Thomas, Walt Garrison (14 carries for 74 yards), and his offensive line, "everything else opens up and we're an explosive team."[2]

They had not yet been dubbed "America's Team." Finally, however, the Cowboys were America's best team.

over the Jets. Duane Thomas raced for 112 yards and a score, and Roger Staubach was an efficient 10-of-15 for 168 yards and three TDs before Coach Tom Landry turned to his reserves.

The Cowboys outgained New York 439–149 and pounced on six Jets turnovers.

GAME 13: Another N.Y. Foe, Another Rout

Cowboys 42 at N.Y. Giants 14

December 12: Dallas clinched a playoff berth for the sixth consecutive season by blasting a New York club for the second straight week. Roger Staubach found Bob Hayes for two long TDs

and enjoyed another sizzling game, going 10-of-14 for 233 yards and three scores while extending his string of attempts without an interception to 125.

The Cowboys could do no wrong on this day. Duane Thomas ran for 94 yards and two scores, and Calvin Hill added 89 rushing yards and a TD. The Giants managed just 64 rushing yards as a team.

GAME 14: Another NFC East Title

Cowboys 31 vs. St. Louis 12

December 18: Dallas captured a division or conference crown for the sixth year in a row with a matter-of-fact, season-ending win over the Cardinals. Duane Thomas tied a club record by scoring four TDs—three in the first half.

Roger Staubach's string of 134 pass attempts without an interception was snapped, but the outcome was never in doubt after Dallas opened a 21–3 advantage.

GAME 15: Merry Christmas, Dallas

Cowboys 20 at Minnesota 12

December 25: Coach Tom Landry called it his team's best defensive effort all season. It came on Christmas Day at Metropolitan Stadium, where the previous day's bitter temps settled near the freezing mark, and the Cowboys put a chill on the Vikings' attack.

Dallas led 6–3 at halftime in a battle of field goals. Then Duane Thomas ran for a 13-yard score and Bob Hayes caught a nine-yard TD pass from Roger Staubach to break the game open in the third quarter. Minnesota did not cross the goal line until late in the game when it

no longer mattered, committing five turnovers to the Cowboys' none.

GAME 16: Dallas Returns to Super Bowl

Cowboys 14 vs. San Francisco 3

January 2, 1972: Yet another potent offense fell at the hands of the Doomsday Defense, and Dallas reached the Super Bowl for the second straight year. The Cowboys kept John Brodie and the 49ers out of the end zone and kept mistakes to a minimum to fulfill the goal they had set for themselves after falling to the Colts in Super Bowl V.

Short TD runs by Calvin Hill in the second quarter and Duane Thomas in the fourth were more than enough at Texas Stadium, where 66,311 fans celebrated the first playoff game at the venue. The Cowboys picked off three Brodie passes, thwarting an offense that scored 300 points in the regular season.

1972

WILD, WILD CARDS

Hill, Dallas Blaze New Path to Playoffs

The Cowboys made the playoffs for the seventh straight time in 1972 but this time they got there under the wild-card format. Two years earlier, when the AFL and NFL merged, a wild-card postseason spot was introduced for an even four teams per conference.

Dallas' 10–4 record was one game short of the Redskins' mark, but it was good enough to claim that bonus playoff berth, giving the Cowboys the opportunity to upset San Francisco in a postseason opener before falling to Washington in the NFC title game.

Perhaps a more significant first came out of the Dallas backfield. Calvin Hill, with 1,036 yards on 245 carries, became the first player in franchise history to rush for 1,000 yards. Craig Morton displaced Roger Staubach as the starting QB during the season, but he lost the job midway through the Staubach-sparked playoff win over the 49ers.

GAME 1: Eagles Again No Match

Cowboys 28 vs. Philadelphia 6

September 17: Dallas opened defense of its Super Bowl title in familiar fashion, topping Philadelphia for the 10th straight time. It took the Cowboys some time to get started. They trailed 6–0 in the second quarter before scoring four unanswered TDs—two on Craig Morton passes and two on short runs.

Morton passed for 235 yards on a humid Texas afternoon. The Cowboys limited the Eagles to 70 yards on 30 carries.

GAME 2: Dallas Survives in Big Apple

Cowboys 23 at N.Y. Giants 14

September 24: The defending Super Bowl champs were in a dogfight until a late fourth-quarter TD drive put the scrappy Giants away. Dallas never trailed, but a 94-yard bomb from Norm Snead to Rich Houston in the fourth quarter made it a 16–14 game and had the New York crowd smelling an upset.

However, the Cowboys staged one of their best drives, culminated by a TD pass from Craig Morton to Lance Alworth to seal the win. Toni Fritsch kicked three Dallas field goals, including a franchise-record 54-yarder, and Calvin Hill rushed for 91 yards.

GAME 3: Miscues Hurt in Milwaukee

Green Bay 16 vs. Cowboys 13

October 1: Dallas threw three interceptions and lost two fumbles against a Green Bay team that did not commit a turnover in Milwaukee. The result was a win for the Packers that was not decided until Chester Marcol kicked his third field goal of the game, a 22-yard game-winner in the fourth quarter.

The Cowboys could have tied it in the final minutes but bypassed a 47-yard field-goal attempt to go for a first down on fourth-and-1. A controversial spot on Walt Garrison's run left the visitors short. Calvin Hill paced Dallas with 87 rushing yards.

GAME 4: Trick Play Lifts Dallas

Cowboys 17 vs. Pittsburgh 13

October 8: Calvin Hill threw for a 55-yard TD on a halfback pass as Dallas pulled out all the stops to get back in the win column. Hill was also a workhorse at his usual trade, carrying 23 times for 108 yards and a score.

The trick play came in the third quarter and proved to be the winning TD, erasing a 13–10 Pittsburgh lead built on a 35-yard Mel Blount fumble return. Terry Bradshaw aired it out 39 times for the Steelers, completing only 12 and driving Pittsburgh to the Dallas 22-yard line late before turning it over on downs.

GAME 5: Colts Succumb to Shutout
Cowboys 21 at Baltimore 0

October 15: Dallas dominated the once-proud Colts, limiting Johnny Unitas and Co. to 175 offensive yards and riding a crisp passing performance from Craig Morton. Morton completed 22-of-30 aerials for 279 yards and two TDs, and he tied a club record with 10 consecutive completions.

Calvin Hill scored on a run and a reception. It marked the first time in seven years the Colts had been shut out.

GAME 6: Brown Leaves 'Boys Feeling Blue
Washington 24 vs. Cowboys 20

October 22: Larry Brown was a one-man wrecking crew as the Redskins took control of the NFC East. He rushed for 95 yards and a TD and caught seven passes for 100 yards and a score as the game's most productive weapon via ground and air. Brown was too much for the Cowboys on this day.

Dallas led 20–7 after Walt Garrison's TD plunge opened the second-half scoring, but the Cowboys offense then packed it in. Brown raced 34 yards for a TD, Curt Knight kicked a 42-yard field goal for Washington, and the winner came on a 13-yard dash by Charlie Harraway in the fourth quarter.

GAME 7: Morton Passes Dallas Past Lions
Cowboys 28 vs. Detroit 24

October 30: Impending storms held off on *Monday Night Football* much like the Cowboys held off the Lions' late charge. Dallas took two 14-point leads and led by 11 in the fourth quarter before surviving against the Lions.

Craig Morton threw TD passes to three different receivers, and the Cowboys held Detroit to 59 rushing yards on 28 carries. Calvin Hill rushed for 81 yards and caught a TD pass.

GAME 8: Here We Go Again
Cowboys 34 at San Diego 28

November 5: Nothing, it seemed, could be easy for the defending Super Bowl champs. The Cowboys erupted for the game's 31 points en route to an apparent blowout, then let up just enough to let the Chargers make a game of it late.

Craig Morton was an accurate 15-of-21 passing. He threw for one TD and ran for another. In the end, San Diego came back to outgain Dallas 346–269 in total yardage, but John Hadl and his Chargers could not overcome four different Cowboys who reached the end zone in the first three quarters.

GAME 9: Dallas Rides Waters to Win

Cowboys 33 vs. St. Louis 24

November 12: Charlie Waters intercepted two passes, returning one for a TD and setting up a field goal with another as Dallas turned back the Cardinals at Texas Stadium. The Cowboys raced to another big lead at 30–10 early in the third quarter and held on, similar to the pattern of their previous two wins.

Toni Fritsch kicked four field goals, including a 50-yarder, while Calvin Hill (93 yards) and Walt Garrison (83) helped Dallas to a huge edge in rushing yards. But it was Waters' picks that ultimately made the difference.

GAME 10: Ho-Hum—Another Win Over Philly

Cowboys 28 at Philadelphia 7

November 19: Dallas scored two safeties—an NFL rarity, to be sure. That was about the only thing memorable about this afternoon. Dallas got another defensive score when John Niland recovered a fumble in the end zone, and Calvin Hill ran for 100 yards and a score.

It was a cold, dreary, rainy day at Veterans Stadium, but the Cowboys wore smiles after their 11th consecutive defeat of the Eagles.

Quarterback Roger Staubach (No. 12) of the Dallas Cowboys sets the offense against the Washington Redskins at RFK Stadium in the 1972 NFC Championship Game on December 31, 1972, in Washington, D.C. The Redskins defeated the Cowboys 26–3. (Photo by Nate Fine/NFL Photos/Getty Images)

GAME 11: A Day of Firsts

San Francisco 31 at Cowboys 10

November 23: Dallas had never been beaten in Texas Stadium and had never lost on Thanksgiving Day. But that was before the Cowboys faced the surging 49ers and were thoroughly handled in most facets of the game.

Craig Morton threw two interceptions, and Dallas lost two fumbles. After Walt Garrison gave the Cowboys a 7–0 first-quarter lead, it was all San Francisco. Skip Vanderbundt gave the 49ers TDs on both interception and fumble returns to make it a rout.

GAME 12: Dallas Beats Cold, Cards

Cowboys 27 at St. Louis 6

December 3: On the day Washington clinched the NFC East, the Cowboys took a step toward a wild-card playoff berth with a win over slumping St. Louis on a cold, windy day at Busch Stadium. It was no contest, really, as Walt Garrison scored three TDs and Dallas held the Cardinals to 141 yards of total offense.

Calvin Hill rushed for 120 yards—more than twice the total St. Louis managed as a team. The teams combined for 11 fumbles, losing seven, and 10 turnovers.

GAME 13: Hill Runs to Milestone

Cowboys 34 vs. Washington 24

December 9: Calvin Hill became the first man in Cowboys history to rush for 1,000 yards in a season, scoring two first-quarter TDs to put Dallas on the road to a win over the rival Redskins. Both Hill and teammate Walt Garrison topped 100 ground yards on a rainy afternoon at Texas Stadium.

Washington chiseled away at a 28–3 half-time deficit to pull within a touchdown in the fourth quarter, but its four turnovers and the Dallas ground game proved too much. The Cowboys rushed for 246 yards.

GAME 14: New Yorkers Dominate in Finale

N.Y. Giants 23 at Cowboys 3

December 17: Dallas played like a team with a playoff berth assured and no chance to improve its postseason lot. Fortunately for the Cowboys, that was precisely the case. The Giants outgained them 349–132 and dominated virtually every facet of the regular-season finale at Texas Stadium.

Vince Clements ran 23 times for 105 yards for the Giants, while Norm Snead was 16-of-28 for 175 yards and two TDs. Toni Fritsch kicked his 21st field goal of the season, setting a Cowboys record.

GAME 15: Staubach Engineers Thrilling Comeback

Cowboys 30 at San Francisco 28

December 23: Left for dead by 49ers fans who were heading for the exits to celebrate a first-round playoff win, the Cowboys rallied behind

Milestone Man Hill Is First to 1,000
Calvin Hill Makes Sudden Impact in the Backfield

If a man is to be judged by those around him, Calvin Hill is an unqualified success. One of his fraternity brothers at Yale University, George W. Bush, went on to become a two-term president of the United States. Calvin's son, Grant, attended Duke University and has been an NBA All-Star regular. And since completing his football career, Hill has surrounded himself with civic leaders while chairing or serving on hospital, community, and charity boards far and wide.

Becoming the first player in Cowboys history to rush for 1,000 yards in a season, in the grand scheme of things, was not close to the greatest thing Calvin Hill has accomplished in his life. When it happened, however, it made him an instant favorite among Dallas fans.

Hill thought someone was playing a practical joke on him the day he received a call from the Cowboys informing him he had been drafted with the 24th pick in the first round in 1969. He had been a two-time All-Ivy League performer, Yale's career scoring leader, and one of the best long- and triple-jumpers in school history, but he had never pinned his career hopes on sports. Hill planned on putting his history degree to use.

Instead, he joined the Cowboys and dashed for 942 yards—second in the NFL—on 204 carries in 1969, taking over for Don Perkins as the team's top runner. He was a unanimous NFL Offensive Rookie of the Year choice and the first player in Dallas history to make the AP All-Pro first team as a rookie. "He might be the best ball-carrier I've seen in 20 years of pro football," Cowboys coach Tom Landry said.[1]

Running back Calvin Hill (No. 35) of the Dallas Cowboys leaps over a teammate on a carry against the San Diego Chargers at San Diego Stadium on November 5, 1972, in San Diego, California. The Cowboys defeated the Chargers 34–28. (Photo by James Flores/NFL Photos/Getty Images)

After dividing time with Duane Thomas for two seasons, Hill exploded into the history books again in 1972. He rushed for 1,036 yards, becoming the first in franchise history to break the 1,000-yard barrier, and he eclipsed the mark the following year with 1,142 yards.

Hill ran for 844 yards in 1974, raising his Cowboys career total past 5,000 before jumping to the World Football League. He returned to the NFL with Washington and finished his career with Cleveland. However, Hill's contributions were only beginning. He has spent the last three decades making a positive impact in community, civic, and charity endeavors and doing sports management and consulting work.

One of Hill's most lasting contributions bears his name and receives regular visits from the former Cowboys star. The Calvin Hill Daycare Center, which he helped found in 1970, continues to offer childcare for Yale University employees and other working parents.

Roger Staubach for two TDs in the final 90 seconds—a finish that defied logic.

Staubach had been on the sideline until the third quarter, when it became apparent it was not Craig Morton's day. San Francisco led 28–16 with 1:53 remaining in the game when Staubach started a scoring drive from his own 45. It culminated with a 20-yard pass to Billy Parks.

Mel Renfro recovered the ensuing onside kick with just more than a minute to play after the 49ers were unable to corral the ball, and a 21-yard scramble by Staubach put Dallas in striking range again. Finally, he delivered a 10-yard strike down the middle to Ron Sellers for a TD, and the Cowboys had done the impossible.

GAME 16: Rival Redskins Claim NFC Title

Washington 26 vs. Cowboys 3

December 31: A third straight trip to the Super Bowl was not in the cards for the Cowboys. The Redskins dominated the third meeting of the season between the rivals, using a dominant defense to claim the rubber match and earn a Super Bowl date against Miami.

Dallas could not rekindle the magic of the previous week's comeback at San Francisco, failing to reach the end zone and managing just 169 offensive yards. Tackle Bob Lilly said the Redskins "just beat the hell out of us."

Billy Kilmer dissected the Dallas pass defense, going 14-of-18 for 194 yards and two scores, while Larry Brown ran for 88 yards.

1973

CENTURY MARK

Dallas Wins 100th Game, Keeps Playoff Streak Alive

With Roger Staubach back under center and the Craig Morton experiment over, the Cowboys returned to the top of the division and made the playoffs for the eighth straight season. It was an amazing feat for a franchise that put just its 100th win in the books during this 1973 campaign, its 14th season of existence.

Staubach completed 62.6 percent of his passes, second in the NFL, and led the league in passer rating and yards per attempt. Calvin Hill topped 1,000 rushing yards for the second straight year and also led the team with 32 receptions. Staubach and Hill combined to give the Cowboys the second-best offensive attack in the NFL.

For the second straight year, though, Dallas lost in the NFC title game. After knocking off a Rams team that went 12–2 in the opening round, the Cowboys stumbled against the Vikings just one game short of the Super Bowl.

GAME 1: Bears Trickery Backfires

Cowboys 20 at Chicago 17

September 16: Facing fourth-and-1 from his own 29-yard line late in a 17–17 game, Bears coach Abe Gibron called for a fake punt—a ploy that had worked earlier in the game. This time though, up-man Bob Parsons was pegged for a three-yard loss by Billy Joe DuPree, setting up Toni Fritsch's winning 11-yard field goal for the Cowboys.

"I was a little surprised," Dallas coach Tom Landry said of the Bears' late risk. "They decided to go for the win." Calvin Hill accounted for more than half of the Cowboys' offense in this rainy opener, rushing for 130 yards and catching four passes for 28. Chicago managed just 202 yards and committed six turnovers.

GAME 2: Lowly Saints Go Marching Out

Cowboys 40 vs. New Orleans 3

September 24: A New Orleans team that suffered a 62–7 opening loss to Atlanta was merely scrimmage fodder for Dallas on a nationally televised Monday night game. Craig Morton replaced an injured Roger Staubach in the third quarter, and both QBs moved the Cowboys with ease.

Robert Newhouse scored two TDs, and Calvin Hill rushed for 71 yards and a score.

GAME 3: Dallas Slows High-Powered Cards

Cowboys 45 vs. St. Louis 10

September 30: With machine-like precision, Dallas stifled a St. Louis attack that had averaged 34 points in two straight victories and left little doubt as to its superiority. The Cardinals never had a chance as the Cowboys stormed to a 24–0 halftime lead.

Roger Staubach was 17-of-22 for 276 yards and two TDs, and Craig Morton also threw for two scores in relief duty. Three of Billy Joe DuPree's six receptions ended with the Cowboys wideout celebrating in the end zone.

GAME 4: Redskins Rally for Big Win

Washington 14 vs. Cowboys 7

October 8: It was an early season game with a playoff feel, and the Redskins won it in dramatic fashion. Two TDs in the final four minutes lifted Washington to victory, pulling the hosts even with the Cowboys in the NFC East.

Trailing 7–0, Redskins QB Sonny Jurgensen hit Charley Taylor from the 1-yard line for the tying score with 3:39 remaining. The winning points came one minute later when Brig Owens intercepted a Craig Morton pass and returned it 26 yards for a TD. Morton had replaced a banged-up Roger Staubach for most of the second half. Calvin Hill was also shaken up, but he managed to lead the Cowboys with 103 rushing yards. Dallas' lone score came on a second-quarter TD pass from Staubach to Otto Stowe.

GAME 5: Jackson, Rams Outrace Dallas

Los Angeles 37 vs. Cowboys 31

October 14: The Cowboys could not catch speedster Harold Jackson, and their failure to do so cost them a victory. Jackson was a big-play machine for the Rams, catching seven passes for 238 yards and four TDs—two covering more than 60 yards.

Jackson's TDs all came in the first half, sparking L.A. to a 34–14 cushion. Although the Cowboys did a better job against him after the break, the damage had been done. Otto Stowe caught two second-half TD passes from Roger Staubach to narrow the final margin.

GAME 6: Dallas Ends Two-Game Skid

Cowboys 45 vs. N.Y. Giants 28

October 21: Calvin Hill rushed for 95 of his 123 yards in the first half and helped Dallas move the ball seemingly at will for its first win in three weeks. The Cowboys ran for 234 yards, with Walt Garrison scoring twice and Hill once against a Giants defense that appeared helpless to do anything about it.

Roger Staubach passed just 11 times in the win, completing eight. Two went for TDs.

GAME 7: Eagles Celebrate Big Win

Philadelphia 30 vs. Cowboys 16

October 28: Veterans Stadium fans stormed the field and attacked the goal posts as if their team had just won a championship. In reality, the Eagles had merely won their second game of the season, but it was an impressive triumph against a struggling rival.

The Cowboys lost for the third time in four games, thanks largely to four turnovers. Philly, protecting the football, raced to a 10–0 lead and stretched it to 27–13 by halftime. Calvin Hill's 100-yard rushing day and Roger Staubach's 250-yard passing performance were for naught. Eagles QB Roman Gabriel threw for two TDs and ran for another.

GAME 8: Jordan Steals the Show

Cowboys 38 vs. Cincinnati 10

November 4: Lee Roy Jordan intercepted three Cincinnati passes in the first quarter, returning one 31 yards for a score and setting up a TD with another as Dallas righted its course against Ken Anderson and the Bengals.

The picks led the Cowboys to a 24–0 halftime lead. While Anderson struggled, his counterpart Roger Staubach was a precise 14-of-18 for 209 yards and three TDs.

GAME 9: Defense, Special Teams Carry Dallas

Cowboys 23 at N.Y. Giants 10

November 11: With their offense flailing, the Cowboys found another way to prevail. A blocked punt and blocked field goal led to two Dallas TDs, and the defense forced six turnovers to overcome the team's offensive ineptitude. The result was that the Cowboys never trailed despite gaining only 195 yards. Charlie Waters

came up with two of Dallas' four interceptions of Randy Johnson.

GAME 10: Dallas Avenges Upset Loss

Cowboys 31 vs. Philadelphia 10

November 18: For a while, it looked like the Eagles might have another shocker in them. They led 10–0 over a Dallas team they had upset

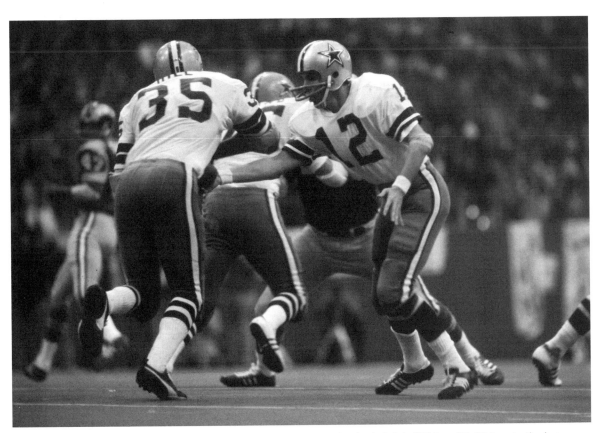

Future Hall of Fame quarterback Roger Staubach hands off to running back Calvin Hill in a 37–31 loss to the Los Angeles Rams on October 14, 1973, at Los Angeles Memorial Coliseum. (Photo by George Long/NFL)

Wright Tackle

With a Little Help from Above, Rayfield Wright Rose to Prominence

At age 10, Rayfield Wright fell to his knees in prayer. A poor, fatherless African American child in segregated Griffin, Georgia, Rayfield had all the odds stacked against him. But he did have a loving, faith-filled family and the desire to do good.

As he knelt in prayer, Wright asked God for a little help. "I asked Him if He would just give me the ability that I could do something…that I could help my mother and my grandmother, and I could help other people," he recalled in his 2006 Pro Football Hall of Fame acceptance speech.

As his body developed as a teenager, Wright realized that he had an extraordinary gift for sports. At Fort Valley State College, the 6'7", massive-framed athlete excelled in football and, more famously, in basketball, averaging 20 points and 20 rebounds a game. The NBA's Cincinnati Royals tried to sign him after his junior season in 1966, but he stayed in school until graduation.

In July 1967, Wright and 136 other rookies attended the Cowboys' training camp. Rayfield, while looking forward to the Royals' camp in August, surprisingly made the Cowboys' roster. He remained in Dallas for 13 seasons.

Wright started his career as a tight end, but he caught just one pass in his first two seasons. In 1969, coach Tom Landry told Rayfield that he was moving him to offensive tackle. A surprised Wright responded that he had never played that position in his life. "I know," Landry said, as Wright recounted in his acceptance speech, "but you're quick, you learn fast. Besides, we got a young quarterback coming to the team this year, and his name is Roger Staubach, and he don't stay in the pocket. He runs around a lot, and he needs a little bit more protection."

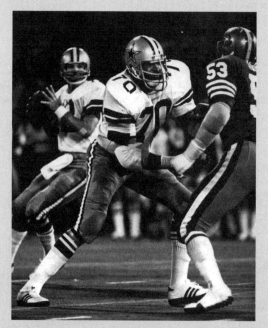

Dallas Cowboys offensive tackle Rayfield Wright protects quarterback Roger Staubach in a 42–35 win over the San Francisco 49ers on December 12, 1977, at Candlestick Park. (Photo by Russ Russell/NFL)

At right tackle, Wright protected "Roger the Dodger" while blowing open holes for halfbacks. From 1971–73, he earned first-team All-Pro honors each year, and he made the Pro Bowl from 1971–76. He was the premier lineman for an offense that ranked in the NFL's top 10 in scoring every year in the 1970s. Moreover, he helped power the Cowboys to five Super Bowls.

Wright, who considered himself a secret service agent protecting his "president" (i.e., Staubach), retired after the 1979 season—the same year that Roger turned in his helmet. Wright was inducted into the Cowboys Ring of Honor in 2004.

three weeks earlier. Then Walt Garrison, Calvin Hill, and Robert Newhouse went to work, and their 240 combined rushing yards propelled the Cowboys to 31 unanswered points.

Roger Staubach threw for two TDs and ran for another, and the Dallas defense overcame his three interceptions.

GAME 11: Dolphins Ride "D" Past Dallas

Miami 14 at Cowboys 7

November 22: Two first-quarter TDs were all mighty Miami needed in a defensive slugfest with Dallas. Larry Csonka plowed in from the 1-yard line and Paul Warfield caught a 45-yard strike from Bob Griese to give the Dolphins defense all the cushion they needed.

The Cowboys were kept off the scoreboard until a 16-play, 94-yard drive that culminated with Walt Garrison's one-yard TD blast in the fourth quarter. That was all, however. The Dolphins had the ball at the Dallas 1-yard line as time expired in what combatants on both sides agreed was a great game.

GAME 12: Dallas Takes Care of Business

Cowboys 22 at Denver 10

December 2: There was no looking ahead to a big showdown with Washington. Dallas knew it needed a win over a tough Denver team first, and it earned one with stellar defense and a 240-yard passing effort from Roger Staubach.

The defense pounced on three Broncos turnovers and scored on a safety, while Staubach hit 14-of-18 passes—two for TDs to Jean Fugett.

GAME 13: Playoffs Become a Reality

Cowboys 27 vs. Washington 7

December 9: Needing to beat the Redskins by more than seven—the margin of Washington's win in their previous meeting—to take command of the NFC East, the Cowboys made sure there would be no nail-biting. They scored the first 27 points in one of their most complete games.

Calvin Hill rushed for 110 yards and two TDs. The Dallas defense was even more impressive, limiting the Redskins to 155 total yards. The Cowboys could have run up the score on their rivals, but they let the clock expire with the ball at the Washington 2.

GAME 14: Dallas Sets NFL Record

Cowboys 30 at St. Louis 3

December 16: By winning its last three regular-season games, the Cowboys reached the playoffs for the eighth straight season—an unprecedented feat in NFL annals. The last of those wins was the easiest, as the Cardinals provided little resistance.

Roger Staubach hit 14-of-19 passes for 256 yards and three TDs, including two scoring strikes to Drew Pearson. The Dallas defense allowed just 30 passing yards and 141 total yards in a dominant effort.

GAME 15: Dallas Survives Opening Scare

Cowboys 27 vs. Los Angeles 16

December 23: Dallas raced to a 17–0 lead, then watched the Rams rally for 16 straight points. But the Cowboys held on to reach the NFC title game for the fourth straight season. Rams receiver Harold Jackson, who caught four TDs in a regular-season win over the Cowboys, was held to one reception this time. And the Rams mustered just 192 yards as a team.

Still, the Cowboys did not cruise to victory as easily as it looked like they might. Roger Staubach's 83-yard bomb to Drew Pearson in the fourth quarter regained the momentum after the Rams had pulled within a single point. Calvin Hill ran for 97 yards and a TD.

GAME 16: Another Heartbreaking Title Game

Minnesota 27 at Cowboys 10

December 30: The visiting Vikings dominated the battle for NFC supremacy, advancing to their first Super Bowl and leaving the Cowboys on the outside once again. Chuck Foreman and Oscar Reed each rushed for 75-plus yards, and Fran Tarkenton quarterbacked Minnesota to a 10–0 halftime lead.

Despite gaining only 153 yards against the Purple People Eaters, Dallas did make it interesting in the second half when Golden Richards scored on a 63-yard punt return. The score sliced the deficit to 10–7, but Minnesota later got a 63-yard interception return from Bobby Bryant that sent many Texas Stadium patrons toward the exits. It was one of four interceptions thrown by Roger Staubach on a dismal 10-for-21, 89-yard passing day, and two of those picks were snared by Bryant.

1974

STREAK ENDS AT EIGHT

Failure to Reach Playoffs Does Not Sit Well

In 1974, the NFL playoffs went on without the Cowboys for the first time since 1965. Their run of eight consecutive postseason berths came to a halt thanks to an 8–6 record that included four straight early losses.

Dallas struggled on both sides of the ball, but its offensive woes were most noticeable. Their production slipped by six points per game compared to the previous season, with Calvin Hill's 844-yard rushing total marking a huge drop-off from the prior two years. Defenses also started to solve QB Roger Staubach, whose completion rate tumbled almost 10 points to 52.8.

Dallas followed the four-game losing streak with four straight wins, but the hole was too deep for recovery...that is, until the next season.

GAME 1: Birds Blanked

Cowboys 24 at Atlanta 0

September 15: Coach Tom Landry called it "great defense," and no one was arguing. His club pitched a shutout on the road, limiting the Falcons to an unthinkable 108 yards and keeping them off the board even when they started possessions in Dallas territory.

Roger Staubach nearly tripled Atlanta's yardage output on his own, running for one TD and passing for another. He threw for 252 yards and rushed for 24.

GAME 2: Dempsey's Boot Kicks Cowboys

Philadelphia 13 vs. Cowboys 10

September 23: The NFL added 10 yards to each field goal and extra-point try by moving the goal posts to the back of the end zone, but that didn't bother Tom Dempsey in his second game kicking under those conditions. The veteran sent a 45-yarder through the uprights with 25 seconds left as the Eagles upset the Cowboys on Monday night.

It was an improbable loss for Dallas, which outgained Philadelphia 385–165 and compiled 20 first downs to the Eagles' five. But missed opportunities kept the Cowboys from building on a 7–0 halftime lead. Joe Lavender's 96-yard return of a Doug Dennison fumble tied the game in the third quarter and gave the Eagles life. Roger Staubach's second interception of the game set up Dempsey's winning boot.

GAME 3: Dallas Self-Destructs Again

N.Y. Giants 14 at Cowboys 6

September 29: The Cowboys continued to be their own worst enemy in an upset loss to the Giants at Texas Stadium. Roger Staubach threw three interceptions and Dallas lost two fumbles, negating a slight yardage advantage over the visitors.

It wasn't until Staubach hit Bob Hayes for a meaningless 35-yard TD hookup with 11 seconds left in the game that the Cowboys ended the shutout bid from their rivals.

GAME 4: Controversial Kick Lifts Vikings

Minnesota 23 at Cowboys 21

October 6: For the second time in three games, a last-second field goal doomed the Cowboys. This time, it was accompanied by protests and profanity. Fred Fox kicked a 27-yarder high over the top of the right upright. Cowboys players and coaches signaled "no good," seeing the ball either directly in line with the post or just outside of it. The Vikings signaled "good." After a pause, the referees agreed with the latter.

The Cowboys were fortunate the game was as close as it was, considering they were significantly outgained and had a minus-four turnover margin. They overcame a 20–7 deficit on Walt Garrison and Calvin Hill TDs in the fourth quarter. Vikings QB Fran Tarkenton threw for 283 yards and two scores.

GAME 5: Dallas Dumped Again

St. Louis 31 vs. Cowboys 28

October 13: Another week, another late kick that beat the Cowboys. This time, St. Louis stymied Dallas' comeback efforts on a 31-yard Jim Bakken boot with one minute to play. The Cardinals had squandered a 28–14 fourth-quarter lead before recovering to send the Cowboys to their fourth loss in a row.

Roger Staubach led the Dallas comeback, throwing for 236 yards and a score. Drew Pearson caught eight balls for 118 yards, and Calvin Hill ran for 92.

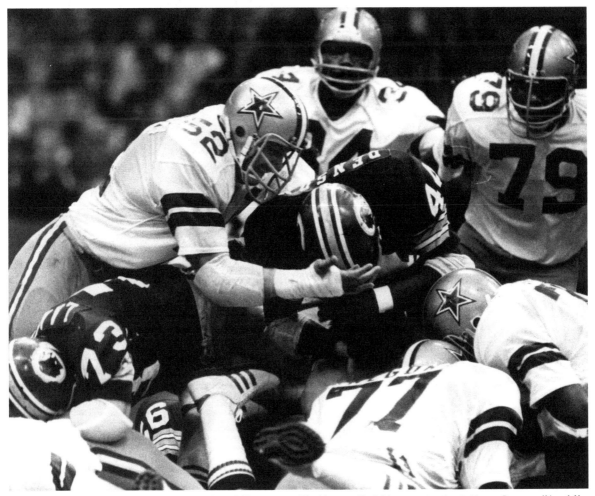

Dallas Cowboys linebacker Dave Edwards (No. 52) wraps up Washington Redskins running back Moses Denson (No. 44) during a 24–23 Cowboys victory on November 28, 1974, at Texas Stadium in Irving, Texas. (Photo by Russ Russell/NFL)

Captain Comeback
Roger Staubach was the "Stars and Stripes" of America's Team

By the time Roger Staubach earned the starting quarterback job with the Cowboys in 1971, he was at an age, 29, when most NFL players had already retired. Nevertheless, he packed a Hall of Fame career into his remaining nine seasons in Big D.

A man of the highest integrity and a natural-born leader, Staubach reigns as the most revered player in Cowboys history. As sportswriter Tom Melody put it, "When somebody raised the flag over Dallas and proclaimed the Cowboys to be America's Team, Roger Staubach was the stars and stripes."[1]

Upon joining the 'Boys in 1969, Staubach was already an American idol, having won the 1963 Heisman Trophy with Navy and honoring his obligation to the academy with four years of service—including a year in Vietnam. It was with the 'Boys that Roger earned the rank of "captain"—Captain Comeback.

After backing up Craig Morton for two years in Dallas, Roger earned his shot in 1971. Of course, he made the made the most of it, throwing 15 touchdown passes and just four interceptions, earning NFL Player of the Year honors, and leading Dallas to victory in Super Bowl VI.

Staubach led the Cowboys to four Super Bowls in all, and he posted a record of 85–29 as starting quarterback. Famous for operating under the shotgun formation, Roger rallied his troops to 23 victories after trailing in the fourth quarter. Incredibly, 14 of those come-from-behind wins came in the last two minutes or in overtime.

Roger earned the "Comeback" nickname after shocking San Francisco with two touchdown drives in the final two minutes in the

Roger Staubach accumulated more than 22,000 passing yards in his Hall of Fame career. (Photo by Focus on Sport/Getty Images)

1972 playoffs. Three years later, he launched the original "Hail Mary" pass—a 50-yarder to Drew Pearson with seconds remaining—to defeat the Vikings in the playoffs. "I closed my eyes and said a Hail Mary prayer," he told reporters afterward.

Staubach led the NFL in passer rating four times and was named to six Pro Bowls. In January 1978 he led Dallas over Denver 27–10 in Super Bowl XII with a typically efficient performance (17-of-25, 183 yards, 1 TD, 0 INT).

In 1979, his final NFL season, Staubach went out with a bang, setting career highs in passing yards (3,586) and touchdown passes (27) and posting an NFL-best 92.3 passer rating. When he left the game, he held the highest passer rating (83.4) in NFL history. He retired with 22,700 passing yards and, as "Roger the Dodger," 2,264 yards rushing. He was inducted into the Pro Football Hall of Fame in Canton, Ohio, in 1985, his first year of eligibility.

GAME 6: Dallas Halts Four-Game Slide

Cowboys 31 vs. Philadelphia 24

October 20: Getting back to basics, Dallas rushed for 246 yards—140 by Calvin Hill—and snapped a four-game losing streak when Roger Staubach ran one yard for the winning score in the fourth quarter. Hill was brilliant, carrying 26 times and scoring three TDs. Still, victory did not come easily.

Philadelphia rallied three times from deficits to tie the game, and it took a 24–17 lead on a 64-yard TD strike from Roman Gabriel to Don Zimmerman in the third quarter. From there, the Cowboys defense and running game came to the rescue.

GAME 7: Defense, Trick Play Boost Dallas

Cowboys 21 at N.Y. Giants 7

October 27: The Giants failed to score against the Dallas defense, getting their only TD on a 71-yard fumble return by Roy Hilton in the third quarter at the Yale Bowl. The score cut the deficit to 14–7 and had the Cowboys sweating out another one. Then, in the final quarter, Drew Pearson threw a 46-yard TD pass to Golden Richards on a flanker option pass to clinch the Dallas victory.

Pearson had caught a TD toss from Roger Staubach in the first half to give the Cowboys a 14–0 edge at the break.

GAME 8: Tables Turn Toward Cowboys

Cowboys 17 vs. St. Louis 14

November 3: After losing three earlier games on late field goals, it was the Cowboys' turn to win one. Efren Herrera popped a 20-yarder through the uprights with four seconds to go as Dallas avenged a three-point loss in St. Louis three weeks earlier. The effort capped a comeback from a 14–7 deficit after three quarters.

Calvin Hill, shuffling in and out of the game with an injured leg, scored earlier in the final quarter to tie the game. It was a balanced offensive effort from Dallas, which got 52 rushing yards from Walt Garrison and 51 from Hill, along with a 154-yard, no-interception passing performance from Roger Staubach.

GAME 9: Hill Sets Records, Sparks Win

Cowboys 20 vs. San Francisco 14

November 10: The Cowboys kept their postseason hopes alive—for the time being—by covering 70 yards in seven plays for the winning TD in the fourth quarter. While Roger Staubach directed the drive, Calvin Hill, Drew Pearson, and Walt Garrison made big plays, setting up Hill's score with 1:58 remaining to erase a 14–13 deficit.

It was a record-breaking day for Hill, who scored both Cowboys TDs. The running back set club marks for carries (32) and rushing yards (153) in a game.

GAME 10: Comeback Can't Save Cowboys

Washington 28 vs. Cowboys 21

November 17: In a true tale of two halves, Dallas spotted Washington a seemingly safe 28–0 halftime lead, then came roaring back to make a game of it. Unfortunately for the Cowboys, their inspired second half left them six yards short of a potential tying TD.

Roger Staubach and Billy Joe Dupree hooked up for two second-half TD strikes, and Robert Newhouse ran for a score as the Cowboys came roaring out of the locker room after a first half in which they could do little right. However, late incompletions on third and fourth downs from the Redskins' 6-yard line prevented Dallas from finishing its comeback.

GAME 11: Dallas Claims Texas Tussle

Cowboys 10 at Houston 0

November 24: The largest regular-season crowd for the Oilers in the Astrodome (49,775) witnessed one of the best defensive performances in Cowboys history. Not only did the visitors keep Houston off the scoreboard, they held the hosts to 81 total yards (26 rushing yards) and registered seven sacks in ending the Oilers' four-game win streak.

The Cowboys' attack was not prolific, but it didn't need to be. With Calvin Hill limited, Robert Newhouse and Charley Young combined for 148 rushing yards. Doug Dennison scored the game's only TD on a short first-quarter run.

GAME 12: "Mad Bomber" Rescues Dallas

Cowboys 24 vs. Washington 23

November 28: Clint Longley was the most unlikely Thanksgiving Day hero. Nicknamed the "Mad Bomber" for his aggressive, erratic throwing in training camp and never having taken an NFL snap, the rookie from Abilene Christian replaced a shaken-up Roger Staubach and led the Cowboys from a 16–3 deficit to a memorable victory.

Longley went 11-of-20 for 203 yards and two TDs in his debut, sparking a desperate club in the second half. "He was unbelievable for a guy who hasn't played," said teammate Walt Garrison. Longley hit Drew Pearson for the winning 50-yard score in the final seconds with no timeouts to work with.

GAME 13: Browns Trampled

Cowboys 41 vs. Cleveland 17

December 7: Roger Staubach returned from a Thanksgiving Day injury to throw for 230 yards

and three TDs, and the Dallas running game smashed the Browns for 252 yards in a one-sided affair. Golden Richards caught two first-quarter TD passes, and Walt Garrison ran for two third-quarter scores.

Cornell Green picked off two of Cleveland QB Mike Phipps' four interceptions as Dallas kept its playoff hopes alive.

GAME 14: Dallas on Outside Looking In

Oakland 27 vs. Cowboys 23

December 14: Oakland made official what the Cowboys' four-game losing streak early in the season intimated—that Dallas would miss the playoffs for the first time in nine years. It was a bitter setback for the Cowboys, who gained 400 yards to the Raiders' 267.

Two lost fumbles were costly for the visitors, who trailed 24–9 early in the third quarter before mounting a comeback that came up just short. Roger Staubach passed for 266 yards in the finale but could not match Ken Stabler's two TD passes for the playoff-bound Raiders.

1975

HAIL MARY!

Milestone Play Caps Cowboys Comeback

One of the most memorable plays in NFL history gave the Cowboys a last-second playoff win in Minnesota, blazing their way to the Super Bowl. It was the original "Hail Mary," a timeless connection between Roger Staubach and Drew Pearson that covered half the gridiron and will never be forgotten.

The 1975 Dallas Cowboys season featured more than miracles. After a rare season out of the playoffs, the team returned as a wild-card entry at 10–4. Fullback Robert Newhouse bulled through defenses for a team-leading 930 rushing yards, and a four-game winning streak to open the year helped fans put the previous season's early ending behind.

While the Pittsburgh Steelers were dominating the AFC, eventually defeating the Cowboys in Super Bowl X, Dallas was never out of the mix among the top NFC clubs. The Cowboys suffered three of their four losses by less than seven points, and they won several close games, too.

But no games were closer than the one decided on a prayer.

GAME 1: Dallas Dominates Opener
Cowboys 18 vs. Los Angeles 7

September 21: Dallas stifled a talented Rams team from start to finish, holding the visitors to 148 yards and a 4-of-17 passing rate. The fact that the Cowboys settled for Toni Fritsch field goals on four of their five scoring drives kept the score closer than the game.

Mel Renfro intercepted two Rams passes, and Roger Staubach, while putting up modest passing numbers, directed a methodical offense and scrambled seven times for 56 yards. Robert Newhouse ran for a game-high 88.

GAME 2: First OT Game Goes to Dallas
Cowboys 37 vs. St. Louis 31 (OT)

September 28: The first OT game in Cowboys history was there for the Cardinals' taking, but their big gamble backfired. In position to try a winning field goal in the extra session, the visitors instead put the ball in the air, and Lee Roy Jordan intercepted a Jim Hart pass and returned it 38 yards to the St. Louis 37-yard line. That set up Roger Staubach's winning three-yard TD pass to Billy Joe Dupree.

The Dallas offense was terrific for most of the day. Staubach threw for 307 yards and three scores and directed three long TD drives in regulation time. Robert Newhouse ran for 90 yards on 23 carries. But Hart and the Cardinals erased a 31–17 fourth-quarter deficit to force overtime.

GAME 3: At Home in the Dome
Cowboys 36 at Detroit 10

October 6: The new Pontiac Silverdome hosted nearly 80,000 fans and a dominant Dallas pass rush on this Monday night. The Cowboys were all over Lions QB Greg Landry, getting to him 11 times for minus-84 yards.

Still, Detroit led 10–9 in the third quarter before Dallas took control. Charley Young ran for the go-ahead TD in the third quarter and caught a Roger Staubach TD pass early in the fourth. Drew Pearson then hauled in two long TD passes—one from Staubach and another on a trick play from Robert Newhouse.

GAME 4: Late Pick Lifts Cowboys
Cowboys 13 at N.Y. Giants 7

October 12: Trailing 7–6 in the fourth quarter, Dallas devastated an old friend to pull out a thriller at Shea Stadium. Mark Washington intercepted a throw from former Cowboys QB Craig Morton to set up the winning score, a four-yard strike from Roger Staubach to Jean Fugett.

Until the late turn of events, it appeared the Giants were poised for an upset. They nearly had one despite Morton's three interceptions and a Dallas defense that yielded just 173 yards. Charley Young ran for 93 yards for the Cowboys.

GAME 5: Pack Ruins Perfect Start
Green Bay 19 at Cowboys 17

October 19: The Cowboys had been living on the edge in four straight wins to open the season. Against the Packers, they toppled over it in heartbreaking fashion. Leading 17–12, Dallas return man Golden Richards fumbled a punt with 2:12 to go. Green Bay recovered and won the game on John Hadl's 26-yard pass to Rich McGeorge.

That was one of the five turnovers that kept the Cowboys from victory despite 101 rushing yards from Preston Pearson and 92 from Robert Newhouse. Dallas led 17–9 early in the fourth quarter.

GAME 6: Fritsch Boots Eagles
Cowboys 20 at Philadelphia 17

October 26: Having missed from 49 and 41 yards and having bounced a 20-yarder off the upright, Dallas kicker Toni Fritsch was not at the height of his confidence as he lined up a 42-yard game-winner in the final seconds. It didn't matter, though. The kick sailed through, and a hard-fought game with the Eagles finished in the win column.

Fritsch's field goal gave Dallas its only lead of the day. The Cowboys struggled to run against their bitter rivals, but Roger Staubach passed for

314 yards and a TD, moving his team into position for the win after getting the ball at his own 40 with 35 seconds remaining.

GAME 7: Dallas Misfires Against Redskins
Washington 30 vs. Cowboys 24 (OT)

November 2: Dallas missed several chances to put this one away. Its most obvious blunder came when Toni Fritsch missed badly on a 38-yard field goal in the final seconds of regulation time. That paved the way for an overtime win for the Redskins, secured on a one-yard Billy Kilmer run.

Cliff Harris had given the Cowboys a 24–17 fourth-quarter lead when he returned his second interception 27 yards for a TD. But Kilmer, who passed for 301 yards, directed a tying drive for the Redskins. Drew Pearson caught seven passes for 114 yards and a Cowboys score.

GAME 8: Turnovers Doom Dallas
Kansas City 34 at Cowboys 31

November 10: Dallas did everything in its power to give this one away, losing five fumbles and two interceptions. Finally, early in the fourth quarter, Kansas City took control, erasing a 31–27 deficit on Ed Podolak's third TD of the game. From there, the Cowboys continued to be their own worst enemy.

Their 436 offensive yards, compared to 296 for the Chiefs, were no match for their miscues, which included erratic passes, inexcusable drops, and an inability to pounce on a bouncing football. Roger Staubach ran for two TDs and threw for two others.

GAME 9: Dallas Hangs On
Cowboys 34 at New England 31

November 16: No lead seemed safe for the Cowboys, who raced to 24–10 and 34–17 advantages before surviving two late TD hookups between Jim Plunkett and Darryl Stingley to end a two-game skid.

Roger Staubach was sharp in victory, hitting 10-of-14 passes for 190 yards and three TDs. Drew Pearson caught two of those scoring tosses in the first half. Plunkett also threw for three TDs, but he was intercepted twice.

GAME 10: Ground Attack Prevails
Cowboys 27 vs. Philadelphia 17

November 23: Robert Newhouse rushed for 82 yards, and Roger Staubach, Preston Pearson, and Doug Dennison all ran for TDs as the Cowboys ground out a win against the Eagles.

Dallas Cowboys wide receiver Drew Pearson catches a scoring pass behind New England Patriots cornerback Ron Bolton in a 34–31 win on November 16, 1975, in Foxboro. (Photo by Russ Russell/NFL)

Super Bowl X: Comeback Falls Short Against Steel Curtain
Swann, Pittsburgh Defend Title in Memorable Matchup

America entered its bicentennial celebration with one of the most memorable Super Bowls ever played. Some of its highlights remain among the most replayed in the game's history. There was Lynn Swann catching a pass by tipping the ball to himself while falling over Cowboys defender Mark Washington. There was Swann getting behind Washington for a 64-yard, final-quarter TD grab on a play that a) determined the game's outcome and b) knocked QB Terry Bradshaw out of the game. And there was Roger Staubach nimbly scrambling in the pocket, trying to pull off an amazing comeback, only to be sacked by the future Hall of Famers on the "Steel Curtain" defense.

"What hurts is that you come so far, make it to the Super Bowl and then have a chance to win and don't," noted Drew Pearson, who gave Dallas an early 7–0 lead on a 29-yard TD catch. "This game means so much, it can make you forget for a while what a good season you had."[1]

The Steelers' 21–17 victory made them the third team in NFL history to win back-to-back Super Bowls. Perhaps lost in the shuffle was the fact the Cowboys reached the big game for the third time, something only Miami and Minnesota had managed before them.

Swann's scoring reception headlined a 161-yard MVP performance and gave Pittsburgh a 21–10 cushion with three minutes to play in the game. The underdog Cowboys, however, refused to duck out of the Orange Bowl quietly.

Staubach fired a 34-yard scoring pass to wide-open rookie Percy Howard—Howard's

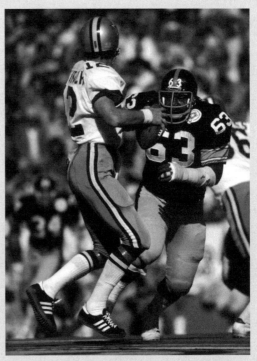

Pittsburgh defensive tackle Ernie Holmes pressures Dallas quarterback Roger Staubach as he gets ready to pass the ball in the Steelers' 21–17 win over the Cowboys in Super Bowl X on January 18, 1976, at the Orange Bowl in Miami, Florida. (Photo by Vernon Biever/NFL)

first career catch—to trim the deficit and got a shot at a winning drive when the Dallas defense stopped the Steelers and gave him the ball back with 1:22 left. With no timeouts, the Cowboys reached the Pittsburgh 38 before a desperation pass was intercepted by Steelers safety Glen Edwards. Unlike in an earlier win at Minnesota, this Hail Mary went unanswered.

Bradshaw completed just nine passes before he was knocked from the game, but they went for 209 yards and two TDs. Staubach also threw two TD passes but had three intercepted and was sacked seven times—four times by L.C. Greenwood.

Pittsburgh turned the tide on a special-teams play, blocking a Mitch Hoopes punt out of the back of the end zone for a fourth-quarter safety. Dallas had entered the final frame leading 10–7.

"That was the key," Cowboys coach Tom Landry admitted. "We were holding our own until then."[2]

In total, Dallas rushed for 205 yards on 48 carries.

"I believe our offense is as good as there is right now," said Staubach, who was 11-of-15 passing but was intercepted on two of his four mistakes.

GAME 11: Morton Misfires vs. Old Team

Cowboys 14 vs. N.Y. Giants 3

November 30: For the second time, Craig Morton could not solve the problem of his old Dallas teammates. The Giants QB threw three interceptions and could not lead his club to the end zone as Dallas ran to another victory.

Roger Staubach was not much better, going 13-of-22 with two picks. However, he did throw a 54-yard TD pass to Jean Fugett and contributed to a 181-yard team rushing effort. All of the scoring came in the first quarter.

GAME 12: Cardinals Win Battle for First

St. Louis 31 vs. Cowboys 17

December 7: The defending NFC East champs took a giant step toward repeating, racing to a 28–3 halftime lead and outplaying Dallas on a cold day at Busch Stadium. Roger Wehrli set the tone, picking off three Roger Staubach passes.

Jim Otis and Terry Metcalf each ran for more than 80 yards against the Cowboys. Staubach threw for 222 of his 268 yards in the second half.

GAME 13: Dallas Rumbles into Playoffs

Cowboys 31 vs. Washington 10

December 13: After spotting the Redskins a 10-point lead, the Cowboys scored 31 unanswered points to secure a playoff berth. They did it on the ground, rushing for 207 yards, with 90 yards coming from Robert Newhouse.

Roger Staubach hit Golden Richards from 57 yards in the second quarter to get Dallas on the board, and Staubach ran for the go-ahead score before halftime. Charlie Waters returned an interception 20 yards for a TD in the fourth.

GAME 14: Backups Produce Win

Cowboys 31 at N.Y. Jets 21

December 21: Resting Roger Staubach, Rayfield Wright, Mel Renfro, and several other regulars in a meaningless finale, Cowboys coach Tom Landry still had enough weapons to defeat the Jets. Robert Newhouse accounted for 108 of the team's 243 rushing yards, and Clint Longley quarterbacked a rally from a 14–0 deficit.

Newhouse finished the season 70 yards short of the 1,000-yard barrier.

GAME 15: Hail Mary Saves Dallas

Cowboys 17 at Minnesota 14

December 28: It was simply the greatest play in Cowboys history. And it might never be topped. Roger Staubach needed a miracle TD in the final seconds of a playoff game at Minnesota, so he faded, pump-faked, and launched what he later dubbed a "Hail Mary" toward the end zone.

Somehow—Minnesota fans claim it was with the help of a push-off on defender Nate Wright—Drew Pearson cradled the ball on his hip, ran into the end zone past the fallen Wright, and threw the ball into the stands in celebration. Another throw followed. A Vikings fan hit referee Armen Terzian in the head with a whiskey bottle in protest, bloodying one of the most memorable playoff games in NFL history.

If it was a miraculous play that made the difference, it was the Dallas defense that made it possible. The potent Vikings managed just 215 total yards to 356 for the Cowboys. But it was the final 50 of those yards that will never be forgotten.

GAME 16: Wild Card Reaches Super Bowl

Cowboys 37 at Los Angeles 7

January 4, 1976: In dominant fashion, the Cowboys became the first wild-card team to ever reach the Super Bowl. They did so behind a potent passing attack and relentless defense.

Roger Staubach threw four TD passes—three to Preston Pearson—and led the Cowboys to the game's first 34 points. Dallas compiled 441 yards to the Rams' paltry 118, sending thousands of the 84,000 fans at the Los Angeles Coliseum to the exits early.

1976

QUICK START FADES

Dallas Loses Steam as Another Winning Season Ends

Their Super Bowl loss to the Steelers the year before had the Cowboys on a mission in 1976, and they opened the year on fire. Five straight wins to begin the season led to nine victories in their first 10 games and a return to the top as NFC East champions.

However, something went awry once the weather turned cold. The Cowboys lost two of their last four regular-season games to finish at 11–3, and they were upset 14–12 by the Rams in their first playoff game. It was a dreary finish to their 11th consecutive winning season and a year in which three Dallas runners topped 400 yards.

The Doomsday Defense was the key to the team's success. Opponents averaged less than 14 points per game against Harvey Martin, Ed "Too Tall" Jones, and the Dallas stop troops.

GAME 1: Dallas Dominates Opener

Cowboys 27 vs. Philadelphia 7

September 12: Second-year fullback Scott Laidlaw ran for 109 yards and caught seven passes for 66 more to power an impressive opening-day attack. Dallas was in control from start to finish, racking up 445 yards while keeping the visiting Eagles off the scoreboard until the fourth quarter.

Roger Staubach was 19-of-28 for 242 yards and threw TD passes to Drew Pearson and Golden Richards.

GAME 2: Saints No Match

Cowboys 24 at New Orleans 6

September 19: Not even losing four fumbles could derail the Cowboys in New Orleans. For the second straight week, they shut out their opponent through the first three quarters and cruised to an easy victory.

Scott Laidlaw ran for two TDs and Billy Joe Dupree caught five passes for 108 yards in the one-sided affair.

GAME 3: Quick Strikes Down Colts

Cowboys 30 vs. Baltimore 27

September 26: Just 23 seconds remained when the Cowboys got the ball at their own 32 in a tie game. It turned out to be plenty of time. Two hookups from Roger Staubach to Drew Pearson and a pass-interference penalty set up Efren Herrera for his 32-yard winning field goal with three seconds remaining at Texas Stadium.

The game was an offensive showcase featuring 857 total yards. Staubach was sensational, completing 22-of-28 throws for 339 yards and two scores without an interception. Pearson also threw a TD pass to Golden Richards.

GAME 4: Wake-Up Call Arrives in Time

Cowboys 28 at Seattle 13

October 3: The expansion Seahawks put up a game effort, scoring the first 13 points and making a surprising game of it into the third quarter. But the Cowboys woke up in time to pull away late, riding Robert Newhouse to another win.

Newhouse needed just 19 carries to amass 120 yards and a third-quarter score that gave Dallas a 21–13 edge. Roger Staubach threw for 200 yards and two TDs.

GAME 5: Giants Fall in Stadium Opener

Cowboys 24 at N.Y. Giants 14

October 10: More than 76,000 fans packed the new Giants Stadium for New York's first game there, but Dallas spoiled their party. The Cowboys grabbed a 17–0 halftime lead and never looked back in winning their fifth straight to start the season.

Roger Staubach attempted just 15 passes but completed 13 of them. His 40-yard TD toss to

Quarterback Roger Staubach (No. 12) of the Dallas Cowboys turns to hand off against the Washington Redskins at RFK Stadium on October 31, 1976, in Washington, D.C. The Cowboys defeated the Redskins 20–7. (Photo by Nate Fine/NFL Photos/Getty Images)

Drew Pearson in the second quarter made it a 14–0 game. Three Cowboy runners toted at least 10 times for 40-plus yards.

GAME 6: Streak Ends in St. Louis

St. Louis 21 vs. Cowboys 17

October 17: A shotgun formation–fueled comeback nearly kept the Cowboys perfect, but a last-second pass from Roger Staubach went off the fingertips of Billy Joe Dupree in the end zone as the Cardinals halted a five-game Dallas winning streak. Jim Hart threw for 346 yards and three TDs for St. Louis, but the Cowboys threatened to rally from 21–10 down in the final quarter.

Staubach, taking snaps in the shotgun, drove Dallas downfield and hit Drew Pearson for a score. Then, needing to cover 75 yards in the final 45 seconds for a potential winning TD, the Cowboys came within a fingertip catch of victory in a game in which their defense yielded 436 yards.

Sunday was Doomsday for Dallas Foes

Doomsday Defense One of the Best, and Best-Named, in NFL Annals

Every great defense, it seems, needs a great nickname. There were the "Steel Curtain" (Pittsburgh), "Purple People Eaters" (Minnesota), "Orange Crush" (Denver), and "No-Name Defense" (Miami), to name a few. So dominant was the "Doomsday Defense" of the Dallas Cowboys, it earned its mighty moniker twice. "Doomsday I" smashed opponents in the late 1960s and early '70s, and "Doomsday II" continued the job in the late '70s.

The stars on those teams read like a Who's Who of NFL defensive greats. Bob Lilly, George Andrie, Chuck Howley, Lee Roy Jordan, Herb Adderly, Cornell Green, and Mel Renfro were among the first to wreak havoc on opposing offenses. Charlie Waters, Harvey Martin, Ed "Too Tall" Jones, Randy White, Thomas "Hollywood" Henderson, and Everson Walls led the group that made sure the nickname lived on.

"Coach Landry used to tell us that if we held our opponents to 17 points, we'd win about 90 percent of our games," said Lilly, who anchored a 1971 unit that allowed just 18 total points in three playoff games.[1]

The Doomsday Defense between plays during Super Bowl X on January 18, 1976. (Photo by Focus on Sport/Getty Images)

That was the formula the Cowboys rode to more than a decade of dominance. Keeping their foes from lighting up the scoreboard allowed Dallas to win with a largely conservative, ball-control offense. That style, in turn, forced defenses to load up the line of scrimmage, opening big-play chances for Roger Staubach and Danny White to throw downfield.

Between 1968 and '71, the Cowboys never ranked lower than fourth in the NFL in yards allowed. They finished second in that category in '71, the year they won the Super Bowl for the first time and made Doomsday Defense a household term.

Doomsday II gave the Cowboys their first season-ending No. 1 NFL defensive ranking in 1977, when Dallas finished 12–2 and again won the Super Bowl. Fittingly, defensive stalwarts Martin and White were named co–Super Bowl MVPs that year. It was just the second time in history the award did not go to an offensive player. The only previous time was when Howley earned it seven years earlier on Doomsday I.

The nickname gained popularity among the press beginning in 1968, when Dallas held opponents to the second-fewest points in the NFL before falling to the Packers in the NFL title game. Lilly contends he and his mates did not truly deserve it until after they suffered a 38–0 pasting at the hands of the Cardinals in 1970. A loud defensive team meeting was held the following day, at which the Cowboys resolved to clamp down on all comers.

The rest, as they say, is history. Or is it? In shutting out their last two regular-season opponents to win the NFC East, the 2009 Cowboys had some headline writers using the phrase "Doomsday III." Stay tuned.

GAME 7: Staubach Hurt in One-Sided Win

Cowboys 31 vs. Chicago 21

October 24: The 10-point margin masked a dominant Dallas performance. With a gaudy yardage advantage of 529–110, the Cowboys could have—and should have—won this game by 40. As it was, they gained a victory but lost a QB, as Roger Staubach fractured the small finger on his throwing hand in the first half and gave way to Danny White.

The two QBs combined for 307 passing yards. Three Dallas turnovers, one of which produced a Chicago TD, played a large role in keeping the score close.

GAME 8: Redskins Fall at RFK

Cowboys 20 at Washington 7

October 31: For the first time since 1971, the Cowboys downed the Redskins at RFK Stadium. They did so in dominating style, losing their shutout bid only in the final minute.

Doug Dennison's early TD provided the only points of the first half, and a Roger Staubach run made it a 14–0 game in the third quarter. Two Efren Herrera field goals padded the margin and stole all hope from Washington.

GAME 9: Three Kicks Beat One

Cowboys 9 vs. N.Y. Giants 3

November 7: In a TD-less battle with the winless Giants, the Cowboys felt fortunate to emerge with a win. They were outrushed and outgained by the Giants in a strange game at Texas Stadium, but Efren Herrera's three field goals proved to be just enough.

Craig Morton, the former Dallas QB, drove the Giants to the Dallas 6-yard line with less than two minutes to play, but Harvey Martin sacked him on fourth down. Larry Csonka ran for 89 yards for the Giants—three times as many rushing yards as any Cowboy managed.

GAME 10: Another Lackluster Win

Cowboys 17 vs. Buffalo 10

November 15: A *Monday Night Football* game following an ugly win over the Giants was not enough to inspire greatness from the Cowboys, but it did provide another win. A two-win Bills team compiled more yardage than its favored foe, but Dallas prevailed.

Butch Johnson's 74-yard kickoff return was the biggest play for the Cowboys, who got 202 passing yards from Roger Staubach but again struggled to run the ball. Drew Pearson caught nine passes for 135 yards and a TD.

GAME 11: Mistakes Cost Cowboys

Atlanta 17 vs. Cowboys 10

November 21: Four turnovers, eight penalties, and a nonchalant fourth-quarter defense caught up to the Cowboys in Atlanta. The Falcons stormed back from a 10–0 deficit with 17 points in the final period to beat a Dallas team that had been barely getting by.

Mike Esposito's 35-yard run tied the score, and QB Scott Hunter's one-yard plunge put the hosts ahead. The Falcons then held off the Cowboys in the final minutes, handing them just their second loss of the year.

GAME 12: Dallas Holds On

Cowboys 19 vs. St. Louis 14

November 25: The Cardinals had made a habit of winning games in the final minute, and they nearly did it again. This time, though, the Cowboys held on to avenge an earlier setback and post their most impressive win in more than a month.

St. Louis got to the Dallas 13-yard line but could not score on four late tries. The Cowboys finally got their ground game going. Roger Staubach ran for one score and threw for another, and his 54 rushing yards were a game high.

GAME 13: Dallas Clinches NFC East

Cowboys 26 at Philadelphia 7

December 5: Overcoming a "chippy" game with their bitter rivals, the Cowboys secured the NFC East crown with an impressive second half. Roger Staubach threw for 259 yards and a TD, and his defense held the Eagles to 176 yards.

To win, the Cowboys had to overcome 105 yards on nine penalties. Once they put their mind to football, however, they pulled away by scoring the game's last 17 points.

GAME 14: Redskins Make Playoffs

Washington 27 at Cowboys 14

December 12: The Redskins needed a win to make the playoffs. The Cowboys did not, and it showed. Washington overcame a 14–10 third-quarter deficit to gain a wild-card berth, while Dallas looked like a team content with having won its division a week earlier.

Mark Washington sparked Dallas with two interceptions, but the Redskins simply relied on their ground game. John Riggins ran for 95 yards to power Washington's potent rushing attack.

GAME 15: One and Done

Los Angeles 14 at Cowboys 12

December 19: Dallas again struggled to move the ball on the ground, but a Scott Laidlaw plunge gave the Cowboys a 10–7 halftime lead. The Rams, no offensive juggernaut either, took the lead for good on a Lawrence McCutcheon dive in the fourth quarter.

Mere inches kept Dallas from keeping its dreams of a deep playoff run alive, but it was not for a lack of opportunities. Trailing 14–10, the Cowboys failed to score after Charlie Waters' second blocked punt set them up at the Rams 17-yard line in the final two minutes.

Butch Johnson nearly had a winning TD catch, but he could not keep both feet in bounds, and a fourth-down reception by Billy Joe Dupree was marked just short of a first down. Los Angeles gave up an intentional safety as time expired rather than punt.

Roger Staubach's struggles set the tone for the Cowboys. The QB completed just 15-of-37 passes and was intercepted three times.

1977

TONY D BURSTS ONTO SUPER SCENE

Runner-By-Committee Approach Gives Way to a Star

Through many of the Cowboys' early years, Coach Tom Landry fielded a three-headed-monster style of running the football. Calvin Hill's back-to-back 1,000-yard seasons were the exception; a committee approach was the rule. That came to an end in 1977, when a rookie named Tony Dorsett arrived.

The fleet-footed Pitt product won the AP Offensive Rookie of the Year Award with a 1,007-yard debut that sparked Dallas to a 12–2 record, tops in the NFC. The Cowboys ran over their playoff opponents as well, trampling the Bears and Vikings in the NFC and the Broncos to claim the second Super Bowl title in their history.

If Dorsett was a sparkplug, then defense was the team's engine. The Cowboys gave up fewer yards than any team in the NFL. They ranked second against the pass and third against the run. In 17 games, counting the playoffs, 10 of their opponents scored 10 points or less.

It was a championship formula for a franchise fast becoming one of the most popular in the land—and one now loaded with star power.

GAME 1: Opener a Classic
Cowboys 16 at Minnesota 10 (OT)

September 18: Minnesota marched for a TD on its opening possession and drove for a tying field goal late in the fourth quarter. In between, Dallas showcased a dominant defense and managed 10 points of its own. And in the end, an opener between two talented teams required extra time to decide.

Roger Staubach, whose pass to Preston Pearson accounted for the Cowboys' only TD in regulation, made a gutsy scramble from the 4-yard line and crossed the goal line for the winning TD just 6:14 into overtime. Cliff Harris intercepted two passes for the Cowboys, who benefited from five Vikings turnovers.

GAME 2: Dorsett Debuts in Dallas
Cowboys 41 vs. N.Y. Giants 21

September 25: In his first home game, rookie Tony Dorsett ran for two TDs as Dallas dominated New York. The Giants fell behind 28–0 in the second quarter, when Dorsett scored from 11 yards out. He later added a 34-yard dash to the end zone.

Roger Staubach ran for one TD and threw for another, while the Dallas defense held the Giants to 161 total yards.

GAME 3: Hollywood a Hit
Cowboys 23 vs. Tampa Bay 7

October 2: Thomas "Hollywood" Henderson returned an interception 79 yards for the game's first TD, and the Cowboys cruised to an expected victory over the Buccaneers. It was the first career TD for Henderson, who later picked off a second pass and knocked two Tampa Bay players out of the game.

Tony Dorsett and Robert Newhouse each contributed 70-plus yards to the Cowboys' 205-yard team rushing effort.

GAME 4: Dallas Keeps Rolling
Cowboys 30 at St. Louis 24

October 9: Another hotly contested game between these two clubs produced a combined 20 penalties for 275 yards. There were certainly too many flags to call it a classic game, but Dallas gladly left with a hard-fought win over a bitter rival.

The explosive Tony Dorsett was the difference, carrying 14 times for 141 yards and two TDs. He broke a 77-yarder for a second-quarter score, and his one-yard score in the final frame brought the Cowboys within 24–23. The winning score came on Roger Staubach's

17-yard pass to Golden Richards with 13:15 remaining.

GAME 5: Pearson Gets Deep

Cowboys 34 vs. Washington 16

October 16: Dallas trailed 16–14 in the third quarter before breaking it open, thanks largely to a 59-yard TD bomb from Roger Staubach to Drew Pearson. The Cowboys sacked Redskins QBs eight times for minus-63 yards. That was just one yard less than the visitors covered on completions.

Staubach passed for 250 yards and two scores, while Pearson caught six balls for 157 yards.

GAME 6: Dallas Escapes with a Win

Cowboys 16 at Philadelphia 10

October 23: Eagles fans had plenty to boo—Dallas, of course; their own team's mere 186 yards of offense; even a Frisbee-catching dog during halftime who missed a few times. The Cowboys did not play well, but they did play turnover-free football and took care of business.

Charlie Waters returned a blocked punt 17 yards for a third-quarter TD that put Dallas ahead for good in a defensive struggle.

GAME 7: Lions Run Into Wall

Cowboys 37 vs. Detroit 0

October 30: Statistically, it was one of the greatest defensive efforts in Cowboys history. They held the Lions to 120 yards and seven first downs and registered six sacks in a Texas Stadium shutout.

Any one of Efren Herrera's three field goals would have been enough offense for a seventh-straight Dallas win. Roger Staubach added TD passes to three different receivers.

GAME 8: Dallas Wins Eighth Straight

Cowboys 24 at N.Y. Giants 10

November 6: One week after holding Detroit to 120 yards, the Cowboys limited the Giants to 121 in another defensive gem. The Harvey Martin–led stop troops chalked up eight more sacks and opened the scoring on an eight-yard fumble return by Jay Saldi in leading the club to its eighth consecutive victory.

Offensively, Dallas struggled on the ground, but it didn't matter much against the Giants. Roger Staubach threw a five-yard TD pass to Billy Joe Dupree, and Tony Dorsett ran for a score.

GAME 9: Cardinals Halt Torrid Streak

St. Louis 24 at Cowboys 17

November 14: The best start in team history ended at eight in a row for the Cowboys, as their rivals from St. Louis delivered a setback in a Monday night game at Texas Stadium. Jim Hart threw two fourth-quarter TD passes to erase a 17–10 deficit, and Roger Staubach's comeback attempt was intercepted with less than two minutes to go.

Though they led for much of the way, the Cowboys struggled to get anything going on offense, managing just 236 yards from scrimmage.

GAME 10: Steelers Dominate

Pittsburgh 28 vs. Cowboys 13

November 20: Coach Tom Landry said his team was beaten in every facet by the Steelers. Nowhere was that more true than in the Cowboys' efforts to stop Franco Harris. The Pittsburgh workhorse powered for 179 yards and two TDs at Three Rivers Stadium.

So strong was the Steelers' running attack that QB Terry Bradshaw attempted just 12 passes. He completed seven, including TDs to John Stallworth and Lynn Swann. Tony Dorsett opened the scoring for the Cowboys, but it was all Pittsburgh thereafter.

Running back Tony Dorsett (No. 33) runs behind the blocking of offensive linemen Burton Lawless (No. 66) and Tom Rafferty (No. 64) after taking a handoff from quarterback Roger Staubach (No. 12) during a game against Mel Blount (No. 47) and Steve Furness (No. 64) of the Pittsburgh Steelers at Three Rivers Stadium on November 20, 1977, in Pittsburgh, Pennsylvania. (Photo by George Gojkovich/Getty Images)

Super Bowl XII: Orange Crushed
Doomsday Defense Dashes Denver's Dreams

The 1977 NFL season would conclude with at least two notable firsts. Super Bowl XII was the first to be played indoors, with the Louisiana Superdome in New Orleans providing a setting for 76,400 fans. And a team from Denver, for the first time in the city's major professional sports history, would be playing for a championship.

Unfortunately for fans of the orange-clad Broncos, their team was facing a Dallas squad that gained more yards and allowed fewer than any team in the NFL that season. The Cowboys' might quickly turned the first prime-time Super Bowl into a rout.

A Tony Dorsett TD run and two Efren Herrera field goals carried Dallas to a 13–0 halftime lead, and Butch Johnson's diving grab of a Roger Staubach TD pass in the third quarter made it 20–3 before the Broncos could reach the end zone. After they did, Robert Newhouse hit Golden Richards on a 29-yard, halfback-option pass for a fourth-quarter TD that set the final score at 27–10.

Some fans, particularly those from Denver, thought the underdog Broncos might be able to stay in the game thanks to their "Orange Crush" defense, a group that allowed only 10.6 points per game during a 12–2 regular season. It was the "Doomsday II" defensive unit of the Cowboys, however, that controlled the game.

"Orange Crush is soda water, baby," exclaimed Dallas defensive end Harvey Martin, who was voted the game's co-MVP along with defensive tackle Randy White. "You drink it. It don't win football games."[1]

Cowboys linebacker Thomas "Hollywood" Henderson sacks Broncos quarterback Norris Weese in a 27–10 win over the Denver Broncos in Super Bowl XII on January 15, 1978, at the Louisiana Superdome. (Photo by Takashi Makita/NFL)

Aside from the matchup of two great defenses, the other big storyline was Staubach against Craig Morton, the man he once competed against for the Cowboys' starting QB job. This, too, was a one-sided affair.

Morton, traded by the Cowboys to the Giants three years earlier, set a dubious Super Bowl record by throwing four interceptions, all before halftime. He had been picked off only eight times during the regular season. The Broncos also lost four fumbles for a record eight turnovers in the game. It was only their defense that kept Dallas from winning by 40 points.

Staubach finished 17-of-25 for 183 yards, the highlight-reel score to Johnson and no interceptions. Tony Dorsett rushed for 66 yards, all in the first half, before a knee injury forced him out of the game in the third quarter. Newhouse added 55 on the ground in addition to his rare TD toss. And the Cowboys' 325 total yards more than doubled Denver's output.

GAME 11: Dallas Bounces Back

Cowboys 14 at Washington 7

November 27: It wasn't pretty, but Dallas snapped a two-game losing streak with a pair of second-half TDs to sweep the season series with Washington. Scoring drives of 61 and 55 yards spoiled an otherwise stingy Redskins defensive performance.

Roger Staubach capped the first with a four-yard toss to Golden Richards, and Tony Dorsett scored the winner from the 1-yard line in the fourth quarter. Thomas "Hollywood" Henderson made a club-high nine tackles.

GAME 12: Dorsett Runs Roughshod Over Philly

Cowboys 24 vs. Philadelphia 14

December 4: Dallas clinched the NFC East early on a record-shattering day from Tony Dorsett.

The rookie running back broke club marks with 206 rushing yards and an 84-yard scoring scamper.

The Eagles tied the game at 14 on a TD pass from Ron Jaworski to Harold Carmichael in the third quarter. But an Efren Herrera field goal put the Cowboys up for good, and Dorsett's long run broke Philly's back in the fourth quarter.

"He's just like he was when they drafted him," Eagles coach Dick Vermeil said. "The best in the country."

GAME 13: Staubach Outduels Plunkett

Cowboys 42 at San Francisco 35

December 12: Jim Plunkett passed for 263 yards and four TDs for the 49ers. While Roger Staubach did not match those numbers, the Dallas QB was even better. Staubach hit 14-of-19 passes for 220 yards and three scores and also ran for a TD as Dallas won a high-scoring game that featured 760 offensive yards and no turnovers by either team.

Not until Tony Hill secured a late onside kick was the victory secure. With it came home-field advantage in the NFC playoffs.

GAME 14: Dorsett Goes for 1,000

Cowboys 14 vs. Denver 6

December 18: In a game that meant nothing to the Cowboys in the standings, Tony Dorsett became just the eighth rookie in NFL history to rush for 1,000 yards in a season. He did so with 50 yards on 17 carries as Dallas completed a 12–2 regular season.

Roger Staubach hit Preston Pearson and Robert Newhouse for TDs that gave the Cowboys a 14–0 lead and left the rest up to his defense. Denver managed just 178 yards.

GAME 15: Dallas Drubs Bears in Opener

Cowboys 37 vs. Chicago 7

December 26: Losing fumbles on their first two possessions did not keep the Cowboys from corralling Walter Payton and the Bears. They held Payton to 31 yards over the first three quarters while amassing a 34–0 lead over the visitors from the Windy City.

In fact, both Tony Dorsett (85 yards) and Robert Newhouse (80 yards) outrushed the Chicago star, and Dallas totaled 233 ground yards as a team. In addition to shutting down Payton, the Cowboy defense got three Charlie Waters interceptions and four total picks against Bob Avellini.

GAME 16: Less Drama the Second Time Around

Cowboys 23 vs. Minnesota 6

January 1, 1978: Dallas opened this super season with an overtime win over the Vikings. In the NFC title game, regulation time sufficed. A dominant Cowboys defense yielded just 66 rushing yards on 30 carries and kept Minnesota out of the end zone while advancing to the Super Bowl for the fourth time.

A TD pass from Roger Staubach to Golden Richards plus a Robert Newhouse TD run staked the hosts to a 13–0 lead in the second quarter, and all the Vikings could muster was a pair of field goals after that. Newhouse ran for 81 yards, and Tony Dorsett added 71 while their defensive teammates recovered three Minnesota fumbles.

1978

STEELERS PREVENT REPEAT

Dallas Dashes to Fifth Super Bowl Berth

The road to the Super Bowl became longer in 1978, with the NFL schedule expanding to 16 games. The Cowboys were the team most thankful for the extra games, having opened defense of their championship by losing four of their first 10 starts. A run of six straight wins followed, and it wasn't until Pittsburgh put up a wall in the Super Bowl that the Cowboys' momentum was halted.

Roger Staubach, who earned the NFL Man of the Year Award, threw a career-high 25 TD passes while directing the highest-scoring offense in the NFL (24 points per game). He also set a team record for passing yards in a season with 3,190. Tony Dorsett took advantage of the longer slate to run for 1,325 yards, also a club record.

And the Dallas defense remained one of the NFL's elite, yielding just 13 points per game. A 35–31 shootout loss to the Steelers in the Super Bowl was not what either of those two defensive powers expected, but it was a classic finish to a memorable campaign.

GAME 1: Champs Impress in Opener
Cowboys 38 vs. Baltimore 0

September 4: Dallas defended its Super Bowl title with precision. Roger Staubach completed 11 straight passes at one point and finished with 280 aerial yards and four TDs before giving way to Danny White in the fourth quarter.

The Colts had no chance. They surrendered 583 yards, including 147 rushing from Tony Dorsett. The Cowboys star also caught a 91-yard TD pass in the second quarter.

GAME 2: Dallas Wins Shootout
Cowboys 34 at N.Y. Giants 24

September 10: Productive offense was enough to overcome shaky defense in New York as the Cowboys outscored the Giants. Tony Dorsett ran for 111 yards and Robert Newhouse scored two TDs in the winning effort.

The Giants moved the ball with ease at times, particularly through the air. Joe Pisarcik threw for 261 yards and a score. However, his three interceptions—two by Benny Barnes—were costly.

GAME 3: Rams Win Battle of Unbeatens
Los Angeles 27 vs. Cowboys 14

September 17: The Rams shut down Tony Dorsett and the Dallas running game and burned the Cowboys through the air to win an early battle of undefeated teams in L.A. Half of Pat Haden's 14 completions went to Ron Jessie, who covered 144 yards and scored on a 21-yard TD toss.

Dorsett, after back-to-back 100-yard rushing games, was kept to 38 yards on 19 carries. Roger Staubach tried to make up the difference through the air, but his 246 passing yards were tainted by four interceptions. Rod Perry returned his second pick for a score as the Rams broke open a 14–14 game in the fourth quarter.

GAME 4: Dallas Awakens Just in Time
Cowboys 21 vs. St. Louis 12

September 24: Trailing 12–7 entering the final 15 minutes, the Cowboys drove 73 and 88 yards for fourth-quarter TDs to avoid dropping back-to-back games. Robert Newhouse capped both marches—once on a short run and finally on a 15-yard pass from Roger Staubach.

Tony Dorsett carried the load for the Cowboys, running 21 times for 154 yards and a second-quarter score.

GAME 5: Redskins Have Friends in High Places

Washington 9 vs. Cowboys 5

October 2: President Jimmy Carter was among a crowd of 55,000-plus who witnessed the fifth Redskins victory in as many games. Washington did it with three Mark Moseley field goals, including a 52-yarder, and terrific goal-line defense.

Despite outgaining the Redskins and piling up three more first downs, the Cowboys managed only a short Rafael Septien field goal through the first three quarters. The Cowboys' late safety, when Redskins QB Joe Theismann was tackled in the end zone, was meaningless to everything but the final score. Washington bruiser John Riggins rushed for a game-high 96 yards.

GAME 6: Dallas "D" Steps Up

Cowboys 24 vs. N.Y. Giants 3

October 8: The Cowboys stretched their defensive streak of not allowing an opposing TD to 11 consecutive quarters. Tony Hill, on the other hand, reached the end zone twice in an impressive win at Texas Stadium.

Hill caught seven Roger Staubach passes for 112 yards and TDs of 17 and 30 yards. Staubach passed for 246 yards and three scores, while the Giants managed just 142 total yards as a team.

GAME 7: Wild OT Win Boosts 'Boys

Cowboys 24 at St. Louis 21

October 16: Rafael Septien kicked a 47-yard field goal 3½ minutes into overtime to end a wild game. Dallas won despite coughing up four turnovers and having QB Roger Staubach knocked woozy late in the game.

Coach Tom Landry called it a great game for fans but taxing for coaches—particularly himself. His defense gave up 264 passing yards to Jim Hart and 88 rushing yards to Jim Otis. Staubach offset that with two second-half TD tosses to Tony Hill and 289 aerial yards. Strangely, each team missed a field goal in the final three minutes of regulation time.

GAME 8: Landry Benches Dorsett, Wins Anyway

Cowboys 14 vs. Philadelphia 7

October 22: Tony Dorsett overslept and missed a practice without notifying the Cowboys, and Tom Landry took action. Benching his star running back in favor of Preston Pearson, Landry still saw his club handle the Eagles to grab a share of first place in the NFC East. Dorsett was not pleased with the demotion, but his teammates played inspired football.

Pearson and Robert Newhouse combined for 128 rushing yards, while Dorsett added 24 on seven carries off the bench. Newhouse and Pearson scored second-quarter TDs, and the Dallas defense took care of the rest.

The Cowboys' Dennis Thurman (No. 32) tackles Ron Jessie (No. 81) of the Rams during the 1978 NFC Championship Game on January 7, 1979, at the Los Angeles Memorial Coliseum in Los Angeles, California. The Cowboys shut out the Rams 28–0. (Photo by Andy Hayt/Getty Images)

GAME 9: Dorsett's Return No Spark for Dallas

Minnesota 21 at Cowboys 10

October 26: Tony Dorsett's return to the starting lineup did not have nearly the impact on the rushing stat sheet as did Chuck Foreman's bulldozing play. The Vikings standout ran for 101 yards on 22 carries and caught a TD pass in Minnesota's convincing victory.

Dorsett carried just 11 times for 38 yards and lost a fumble that led to a Minnesota TD. Roger Staubach did not fare much better, throwing two interceptions and no TDs. Dallas lost the turnover battle 4–0 and trailed 21–3 at halftime.

GAME 10: Turnovers Doom Dallas

Miami 23 vs. Cowboys 16

November 5: There was no secret to Dallas' back-to-back losses to the Vikings and Dolphins. In those games, the Cowboys gave up nine turnovers against zero takeaways. Four fumbles—three lost—and two interceptions doomed them against Miami. The Dolphins raced to a 17–0 lead and were never challenged.

Dallas settled for field goals three times after advancing inside the Miami 12. Roger Staubach passed for 275 yards and had a chance to lead Dallas to a tying score in the final minutes, but tight end Billy Joe Dupree fumbled after catching a pass and the Dolphins recovered.

GAME 11: Packers in Wrong Place at Wrong Time

Cowboys 42 at Green Bay 14

November 12: After back-to-back losses, the Cowboys were ready to unload on someone. That someone was mighty Green Bay, who was overwhelmed from start to finish by the defending Super Bowl champs.

Tony Dorsett and Robert Newhouse each ran for 100-plus yards and two TDs as Dallas set a franchise record with 313 rushing yards. Roger Staubach also threw for 200 yards, and Billy Joe Dupree caught two TD passes.

GAME 12: Dallas Intercepts Another Win

Cowboys 27 vs. New Orleans 7

November 19: The Cowboys picked off Archie Manning three times in a dominant defensive performance, while Tony Dorsett ran for 152 yards and a TD. It was a recipe for a one-sided win at Texas Stadium.

Dorsett's success allowed Dallas to keep it on the ground in a conservative attack. The Cowboys did not commit a turnover and ran for 198 yards as a team. Meanwhile, their defense piled up five takeaways.

Super Bowl XIII: Loss to Steelers Smarts

Spelling Ability Aside, Bradshaw Delivers Pittsburgh a Third Ring

The Dallas-Pittsburgh rivalry grew white-hot in the days leading up to Super Bowl XIII. The Steelers' claim to "Team of the '70s" status and their Super Bowl win over the Cowboys three years earlier made them burgeoning rivals of Dallas. Then the Cowboys' Thomas "Hollywood" Henderson raised the stakes by questioning All-Pro QB Terry Bradshaw's intelligence as the championship rematch in Miami approached.

"He couldn't spell 'cat' if you spotted him the 'c' and the 't,'" Henderson famously claimed of Bradshaw before the game.[1]

Bradshaw could certainly read a defense. If the Cowboys weren't convinced of that before the game, they were after the Pittsburgh signal-caller threw for 318 yards and four TDs—both Super Bowl records—in a 35–31 victory that made the Steelers the first team to win three Super Bowl titles. Bradshaw became the first player since the AFL-NFL merger to claim the regular-season MVP and Super Bowl MVP awards in the same year.

The Cowboys also set an NFL record by appearing in their fifth Super Bowl. And though it was no consolation after suffering their third defeat on football's grandest stage, they played a significant part in making Super Bowl XIII one of the greatest ever.

Roger Staubach matched Bradshaw throw for throw in the early going. He hit Tony Hill on a 39-yard TD pass in the first quarter, and Dallas took a 14–7 lead when Mike Hegman picked up a Pittsburgh fumble and returned it 37 yards to the end zone. The Steelers, though, scored 28 of the game's next 31 points to seize control.

John Stallworth turned a 10-yard throw from Bradshaw into a 75-yard scoring play—his second TD of the game—to tie the score at 14. Lynn Swann and Rocky Bleier also caught TD

Dallas Cowboys quarterback Roger Staubach makes a pass in a 35–31 loss to the Pittsburgh Steelers in Super Bowl XIII on January 21, 1979, at the Orange Bowl. (Photo by NFL/NFL)

passes from Bradshaw, and Franco Harris ran for a score. The Steelers' surge was aided by two controversial calls in the fourth quarter, a shaky pass interference flag on Benny Barnes and a delay-of-game penalty on Pittsburgh that nullified an apparent Henderson sack.

Just as they did in their Super Bowl X loss to the Steelers, the Cowboys responded to Pittsburgh's celebrating players and fans by nearly making a miracle comeback. Staubach, whose 17-of-30 passing rate matched Bradshaw's exactly, threw fourth-quarter TD passes to Billy Joe Dupree and Butch Johnson—the second one after the Cowboys recovered an onside kick. A second onside kick try failed, and Bradshaw fell on the ball to run out the clock.

Tony Dorsett rushed for 96 yards for Dallas, topping Pittsburgh's team rushing total by 30 yards. Bradshaw made up the difference, spelling victory for the Steelers.

"I never questioned his ability," Henderson said after the game.

GAME 13: Dallas Takes Control of NFC East

Cowboys 37 vs. Washington 10

November 23: A war of insults leading up to this Thanksgiving Day battle for first place had Thomas Henderson calling the Redskins "turkeys" and John Riggins declaring Henderson a "hot dog." On the field, Henderson and Dallas had the last word.

"Their feathers are all over the place," Henderson said after removing a piece of tape from across his mouth in the postgame interview area. The Redskins were no match on this day. They were outgained 507–201, gave up 122 rushing yards and two TDs to backup running back Scott Laidlaw, and racked up 100 penalty yards—more than they managed to gain on the ground.

GAME 14: Dallas Darts Past Pats

Cowboys 17 vs. New England 10

December 3: Roger Staubach threw two TD passes to rally Dallas from a 10–3 halftime deficit as the Cowboys showed they remembered how to win the close ones. After three-straight lopsided wins, they needed a 36-yard, fourth-quarter throw from Staubach to Billy Joe Dupree to break a 10–10 tie against the Patriots.

The earlier TD came on a flea-flicker as Staubach took a pitch from Scott Laidlaw and fired a 40-yard, game-tying strike to Tony Hill. New England got 93 rushing yards from Sam Cunningham and held the Dallas running game in check, but Staubach's late flurry gave him 243 passing yards.

GAME 15: Records Fall as Dallas Rolls

Cowboys 31 at Philadelphia 13

December 10: Roger Staubach and Tony Dorsett set single-season club records for TD passes and rushing yards, respectively, and the Cowboys clinched home-field advantage in the first round of the NFC playoffs with a romp in Philadelphia.

Dorsett and Scott Laidlaw each rushed for one score and caught a Staubach pass for another. Staubach's last TD throw was his 25th of the season, topping Don Meredith's old record. Dorsett ran past Calvin Hill, upping his season rushing yardage to 1,204 by game's end.

GAME 16: White Wins First Start

Cowboys 30 at N.Y. Jets 7

December 17: Danny White started at QB for a Cowboys team that rested Roger Staubach. Spending much of the day handing off to Tony Dorsett (121 yards on 29 carries), White engineered an easy win, throwing for 156 yards in the process.

Dallas intercepted Matt Robinson three times and held the Jets to 137 total yards on a cold, windy day. Dorsett finished his team record-breaking regular season with 1,325 rushing yards.

GAME 17: Dallas Survives Scare

Cowboys 27 vs. Atlanta 20

December 30: Favored by more than two TDs in their playoff opener, the defending Super Bowl champion Cowboys weathered a storm against the Falcons. They overcame a 20–13 halftime deficit behind backup QB Danny White, getting the winning TD on a one-yard Scott Laidlaw run with 9:46 remaining.

Atlanta linebacker Robert Pennywell knocked QB Roger Staubach out of the game late in the second quarter with a big blow. White came in and handled the club coolly, tying the score on a short, third-quarter TD pass to Jackie Smith. The Cowboys won despite allowing 164 rushing yards and losing four turnovers.

GAME 18: Super Bowl–Bound Again

Cowboys 28 at Los Angeles 0

January 7, 1979: A scoreless first half gave way to a Doomsday Defense outburst that knocked out the Rams. Thomas Henderson returned an interception 68 yards for a TD, and Dallas amassed seven takeaways to secure another ticket to the Super Bowl.

Although Henderson got the defensive score, it was Charlie Waters leading the way with two interceptions and a fumble recovery. Both of Waters' interceptions set up short TD drives. Tony Dorsett compiled 101 yards and a TD on just 17 carries for a Cowboys team that captured its eighth consecutive game.

1979

COWBOYS CELEBRATE 20TH ANNIVERSARY

Dallas Closes 1970s on Remarkable Run

They fell well short of their goal, of course, which by this point was always winning the Super Bowl. Still, it was hard for Dallas fans to look back on 20 years of NFL football and be anything but amazed as their team's standing.

Tom Landry, the coach for all 20 of those seasons, took his team to a 14th consecutive winning record in 1979. The Cowboys won their 11th division title and fourth NFL East crown in a row. And even though their 13th trip to the playoffs ended with an upset loss at the hands of the Rams, their star shone brightly as a nation turned to a new decade.

Roger Staubach directed an 11–5 record in his final season as Cowboys QB. Tony Dorsett topped 1,000 rushing yards for the third time in as many years in the league, and Tony Hill and Drew Pearson gave Dallas two 1,000-yard receivers for the first time in franchise history.

GAME 1: Opening Win a Wild One

Cowboys 22 at St. Louis 21

September 2: Dallas' 15th-straight opening-week win did not come easily. The Cowboys overcame a 14–13 deficit entering the final quarter, gave up a 76-yard Ottis Anderson TD run to fall behind again, and scored the winning points when Rafael Septien's 27-yard field goal bounced off the upright and through with 1:16 remaining.

Even then, the Cowboys had to sweat out a 60-yard, last-second field goal try by Mike Wood that barely missed. Anderson finished with 193 rushing yards to outduel Robert Newhouse (108) of the Cowboys. Ron Springs threw Dallas' only TD pass—a 30-yard halfback option toss to Tony Hill.

GAME 2: Yellow Flags Mark Ugly Win

Cowboys 21 at San Francisco 13

September 9: Dallas tied a club record with 14 penalties and generally struggled before surviving against a heavy underdog. The Cowboys failed to reach 100 rushing yards as a team, and they trailed 10–6 at halftime after O.J. Simpson scored on a short run for the 49ers.

Two second-half Roger Staubach TD passes secured the victory. Staubach passed for 259 yards, while San Francisco's Steve DeBerg nearly matched him with 239.

GAME 3: Staubach Sparks Dramatic Comeback

Cowboys 24 vs. Chicago 20

September 16: Roger Staubach drove the Cowboys 71 yards on four plays in 57 seconds, capping a last-minute, game-winning drive with a 22-yard TD pass to Tony Hill. It was the third TD toss of the game for Staubach and the second to Hill.

Tony Dorsett contributed 108 ground yards to the Cowboys' attack but also fumbled the ball three times to the Bears. Chicago's Walter Payton was even better—"Sweetness" ran for 134 on 22 totes for a Bears team that held three leads in the back-and-forth battle.

GAME 4: Browns Blitz 'Boys

Cleveland 26 vs. Cowboys 7

September 24: A crowd of 80,000-plus, a national TV audience, and former President Gerald Ford witnessed a Cowboys collapse in Cleveland. After winning three straight nail-biters, Dallas ran out of magic in a five-turnover debacle against the Browns.

Roger Staubach's 300-yard passing game was tainted by two interceptions, one of which was returned for a score, and a fumble. Counterpart Brian Sipe capped Cleveland's first two possessions with TD passes as the Browns bolted to a 20–0 lead in the first quarter.

GAME 5: Dorsett, Defense Lead Way
Cowboys 38 vs. Cincinnati 13

September 30: Tony Dorsett rushed for 119 yards on 20 carries and the Dallas defense set up three TDs with interceptions as the Cowboys cruised at home. Randy Hughes, Aaron Mitchell, and Bruce Thornton picked off passes for a defense that disrupted Cincinnati from the outset.

While Dorsett kept the chains moving, Scott Laidlaw finished drives with the game's first two TDs, and Dallas was never threatened.

GAME 6: TD Tony Scores Three
Cowboys 36 at Minnesota 20

October 7: A winning pattern was emerging for the Cowboys—opportunistic defense and a steady diet of Tony Dorsett. Dallas scored a TD on a fumble return by Benny Barnes and set up one of Dorsett's three TDs with another fumble recovery.

Dorsett ran for 145 yards and added five receptions for 47 more. Two Dorsett TD dashes and Barnes' first career score gave the Cowboys a 20-point second quarter and a 23–7 lead. The Vikings rallied to within a field goal in the third quarter when Dorsett scampered 30 yards to halt the flurry.

GAME 7: Dallas Puts it All Together
Cowboys 30 vs. Los Angeles 6

October 14: Sharp on offense, defense, and special teams, the Cowboys dominated the Rams at Texas Stadium. Roger Staubach threw for three TDs, Tony Dorsett ran for 100 yards for the third straight week, and the defense held L.A. to 158 total yards and two field goals.

It was one of the best all-around efforts in some time for Dallas, which ran for 201 yards while passing for 202.

GAME 8: Defense Digs Deep
Cowboys 22 vs. St. Louis 13

October 21: The Cowboys took over sole possession of first place in the NFC East thanks to their stout defense, which tallied a safety and used a fierce pass rush to make life troublesome for Cardinals QB Jim Hart.

Ottis Anderson rushed for 105 yards for St. Louis, but Tony Dorsett was six yards better in his fourth-consecutive 100-yard game. Roger Staubach threw second-quarter TD passes to Billy Joe Dupree and Tony Hill to give the Cowboys a 17–6 cushion.

GAME 9: Steel Curtain Stymies Dallas
Pittsburgh 14 vs. Cowboys 3

October 28: The Steelers became the "Team of the '70s" with their dominant defense, and that defense was on full display at Three Rivers Stadium. Dallas managed only a second-quarter field goal and 79 rushing yards against a ferocious front seven.

The Cowboys' defense was no slouch but yielded two Franco Harris TD runs—one covering 48 yards in the third quarter. Harris finished with 102 yards on just 18 carries, and his ability to move the chains was the difference in the game. Tony Dorsett ran for 73 yards—his first game with less than 100 yards in more than a month.

GAME 10: Dallas Rallies Past Giants
Cowboys 16 at N.Y. Giants 14

November 4: Rafael Septien's 22-yard field goal with six seconds remaining capped a 10-point, fourth-quarter rally that allowed Dallas to fend off Phil Simms and the emerging Giants. Simms' two TD passes had given New York a 14–6 edge in the final period, providing Giants fans a reason to believe a fourth-straight win was in the works.

Running back Tony Dorsett (No. 33) runs the ball against the New York Giants at Giants Stadium in East Rutherford, New Jersey, in November 1979. (Photo by Bruce Bennett Studios/Getty Images)

Roger Staubach (266 passing yards) buried those dreams by hitting Drew Pearson for a 32-yard TD and driving the Cowboys into position for the winning field goal. Pearson made six catches for 124 yards on a day when the Cowboys ran for just 106.

GAME 11: Eagles Tighten NFC East Race

Philadelphia 31 at Cowboys 21

November 12: Rather than collapse under the weight of a three-game slump, the Eagles stormed into Texas Stadium and rode Wilbert Montgomery to an upset win. Montgomery ran for 127 yards and a TD as Philly pulled within one game of Dallas in the NFC East.

The Cowboys took a 7–0 lead on the first of two long TD hookups between Roger Staubach and Tony Hill, but the Eagles responded with 24 consecutive points to take control. Staubach threw for 308 yards and three scores without an interception and Hill had 213 receiving yards, but Dallas was plagued by three turnovers.

GAME 12: Miscues Prove Costly

Washington 34 vs. Cowboys 20

November 18: Roger Staubach threw three interceptions and Dallas also lost two fumbles in a loss at Washington that forged a three-way tie atop the NFC East among the Eagles, Redskins, and slumping Cowboys. For the second-straight game, Dallas did not cause a turnover while giving up plenty of them.

Joe Theismann was largely responsible for that. The Redskins QB threw for 210 yards and three scores without an interception. The Cowboys again struggled to move the ball on the ground, rushing for just 85 yards.

GAME 13: Dallas Drops Third Straight

Houston 30 at Cowboys 24

November 22: "They may be America's Team," Houston coach Bum Phillips said after the Oilers' first regular-season win over the Cowboys. "But we're Texas' team." Houston's upset win at Texas Stadium gave Dallas its first three-game losing streak since 1974.

There was no secret to the outcome. Bruising back Earl Campbell plowed through the Cowboys' defense for 195 yards and two TDs on 33 carries, and his 61-yard scoring burst in the first quarter erased a 7–0 Dallas lead. Dallas held a 21–17 halftime edge, but Dan Pastorini fired two second-half scores to lift the Oilers. Roger Staubach also threw for two TDs, but he was also intercepted twice.

GAME 14: Dallas Finds Form

Cowboys 28 vs. N.Y. Giants 7

December 2: Dominant defense, a 100-yard game for Tony Dorsett, and Drew Pearson TD

Captain Crash

Cliff Harris Laid Heavy Hits and Asked, "Was It Worth It?"

Up through the 1960s, free safeties resembled center fielders. These speedy defensive backs would break to the ball, hoping for a catch or disruption. They rarely made a physical impact. But then came "Captain Crash."

In his 10 seasons with the Cowboys (1970–79), Cliff Harris redefined the position. This free safety was all over the field—defending the pass, yes, but also racing to the line of scrimmage to lay a bruising hit on the halfback. Moreover, Harris "crashed" into receivers so hard, they began to ponder their approach to the game.

"If you step in front of a receiver and intercept a pass, he'll be a little upset," Harris said, as recounted by Roger Staubach. "But if you blast him, turn his helmet around, then he'll be looking for you. A good hit just makes my job easier. After a hit, I ask [the receiver], 'Was it worth it?'"[1]

Incredibly, the free safety on the NFL All-Decade Team for the 1970s was never even drafted. Harris had starred on the gridiron at Ouachita Baptist College in Arkansas, but that school was so small that it didn't even qualify for the NCAA. But after viewing game film of Harris, the Cowboys invited him to training camp in 1970. Harris not only made the team, but he beat out third-round rookie Charlie Waters for the free safety job his rookie year.

Together, Harris and Waters (who played safety and cornerback) would develop into a dynamic duo in the defensive backfield, earning a combined nine trips to the Pro Bowl. Harris earned six such invites (1974–79). More impressively, he was named first-team All-Pro at the position from 1975–78.

Free safety Cliff Harris redefined the position and earned six trips to the Pro Bowl. (Photo by Tony Tomsic/Getty Images)

Because he could cover both the run and pass, Harris added flexibility to the Cowboys' defense. He was a major factor in helping the Cowboys—for each year in the 1970s—rank in the top eight in the NFL in fewest yards allowed.

In some ways, Crash wasn't the most prudent bear in the woods. He suited up in skimpy place-kicker pads to optimize his speed (although he never missed a game due to injury). Also, in Super Bowl X, he made the mistake of taunting Steelers placekicker Roy Gerela by patting him on the helmet after he missed a short field goal. Enraged Steelers linebacker Jack Lambert responded by slamming Cliff to the turf.

Harris was inducted into the Cowboys Ring of Honor in 2004.

catches once again spelled victory for Dallas, ending a three-game slump and keeping the Cowboys in the playoff hunt. Dorsett rushed for 108 yards and a score—his first game over the century mark since October.

Roger Staubach hooked up with Pearson for three TDs to erase a 7–0 Giants lead. It was the first three-TD game of Pearson's career, and he earned more than 1,000 receiving yards for the year in the process. Dallas limited New York to 197 yards and snatched three turnovers.

GAME 15: Dallas Seals Playoff Spot

Cowboys 24 at Philadelphia 17

December 8: Coach Tom Landry called it Dallas' most important regular-season win in years. Before a record crowd of 71,434 at Veterans Stadium, the Cowboys clinched at least a wild-card playoff spot with a physical, line-controlled win over the Eagles.

Dallas smashed for 185 ground yards while holding Philly to 80, and that was the difference. Ron Springs and Robert Newhouse each carried 12 times for 60-plus yards in place of Tony Dorsett, who injured his shoulder early in the game. The Cowboys never trailed, pulling out of a 10–10 halftime tie on Newhouse and Butch Johnson TDs.

GAME 16: Call it a Miracle Finish

Cowboys 35 vs. Washington 34

December 16: For the Cowboys to win their fourth straight NFC East title, they needed to storm back from a 34–21 deficit in the final three minutes against a Washington team fighting for its own playoff life. Thanks to Roger Staubach, they did just that.

Staubach's 26-yard TD pass to Ron Springs with 2:20 remaining gave Dallas life, and his eight-yard lob to Tony Hill with 39 seconds left sent Texas Stadium into a frenzy. It set Staubach's final tally at 336 passing yards, his second-best career performance.

John Riggins ran for 151 yards for the Redskins, who at 10–6 failed to make the playoffs.

GAME 17: Rams Avenge Earlier Rout

Los Angeles 21 at Cowboys 19

December 30: A Rams team that suffered a 30–6 regular-season setback to Dallas turned the tables on a 50-yard pass from Vince Ferragamo to Billy Waddy in the final minutes at Texas Stadium. The ball was tipped by a Cowboys defender, but Waddy pulled it in and outraced the defense. Ferragamo was tackled by Randy White for a first-quarter safety and completed just nine passes in the game, but three went for scores.

Meanwhile, Dallas failed to mount a consistent attack. Roger Staubach was just 12-of-28 through the air, and the Cowboys were out-rushed 159–156 by the Rams.

1980

NEW QB OPENS 1980s

White Takes Over for Staubach, with Distinction

Danny White took over the spotlight for "America's Team" when QB Roger Staubach announced his retirement in March 1980. White followed a proven formula to success—get the ball to Tony Dorsett.

Dorsett rushed for his fourth straight 1,000-yard season, and White completed nearly 60 percent of his passes in engineering a 12–4 campaign. The new QB threw for 28 TDs, more than Staubach ever fired in a season, with Tony Hill and Billy Joe Dupree combining to catch 15 of them.

How smooth was the QB transition? White's Cowboys led the NFL in scoring, averaging 28.4 points per game. They also gave Tom Landry his 200th career victory as head coach. A loss to Philadelphia in the NFC title game was not the ending Dallas or its new QB were looking for, but it was one whale of a debut nonetheless.

GAME 1: No Redskins Revenge

Cowboys 17 at Washington 3

September 8: Eager to avenge a loss to Dallas that ended their 1979 season in the final minutes of the final week, the Redskins ran into a buzz saw of a defense and did not come close. They rushed for just 58 yards against the Cowboys in a one-sided opener.

Tony Dorsett's six-yard TD run in the first quarter was all the offense Dallas needed. Ron Springs tacked on a fourth-quarter TD, and Danny White, beginning his first season as the full-time starting QB, was 10-of-18 with two interceptions. Only a 45-yard fourth-quarter field goal spared Washington from a shutout.

GAME 2: A Mile-High Mismatch

Denver 41 vs. Cowboys 20

September 14: The highest point total put up on Dallas in a decade was no fluke. The Broncos had their way from start to finish, racing to a 17–0 lead and never looking back in a rout witnessed by nearly 75,000 fans at Mile High Stadium.

Denver went 7-of-15 on third-down conversions and took advantage of three Cowboys turnovers. Broncos QB Matt Robinson ran for two scores, completed half of his 20 pass attempts, and directed an opportunistic attack. Danny White threw for 292 yards and a pair of Cowboys TDs, but much of the yardage came with the game out of reach.

GAME 3: Dallas Claims Shootout

Cowboys 28 vs. Tampa Bay 17

September 21: The Buccaneers set a club record with 442 yards of total offense but managed just 17 points and fell to a Cowboys team that proved much better at finding the end zone. Running for one score and passing for another, Doug Williams led Tampa Bay to a 17–7 lead in the second quarter.

But Danny White had other plans, leading the Cowboys on four TD drives of 70-plus yards. His two TD passes to Billy Joe Dupree and a TD run from Robert Newhouse erased the deficit and put Dallas over the top. Tony Dorsett carried 20 times for 100 yards.

GAME 4: Dallas Drives Again

Cowboys 28 at Green Bay 7

September 28: One week after staging four TD drives of 70 or more yards, Dallas did it three more times in an impressive win over the Packers. Danny White's accuracy was astounding. The Cowboys QB hit 16-of-20 passes for 217 yards and two TDs.

It was Green Bay's third consecutive loss.

GAME 5: Dallas Wins Comedy of Errors

Cowboys 24 vs. N.Y. Giants 3

October 5: Dallas kicker Rafael Septien recovered a Giants fumble on the opening kickoff, setting up his own field goal a few plays later in a game that featured several miscues on both sides. The Cowboys simply made fewer of them, benefiting from four N.Y. turnovers.

Danny White threw for 266 yards and two TDs on a day when Dallas struggled to run. The Cowboys got their final TD on a 38-yard interception return by John Dutton.

GAME 6: White Dissects 49ers
Cowboys 59 vs. San Francisco 14

October 12: Danny White completed 16-of-22 passes for 239 yards and a career-high four TDs—three to Drew Pearson—in a rout of the 49ers. Dallas' 460 total yards more than doubled San Francisco's total.

White was not intercepted and could have easily had a bigger yardage day had Coach Tom Landry not decided to work on the ground game. Ron Springs rushed for 81 yards, and Tony Dorsett added 75.

GAME 7: Eagles Win Defensive Struggle
Philadelphia 17 vs. Cowboys 10

October 19: Neither team gained 250 yards in a game that was settled on a controversial no-call down the stretch. Facing fourth down in the final minute, Danny White threw a pass to a blanketed Tony Hill in the end zone, and the Cowboys screamed for an interference call on cornerback Roynell Young. However, no flag was thrown.

Dallas got its TD on defense when Mike Hegman recovered a first-quarter fumble in the end zone for a 7–0 lead. Ron Jaworski threw two TD passes for the Eagles, including the winner to Charlie Smith in the fourth quarter.

GAME 8: Shootout Goes to Dallas
Cowboys 42 vs. San Diego 31

October 26: Rather than trying to slow the high-flying Chargers and their aerial circus, the Cowboys played along and outgunned them. The teams combined for 874 total yards and 50 first downs, but San Diego was doomed by seven turnovers in an entertaining game at Texas Stadium.

Dan Fouts and Danny White each threw three TDs, but Fouts tossed four interceptions. John Jefferson caught eight passes for 160 yards for the Chargers, while the Cowboys had seven players make multiple receptions. Dallas overcame a 24–14 halftime deficit by scoring the first 28 points of the second half, including two short Timmy Newsome TD runs.

GAME 9: White Leads Clutch Finish
Cowboys 27 at St. Louis 24

November 2: For the first time in his career as the Cowboys' QB, Danny White became a comeback kid by leading Dallas from a

Defensive end Harvey Martin of the Dallas Cowboys in a game against the Philadelphia Eagles on October 19, 1980. (Photo by George Gojkovich/Getty Images)

seemingly certain defeat to a victory. He drove the team 69 yards in the final two minutes, hitting Tony Hill for a 28-yard TD on a fourth-down pass to leave a big Busch Stadium crowd stunned.

The lead changed hands three times in the fourth quarter. Dallas went up 20–17 on a 78-yard interception return by Dennis Thurman. St. Louis then reclaimed the edge when Jim Hart, who matched White with 258 passing yards, found Mel Gray for a 38-yard TD.

GAME 10: Errors Abound in N.Y.

N.Y. Giants 38 vs. Cowboys 35

November 9: Danny White tied a club record with five interceptions, four of which led to Giants TDs, and yet Dallas somehow still had a chance to win. Tied 35–35 with 2:28 remaining, Coach Tom Landy elected to go for a first down on fourth-and-inches from his own 47, but Robert Newhouse was stuffed at the line of scrimmage. Phil Simms then capped a 351-yard, three-TD passing day by driving the Giants to a winning field goal.

The Giants, big underdogs, compiled 462 total yards in the rain. Their effort spoiled Tony Dorsett's best day of the season. The Cowboys' running back went for 183 yards and two TDs on 24 carries. Newhouse also ran for two scores.

GAME 11: Defense Regains Form

Cowboys 31 vs. St. Louis 21

November 16: One week after allowing 351 passing yards to Phil Simms and the Giants, Dallas held Jim Hart to 12-of-30 passing in a strong defensive effort that led to victory against the Cardinals. Trailing 14–0 after yielding two long first-quarter TDs, the Cowboys sprang to life and dominated the rest of the game.

Tony Dorsett offset a 100-yard rushing game from the Cardinals' Ottis Anderson with 122 yards on 26 carries. Danny White threw for 296 yards and fired TDs to three different receivers.

GAME 12: Cole Delivers Victory

Cowboys 14 vs. Washington 10

November 23: Veteran defensive tackle Larry Cole got his big mitts on an interception in the fourth quarter and returned it 43 yards for his first TD in more than 10 years, scoring the points that rescued the favored Cowboys from a 10–7 deficit. Dallas won despite managing just 199 offensive yards.

It was fitting then that a defensive lineman intercepted a backup QB (Mike Kruczek) to claim an ugly contest. The Cowboys' offense certainly wasn't doing anything to secure a victory. QB Danny White threw four interceptions, and no Dallas runner reached 60 yards. Wilbur Jackson rushed for 128 yards for the Redskins.

Texas Stadium: A Heavenly View

God Had a Balcony Seat for 38 Seasons of Cowboys Football

Dallas fans were fond of telling outsiders that Texas Stadium had a hole in the roof for one reason: so God could watch his favorite football team. Anyone who enjoyed the view, whether from above or from the 65,000-plus seats, witnessed five Super Bowl championship teams, seven conference championship clubs, and Emmitt Smith's run to the all-time NFL rushing mark. They suffered through just 10 losing seasons over 38 years, ogled the most famed collection of cheerleaders in pro football history, and fell in love with the notion that their team was, unquestionably, "America's Team."

"I came to the stadium at night and it was dark except for a light shining through the hole in the roof," Smith told Texas Stadium fans in a final-game ceremony at the Irving, Texas, venue in 2008, recalling his first visit there after being drafted out of Florida. "There was dirt on the ground because there was a tractor pull the next day.

"I read the names on the Ring of Honor: Lilly, Meredith, Dorsett, and I thought, *'These guys have paved the way for young guys like me, and I do not want to disappoint. Every time I step on that field I have to represent the star.'*"[1]

Sun comes through the roof of Texas Stadium during the game between the Philadelphia Eagles and the Dallas Cowboys on December 16, 2007, in Irving, Texas. Texas Stadium served as the home of the Cowboys from 1971–2008. (Photo by Drew Hallowell/Getty Images)

God's loyalties aside, it was initially a domed stadium that was to replace the Cotton Bowl as the Cowboys' $35 million home field in 1971. However, Texas Stadium's structure was unable to support the weight of a full roof, and funding did not permit the reinforcement of the building. As a result, Texas Stadium was destined to stand partially enclosed. Most of the stands were covered, but the unique opening in the roof caused shadows that played havoc during afternoon games and gave the stadium its signature look.

Opponents complained about the Texas Turf that covered the field for most of the stadium's existence and the severe "crown" of the field, which helped drainage. It's safe to say, though, that those imperfections might have been easier for visitors to overlook had their teams not fared so poorly at Texas Stadium.

The Irving-owned facility hosted 213 Cowboys victories against just 99 defeats. Dallas also compiled a 16–6 postseason record there.

Former QB Roger Staubach told the crowd before the Cowboys lost to Baltimore in the last game at Texas Stadium, "We won a lot of games because we were a good team, but also because you were our fans. Thank you."[2]

GAME 13: A Thanksgiving Rout
Cowboys 51 vs. Seattle 7

November 27: As compelling games go, this one was for the birds. The Cowboys gobbled up the Seahawks as the nation gobbled up its Thanksgiving meals, scoring the fifth-most lopsided win in franchise history.

Seattle made its own misery with seven turnovers that the Cowboys routinely turned into points. Tony Dorsett carried 24 times for 107 yards and two TDs, and the Dallas defense pitched a shutout until the Seahawks finally scored in the last three minutes.

GAME 14: Kicks Power Dallas
Cowboys 19 at Oakland 13

December 7: Rafael Septien kicked two clutch field goals, including a 52-yarder, and the Cowboys took control of their divisional destiny with a hard-fought win at Oakland. The AFC West co-leaders put up a strong fight, but Dallas had just enough defense—and offensive power thanks to the legs of Septien and Tony Dorsett—to prevail.

Dorsett rushed for a game-high 97 yards and a TD, and the Cowboys never trailed. Septien's long boot snapped a 7–7 tie in the first half, and his second one gave the Cowboys a 19–10 cushion in the third quarter.

GAME 15: Dallas Deflates

Los Angeles 38 vs. Cowboys 14

December 15: A national TV audience and more than 65,000 fans in Anaheim witnessed a Cowboys Monday night meltdown as the Rams scored the first 38 points and racked up 517 yards of offense against their helpless visitors. Vince Ferragamo threw for 275 yards and three TDs, and Jewerl Thomas added 147 yards on the ground.

Danny White was intercepted three times for Dallas, which averted a shutout with two fourth-quarter TDs.

GAME 16: Eagles Win by Losing

Cowboys 35 vs. Philadelphia 27

December 21: In an odd twist of fate, the Eagles merely had to prevent Dallas from beating them by 25 or more points to secure the NFC East title. The Cowboys reached that magic number by building a 35–10 lead early in the fourth quarter, but a late flurry brought Philadelphia the crown on the strength of an eight-point loss.

The Cowboys, settling for a wild-card berth, became the first team in 128 games to prevent Harold Carmichael from catching a pass. Danny White threw for four Dallas TDs and ran for another.

GAME 17: A Total Turnabout

Cowboys 34 vs. Los Angeles 13

December 28: Two weeks after being humiliated by the Rams in California, the Cowboys put a Texas-sized beating on their wild-card playoff foe in Dallas. L.A. led 13–6 midway through the second quarter but failed to score again while the Cowboys ran away.

Tony Dorsett tore through the Rams for 160 yards on 22 carries. He tied the score on a 12-yard TD dash before halftime and started his team's 21-point second half on a 10-yard scoring scamper in the third quarter. With 528 total yards, Dallas more than doubled its visitor's total.

GAME 18: On a Wing and a Pearson

Cowboys 30 at Atlanta 27

January 4, 1981: Trailing by as much as two TDs in the third quarter and 10 points midway through the fourth, the Cowboys turned to Drew Pearson and hoped beyond hope for a miracle. Pearson delivered.

Pearson caught a pass despite double-team coverage—his third big catch of the drive—to bring the Cowboys within three. After his team got the ball back in the last minutes, the speedy receiver snared the 23-yard game-winner to cap a 70-yard, six-play drive.

Danny White delivered those clutch passes, finishing with 322 aerial yards and three scores. Pearson made five catches for 90 yards. Steve Bartkowski led the Falcons with 320 passing yards and two TD tosses.

GAME 19: Eagles Claim NFC Crown

Philadelphia 20 vs. Cowboys 7

January 11, 1981: Philadelphia won the NFC East title on the strength of a narrow loss at Dallas. The win wound up earning the Eagles home-field advantage for the NFC title game and the "right" to play in 17-below wind chills. Certainly, the hosts handled the conditions better.

Philadelphia powered for 263 yards on the ground while holding Dallas to 90 in a dominating performance. Wilbert Montgomery rushed for 194 yards and a TD. Add in his reception for 14 yards and he accounted for more total offense than the Cowboys mustered as a team.

It was a 7–7 game at halftime, but Philadelphia pounced on two third-quarter Dallas fumbles and turned them into 10 points for a commanding lead.

1981

"THE CATCH" TRUMPS ALL

Another Banner Year Falls One Play Short

"The Catch"—that's all one has to say to bring smiles in San Francisco and grimaces in Dallas. Joe Montana, Dwight Clark, and the 49ers spoiled the Cowboys' 1981 Super Bowl dreams on a play that will never be forgotten.

Getting there, for Dallas, was yet another story of success, perseverance, and consistency. The Cowboys won their 12th division title since 1966 with a 12–4 mark. It was their 16th consecutive winning season. Back-to-back losses to start October became a blip on the radar when Danny White and Tony Dorsett ignited a run of eight wins over their next nine games.

It was an All-Pro year for Dorsett. He rushed for a career-high 1,646 yards, second in the NFL, and gained 1,971 yards from scrimmage. It looked for a while like the Cowboys might just be on their way back to the Super Bowl.

That is, until "The Catch."

GAME 1: Dallas Picks Off Opening Win

Cowboys 26 at Washington 10

September 6: A stunned RFK Stadium crowd watched Joe Theismann fire four interceptions. Dennis Thurman returned the last one 96 yards to seal a one-sided opening game in which his Cowboys took advantage of six Washington turnovers.

Tony Dorsett, in his first game since being named offensive team captain, carried 21 times for 132 yards. Danny White threw two TD passes and Rafael Septien kicked four second-half field goals in the win.

GAME 2: Septien Matches Mark

Cowboys 30 vs. St. Louis 17

September 13: Rafael Septien kicked three field goals and tied a club record by connecting on seven in a row, Tony Dorsett ran for 129 yards, and Ron Springs made three TD dashes to turn back the Cardinals.

Though St. Louis topped 400 offensive yards, including a 275-yard passing effort from rookie Neil Lomax, the visitors never held a lead. Springs scored all three of his TDs in the first half as Dallas grabbed a 24–7 cushion in the second quarter.

GAME 3: Dorsett Does it Again

Cowboys 35 at New England 21

September 21: Continuing his torrid start, Tony Dorsett dashed for 162 yards, including a 75-yard scoring scamper, and carried the Cowboys to a Monday night win. Dorsett also caught four passes and Danny White threw for two TDs to highlight a 455-yard team offensive performance.

The Cowboys intercepted Matt Cavanaugh four times, turning three of those picks into points. They also recovered three New England fumbles.

GAME 4: Defense Carries Dallas

Cowboys 18 vs. N.Y. Giants 10

September 27: What the game lacked in artistry it made up for in grit, as Dallas intercepted Phil Simms three times and threw him for a safety in a defensive-minded victory. Rafael Septien kicked three field goals, the last one providing an 18–3 fourth-quarter lead.

Danny White's 41-yard TD pass to Butch Johnson in the second quarter gave the Cowboys the lead for good and marked the only time all day that Dallas found the end zone. Tony Dorsett, who had run for 100 yards in three straight games, was held to 70.

GAME 5: Cardinals Kick Cowboys

St. Louis 20 vs. Cowboys 17

October 4: Neil O'Donoghue's 37-yard field goal with 23 seconds remaining sent Dallas its first loss of the year. The Cowboys never led, but Tony Dorsett's second TD had tied the score at 17 before St. Louis drove from its own 22 for the winning boot.

Dorsett ran for 99 yards and also caught four Danny White passes. But the Dallas offense was plagued by dropped balls and miscommunication for much of the day.

GAME 6: A California Nightmare

San Francisco 45 vs. Cowboys 14

October 11: Coach Tom Landry harkened back to his team's early years in trying to explain this one. His Cowboys were manhandled at Candlestick Park, surrendering 440 yards,

Wide receiver Butch Johnson (No. 86) makes a catch in a 30–17 win over the St. Louis Cardinals on September 13, 1981, at Texas Stadium in Irving, Texas. (Photo by Al Messerschmidt/Getty Images)

committing four turnovers, and never mounting a threat.

The 49ers scored the first 24 points and were never headed. Joe Montana threw for 279 yards and two TDs, while the Cowboys gained just 192 yards as a team.

GAME 7: Dallas, Dorsett Recover
Cowboys 29 vs. Los Angeles 17

October 18: Tony Dorsett had been down with the flu during the week, and his team was simply trying to get well after its 31-point loss in San Francisco. The Cowboys got well on both counts, putting up 26 points in the first half and holding on for a big win.

Dorsett looked as healthy as ever, running for 159 yards and a TD. Danny White threw for 277 of his team's 496 total yards. Harvey Martin was a defensive force, registering two sacks and a first-half safety.

GAME 8: White Rallies Troops
Cowboys 28 vs. Miami 27

October 25: Trailing 27–14, Danny White threw two TD passes in the last four minutes to lift Dallas past the Dolphins. First, the QB capped a long drive with a five-yard scoring toss to backup tight end Doug Cosbie with 3:48 to play. After Dennis Thurman picked off a David Woodley pass and returned it to the Miami 32, White connected with Ron Springs from that distance to give the Cowboys a sudden lead.

In the end, it was a missed extra point early on from the normally automatic Uwe von Schamann that cost Miami. Tony Dorsett's 122 rushing yards helped offset a remarkable 408-yard passing performance from Woodley. The Dolphins QB threw three TD passes but was intercepted five times.

GAME 9: Late Surge Lifts Dallas
Cowboys 17 at Philadelphia 14

November 1: For three quarters, the Cowboys looked like certain losers at Veterans Stadium. However, their 14-point outburst in the fourth erased a 14–3 deficit and hoisted Dallas into a first-place tie with the Eagles.

An 85-yard pass from Ron Jaworski to Harold Carmichael gave Philadelphia its biggest lead in the third quarter. But Danny White started the rally by hitting Doug Cosbie for a TD for the second straight week, and Tony Dorsett provided the power behind the winning drive, scoring from the 9-yard line with 7:36 to go.

Philly's Tony Franklin missed a 34-yard field goal try that could have tied the game.

GAME 10: Bills Come Due in Second Half
Cowboys 27 vs. Buffalo 14

November 9: If Buffalo's 14–7 halftime lead was something of a shock, it was enough to wake up the Cowboys in time for a big second

America's Team

Love 'Em or Loathe 'Em, The Cowboys Have a Fan Base to Rival Any in Sports

Just as the most famous entertainment icons need only one name to be recognized—Elvis, Prince, Madonna, et al—the phrase "America's Team" brings unmistakable recognition to one team and one team only. The Dallas Cowboys.

Oh, sure, others have tried to make the claim: baseball's Yankees, Braves, or Brooklyn Dodgers; the NFL's Patriots in the aftermath of 9/11; or the Saints after the floods of Hurricane Katrina. Such attempts to share the label are merely fodder for sports talk radio. The Cowboys remain America's Team more than 30 years after the nickname was coined by an NFL Films employee who needed to come up with a catchy title for a video highlights package.

Bob Ryan, who went on to become editor-in-chief of NFL Films, wanted to come up with a unique twist for the Cowboys footage he was putting together in 1979. He had no idea he was about to come up with a phrase with such staying power.

He settled on, "The Dallas Cowboys: The Complete History of America's Team," the result of Ryan's noting that the Cowboys were frequently the national TV game of the week and that wherever they traveled the stands were filled with their star logo on hats, T-shirts, and signs. TV and radio announcers latched onto the moniker, and soon "America's Team" came to be a household phrase among sports fans.

Dallas fans waved towels prior to the opening kickoff against the Philadelphia Eagles during the NFC wild-card playoff game at Cowboys Stadium on January 9, 2010, in Arlington, Texas. (Photo by G. Newman Lowrance/Getty Images)

"Whenever the Cowboys are playing well," Ryan said, "the nickname comes up again. It's probably one of the most high-profile nicknames for a team in history."[1]

With such a nickname, of course, come accusations of vanity from rival players and fans. It's a dynamic fans of baseball's Yankees or the Fighting Irish of Notre Dame know well. With such widespread national appeal comes widespread national disdain. These are teams either loved or loathed by sports fans with very small numbers on the fence.

"They ain't my team," said Vikings defensive tackle Pat Williams, a Texas A&M product, before a 2009 playoff meeting with the Cowboys. "Our fans couldn't care less. America's Team? They ain't Houston, Texas' team. Just the Dallas area."[2]

Williams' sentiments aside, the Cowboys are America's Team. It doesn't mean everyone roots for them, because that's far from the case. It simply means that they had the nickname first, it stuck, and there's no cause for taking it away considering their national—even international—following is among the most intense in sports.

"They are America's team," said TV analyst Mark Schlereth, a former Cowboys opponent. "I don't care where you go, you'll find Cowboys fans. Cowboys fans are all over the place. As a former Redskin, it hurts me to say they're still America's Team. It has stuck, and there's no getting rid of it, and people believe it."[3]

half. Dallas scored 20 unanswered points in the third quarter and rode a 117-yard rushing effort from Tony Dorsett to victory.

Bills QB Joe Ferguson passed for 301 yards but threw four interceptions. Everson Walls snared two of those picks.

GAME 11: Lions Roar Late

Detroit 27 vs. Cowboys 24

November 15: Eddie Murray kicked a 47-yard field goal as time expired to the delight of nearly 80,000 fans at the Pontiac Silverdome. The result was a come-from-behind win for the Lions, who trailed 17–0 early and 24–17 in the fourth quarter.

Detroit speedster Billy Sims tied the score on an 81-yard catch and run from Eric Hipple, putting his team in position for the late kick. Sims also outshone Tony Dorsett in a battle of top runners, gaining 119 ground yards to Dorsett's 55. Danny White threw for three Cowboys TDs but was intercepted twice. Dallas was outgained in total yardage 429–323.

GAME 12: Offense Comes Alive

Cowboys 24 vs. Washington 10

November 22: Dallas piled up yardage worthy of a much higher score in beating the Redskins for the fifth straight time. Tony Dorsett ran for 115 yards, Ron Springs rushed for 85, Drew Pearson caught passes for 111, and Danny White threw for 222 and two scores.

The Cowboys, it seemed, were in scoring position all day and took only moderate advantage of it. They compiled 470 yards to Washington's 256. Doug Cosbie's 10-yard TD catch in the third quarter broke a 10–10 tie and sent Dallas toward another win.

GAME 13: Blocked PAT Spells Victory

Cowboys 10 vs. Chicago 9

November 26: As it turned out, a blocked extra-point try was the difference between the 10-win Cowboys and the three-win Bears. After Chicago snapped a 3–3 Thanksgiving tie in the fourth quarter with the game's first TD, Ed "Too Tall" Jones got a hand on the PAT to limit the Bears' lead to 9–3.

When Dallas successfully converted its six-yard Ron Springs TD run with 5:09 to play, it meant a narrow victory against a team that rode the great Walter Payton for 38 carries and 179 yards. Neither team gained 275 offensive yards, and each committed three turnovers.

GAME 14: Colts Drop 13th Straight

Cowboys 37 at Baltimore 13

December 6: Following a lackluster victory over Chicago, the Cowboys had no trouble against Baltimore. The Cowboys handed the Colts their 13th consecutive loss, piling up 464 yards and taking a 27–6 halftime lead in a laugher.

Tony Dorsett carried 30 times for 175 yards, and James Jones ran for a 59-yard score for the winners. Glenn Carano, filling in for Danny White at QB, attempted just 18 passes. Curtis Dickey led the Colts with 130 yards and two TDs on just 15 carries.

GAME 15: Another NFC East Title For Dallas

Cowboys 21 vs. Philadelphia 10

December 13: After spotting the Eagles 10 points, Dallas scored 21 unanswered to claim its 12th NFC East crown in 16 years. Danny White threw two TD passes—one to close the first-half scoring, and another to start the second half.

Tony Dorsett fumbled three times during his 101-yard day, but teammate Dennis Thurman made up for it with three interceptions. One of them set up the TD that got the Cowboys going in the second quarter, and Dallas dominated from there.

GAME 16: Giants Come Up Big
N.Y. Giants 13 vs. Cowboys 10 (OT)

December 19: New York fought its way into the playoffs with a chilly overtime win against a Cowboys team that looked like nothing rode on the outcome. The truth is, Dallas missed a chance to get Tony Dorsett a rushing title (he finished second by 28 yards to George Rogers) and could have secured home-field advantage throughout the NFC playoffs.

Instead, Giants kicker Joe Danelo tied the game on a 40-yard field goal in the fourth quarter and won it on a 35-yarder in OT. The Cowboys ran for just 90 yards, with Dorsett held to 39 on 20 carries by a stout Giants defense.

GAME 17: Dallas Blanks Bucs
Cowboys 38 vs. Tampa Bay 0

January 2, 1982: The Cowboys clamped down on Tampa Bay in their playoff opener, matching a 14-year-old club record for margin of victory in a playoff game. The Bucs never had a chance thanks to four Doug Williams interceptions and just 222 total yards.

Ron Springs, Tony Dorsett, and James Jones all ran for third-quarter TDs as the Cowboys, who held a 10–0 halftime lead, turned the game into a rout. Dorsett rushed for 86 yards, and Springs added 70. Dennis Thurman intercepted Williams twice.

GAME 18: "The Catch" Dooms Dallas
San Francisco 28 vs. Cowboys 27

January 10, 1982: It has come to be known as "The Catch," and to the 49ers it was worthy of such stature in football lore. Joe Montana rallied San Francisco from a 27–21 deficit on an 89-yard drive for the ages. The culmination was a six-yard pass to a leaping Dwight Clark in the back of the end zone as the tight end broke free against double coverage with 51 seconds on the clock.

One of the most memorable moments in NFL playoff history decided a game that featured nine turnovers, including six by the 49ers. Everson Walls got his hands on two of Montana's three interceptions. Montana also threw three TD passes, including two to Clark.

The lead changed hands six times. Tony Dorsett (91 rushing yards) gave the Cowboys a 17–14 halftime lead on a five-yard score, and a 21-yard pass from Danny White to Doug Cosbie in the fourth quarter gave Dallas its final edge.

After the winning drive, the Cowboys moved the ball to within 20 yards of Rafael Septien's field goal range, but White was sacked by Lawrence Pillars and fumbled to San Francisco with 30 seconds to play.

1982

STRIKING OUT

Work Stoppage Causes Contention

The 1982 season was a strange one in the NFL. A players' strike stopped play for two months, chasing away fans and breeding hostility between players and owners. In Dallas, the strike caused more angst than in most NFL towns. QB Danny White was among the players who publicly spoke in support of the owners, causing bruised feelings in the locker room and even more confusion among fans.

After splitting the season's first two games, the Cowboys returned to action in November and won five straight. It was good enough to overcome two late losses for a 6–3 record and a playoff berth, the team's 16th in a 17-year span.

Wins over Green Bay and Tampa Bay led Dallas to another NFC title game, where Washington's "Hogs" prevailed on their way to a Super Bowl crown.

The Cowboys' nine-point average victory margin was tops in the NFL during this tumultuous year, and Tony Dorsett gave fans something to celebrate upon the game's return with a record 99-yard scoring sprint against Minnesota.

GAME 1: Opening Streak Ends at 17
Pittsburgh 36 at Cowboys 28

September 13: A 17-year winning streak in season openers came to an end at the hands of the Steelers. The loss also ended an 18-game win streak at Texas Stadium.

Though two late Cowboys TDs made the score more respectable, there was little doubt about this one. Pittsburgh got three TD tosses from Terry Bradshaw and 103 rushing yards from Franco Harris. They also obliterated a 14–13 halftime deficit with 20 successive points in the second half. Danny White threw for 347 yards and four TDs in the loss.

GAME 2: Dallas Enters Strike Upbeat
Cowboys 24 at St. Louis 7

September 19: With a players' strike looking more and more probable, the Cowboys made sure any long delay would give them time to reflect on a solid performance. They outscored St. Louis 17–0 in the second half at Busch Stadium to even their mark at 1–1.

Danny White was 20-for-32 with two TD passes, and Tony Dorsett ran for 98 yards on 22 carries. Meanwhile, the defense held the Cardinals to 62 rushing yards.

GAME 3: Dallas Returns…Barely
Cowboys 14 vs. Tampa Bay 9

November 21: In the first game after the strike, Dallas drew its smallest home crowd since 1975 (49,578) and had its 44-game Texas Stadium sellout streak halted. If the fans were slow to show up, the same could also be said of the Cowboys. They won despite gaining just 185 yards, while Tampa Bay totaled 382.

What saved Dallas was the Buccaneers' inability to reach the end zone. While the visitors settled for three short field goals, the Cowboys got second-half TDs from Drew Pearson and Robert Newhouse to win a game they had little business winning. At least NFL football was back.

GAME 4: Thanksgiving Good to Dallas
Cowboys 31 vs. Cleveland 14

November 25: Tony Dorsett ran 20 times for 116 yards and two TDs as Dallas dominated on Thanksgiving Day, scoring the first 31 points. Danny White passed for 215 yards and two scores and directed an attack that compiled 496 yards.

Playing twice in a five-day span did not bother the Dallas defense. Cleveland ran for

Running back Tony Dorsett (No. 33) carries the ball during the NFC divisional playoff game, a 37–26 victory over the Green Bay Packers on January 16, 1983, at Texas Stadium in Irving, Texas. (Photo by Jay Dickman/NFL)

just 82 yards and committed five turnovers, including four interceptions, while Everson Walls picked off two Browns passes.

GAME 5: Dallas Dominates in D.C.

Cowboys 24 at Washington 10

December 5: There was nothing fancy about the Cowboys' sixth consecutive win over the Redskins. Dallas controlled the game on the ground, became remarkably efficient through the air, and played stifling defense at RFK Stadium.

Danny White completed 21-of-29 passes for 216 yards, Ron Springs ran for one TD and caught a pass for another, and the Cowboys intercepted Joe Theismann three times. A 160–66 edge in rushing yards was the big difference.

GAME 6: Hitting on All Cylinders

Cowboys 37 at Houston 7

December 13: The offense clicked, the defense dominated, and Rafael Septien booted a 53-yard field goal. It was that kind of Monday night for the Cowboys, who posted their fifth straight win.

Danny White was 21-of-27 with three TDs and no interceptions in another crisp performance. Butch Johnson caught two TD tosses. While the offense was racking up 416 yards, the defense held Houston to 199 and even scored on an 86-yard fumble return by Michael Downs.

GAME 7: Dallas Wins Sixth Straight

Cowboys 21 vs. New Orleans 7

December 19: The Cowboys wrapped up their eighth consecutive playoff trip by winning for the sixth straight time. It wasn't artistic. In fact, the teams combined for nine turnovers, with Dallas coughing up the ball five times.

Still, Tony Dorsett's 105 yards and two second-quarter TDs were more than enough offense against the mistake-prone Saints. Despite getting 166 rushing yards from George Rogers, New Orleans failed to score until the fourth quarter. By then, it was too late.

GAME 8: Jaworski Leads Eagles

Philadelphia 24 at Cowboys 20

December 26: Ron Jaworski became Philadelphia's career leader in TD passes with a 10-yarder to Harold Carmichael that sank the Cowboys in the fourth quarter. Dallas, which clinched home-field advantage in the playoffs despite the loss, looked like a team with nothing on the line.

The Cowboys matched the Eagles with four turnovers and put the ball on the ground five times in the game (recovering three of those fumbles). Danny White threw two TD passes but was also picked off twice. And after seizing a 20–14 lead in the final frame, Dallas surrendered the final 10 points to lose for the second time at home.

Too Tall
Ed Jones

When Ed Jones was a teenager, they didn't play football—at least not at his high school—in Jackson, Tennessee. That didn't matter much to this amazing athlete, who excelled in both boxing and basketball. As he tells it, the boxing career didn't last long.

"My basketball coach saw on the front page of our local paper that I had knocked a guy out in, like, nine seconds," Jones said. "He called me into his office, showed me the front page, and said, 'What is this all about?' Basically, he gave me an ultimatum: basketball or boxing. I went with basketball."

At Tennessee State University, Jones found that he was even better at football. A towering presence at 6'9", "Too Tall" had the size, strength, and speed to crumple offensive linemen. He developed into a sack machine at TSU, prompting the Cowboys to select him with the first overall pick in the 1974 NFL Draft.

Jones needed just a year to crack the starting lineup of the Doomsday Defense. By the end of training camp in 1975, he had won the starting role at left defensive end. With the exception of

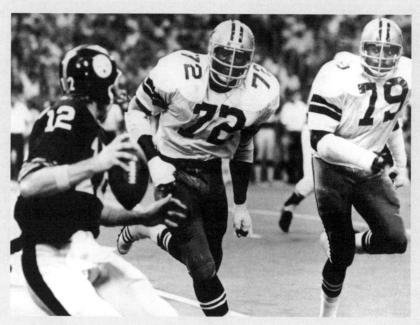

Ed "Too Tall" Jones (center) and Harvey Martin (right), advance toward quarterback Terry Bradshaw (left) of the Pittsburgh Steelers during a game in Pittsburgh, Pennsylvania.
(Photo by Bruce Bennett Studios/Getty Images)

the 1979 season (when he famously retired), he would be a mainstay at the position for 14 years, starting 203 consecutive games. He was the only Cowboy who could claim to play with both Bob Lilly and Troy Aikman.

In his early years in Dallas, Jones corkscrewed quarterbacks into the turf and put the fear of God into halfbacks who attempted to sweep right. In the 1977 NFC Championship Game, Minnesota running back Robert Miller saw Jones in his headlights and dropped the ball. Jones forced two fumbles that day, logged a sack, and made eight unassisted tackles, keying a 23–6 thumping of the Vikings.

The NFL didn't record sacks until 1982, but Jones is unofficially credited with 106 for his career, making him one of the few members of the century club. Too Tall made the Pro Bowl in 1981, '82, and '83, and he was first-team All-Pro in 1982.

Despite his long, prolific career, Jones may be most famous for the year he didn't play football. In 1979, he retired to pursue a professional boxing career. Cowboys fans did not take kindly to his decision. Some sent him hate mail, while others berated him on call-in radio shows. But Jones felt compelled to pursue his boyhood dream. "Barring injuries, I'm sure I would have been a very good fighter," he said. "I mean, why not? I had the hand speed, the power, the dedication, the toughness."

Jones went 6–0 with five knockouts in the ring, although the tomato cans that he knocked off had a combined career record of 37–86–1. For reasons he never revealed, Jones quit boxing and returned to the Cowboys for the 1980 season.

Until his retirement nine years later, Jones was a favorite of fans and teammates. He cherished his Cowboys experience, especially the annual Thanksgiving game. Each year, his large family would trek to Dallas, watch the game, and celebrate Thanksgiving Day together.

Jones never made the Hall of Fame or even the Ring of Honor. But in the hearts and minds of Cowboys fans, he will always stand tall.

GAME 9: Dorsett Makes Record Run
Minnesota 31 vs. Cowboys 27

January 3, 1983: Tony Dorsett set an NFL record that will never be broken when he raced 99 yards to the end zone, helping Dallas overcome a 24–13 deficit in the fourth quarter of the regular-season finale. However, after taking a 27–24 lead, the Cowboys surrendered the deciding score when Tommy Kramer hit Rickey Young with 1:52 remaining.

The outcome meant nothing to Dallas, and Dorsett's run is the lasting memory to come from this contest. It was one of the best plays in the history of *Monday Night Football*, and it covered one more yard than the Cowboys gained on the ground the rest of the night.

GAME 10: White Enjoys Record Day

Cowboys 30 vs. Tampa Bay 17

January 9, 1983: Danny White set Cowboys playoff records with 27 completions and 45 attempts, passing for 312 yards and two TDs in a first-round win. Meanwhile, Buccaneers QB Doug Williams managed only eight completions and was picked off three times.

The most damaging of those interceptions came in the fourth quarter, with Tampa Bay leading 17–16. Monty Hunter stepped in front of a Williams pass and returned it 19 yards for the go-ahead TD. Tony Dorsett ran for 110 yards to edge Tampa Bay's James Wilder (93) for top rushing honors in the game.

GAME 11: Another NFC Title Trip

Cowboys 37 vs. Green Bay 26

January 16, 1983: Reaching the NFC title game for the 10th time in 13 years was no small feat for Dallas. The Cowboys yielded 466 yards to the visiting Packers but took advantage of five takeaways in a wild game that was not settled until late.

Dallas never trailed and held leads as comfortable as 20–7 at halftime and 30–19 in the fourth quarter. The Packers, though, would not go away, thanks largely to Lynn Dickey and his 332 passing yards.

Tony Dorsett rushed for 99 yards for the Cowboys, and Tony Hill caught seven passes for 142. Dennis Thurman, who returned one of his three interceptions 39 yards for a TD, was the Dallas MVP on this day.

GAME 12: Foiled Again

Washington 31 vs. Cowboys 17

January 22, 1983: Road games to decide the NFC title are bad news for the Cowboys. For the third straight season, that situation resulted in a loss that left them one game short of the Super Bowl.

This time, it was the rival Redskins who did the trick. The team that had lost six straight games to Dallas set up TDs by recovering a fumbled punt and returning a kickoff 76 yards. Those special teams plays made the difference.

Dallas outgained Washington by 80 yards but committed three turnovers while forcing none. The Redskins took a 14–3 halftime lead and never fell behind thereafter. John Riggins was a workhorse, carrying 36 times for 140 yards and two TDs in the win.

Cowboys QB Danny White suffered a first-half concussion on a hit by Dexter Manley and was replaced by Gary Hogeboom, who threw two TDs and two interceptions.

1983

OFFENSIVE ERUPTION

Dallas Attack Springs to New Heights

The Cowboys gave scoreboard operators fits during 1983. They averaged nearly 30 points per game (29.9), second in the NFL, and topped 30 points nine times in their first 14 starts. They did the latter three straight times late in their 12–4 season.

However, the offense went relatively quietly in back-to-back losses to conclude the year—costing them a shot at another division title—and in a first-round playoff exit at the hands of the Rams. It was a bitter way to end a season in which Tony Dorsett rushed for 1,321 yards and Danny White threw for 29 TDs. Six different Cowboys caught at least 40 passes.

On the flip side, the Cowboys' defense was becoming a shadow of its former self. Its No. 20 ranking in scoring defense was the lowest in franchise history.

GAME 1: Dallas Wins Wild Opener

Cowboys 31 at Washington 30

September 5: Tony Dorsett's 77-yard TD run was virtually all the offense Dallas could conjure in the first half, but a second-half eruption sent the Cowboys to a Monday night win at RFK Stadium. Danny White threw three second-half TD passes and ran for the go-ahead score with 2:25 to play. That gave the Cowboys a 24–23 lead.

Ron Fellows' 33-yard interception return on Washington's next series set up White's short TD toss to Doug Cosbie, which rendered a late Redskins TD insignificant. Dorsett rushed for 151 yards, and Tony Hill caught two long TD passes.

GAME 2: Cowboys Come Back Again

Cowboys 34 at St. Louis 17

September 11: Dallas spotted St. Louis a 10–0 lead before dominating the rest of the way, winning for the second straight week on the road. Six Cardinals turnovers contributed greatly to their own demise.

Four different Cowboys intercepted Jim Hart passes, and one of them, Dennis Thurman, also scored on a fumble recovery. Offensively, Danny White went 19-for-27 for 234 yards and a score.

GAME 3: Pick Sinks Giants

Cowboys 28 vs. N.Y. Giants 13

September 18: Dextor Clinkscale blew open a tight game when he returned an interception 68 yards for a TD in the fourth quarter to spark the Cowboys in their home opener. It stretched Dallas' 14–13 edge to eight points and kept the Giants at bay.

Otherwise, this was an evenly played game between NFC East Rivals. Danny White threw two TD passes on a day when the Cowboys struggled to run the ball. The Giants fared better on the ground but threw three interceptions, including the back-breaker.

GAME 4: Defense, Return Team Score Big

Cowboys 21 vs. New Orleans 20

September 25: With Dallas struggling to move the ball and trailing 20–13 in the fourth quarter, its special teams and defense came to the rescue. First, with seven minutes to go, Ron Fellows returned a punt 62 yards for a TD. Rafael Septien missed the extra point to leave the Saints up by a point, but the Dallas "D" took care of that.

Anthony Dickerson sacked Saints QB Ken Stabler in the end zone with 1:58 remaining for the most improbable of endings—a game decided by a safety. Tony Dorsett was the only consistent offense the Cowboys managed. He ran 16 times for 124 yards. Wayne Wilson rushed for two New Orleans scores.

GAME 5: Familiar Pattern Holds

Cowboys 37 at Minnesota 24

October 2: Once again, Dallas snoozed early and woke up with a vengeance. The Cowboys fell behind 17–3 and 24–10 in the second quarter, then scored 27 unanswered points for the win.

Ron Fellows returned an interception 58 yards for a third-quarter TD to give Dallas its first lead. Tony Dorsett raced for 141 yards on 26 carries and Ron Springs generated 123 total yards in the winning effort.

GAME 6: Dallas Does it Again

Cowboys 27 vs. Tampa Bay 24 (OT)

October 9: Trailing 24–17 with 1:19 remaining, Dallas raced 74 yards to force overtime on a 52-yard TD pass from Danny White to Timmy Newsome. Then, in the extra period, Rafael

Doug Cosbie (No. 84) scores a touchdown against the Washington Redskins on December 11, 1983, in Irving, Texas.
(Photo by Ronald C. Modra/Sports Imagery/Getty Images)

Septien got a second chance to make a winning kick after being roughed by Thomas Morris on a failed 50-yard try. He split the uprights from 42 yards out.

Danny White passed for 377 yards and two scores, including a career-long 80-yard TD to Ron Springs. He also threw three interceptions, but they did not prevent the Cowboys from posting their first OT win since 1981.

GAME 7: Finally, a Breather

Cowboys 37 vs. Philadelphia 7

October 16: After making a habit of heart-stopping comebacks, the Cowboys finally took care of an opponent with ease. They won their seventh straight by steamrolling the Eagles with 522 total yards while holding Philly to a mere 44 yards on the ground.

The Eagles scored the game's first TD on an 83-yard hookup between Ron Jaworski and Mike Quick, but they failed to score again. Danny White threw for 266 yards and two TDs, and three different Dallas runners gained at least 59 yards.

GAME 8: Raiders End Streak at Seven

L.A. Raiders 40 at Cowboys 38

October 23: After seven consecutive victories, Dallas ran into an offensive juggernaut. The Raiders, now calling Los Angeles home, made themselves comfortable in the Texas Stadium end zones while amassing 519 total yards—200 more than the Cowboys.

Thanks to six Raiders turnovers, though, Dallas took a 38–34 fourth-quarter lead on Mike Hegman's nine-yard fumble return. But the visitors ended this wacky affair on two late 26-yard Chris Bahr field goals, including the winner with 20 seconds to play.

Marc Wilson threw for 318 yards and three Raiders TDs while Frank Hawkins carried 17 times for 118 yards and a score. L.A. bottled up the Dallas running game, keeping Tony Dorsett to 65 yards on 20 carries.

GAME 9: Dallas Rebounds

Cowboys 38 at N.Y. Giants 20

October 30: Coming off their first loss of the year, the Cowboys turned it on when it counted. Danny White threw a career-high five TD passes, including three that helped Dallas pull away from a 17–17 halftime deadlock at Giants Stadium.

White hit fewer than half of his passes (15-of-33) and fired two interceptions, but his completions were big ones totaling 304 yards. Tony Hill caught two TD passes, and Tony Dorsett provided 94 ground yards. The Giants were their own worst enemies with six turnovers, including three Jeff Rutledge interceptions.

GAME 10: Eagles Put Up a Fight
Cowboys 27 at Philadelphia 20

November 6: Thirty-point losers in their last meeting with Dallas, the Eagles flew to a 10–0 lead this time and fought the division-leading Cowboys to the final gun. Their downfall was a failure to stop QB Danny White.

White led the comeback charge, connecting on all but three of his 24 pass attempts and totaling 268 yards and two TDs through the air. His 12-yard toss to Timmy Newsome forged a 10–10 halftime tie, and his 18-yard strike to Tony Hill gave the Cowboys a commanding 27–13 lead in the fourth quarter.

GAME 11: Chargers Fly Without QB
San Diego 24 vs. Cowboys 23

November 13: Even with QB Dan Fouts injured, "Air Coryell" soared. Backup Ed Luther threw for 340 yards for pass-happy Chargers coach Don Coryell as the Cowboys, playing their third straight road game, lost for the second time.

Derrie Nelson started San Diego's barrage by returning a blocked punt 63 yards for a first-quarter TD. Luther then went to work, building a 24–6 third-quarter lead before the Cowboys mounted a Danny White–fueled comeback. White threw for 300 yards and three scores without an interception, but his heroics came up one point shy.

GAME 12: Dallas Dominates
Cowboys 41 vs. Kansas City 21

November 20: The Cowboys finally showed they could win a game without drama. They led from start to finish, racing to a 27–0 lead early in the third quarter and cruising to their 10th win. It was the first game of the year in which the Cowboys never trailed.

Tony Dorsett carried 18 times for 108 yards and two TDs. Kansas City actually gained more total yards (434–421), but the Chiefs did most of their damage after falling into an insurmountable hole.

GAME 13: Cardinals Overrun
Cowboys 35 vs. St. Louis 17

November 24: Dallas overcame an early 71-yard TD pass from Neil Lomax to Roy Green, scoring 35 of the game's next 38 points. Tony Dorsett again carried the load, amassing 102 yards and two TDs on 17 carries.

Although the Cowboys did not commit a turnover, the Cardinals put the ball on the ground five times and lost three. Dallas took advantage and also registered a season-high seven QB sacks. Anthony Dickerson and Randy White had two apiece.

Dynamic Duo

Drew Pearson and Tony Hill Were Double Trouble for Opponents

Sometimes, numbers lie. That's not the case with two of the greatest receivers in Cowboys history. So talented and so close in ability were Drew Pearson and Tony Hill that their statistics line up as though duplicated on a copy machine.

Pearson, in 11 seasons with the Cowboys, caught 489 passes for 7,822 yards and 48 TDs. Hill, in 10 years with the team, grabbed 479 for 7,988 yards and 51 scores. Each made three Pro Bowls. And from 1977–83, they gave Dallas one of the most dangerous 1-2 pass-catching punches in NFL history.

It was a dilemma of nightmarish proportions for defensive coordinators. How do you defend the Cowboys? Do you double-team Pearson, "Mr. Clutch," considered the team's No. 1 receiver and a man whose hands could snatch a speeding bullet out of the sky? Or do you have a safety shadow Hill, "The Thrill," a speedster capable of scoring from anywhere on the field?

In 1979, defenders did not have much success containing either of them. Hill covered 1,062 yards on pass receptions and Pearson 1,026, as they became the first duo in Dallas history to top 1,000 receiving yards in the same year. Not surprisingly, the totals were eerily identical.

"I was the possession guy and Tony was the game breaker," Pearson writes in his autobiography, *Hail Mary: The Drew Pearson Story*. "Every Wednesday, before the next week's game…the first thing the coaches did was pass out the game plans. The first thing Tony and I did was go to the passes and see who was going to be the featured receiver.

"You could tell by our reaction who was going to be the featured receiver because the one who wasn't was mad."[1]

Wide receiver Tony Hill. (Photo by Diamond Images/Getty Images)

They weren't mad at each other, both men are quick to note. It's just that each craved the football and the chance to make a difference. Any competition for the ball only made the Cowboys better. Along the way, both enjoyed their share of signature moments.

No one who saw it will ever forget Pearson's most famous catch. It was the original "Hail Mary," a last-second bomb from Roger Staubach that won a 1975 playoff game at Minnesota. When NFL Films put together a mid-1990s video of the top 75 plays in NFL history, three Pearson receptions were among them.

Landry described Hill as his "home-run hitter." He went deep twice in a 1983 Monday night comeback win against Washington, grabbing TDs of 75 and 51 yards to spark the victory. Hill became the No. 1 receiver when Pearson retired after that season, and he caught a career-high 74 passes for 1,113 yards in '85.

GAME 14: Dallas Sets Up Showdown

Cowboys 35 at Seattle 10

December 4: Showing an ability to focus on a lesser foe rather than looking ahead to a big game against the Redskins, the Cowboys cruised past the Seahawks. They soared to a 28–3 lead in the fourth quarter before turning their attention to Washington and a battle for the NFC East.

Danny White was an accurate 19-of-26 passing for 233 and two TDs, and Tony Dorsett rambled for 117 yards and two scores on 26 totes. Dorsett also caught five passes for 40 yards.

GAME 15: A Big-Game Dud

Washington 31 at Cowboys 10

December 11: With a chance to win the NFC East on their home field, the Cowboys were thrashed by the rival Redskins by a margin that matched their largest ever in a Texas Stadium defeat. Four turnovers doomed Dallas to its fate.

The Cowboys surrendered 89 rushing yards and two TDs to Redskins workhorse John Riggins and allowed Joe Theismann to pass for 203 yards and two scores. A 43-yard TD toss from Theismann to Art Monk in the third quarter stretched a 14–10 Washington edge and sent the Redskins toward a division crown. Danny White threw three interceptions and directed a Dallas offense that scrounged up just 205 total yards.

GAME 16: Faltering in the Finale

San Francisco 42 vs. Cowboys 17

December 19: For the second straight year, the Cowboys finished the regular season with back-to-back losses. It was a disappointing culmination to a year that produced 12 wins in the first 14 games. Dallas committed five turnovers in the loss.

Joe Montana outdueled Danny White, throwing four TD passes for the 49ers. White threw one and was intercepted twice before making way for Gary Hogeboom. Sure-handed running back Roger Craig caught two TD passes for San Francisco.

GAME 17: Early Exit for Cowboys

L.A. Rams 24 at Cowboys 17

December 26: A season that held so much drama and then so much promise ended with a thud for the Cowboys. Danny White threw three interceptions and Dallas set up a Rams TD with a fumbled punt in a wild-card game that was not as close as the final score suggests.

Vince Ferragamo threw three TD passes and directed a Rams offense that did not commit a turnover. Eric Dickerson provided the ground attack, going for 99 yards on 23 carries on a frigid day at Texas Stadium.

White attempted a whopping 53 passes largely out of necessity. The Cowboys were unable to move the ball with any success on the ground and trailed for most of the game. White completed 32 passes for 330 yards, but his miscues overshadowed his two TD tosses.

1984

NOT-SO-BRIGHT LIGHTS IN 1984

New Ownership, Dallas Season Short-Lived

A partnership headed by Dallas businessman H.R. "Bum" Bright gave the Cowboys just their second owner in the team's 25-year history. Bright's stay was a short one compared to that of original owner Clint Murchison, as was the 1984 season by Cowboys standards.

For the first time in 10 years, Dallas failed to make the playoffs. Back-to-back losses to Washington and Miami set the final record at 9–7, a 19th straight winning season but well short of all of the goals the team had set.

The most telling aspect of the season was a QB controversy. Gary Hogeboom got 10 starts to Danny White's six, and the club never developed a consistent offensive identity beyond the usual 1,000-yard season from Tony Dorsett. The Cowboys finished in the NFL's lower half in scoring offense, as well.

GAME 1: Hogeboom Has Record Opener

Cowboys 20 at L.A. Rams 13

September 3: Officially taking over as the starting QB, Gary Hogeboom broke predecessor Danny White's record by completing 33 passes in a game as Dallas took a measure of revenge against the team that knocked it from the 1983 playoffs. Hogeboom was 33-of-47 for 343 yards and a TD. The scoring strike went for 19 yards to Doug Cosbie, ending a string of 13 Rams points to open the game. L.A. did not score again.

Two Rafael Septien field goals forged a tie in the fourth quarter, and Tony Dorsett won it on a seven-yard run with 3:56 to go. Dorsett ran for 81 yards and caught 10 passes for 66. Eric Dickerson led the Rams with 138 yards on 21 carries.

GAME 2: Big Plays Carry Giants

N.Y. Giants 28 vs. Cowboys 7

September 9: New York scored on a 62-yard pass and an 81-yard fumble return in the first half and kept Dallas off the scoreboard until the fourth quarter. Big plays were more than enough to carry the Giants, who were outgained but never headed.

Phil Simms threw for three TDs, including the early bomb to Byron Williams. The defensive score came from Andy Headen, who recovered a Gary Hogeboom fumble and went the distance to produce a 21–0 halftime lead.

Hogeboom, who passed for 242 yards with one TD and one interception, fumbled twice in the second quarter.

GAME 3: Hogeboom Heats Up

Cowboys 23 vs. Philadelphia 17

September 16: Dallas used both trickery and a straight-up attack to turn back the Eagles. Gary Hogeboom threw for 320 yards and a TD without a turnover while engineering the attack efficiently. He also threw a lateral to Mike Renfro in the third quarter, and the receiver heaved a 49-yard TD pass to Doug Donley to give Dallas a 23–10 cushion.

Winning the turnover battle was key. The Cowboys intercepted Ron Jaworski three times while protecting the football themselves. The Eagles were held to 56 rushing yards.

GAME 4: Dallas "D" Dominates

Cowboys 20 vs. Green Bay 6

September 23: The Dallas defense pitched a shutout. If not for a short interception return for a third-quarter TD, the Packers would have left Texas Stadium with a goose egg. It was that kind of day for the Cowboys, who turned four takeaways into an easy win.

Dallas was no offensive force. The Cowboys ran for only 100 yards, and Gary Hogeboom completed fewer than half of his 35 pass attempts. Tony Dorsett's seven-yard TD run in the fourth quarter iced the game.

GAME 5: Miscues Cost Bears

Cowboys 23 at Chicago 14

September 30: Chicago outgained Dallas and got a 155-yard rushing game from Walter Payton. However, the Bears made just enough mistakes to hand the Cowboys a nine-point win. The Bears let the first-half clock expire while inside the Dallas 10-yard line, missed two field goals, and committed two turnovers to the Cowboys' none.

Simply put, Dallas escaped. The Cowboys ran for just 59 yards (barely two yards per carry) but got a 265-yard passing day from Gary

Middle linebacker Mike Singletary (No. 50) of the Chicago Bears pressures quarterback Gary Hogeboom (No. 14) during the September 30, 1984, game at Soldier Field in Chicago, Illinois. (Photo by Focus on Sport/Getty Images)

Hogeboom, who hit Tony Dorsett for a 68-yard TD. The only scoring in the second half came from two short Rafael Septien field goals.

GAME 6: White Returns in Loss

St. Louis 31 at Cowboys 20

October 7: Tom Landry benched Gary Hogeboom in the third quarter, bringing back Danny White, but it wasn't enough to spark his Cowboys against the Cardinals. White did lead a 98-yard TD drive, capping it with a 10-yard pass to Fred Cornwell to set the final score in the fourth quarter. However, a 31–13 hole was far too deep.

Dallas got in that hole by turning over the ball (two Hogeboom interceptions and one lost fumble) and because of its inability to stop Ottis Anderson. The veteran running back carried 25 times for 110 yards. Tony Dorsett rushed for 96 and a score for the Cowboys.

GAME 7: Redskins Roll

Washington 34 vs. Cowboys 14

October 14: There's getting beaten, and there's getting steamrolled. The Cowboys suffered the latter fate against the Redskins, who served up 32 John Riggins runs for 165 yards in a 241-yard team rushing performance that left Dallas reeling. For the second straight game, Danny White replaced Gary Hogeboom at QB. And for the second successive week, it didn't matter.

Washington scored 34 consecutive points after Dallas took a 7–0 lead on a 29-yard Tony Dorsett scamper. Joe Theismann threw for three TDs, including two to Clint Didier.

GAME 8: Dallas Scores Historic Comeback

Cowboys 30 vs. New Orleans 27 (OT)

October 21: It was the greatest comeback in team history. Dallas trailed 27–6 entering the fourth quarter, but Danny White—replacing starter Gary Hogeboom for the third straight week—led an impossible rally to rescue his team from a third-straight loss.

Tony Dorsett scored on a short run to open the fourth quarter, and White hit Mike Renfro on a 12-yard toss, making it a 27–20 game. Then came the wildest part of the comeback. In the closing minutes, Randy White sacked Saints QB Ken Stabler and the ball rolled into the end zone, where Jim Jeffcoat fell on it for the tying TD.

Rafael Septien kicked his third field goal of the game 3:42 into overtime, connecting from 41 yards to end a marathon contest.

GAME 9: Colts No Match

Cowboys 22 vs. Indianapolis 3

October 28: No one was mistaking the Colts for a contender, and they managed just 155 yards against a stout Dallas defense. The only thing preventing Indy from a shutout loss was a 52-yard field goal by Raul Allegre in the fourth quarter.

It took Tony Dorsett nine weeks to rush for 100 yards in a game. The Cowboys star carried 24 times for 104 yards. Dallas scored two TDs, both in the second quarter. Danny White hit Tony Hill and Doug Cosbie for those scores, then Rafael Septien added three short field goals.

GAME 10: Giants Sweep Dallas

N.Y. Giants 19 at Cowboys 7

November 4: Dallas lost twice in a season to the Giants for the first time in 21 years, and the Cowboys did so with gusto. Dallas was outscored 13–0 in the second half and changed QBs three times in the game, yet neither Gary Hogeboom nor Danny White fared well.

The only Dallas score came when Hogeboom and Tony Hill hooked up from 30 yards in the second quarter. However, Hogeboom also threw two interceptions, and White went a dismal 1-of-6. Ali Haji-Sheikh kicked four field goals for the Giants.

GAME 11: An Opportunistic Win

Cowboys 24 at St. Louis 17

November 11: The Cowboys forced six turnovers on defense and special teams and turned them into 21 of their 24 points in a big

road win. Despite being outgained by 185 yards, Dallas never trailed and snapped a 17–17 tie when Gary Hogeboom found Ron Springs for a 26-yard TD early in the fourth quarter.

Neil Lomax burned the Cowboys for 388 passing yards, but he needed 52 attempts to do it, and his two interceptions were costly. Springs also ran for a score, while Tony Dorsett led Dallas with 84 yards on 19 carries.

GAME 12: Bills Come Due in Shocker

Buffalo 14 vs. Cowboys 3

November 18: The winless Bills delivered a dagger to Dallas' playoff hopes, keeping the Cowboys out of the end zone in a colossal upset. Rookie Greg Bell carried 27 times for 206 yards to pound the life out of the visitors.

Tony Dorsett called it "total humiliation," and his teammates weren't arguing after a game in which Dallas ran for just 78 yards on 24 carries as a team. It was the first time in five years the Cowboys had failed to score a TD.

GAME 13: Dallas Holds Off Patriots

Cowboys 20 vs. New England 17

November 22: Looking like a team that meant business, Dallas darted to a 17–3 lead after three quarters before overcoming a late New England charge. The Patriots tied the score with 1:58 to go, but Rafael Septien kicked a 23-yard

In Roger's Shadow: Danny White

Following a Legend is not as Easy as No. 11 Sometimes Made it Seem

He never won Super Bowls, as Roger Staubach and Troy Aikman did. He had the misfortune of falling right between those two on Dallas' quarterbacking timeline. At times, he was not even the most popular QB on his team, a distinction Gary Hogeboom held for some time.

Danny White worked for every ounce of acclaim that came his way, and in the end, it was enough to land him among the most successful signal-callers in franchise history.

Replacing a legend is a thankless task. For every Mickey Mantle-takes-over-for-Joe DiMaggio-in-centerfield story, there are dozens of instances where teams struggle for years to replace the skills and leadership of their greatest heroes. White was never to be mistaken for Staubach in Cowboys annals, but he got to work quickly in establishing his own talents.

In 1980, his first year as a starter, the former Arizona State All-American and College Football Hall of Famer broke Staubach's club record for TD passes in a season, throwing 28. He boosted the mark to 29 in 1983, when he also set franchise records for completions (334) and passing yardage (3,980)—all standards that held up until Tony Romo bettered them in 2007.

Despite leading the Cowboys to the NFC title game in each of his first three years as a starter and making the 1982 Pro Bowl, White was—at times—not even the most popular QB on his team. Some of that had to do with his crossing of the picket line during the 1982 strike season. Losses in all three of those battles for NFC supremacy also played a part. Hogeboom took over as starter to begin 1984, but White reclaimed the job and returned

Danny White helmed the Cowboys to five playoff appearances during his nine seasons with the team. (Photo by Simon Miles/Getty Images)

Dallas to the playoffs in '85. "Danny White was probably as fine a winner as we have had in football," former coach Tom Landry once said.[1]

White also ranked among the most versatile players of his day. How many modern-era starting quarterbacks have also served as their team's regular punter? White did for nine seasons and remains the club's career leader with 610 punts. When he retired in 1988, he did so as the most accurate passer in franchise history and while holding several other aerial records.

No, White was not Roger Staubach. White was not Troy Aikman. He was the man in between them who helped guide the Cowboys to five playoff appearances and three NFC East crowns. He went on to a successful coaching career in the Arena Football League, steering the Arizona Rattlers to two ArenaBowl championships.

field goal with four seconds remaining to secure a win.

For most of the game, a nail-biter did not seem to be in the cards. Michael Downs gave Dallas the early lead when he returned an interception 27 yards for a score, and a TD pass from Danny White to Tony Hill from the 9-yard line gave the Cowboys their 14-point lead. White completed 21-of-41 passes for 288 yards, while Craig James led the Pats with 112 rushing yards on just 19 carries.

GAME 14: Running Game Saves White

Cowboys 26 at Philadelphia 10

December 2: Danny White struggled through his least-accurate game as a starter (8-of-25 passing) and threw four interceptions, but Dallas prevailed thanks to its ground game and defense. Tony Dorsett rushed for 110 yards while the Cowboys totaled 190 ground yards as a team and held the Eagles to an average of two yards per carry.

Dallas led just 7–3 entering the second half, but a 57-yard TD reception by Ron Springs and a safety produced when John Dutton sacked Eagles QB Joe Pisarcik in the end zone blew it open. Philadelphia mustered just 173 total yards.

GAME 15: Dallas Bumbles, Blows It

Washington 30 at Cowboys 28

December 9: Dallas self-destructed after taking a 21–6 halftime lead in a must-win game. The Cowboys coughed up four third-quarter turnovers, and the Redskins parlayed them into 17 points to overcome their deficit. Dallas regained the lead in the fourth on a 43-yard strike from Danny White to Tony Hill, but John Riggins plowed into the end zone to claim victory for Washington with 6:34 remaining.

White finished with 327 passing yards and four TD strikes, but his two interceptions were costly. Riggins outperformed Tony Dorsett, totaling 111 yards on the ground.

GAME 16: No Playoffs This Year

Miami 28 vs. Cowboys 21

December 17: Apparently, the playoffs can go on even without the Cowboys. Dallas missed the postseason for the first time in a decade and suffered a seventh loss for the first time since 1965. It happened suddenly. Mark Clayton got open, caught a Dan Marino pass, and raced unchallenged for a 63-yard winning TD in the final minute.

It was the fourth TD toss of the day for Marino. The first two staked the Dolphins to a 14–0 lead in the third quarter, but Dallas charged back to tie it on two Timmy Newsome TD plunges. After Miami reclaimed the lead, Danny White hit Tony Hill for a 66-yard TD with 1:47 remaining, setting the stage for the dramatic finish.

1985

A WINNING SCORE

20 Consecutive Winning Seasons

Some records stand out more than others in the annals of NFL history. The record for consecutive winning seasons is among them. For 20 straight years, the Dallas Cowboys finished above .500. Considering the parity in the league, especially in the modern era, it's a mark that might stand for some time.

Winning season No. 20 in a row came in 1985, and it was an impressive year indeed. In August, Roger Staubach became just the second player who spent his entire career with the Cowboys to be inducted into the Pro Football Hall of Fame, joining Bob Lilly. Then Staubach's former team, coming off a disappointing 9–7 season, rebounded to win its 13th divisional title and its first NFC East crown since 1981.

The Cowboys did it with a quick start, winning five of their first six games and holding off the Giants and Redskins, also 10–6, on a tie-breaker.

Tony Dorsett enjoyed his eighth and final 1,000-yard rushing season (1,307), and Danny White regained his starting QB job from Gary Hogeboom and threw for 3,157 yards and 21 scores. His favorite target, Tony Hill, enjoyed his finest season with 74 receptions for 1,113 yards.

But it ended all too soon again as the Cowboys fell flat in a 20–0 playoff loss in Los Angeles. Those 20 Rams points, however, could not erase a magical 20-year run that was, as it turned out, finally reaching an end.

GAME 1: On a Mission
Cowboys 44 vs. Washington 14

September 9: Few things feel better than pummeling a heated rival. Dallas did just that in a Monday night season opener, perhaps as a way of saying a year of sitting home during the playoffs is not acceptable. The Cowboys intercepted Redskins QBs six times and returned two—by Victor Scott and Dennis Thurman—for TDs. Joe Theismann, previously a Cowboy-killer, threw five of those picks.

Dallas was not spectacular offensively, but good was sufficient on this night. Danny White threw for 219 yards and a score, while Tony Dorsett rushed for 70 yards on 19 carries.

GAME 2: Lions, Lapses Pain Dallas
Detroit 26 vs. Cowboys 21

September 15: Coach Tom Landry pointed to the fact that no less than 11 Cowboys missed practice time while attending Ron Springs' trial for resisting arrest. It was a short week too, and Dallas was coming off a blowout over Washington. Landry feared a letdown, and he got one when his team committed enough mistakes to nullify a 554–200 total yardage advantage against the Lions.

Five turnovers, 13 penalties, and numerous mental mistakes proved costly. Detroit turned those miscues into a 26–0 lead through three quarters and weathered a furious Cowboys aerial comeback down the stretch. Dallas QBs Danny White and Gary Hogeboom each amassed more than 220 passing yards.

GAME 3: Easy Does It
Cowboys 20 vs. Cleveland 7

September 22: Dallas simplified things, and the Cowboys were simply smashing, particularly on defense, in a one-sided win over the Browns. Cleveland did not reach the scoreboard until the fourth quarter. By then, Dallas owned a 20–0 lead.

By and large, it was an exercise in football basics that carried the Cowboys. The notable exception was a trick play on which James Jones threw a halfback option pass to QB Danny White that produced a 12-yard third-quarter TD. White also fired a TD pass, hitting Doug Cosbie in the second stanza.

GAME 4: Dallas Dominates, Escapes

Cowboys 17 at Houston 10

September 29: An NFL record-tying 12 sacks and five takeaways were not enough to give Dallas an easy win at the Astrodome—far from it, in fact. Thanks largely to four missed field goals in five tries by the normally reliable Rafael Septien, the Cowboys needed to pull out a heart-stopper on a one-yard TD pass from Danny White to Fred Cornwell with 1:47 remaining.

Tony Dorsett ran for 159 yards, including a 31-yard romp in the final minutes that set up the winning score. He was the only Dallas player with as many as 10 rushing yards. The Cowboys' missed kicks and poor execution on third down kept the Oilers in the game despite their dismal offensive production and four Warren Moon interceptions. Ron Fellows made two of those picks.

GAME 5: Septien Wins Surprising Shootout

Cowboys 30 at N.Y. Giants 29

October 6: Two of the NFL's top defenses got together, and offensive fireworks ensued. Rather than try to explain it, Rafael Septien settled for his role of winning it. The Dallas kicker, coming off one of his worst games, booted three fourth-quarter field goals, including the winning 31-yarder with 2:19 remaining.

No one could have predicted the nearly 900 combined yards the teams covered on offense.

The Giants' Phil Simms threw for 432 yards and three scores. The Cowboys' Danny White passed for 342 yards and three TDs, but he was intercepted four times. Mike Renfro gave Dallas 10 receptions for 141 yards and two scores. The Cowboys trailed 26–14 in the second half and 26–21 entering the fourth quarter before Septien put the boot to the Giants.

GAME 6: Milestone Day for Dorsett

Cowboys 27 vs. Pittsburgh 13

October 13: Tony Dorsett became the sixth man in NFL history to reach 10,000 career rushing yards, getting there on a 113-yard day in his first win over the rival Steelers—his "hometown team"—at Texas Stadium. The former Pitt star followed Jim Brown, O.J. Simpson, Walter Payton, Franco Harris, and John Riggins into the exclusive club.

Dorsett also caught a 56-yard TD pass from Danny White to give the Cowboys a 7–3 lead in the first quarter. They stretched it to 20–3 entering the fourth quarter, and Dorsett later rounded out the scoring with a 35-yard TD run.

GAME 7: Jaworski Burns Blitzing 'Boys

Philadelphia 16 vs. Cowboys 14

October 20: Dallas routinely sent seven and eight defenders toward Eagles QB Ron Jaworski. Although the blitz worked for a time, Jaworski eventually solved it and threw for a career-high 380 yards, snapping the Cowboys' four-game winning streak.

Jaworski's only TD pass was the game winner. He lobbed a 36-yarder that Dallas defender Everson Walls tipped right into the hands of Kenny Jackson with 10:07 to play. Tony Dorsett ran for 100 yards and scored both Dallas TDs, giving his team a 14–6 lead entering the fourth quarter. Jaworski completed a 22-of-35 day without an interception, while the Cowboys coughed up four turnovers.

GAME 8: Dallas Finishes Strong
Cowboys 24 vs. Atlanta 10

October 27: The Cowboys dug themselves a 10–0 hole against the one-win Falcons before righting themselves early in the second quarter. Danny White's 35-yard TD pass to Tony Hill and Tony Dorsett's 60-yard TD dash ignited a run of 24 straight points. White also ran for a score.

Hill, matched for much of the game against a rookie cornerback, caught 10 passes for 161

Chicago Bears linebackers Otis Wilson (No. 55) and Wilbur Marshall (No. 58) pressure Dallas Cowboys quarterback Danny White (No. 11) during a 44–0 Bears victory on November 17, 1985, at Texas Stadium in Irving, Texas. (Photo by Don Lansu/NFL)

yards. Dallas overcame its slow start to compile 461 total yards.

GAME 9: Cards Soar in Second Half

St. Louis 21 vs. Cowboys 10

November 4: Things were looking so promising at Busch Stadium. A 93-yard first-half drive that ended on an eight-yard pass from Danny White to Tony Hill jump-started the Cowboys to a 10–0 lead at the break. Then the Cardinals took over…completely.

Dallas failed to cross midfield in the second half until the game's final play. Meanwhile, the Cardinals seized victory on Neil Lomax TD passes to Pat Tilley and J.T. Smith and an eight-yard run by Earl Ferrell. Lomax directed a turnover-free St. Louis attack, while the Cowboys were intercepted once and lost two fumbles in the Monday night contest.

GAME 10: Dallas Sweeps 'Skins

Cowboys 13 at Washington 7

November 10: The score wasn't as lopsided as it was in their 30-point season-opening rout of the Redskins, but the Cowboys again took charge. They intercepted Joe Theismann three times and kept Washington out of the end zone until the fourth quarter. By then, Dallas owned a 13–0 lead on two Rafael Septien field goals and a 48-yard pass from Danny White to Tony Dorsett.

Defensive end Jim Jeffcoat registered a team-record five sacks, and Everson Walls intercepted

Theismann twice. White hit Tony Hill seven times for 136 yards, and the Cowboys did not turn over the ball.

GAME 11: Ouch! Bears Take Laugher

Chicago 44 at Cowboys 0

November 17: The difference between Dallas and the NFL's elite became painfully obvious on this Sunday at Texas Stadium. The Cowboys were shut out for the first time at Texas Stadium, failed to score for the first time in 219 games, and suffered the most lopsided defeat in franchise history. The only consolation came in the fact the bludgeoning came at the hands of the unbeaten Bears, the NFL's best team.

Chicago intercepted four passes by two Cowboys QBs, returning two for TDs. Walter Payton ran for 132 yards, completed a 33-yard throw, and also caught a pass. The Bears were dominant in all facets, stuffing the Dallas running game (52 yards on 16 carries), disrupting the passing attack, and imposing their will from start to finish.

GAME 12: Season Revival

Cowboys 34 vs. Philadelphia 17

November 24: After facing the Bears, even a good team looks mighty beatable. The Eagles were a welcome sight for Dallas after its pummeling the previous weekend, and Dallas rolled behind the 20-for-28 passing of Danny White. The QB threw for 243 yards and three TDs

The Manster

Half Man, Half Monster, Randy White was a Man to Be Feared

Cowboys safety Charlie Waters was the guy who nicknamed Randy White "The Manster." Waters explained, "Randy's charming, innocent demeanor transformed on game day to this despicable, nasty, destructive…well, 'monster.' From this unique combination of split personalities, I spawned the nickname 'The Manster'—part man, part monster, but the perfect football player."[1]

As a child, White's parents simply called him "Hunk," a name that became fitting as he developed into a big, strapping athlete.

Although defensive tackle was his destiny, it always took Randy a while, at each level, to get to that position. At Thomas McKean High School in Wilmington, Delaware, he starred as a fullback and linebacker. Initially a fullback at the University of Maryland, he moved to defensive tackle while increasing his bench-press to 430 pounds. The 6'4", 265-pound Manster eventually would up that figure to 501 pounds.

White won the Outland Trophy before going second overall to Dallas in the 1975 NFL Draft. He was moved to linebacker again until he finally settled at right defensive tackle in 1977. From that position, he would overpower offensive linemen for more than a decade.

Not just strong but smart and relentless, Randy stuffed the running game and ate quarterbacks for lunch. Beginning in 1977, he earned first-team All-Pro honors for nine consecutive seasons, a feat no other Cowboy has ever accomplished. In 1978, White was named the NFC Defensive Player of the Year after totaling 123 tackles and 16 sacks.

Randy White was named an All-Pro for nine consecutive seasons. This image is from 1985. (Photo by Al Messerschmidt/Getty Images)

White's most satisfying performance likely came in Super Bowl XII, when the Cowboys broke the Broncos 27–10. Randy and defensive end Harvey Martin were named co-MVPs after the onrushing Doomsday Defense forced four fumbles, intercepted four passes, and limited Denver's quarterbacks to 61 yards on 25 passing attempts.

Washington Redskins halfback Joe Washington told *Sports Illustrated* that the smartest thing to do when assigned to block White was "to call in sick." Waters told the magazine that White is "like a shark in water. Nothing's wasted. You know those love handles everybody has? The rolls at the waist? I jabbed him there once. His were as hard as biceps."[2]

Seemingly indestructible, Randy missed just one game in 14 seasons with the Cowboys. His career numbers were enormous: 209 games played, 1,114 tackles, 701 solo tackles, and 111 sacks. White was a no-brainer selection for the NFL All-Decade Team of the 1980s, the Cowboys Ring of Honor, and the Pro Football Hall of Fame.

without an interception, bouncing back from a humiliating defeat.

Tony Dorsett ran for 86 yards and two scores against the Eagles, who entered the game with one of the NFL's top defenses. The Cowboys' defense shone on this day, picking off Ron Jaworski three times.

GAME 13: Another Holiday Celebration

Cowboys 35 vs. St. Louis 17

November 28: Dallas improved to 14–3–1 on Thanksgiving Day with its second straight impressive win. The Cowboys overcame a 17–14 second-quarter deficit on two TD grabs by Tony Hill and a Tony Dorsett run to top their winning point total against Philadelphia four days earlier by just one point.

Danny White fired four TD passes and one interception. While Neil Lomax had the better aerial-yardage day with 319, his Cardinals offense put the ball on the ground four times, losing three. They were costly miscues against the opportunistic Cowboys.

GAME 14: Bengals Bruise 'Boys

Cincinnati 50 vs. Cowboys 24

December 8: For the record, these Cincinnati Bengals were not the Chicago Bears. The Cowboys simply made them look like the NFL's best team. Dallas yielded 570 yards, the most in club history, and the second-most points in its existence. And it did so against a team that entered the game with a losing record (6–7).

"Embarrassing," said numerous Cowboys players and coaches after a game in which they allowed 22 points in the first quarter and fell behind 43–10 in the third. Boomer Esiason threw for three Bengals TDs without being intercepted, and James Brooks waltzed through the Dallas defense for 109 yards and two TDs on just 13 carries.

GAME 15: Dallas Regains NFC East Crown

Cowboys 28 vs. N.Y. Giants 21

December 15: A Cowboys team that had been burned for 50 points a week earlier and had lost 44–0 to the Bears was still good enough to win its first NFC East title since 1981. It did so on a Sunday in which three different Cowboys QBs played, none of whom generated as much momentum as a defensive score did.

Trailing 14–7 in the second quarter, Ed "Too Tall" Jones tipped a Phil Simms pass and Jim Jeffcoat ran 65 yards to the end zone with the interception. That play turned the tide. Danny White then hit Mike Renfro with a TD pass to give the Cowboys the lead for good, and third-string QB Steve Pelluer led a key fourth-quarter TD drive.

GAME 16: 49ers a Nemesis Again

San Francisco 31 vs. Cowboys 16

December 22: San Francisco needed a win to ensure a playoff spot, while Dallas had already clinched the NFC East. It showed. The 49ers defeated the Cowboys for the fourth straight time, riding Joe Montana's 322-yard passing effort to a comeback win.

The Cowboys scored the game's first 13 points and led 16–7 late in the first half. San Francisco then clamped down defensively and tallied the last 24 points. Dallas ran the ball 30 times for just 60 yards. Gary Hogeboom passed for 389 yards, but most of his total came too late to rescue his club and earn a first-round home playoff game.

GAME 17: Playoff Whitewashing

L.A. Rams 20 vs. Cowboys 0

January 4, 1986: For much of the season, the Dallas defense had saved the club. But not on this day, when neither offense nor defense clicked against the record-setting Rams.

Eric Dickerson rushed for an NFL playoff record 248 yards and two TDs as L.A. became the first team to shut out the Cowboys in a postseason game. Counting the regular season, it was the second game in which Dallas failed to score a point—another dubious franchise first.

Danny White threw three interceptions, the Cowboys lost three fumbles, and the running attack generated only 61 yards. Gary Jeter notched three of the Rams' five sacks and caused havoc in the Dallas backfield all day.

1986

CHANGE IN THE AIR

Two-Decade Winning Streak Comes to an End

The last time the Cowboys had a losing season prior to 1986, Lyndon Johnson was in the White House. Now, 22 years later, it was Ronald Reagan. Following one .500 campaign and 20 consecutive winning ones, Dallas finally took a step back, slipping to 7–9.

It sure didn't look to be ending. USFL import Herschel Walker made an immediate impact in the backfield, and the Cowboys won six of their first eight games, looking like an NFC East title contender once again. However, the team won just one game in the season's second half, dropping five straight games to finish the year. It was a bitter pill for Coach Tom Landry to swallow after leading one of the most successful runs in pro sports history. Only the Montreal Canadiens and New York Yankees had amassed greater winning stretches in major pro sports.

A minus-6 turnover differential was key. With Steve Pelluer and Danny White each taking their lumps at QB, the Cowboys threw 24 interceptions against just 21 TDs as a team. Tony Dorsett edged Walker for the team rushing lead (each ran for more than 700 yards). but his days as a 1,000-yard man were over, and Landry began looking to construct another winner with young talent.

GAME 1: Memorable Debut for Walker

Cowboys 31 vs. N.Y. Giants 28

September 8: Herschel Walker could not have arrived at a better time. With Tony Dorsett sidelined after suffering a first-half ankle injury, Walker ended his NFL debut by scoring the winning TD on a 10-yard run with 1:16 to play against the Giants.

It was Walker's second TD of the night—a Monday night on which he ran for 64 yards on 10 tries. Dorsett opened the scoring on a 36-yard toss from Danny White in the second quarter, but New York rallied from deficits of 14–0 and 24–21 to claim a 28–24 edge on Phil Simms' third TD pass with 5:24 remaining. Simms threw for 300 yards, but it was Walker, having arrived from the USFL, who made the difference for Dallas.

GAME 2: Dorsett Returns, Runs Wild

Cowboys 31 at Detroit 7

September 14: On crutches for much of the week after spraining his left ankle in the season opener, Tony Dorsett returned to the lineup and trampled the Lions for 117 yards and a TD. Herschel Walker and Danny White also ran for scores in a 197-yard team rushing effort that flattened Detroit at the Pontiac Silverdome.

Only a James Jones TD with three minutes left in the game kept the Lions from suffering a home shutout. Detroit managed only 22 rushing yards through the first three quarters.

GAME 3: Falcons Fly in Final Seconds

Atlanta 37 at Cowboys 35

September 21: In the blink of an eye, the Cowboys' torrid start came crumbling down. They led Atlanta 35–27 in the fourth quarter before a Falcons TD and an improbable field goal with 20 seconds remaining did them in. The final boot was made possible by a 65-yard David Archer bomb to Floyd Dixon, who inexplicably made it behind the Dallas zone coverage when only such a prayer could hurt the Cowboys.

Mick Luckhurst kicked the 18-yarder for the win, deciding a game that featured 835 yards of offense. Danny White starred for the Cowboys, hitting 23-of-30 passes for four TDs to four different receivers. Gerald Riggs rushed for 109

Running back Herschel Walker on a carry in the 24–21 win over the San Diego Chargers on November 16, 1986, at Jack Murphy Stadium in San Diego, California. (Photo by Vic Milton/NFL)

yards and the fourth-quarter TD that got the Falcons back in the game.

GAME 4: Secondary Steps Up

Cowboys 31 at St. Louis 7

September 29: For the second time in as many road games, the Cowboys hung a 31–7 loss on a host. This time, it was the Cardinals in a Monday night game at Busch Stadium, and it was the defense that played the leading role.

Danny White threw for three TDs, and Herschel Walker carried 19 times for 82 yards. The Cowboys secondary intercepted four Neil Lomax passes, with Ron Fellows returning one 34 yards for a fourth-quarter TD. The take-aways negated the need for long drives on a night when St. Louis turned out to be a gracious host.

GAME 5: Orange Crushed!

Denver 29 vs. Cowboys 14

October 5: Mile High Stadium is typically not a friendly place for visitors. Spot the Broncos a 22–0 halftime lead, and you might as well plan to hit the slopes. The Cowboys put themselves in that predicament in Steve Pelluer's first NFL start. The Dallas QB was intercepted three times, and the first of those miscues led to the TD that sent Denver on its way to a romp.

The Cowboys' running attack did nothing to aid the first-time starter. Just 41 yards resulted from 21 carries. John Elway threw for

three scores without an interception to lead the Broncos, while Pelluer went 24-for-44 for 271 yards and a score.

GAME 6: Redskins Handed First Loss

Cowboys 30 vs. Washington 6

October 12: A Redskins team that had won its first five games was no match, on this day, for a Cowboys team trying to find itself. What Dallas found against Washington was its top defensive form—a form that held the visitors to just 184 total yards.

While the Redskins plodded along, the Cowboys struck for a Herschel Walker TD run and three Rafael Septien field goals for a 16–0 halftime lead. Walker added a second TD after the break, and Steve Pelluer finished with 323 passing yards for his first victory as an NFL starter. Walker ran for just 45 yards but caught six passes for 155.

GAME 7: Septien Saves Cowboys

Cowboys 17 at Philadelphia 14

October 19: Steve Pelluer got Dallas started, directing a 74-yard opening drive and finding Doug Cosbie for a TD. But Danny White, banged up but ready to play, had to come off the bench to finish the Eagles. He drove the Cowboys into position for Rafael Septien's winning 38-yard field goal with two seconds remaining.

In between, the Eagles played like two different teams. With Randall Cunningham replacing the injured Ron Jaworski at QB, the Eagles were held scoreless and gained just 62 yards before halftime. However, Cunningham ran for one TD and threw for another in rallying the Eagles to a 14–14 tie in the fourth quarter. White ran into the game with 54 seconds remaining after Pelluer injured his throwing hand and moved Dallas into position for the winning boot.

GAME 8: Cards Put Up No Fight

Cowboys 37 vs. St. Louis 6

October 26: Dallas controlled the ball for more than 41 of the game's 60 minutes in a one-sided scrimmage at Texas Stadium. It was a total mismatch. Herschel Walker rushed for 120 yards and two TDs, Steve Pelluer and Danny White combined on a 22-of-32 completion rate, and the Cowboys scored on seven of their first eight possessions.

The Cardinals, meanwhile, managed only two second-quarter field goals and made only 11 first downs against the Cowboys' 30.

GAME 9: Big Game, Big Losses

N.Y. Giants 17 vs. Cowboys 14

November 2: It was a frustrating day all around for the Cowboys. They lost QB Danny White for the season with a broken wrist. They reached the end zone just twice despite amassing 408 yards to the Giants' 245. And they saw their playoff chances take a crushing blow in a loss at Giants Stadium.

Aside from their inability to capitalize on scoring chances, their downfall was Joe Morris. The shifty back carried 29 times for 181 yards and two Giants TDs on a day when Dallas bottled up Phil Simms (67 passing yards). Steve Pelluer threw for 339 yards and a TD in place of White, but he could not prevent the Giants from taking leads of 10–7 at halftime and 17–7 in the fourth quarter.

GAME 10: Dorsett Trend Finally Falters

L.A. Raiders 17 at Cowboys 13

November 9: For the first time in their history, the Cowboys lost a game in which Tony Dorsett rushed for 100-plus yards. His 101 yards moved him past O.J. Simpson into fifth place on the all-time NFL rushing list, but five Steve Pelluer interceptions prevented Dallas from improving to 28-for-28 with their star runner over the century mark.

Pelluer's picks were the brunt of a six-turnover day by the Cowboys, who led just 10–3 at halftime despite outgaining the Raiders 258–80 before the break. Jim Plunkett hit Dokie Williams for 20- and 40-yard TD passes in the second half, with only a Rafael Septien field goal in between, to prevail.

Touchdown, Tony Dorsett

NFL Defenders Couldn't Catch This Speedy "Rabbit"

Tony Dorsett was so little as a child that he stuffed rocks in his pockets to meet the minimum weight requirement for the football team. On his first-ever carry, he ran scared, trying to out-distance himself from the big guys on his tail. "I took off like a little rabbit," he said. "Ended up running 75 yards for a touchdown."[1]

On January 3, 1983, Dorsett felt trapped again. The Cowboys had the ball inside their own 1-yard line against Minnesota, and confused fullback Ron Springs trotted toward to the sidelines, leaving just 10 men on the field and Dorsett by his lonesome in the Cowboys' end zone. Nevertheless, "T.D." found a hole in the line, zigzagged through the linebackers, and took off like a bunny with its tail on fire. He outraced the secondary to the end zone for the longest run from scrimmage in NFL history.

Raised in the projects of Aliquippa, Pennsylvania, Dorsett was blessed with a loving family and blazing speed. At the University of Pittsburgh, Tony shot through holes faster than defenders could react. He broke or tied 18 NCAA records, including most career rushing yards (6,342), and won the 1976 Heisman Trophy and the national championship.

In the 1977 NFL Draft, the Cowboys selected Dorsett with the No. 2 overall pick (acquired from Seattle). He continued to rock the football world by rushing for 1,007 yards as a rookie, including a career-high 206 in a game against the Eagles, and helping lead Dallas to victory in that season's Super Bowl. Dorsett earned first-team All-Pro honors only once in his career, but he earned four Pro Bowl selections.

Most impressively, T.D. surpassed 1,000 yards rushing eight times in his 11 years with

Tony Dorsett of the Dallas Cowboys carries the ball in the NFC divisional playoff game against the Green Bay Packers on January 16, 1983, in Dallas, Texas. (Photo by Ronald C. Modra/Getty Images)

the Cowboys and eclipsed 1,300 yards four times. In 1981, he ran for 1,686 yards, with a high of 175 against Baltimore.

"Tony was a joy to coach," said Dan Reeves, an assistant coach with the Cowboys. "He's as good a running back as I've ever been around. He's one of those guys that when you're on the opposing team and the ball's handed to him, you kind of lose your breath."[2]

Upon his retirement in 1988 (after a season with Denver), Dorsett had amassed 12,739 yards rushing and 16,326 yards from scrimmage. At the time, he ranked second in the NFL in career rushing yards behind Walter Payton. Six years later, he was inducted into the Pro Football Hall of Fame.

GAME 11: Furious Flurry Lifts Dallas

Cowboys 24 at San Diego 21

November 16: Trailing 21–10 in the fourth quarter and getting beaten up by the Chargers' defense, Dallas somehow rallied for a victory that kept—for the time being—its playoff hopes alive. San Diego tried a 55-yard field goal that would have forced overtime, but Rolf Benirschke's kick drifted wide left with one second on the clock.

Few would have believed it would come down to that after Dan Fouts hit Kellen Winslow for two second-half TDs that put the Cowboys down 11 points midway through the fourth quarter. But a blocked punt put Dallas at the San Diego 2-yard line and set up Herschel Walker's TD with 7½ minutes to play, and QB Steve Pelluer recovered from his day-long beating (12 sacks) to cap the winning drive on a two-yard keeper with 1:37 left.

GAME 12: Redskins Roll

Washington 41 vs. Cowboys 14

November 23: Darryl Clack fumbled the opening kickoff and it never got much better for the Cowboys, who gave up a club-record 34 points in the opening half. The NFC East–leading Redskins had been waiting for this one, having dropped three in a row against the Cowboys, and they made it worth their while.

Jay Schroeder threw for 325 yards and two TDs for Washington. The Redskins were even better on defense, limiting Dallas to 54 rushing yards and shutting out the Cowboys until the third quarter.

GAME 13: Thanksgiving No Holiday This Year

Seattle 31 at Cowboys 14

November 27: Dallas lost on Thanksgiving Day for just the fourth time in 19 years and did so convincingly. Four days after falling into a 34–0 first-half hole at Washington, the Cowboys dug a 24–7 trench against a Seattle club that had lost four of its last five.

The Redskins burned the Cowboys through the air, but this time it was Curt Warner chewing up 122 ground yards on 22 carries. Dave Krieg was also 16-of-24 passing for 214 yards and two scores against a Dallas defense that looked like a shadow of its former self. Steve Pelluer hit 22-of-36 throws for 210 yards in the losing cause.

GAME 14: Slide Continues

L.A. Rams 29 vs. Cowboys 10

December 7: It was a game in which Tom Landry left the field after the third quarter to return in a bulletproof vest after receiving what were deemed serious telephone threats against his life. Dallas' low-key coach took the turn of events in stride and was more concerned with his team's state of mind following its third consecutive loss.

The Rams got two defensive scores—a safety and an interception returned for a TD—in winning their 10th game of the year. They also got a 106-yard rushing effort from Eric Dickerson against a faltering Cowboys defense. Dallas yielded 418 total yards in watching its playoff hopes all but disappear.

GAME 15: Dallas Eliminated

Philadelphia 23 at Cowboys 21

December 14: Herschel Walker broke Tony Dorsett's eight-year-old franchise record with 292 total yards (120 rushing, 172 receiving), but it came as little consolation to a Dallas team that was eliminated from playoff contention and saw its 20-year run of winning seasons snapped. Worse yet, the loss came against a rival that entered the day 4–9–1.

Such was the state of the Cowboys as 1986 neared a close. Backup QB Matt Cavanaugh threw two second-half TD passes, the last one erasing a 21–16 deficit in the final minutes. Walker scored on two 84-yard plays—a first-quarter run and a fourth-quarter pass from Steve Pelluer that gave Dallas its final lead.

GAME 16: Bears Prolong the Misery

Chicago 24 at Cowboys 10

December 21: Dallas posted its first losing season since 1964, losing for the fifth straight week to end the year. How much worse were the Cowboys than the Bears? Well, Chicago tried to give the hosts a chance by throwing three interceptions and losing three fumbles, yet Dallas failed to score until trailing 24–0 in the fourth quarter.

The Cowboys nearly matched the Bears with five turnovers of their own. Doug Flutie attempted just 14 passes for Chicago, but two went for TDs. Ron Fellows intercepted two passes for Dallas.

1987

STRIKE TWO—SCABS IN

Another Work Stoppage Stains NFL

A players' strike chased away fans for the second time in six years, making the term "scab" part of the national sports lexicon. Even though the Cowboys had two notable players cross the picket line—Danny White and Tony Dorsett—it did not spare the club from suffering a 7–8 season.

The strike lasted 24 days and reduced the season by one game. Dorsett became just the fourth player in NFL history to top 12,000 career rushing yards, joining Walter Payton, Jim Brown, and Franco Harris. Dorsett and White helped the Cowboys' offense finish among the NFL's upper half, but the lack of top-line defensive talent showed up as opponents averaged better than 23 points per game.

Once the NFL regulars were back in action, Dallas lost four straight games in November and December to fall out of playoff contention.

GAME 1: Cowboys Collapse
St. Louis 24 vs. Cowboys 13

September 13: Leading 13–3, Dallas gave up three TDs in the final 1:58 of the game to suffer a horrific loss at St. Louis. The Cardinals got within three on a Neil Lomax to Roy Green TD pass, and the Cowboys fell inches short of a first down that could have salted away the game. Instead, they were forced to punt, and St. Louis drove for a second Lomax-to-Green TD pass to take the lead for good.

A late Danny White fumble allowed the Cardinals to tack on seven more points, ruining a strong 3½ quarters from Dallas. White completed 20-of-32 passes for 256 yards and a 20-yard final-quarter TD pass to Gordon Banks that gave the Cowboys a 10-point lead.

GAME 2: Slump Ends Against Champs
Cowboys 16 at N.Y. Giants 14

September 20: The NFL's longest losing streak at the time—six games—came to an end against the defending Super Bowl champions. Roger Ruzek kicked two second-half field goals to lift Dallas from a 14–10 deficit, and New York's Raul Allegre missed a 46-yarder in the final seconds that would have won it for the Giants.

The Cowboys overcame four Danny White interceptions for the improbable victory at Giants Stadium. White gave Dallas a 10–7 halftime lead on a one-yard TD pass to Thornton Chandler. The Giants responded with a Phil Simms scoring strike to Mark Bavaro, but the Cowboys' defense held them to 60 rushing yards on 20 carries.

GAME 3: Send in the Scabs
Cowboys 38 at N.Y. Jets 24

October 4: With the NFL Players Association on strike, replacements took the field and led the Cowboys to a two-TD win in New York. Taking the field after just two weeks of practice, QB Kevin Sweeney found the end zone on three of his six completions and quarterbacked Dallas to victory.

Predictably, the game was sloppy. The teams combined for nine turnovers and 26 penalties for 281 yards. Kelvin Edwards caught two TD passes for the Cowboys.

GAME 4: Quick Strikes Carry Cowboys
Cowboys 41 vs. Philadelphia 22

October 11: Dallas scored three TDs on its first six offensive snaps. Kelvin Edwards ran for a 62-yard score, Alvin Blount went in from the 8-yard line, and Kevin Sweeney hit a 77-yard bomb to Cornell Burbage as the Cowboys took a 21–0 lead midway through the first quarter.

Danny White and Tony Dorsett were among the seven regular players who crossed the picket line for this contest, and both were booed lustily at Texas Stadium when they entered the game in the second half. Each saw very limited action.

Head coach Tom Landry is flanked by Herschel Walker (No. 34), Victor Scott (No. 22), and Vince Albritton (No. 36) on the sidelines during the game against the Washington Redskins on December 13, 1987, in Washington, D.C. (Photo by Ronald C. Modra/Sports Imagery/Getty Images)

GAME 5: Redskins' Replacements Top Dallas Regulars

Washington 13 at Cowboys 7

October 19: Coach Tom Landry opted to go with Danny White, Tony Dorsett, and the rest of his veterans against Washington's all-replacement team in the final game featuring scab players, but the no-names came out on top.

Dorsett rushed for 81 yards but fumbled twice, and White threw for 262 but was sacked six times. In the end, Lionel Vital made the most of his moment in the sun, carrying 26 times for 136 yards in Washington's triumph. The Redskins took a 10–0 lead on Ted Wilson's 16-yard TD run in the third quarter and held on.

GAME 6: Strike Over, Eagles Soar

Philadelphia 37 vs. Cowboys 20

October 25: Dallas was thoroughly defeated by Philadelphia in the first game after the strike. However, that did not prevent the Eagles from taking one extra shot. They tacked on a TD in the final minute with help from a bomb that drew a 32-yard pass-interference penalty, a move that satisfied Eagles head coach Buddy Ryan and had the Cowboys wondering when their chance to counterpunch might come.

It was not on this day. Philly got 94 rushing yards from Keith Byars and two TD passes from Randall Cunningham to John Spagnola. Danny White threw for 257 yards and a TD to Tony Dorsett to pace the Cowboys.

GAME 7: Dallas Rides Record Final Quarter

Cowboys 33 vs. N.Y. Giants 24

November 2: Roger Ruzek tied an NFL record with four field goals in the final frame as the Cowboys scored 19 fourth-quarter points to beat the defending Super Bowl champs for the second time. Trailing 24–14 in the fourth, Ruzek booted a 34-yarder and Jim Jeffcoat tied the game with a 26-yard TD return of a Phil Simms interception.

Ruzek then provided the winning margin with three more kicks. Simms had given New York the lead on two long TD passes to Lionel Manuel. But five Giants turnovers were the difference against a Cowboys club that got a 24-for-33 passing effort from Danny White.

GAME 8: Miscues Cost Dallas

Detroit 27 vs. Cowboys 17

November 8: The third of Danny White's four interceptions led to the TD that broke a 17–17 tie in the fourth quarter and helped the Lions snap an eight-game losing streak, not counting the games played with replacement players.

White, who had been sharp the previous week against the Giants, was erratic in this one. He completed less than half of his throws and did not fire a TD pass. Detroit won despite rushing for just 76 yards.

GAME 9: Walker Ends OT Thriller

Cowboys 23 at New England 17 (OT)

November 15: Herschel Walker burst 60 yards for the winning TD in overtime as Dallas stunned the Patriots. New England led 17–14 late in regulation, but a 43-yard pass from Danny White to Mike Renfro on fourth down set up the tying field goal, and Walker found daylight to finish New England.

Walker replaced an injured Tony Dorsett and carried 28 times for 173 yards, the fourth-highest rushing total in Cowboys history. Throw in five receptions for 59 yards, and Walker racked up more than half his team's 438-yard total.

GAME 10: Dallas Can't Contain Rookie

Miami 20 at Cowboys 14

November 22: Rookie Troy Stradford accounted for 253 yards from scrimmage—169 rushing and 83 receiving—in a one-man rout of the Cowboys. Dan Marino extended his string of games with at least one TD pass to 30, but that wasn't until midway through the fourth quarter.

Until then, it was the Stradford show. Steve Pelluer, named Cowboys starting QB over Danny White, gave Dallas a 7–0 lead with the first of his two TD passes to Timmy Newsome. But a Stradford TD started the Dolphins toward 20 consecutive points.

GAME 11: Comeback Goes to Waste

Minnesota 44 at Cowboys 38

November 26: As Thanksgiving Day turned to Thanksgiving night, it seemed momentum was on the Cowboys' side. They rallied from a 38–24 deficit on two TD passes from Danny White to Mike Renfro in the fourth quarter, forcing overtime against the visiting Vikings.

However, Darrin Nelson got free for a 24-yard TD run midway through the extra session to cap a 476-yard offensive day for Minnesota. The Cowboys also topped 400 total yards, but five turnovers caused their downfall. Danny White threw for four TDs—three to Renfro—but he was also intercepted three times.

GAME 12: Small Crowd Sees Crushing Loss

Atlanta 21 at Cowboys 10

December 6: The smallest regular-season crowd in Texas Stadium history—just more than 40,000—witnessed a low point in the team's progress. The Falcons had lost six straight games since the strike ended, but they were still too much for the once-proud Cowboys on this Sunday.

Atlanta took a 14–0 lead and never looked back. Steve Pelluer was pulled for Danny White in the second half, to cheers from the crowd, but neither QB threw a TD pass. The Falcons' Gerald Riggs rushed for 119 yards, more than three times the totals managed by Cowboys Herschel Walker and Tony Dorsett.

Herschel Walker: Locomotive on Spikes
One of Pro Football's Greatest Runners Had Enormous Impact on Franchise

Herschel Walker, it can be argued, shone as bright a light on the Dallas Cowboys as any player in history. He is not in the Ring of Honor, having played less than six seasons with the team. Unfortunately, he is known more for having left the club in a blockbuster trade than for the 6,000-plus yards he gained with a star on his helmet. That 1989 deal, of course, gave Dallas the ammunition it needed to dominate the 1990s.

Consider the complete package, though, and it's unfair to size up Walker's contributions completely by the bounty it produced. Consider, too, that Walker's athletic career produced:

- the 1982 Heisman Trophy
- more than 25,000 professional all-purpose yards
- nine appearances on the *Sports Illustrated* cover
- a spot on the 1992 U.S. Olympic bobsled team
- College Football Hall of Fame enshrinement

Walker's innate ability was unquestioned. A unique blend of size, strength, and speed, he could run over defenders or around them with equal proficiency. He reached the end zone 86 times as a high schooler, rushed for more than 1,600 yards as a Georgia freshman, and once sprinted 60 yards in a world-class 6.15 seconds.

What set Walker apart, however, was his work ethic. The Augusta, Georgia, native credits

Herschel Walker runs upfield in a 16–14 win over the New York Giants on September 20, 1987, at the Meadowlands in East Rutherford, New Jersey. (Photo by James D. Smith/NFL)

much of his success to starting every day with thousands of push-ups and sit-ups, a routine he has maintained religiously for most of his life.

Before joining the Cowboys, Walker jumped from Georgia early for the United States Football League. He was the face of the fledgling circuit, winning two rushing titles and the 1985 MVP Award with the New Jersey Generals. His 2,411 rushing yards in '85 remain a pro football single-season record. It was not enough for the league to survive.

His anticipated arrival in Dallas the next year gave the Cowboys an added dimension. In addition to his skills as a runner, his soft hands allowed him to be deployed as a top receiving target. Walker caught 76 passes in his first NFL season, a Dallas record that stood for seven years until Michael Irvin broke it. His 1,606 yards from scrimmage in '86 led the NFL.

The trade that made the Cowboys a power in the 1990s sent Walker to Minnesota. He later played for the Eagles and Giants before returning to the Cowboys in 1996 to finish his career as a blocking back and kick-returner. "I went back to the Cowboys," he offered, "because I loved playing football so much that I didn't mind working for the [NFL] minimum wage."[1]

Walker's 25,283 all-purpose yards would stand as an all-time record and have him in the Pro Football Hall of Fame if not for the fact more than 7,000 of them came in the USFL. Instead, Walker may have to settle for his place in history as one of the most exceptional athletes ever to play the game.

GAME 13: Too Little, Too Late

Washington 24 vs. Cowboys 20

December 13: Dallas fell behind 24–3 early in the second half and could not come all the way back, losing for the fourth straight time and watching its slim playoff hopes go up in smoke. Roger Ruzek's second field goal and two Danny White TD passes narrowed the gap, but Washington held on to improve to 10–3.

White threw for 359 yards, but he was again hurt by a poor running game. Neither Tony Dorsett nor Herschel Walker managed 50 yards on the ground. Dallas lost despite outgaining Washington by more than 100 yards.

GAME 14: Dallas Ends Slump

Cowboys 29 at L.A. Rams 21

December 21: Roger Ruzek kicked a Cowboys-record five field goals as Dallas won on the road, ending a four-game losing streak. Four of the kicks came consecutively to break open a 7–7 game, producing a 19–7 Dallas lead by the third quarter. Doug Cosbie then caught a

27-yard TD pass from Steve Pelluer for a 26–7 cushion, and the outcome was decided.

Herschel Walker carried 23 times for 108 yards and a score in a reborn Dallas running attack. The Cowboys took advantage of four Rams turnovers while not giving up one of their own.

GAME 15: Season Ends on High Note

Cowboys 21 vs. St. Louis 16

December 27: With the playoffs a distant dream for the Cowboys, they took whatever consolation they could in eliminating the Cardinals from the postseason. Herschel Walker made two 11-yard TD runs in the second quarter and finished with his second straight 100-yard rushing game, gaining 137 on 25 totes.

His scores gave Dallas a 14–3 cushion that the Cardinals could not overcome. The Cards pulled within 14–13 early in the final quarter, but Steve Pelluer scored on a five-yard keeper for the Cowboys, who were outgained by 137 yards and had just 17 first downs to the Cardinals' 26. St. Louis turned the ball over twice, while Dallas protected it.

1988

LANDRY MATCHES LAMBEAU

NFL Coaching Great Spent 29 Years at Helm of Same Club

Tom Landry's 29th consecutive year coaching the same team matched a feat attained by Curly Lambeau with the Green Bay Packers. It was one of the few positives for Landry in an otherwise dreary year for the Cowboys, his last as their head coach.

Dallas won just three times and only once after September. Opponents scored 116 more points than the Cowboys, the highest such total in the NFL, and both the offense and defense were among the league's worst. With 1,514 rushing yards, Herschel Walker provided the greatest highlights, but defenses knew exactly what was coming and the Cowboys were not equipped to come from behind as they were forced to do all year.

Landry finished his tenure with 250 victories, 162 defeats, and six ties (regular season), along with two Super Bowl championships.

GAME 1: Late Gaffe Costs Upset Chance

Pittsburgh 24 vs. Cowboys 21

September 4: QB Steve Pelluer rolled the wrong way on a third-and-2 near the Pittsburgh goal line late—a busted play that resulted in an interception in the end zone and a blown chance to win the game. Dallas got the ball back, but Luis Zendejas missed a 49-yard field goal try in the final minute as the Steelers survived two scares.

Pittsburgh led 17–7 in the third quarter before Pelluer rallied the Cowboys on TD passes to rookie Michael Irvin and Ray Alexander. Irvin beat double coverage on his 35-yard scoring grab. Dallas gained 414 yards compared to the Steelers' 356.

GAME 2: Walker Tramples Cardinals

Cowboys 17 at Phoenix 14

September 12: The Cowboys' old rivals moved from St. Louis to Phoenix, but they may have left behind the playbook on how to stop Herschel Walker. The bruising back carried 29 times for 149 yards and a TD, rushing for 78 fourth-quarter yards to keep the Cardinals at bay.

QB Steve Pelluer also ran for a score, set up by Walker's fourth-quarter workload. Walker's score just before the half gave Dallas the lead for good, 10–7. The Cowboys ran for 190 yards as a team and survived Neil Lomax's 266-yard, two-TD passing day.

GAME 3: Crazy Safety the Final Margin

N.Y. Giants 12 at Cowboys 10

September 18: Instant-replay official Armen Terzian mistakenly awarded the Giants a safety on the game's very first play when a muffed kickoff by the Cowboys' Darryl Clack should have resulted only in a touchback. The postgame admission of error did nothing to console Dallas, which contributed to its own demise with two Steve Pelluer interceptions and an inept running game.

Following the controversial safety, each team scored on a first-quarter field goal and a third-quarter TD pass in an ugly game. Dallas nearly compiled as many penalty yards (79) as rushing yards (91) and was unable to recover any of the three Giants fumbles.

GAME 4: Cowboys High on Noonan

Cowboys 26 vs. Atlanta 20

September 25: Fittingly, defensive tackle Danny Noonan was the top scorer in a game the Cowboys won on defense. Noonan returned an interception 17 yards for a TD to open the scoring and notched a third-quarter safety that sparked Dallas in overcoming a 20–14 deficit. Then Noonan and his defensive mates preserved the win with high drama.

After falling behind due to a TD pass from Steve Pelluer to Ray Alexander with 1:48 remaining, Atlanta drove to the Dallas 10. A would-be TD pass from Steve Dils zipped right

Quarterback Steve Pelluer scans the field against the New York Giants at Giants Stadium in East Rutherford, New Jersey, on November 6, 1988. The Giants won the game, 29–21. (Photo by T. G. Higgins/Allsport, Getty Images)

through the hands of Aubrey Matthews, and Dils was sacked by the blitzing Cowboys—their seventh sack of the game—on fourth down to end the threat.

GAME 5: Saints Boot 'Boys on Last Play

New Orleans 20 vs. Cowboys 17

October 3: Steve Pelluer's best individual game was not enough to save the Cowboys from the surging Saints on *Monday Night Football*. Pelluer threw for 271 yards and two TDs and ran for 53 yards, but there was nothing he could do as Morten Andersen kicked a 49-yard field goal to carry the Saints as time expired.

The Cowboys never led, but they had rallied from a 14–0 deficit to tie the game twice. The last time came on Roger Ruzek's 39-yard field goal with 24 seconds remaining. But a 39-yard return of the ensuing kickoff and a 26-yard pass from Bobby Hebert to Brett Perriman gave Andersen the final say. Kelvin Martin caught both TD passes from Pelluer.

GAME 6: Redskins Dominate

Washington 35 at Cowboys 17

October 9: Steve Pelluer set up Redskins TDs with two of his three interceptions, and the Cowboys could never get their running game started, dooming them to a lopsided loss at Texas Stadium. Kelvin Bryant rushed for 118 yards for Washington, nearly double the total

Dallas managed as a team (60 yards on 20 carries).

Backup QB Danny White was also intercepted in a five-turnover game for the Cowboys. Washington fell behind 7–0 but used the miscues to build a 28–10 halftime lead in a game that lacked drama thereafter.

GAME 7: Bears Flex Muscle

Chicago 17 vs. Cowboys 7

October 16: Chicago's hard-hitting defense knocked two Dallas QBs out of the game, sending Steve Pelluer (concussion) to the bench early and Danny White (knee) late. In between, no one on the Cowboys' offensive unit could do much to find the end zone. The Bears pitched a shutout until White hit Everett Gay for a meaningless 13-yard TD toss with five minutes remaining in the game.

Chicago scored all of its points in the second quarter. The outburst was highlighted by a 39-yard hookup between Jim McMahon and Ron Morris. Pelluer was decked five minutes into the game, and White came on to throw for 242 yards.

GAME 8: Dallas Blows Big Lead

Philadelphia 24 vs. Cowboys 23

October 23: Victory was there for the taking. So was revenge. But leading the rival that ran up the score on them a year earlier, 20–0, the Cowboys squandered their cushion, gave up the winning TD with four seconds left, and retreated to process one of the most dreary losses in franchise history.

Randall Cunningham directed TD drives of 99 and 85 yards in the fourth quarter to pull out the win for the Eagles. The former ended on a seven-yard Anthony Toney dash, the latter on a two-yard toss from Cunningham to Toney on the game's next-to-last play. The Eagles entered the fourth quarter trailing 23–10. Cowboys QB Steve Pelluer went 32-of-46 for 342 yards and a TD with one interception.

GAME 9: Another Losing Letdown

Phoenix 16 at Cowboys 10

October 30: For the second straight week and the fifth time on the season, Dallas allowed victory to morph into defeat. Leading the Cardinals 10–0 midway through the third quarter, the Cowboys yielded a field goal and two fourth-quarter TDs, both to Earl Ferrell.

Ferrell, who ran for 110 yards on just 19 carries, tied the score 10–10 on a 14-yard scoring reception from Neil Lomax. After a Steve Pelluer interception, he capped the winning drive on a one-yard burst. Pelluer struggled mightily, going 9-of-31 for 102 yards with two picks. Almost half of his passing yards came on a 50-yard TD toss to Ray Alexander that gave Dallas a 10–0 lead after a scoreless first half.

GAME 10: Sweeney Can't Change Fate

N.Y. Giants 29 vs. Cowboys 21

November 6: The backup QB is usually the most popular player on a struggling team. Such was the case with Kevin Sweeney, who scrambled all over Giants Stadium, threw three TD passes with no interceptions, and generally performed well for the Cowboys. However, he could not save them from their sixth consecutive loss.

Sweeney provided a second-half spark, but the same could not be said for many on the Dallas defense in the first half. Phil Simms connected with Stephen Baker on two second-quarter TD passes to blow open the game. Herschel Walker ran for 96 yards and caught passes for 40 more yards in the losing cause.

GAME 11: Vikings Overpowering

Minnesota 43 at Cowboys 3

November 13: It was Kevin Sweeney's first start at QB in a non-replacement game, but not even Johnny Unitas in his prime could have saved the Cowboys on this day. The Vikings took advantage of four Sweeney interceptions and three fumble recoveries, pummeling Dallas at Texas Stadium.

It was the second-worst home loss in history for the Cowboys. Sweeney was just 10-of-28 with four picks. Wade Wilson threw three TD passes for Minnesota, which got defensive scores on a fumble recovery and a safety.

Pickin' It: Everson Walls

The Great Interceptor Thwarted Many a Game Plan

For someone who carved a career out of taking away, Everson Walls made his greatest impact by giving. Former teammate Ron Springs, suffering from severe diabetes in 2006, was in need of a kidney to live. Walls, as he so often was on the football field, was Johnny on the spot.

The transplant took place in the winter of 2007. It was not something Walls had to stop and ponder for long. "My giving a kidney to Ron wasn't about Ron and me," Walls writes in his book, *A Gift for Ron*. "What Ron and I did was about the families and loved ones and friends and co-workers in need of the gift for a continued and better life."[1]

If Walls had made life better for individuals off the field, he sure made it hell on QBs and offensive coordinators. His 57 career interceptions place him among the all-time NFL leaders in that category, and his 44 picks in a Cowboys uniform rank second to Mel Renfro's 52.

Just as he snuck up on QBs and receivers for years from his cornerback position, no one saw Walls coming before he made his big NFL splash. The Dallas native was bypassed several times by every team in the league in the 1981 NFL Draft after clocking "slow" 40-yard dash times in workouts. This, despite the fact he led the nation with 11 interceptions as a Grambling senior.

The hometown Cowboys gave Walls a chance, signing him as a free agent. And one chance was all Walls needed. He worked to make the team and then went about the business of making an immediate impact.

Walls broke a franchise record by picking off a league-leading 11 passes as a rookie in 1982. He made seven more in just nine games during the following, strike-shortened slate,

Everson Walls during the game against the Los Angeles Raiders on August 13, 1988, at the LA Memorial Coliseum in Los Angeles, California. (Photo by Allen Dean Steele/Getty Images)

again leading the NFL. And in 1983 he joined Renfro and Don Perkins as the third player in Cowboys history to make the Pro Bowl in each of his first three seasons.

Walls' knack for being in the right place at the right time, great hands, and deceptive closing speed made him a nightmare for opposing attacks. He led the NFL in interceptions for a third time and was named to his fourth Pro Bowl in 1985. Playing on the left side while Dennis Thurman handled the right, Walls became the more celebrated member of one of the best cornerback tandems in NFL history.

Walls added a Super Bowl title to his career résumé as a member of the 1990 New York Giants. Playing safety, his open-field tackle of Thurman Thomas in Super Bowl XXV was a key play late in the game that his Giants won when Buffalo's Scott Norwood missed a last-second field goal— yet another example of Walls being in the right place at the right time.

GAME 12: Slump Reaches Eight

Cincinnati 38 at Cowboys 24

November 20: The Bengals amassed more than 300 yards in the first half alone, roaring to a 24–3 lead toward stretching the Cowboys' losing streak to eight games. Just 37,865 fans turned out, the second-smallest Texas Stadium crowd to watch a Cowboys game.

The no-shows missed a dominant rushing performance from the Bengals' James Brooks. He amassed 148 yards and a TD on just 16 carries, while Boomer Esiason threw three Bengals TD passes. Herschel Walker carried 27 times for 131 yards and a Cowboys TD.

GAME 13: Thanksgiving Brings No "W"

Houston 25 at Cowboys 17

November 24: About the only thing Cowboys fans could be thankful for, football-wise, on this Thanksgiving was the prospect of getting the first pick in the 1989 NFL Draft, a possibility that could bring UCLA's star QB Troy Aikman to Dallas. For the time being, Turkey Day simply meant their ninth consecutive loss. Houston rallied from a 17–10 deficit to score the game's final 15 points.

Herschel Walker and Steve Pelluer ran for scores to put Dallas up by a TD in the third quarter. However, Warren Moon hit Drew Hill for Houston's go-ahead TD in the fourth quarter, and Tony Zendejas kicked three second-half field goals for the Oilers, whose offense played turnover-free football.

GAME 14: Dubious Distinction for Dallas

Cleveland 24 vs. Cowboys 21

December 4: The Cowboys set a club record with 17 penalties, two of which nullified Roger Ruzek field goals, in suffering their 10th loss in a row. The last of the wiped-out field goals, a 40-yarder, would have tied the game in the final two minutes, but Randy White was flagged for tripping, and Ruzek's 50-yard try fell short.

When Dallas wasn't aiding Cleveland scoring drives with penalties, it was aiding them with poor pass defense. Bernie Kosar went 19-of-27 for 308 yards and three TDs without an interception. Herschel Walker ran 25 times for 134 yards and a Cowboys score, but a portion of Dallas' 142 penalty yards cut into the club's 410-yard offensive effort. Steve Pelluer threw two TD passes.

GAME 15: Slump Ends at 10

Cowboys 24 at Washington 17

December 11: A team record–tying losing streak ended at 10 games for the Cowboys, thanks to their dominance on the ground. Dallas ran (Herschel Walker had 27 carries for 98 yards) and stopped the Redskins from doing so (24 yards on 14 carries as a team), and that was the difference as the Cowboys won for the first time since September.

Steve Pelluer threw for 333 yards and three TDs to rookie wideout Michael Irvin. Irvin enjoyed a breakout game with six catches for 149 yards, including a 61-yarder for a third-quarter score that gave his team a 17–3 edge. Washington QBs Doug Williams and Mark Rypien combined for three interceptions, and the Redskins also lost two fumbles.

GAME 16: Misery Ends with Loss

Philadelphia 23 at Cowboys 7

December 18: Green Bay's win over Phoenix later in the day, combined with the Cowboys' lackluster performance against the Eagles, gave Dallas the edge over the Packers in the "Troy Aikman Sweepstakes." By virtue of their 3–13 record, the Cowboys earned the right to draft the UCLA star first overall in 1988.

Getting there was an easy task in the finale. All Dallas had to do was let Steve Pelluer throw three interceptions and allow Eagles QB Randall Cunningham to throw two TD passes without a pick. That's not to say the Cowboys didn't try. They simply came up short, as they had for most of the season. Herschel Walker's first-quarter TD plunge turned out to be their lone score.

1989

NEW ERA BEGINS

New Owner Jones Brings in New Coach, New Attitude

The Tom Landry era could not have given way to a more stark contrast in 1989. Brash new owner Jerry Jones hired brazen college coach Jimmy Johnson, and the two University of Arkansas alumni proceeded to turn things upside down following the successful and mostly stoic 29-year run of Tom Landry walking the sidelines and Tex Schramm manning the front office.

Johnson had been highly successful with the bravado-filled Miami Hurricanes of the college ranks, and he was confident that a tough, physical, in-your-face style would succeed in Dallas, too. It did not happen overnight, although the drafting of Troy Aikman provided a young QB around whom to build a dynasty.

Their 1989 debut produced just one victory—a 13–3 midseason triumph at Washington. Still, the pieces were coming together, and a dominant decade was on the horizon.

GAME 1: Embarrassing Start

New Orleans 28 vs. Cowboys 0

September 10: The Jimmy Johnson Era opened with a thud, and Dallas suffered its first regular-season shutout loss in four years. Unless the new head coach could have lined up at offensive guard and opened an actual hole for a ball-carrier, there was nothing he could do.

The Saints literally stuffed the Cowboys, holding them to 20 yards on 10 carries in the game. Dallas gained just 10 first downs to New Orleans' 26, and rookie QB Troy Aikman completed less than half of his passes with two interceptions in his debut. Saints QB Bobby Hebert, meanwhile, completed 16-of-19 passes.

GAME 2: Victory Chance Slips Away

Atlanta 27 vs. Cowboys 21

September 17: This was more like it. Though first-year Dallas coach Jimmy Johnson admitted his club had a long way to go, it dashed to a 21–10 halftime lead and appeared to be on the verge of an early win. Then its inexperience began to show.

Atlanta pounced on miscues and scored 17 unanswered second-half points, snatching victory when Scott Case made an easy interception of a Troy Aikman pass with 2:59 to go. Dallas got 85 yards and two TDs on 23 Herschel Walker carries. Aikman threw for 241 yards and his first TD (a 65-yarder) to Michael Irvin, but his two interceptions were costly against a Falcons team that did not commit a turnover. Bobby Butler returned a Walker fumble 29 yards for a Falcons TD.

GAME 3: "Awful" Cowboys Routed

Washington 30 at Cowboys 7

September 24: Jimmy Johnson called his club "awful" after a game in which he turned to his former University of Miami QB, Steve Walsh, to try to ignite the offense. It didn't work. Dallas got its only points on a defensive score—Jim Jeffcoat's 77-yard fumble return in the opening quarter—and rushed for just 34 yards in the home opener.

Walsh replaced Troy Aikman under center, but each man threw two interceptions. Alvin Walton returned one of Aikman's 29 yards for a TD. Jamie Morris ran for 100 yards and a Washington score.

GAME 4: Aikman's Progress Halted by Injury

N.Y. Giants 30 at Cowboys 13

October 1: Rookie QB Troy Aikman broke his left index finger, leaving the Dallas offense in Steve Walsh's control. As it stood, the QB spot was the least of the Cowboys' worries. A visitor scored 30 points for the second straight week as Phil Simms threw for 211 yards and two TDs in a game the Giants never trailed.

Steve Walsh replaced the injured Aikman in the second quarter. By the time he marched the team to its first offensive TD in two weeks—a

27-yard scoring strike to Herschel Walker—New York had rolled to a 30–6 lead. The Giants won despite three Simms interceptions and five turnovers.

GAME 5: Packers Prevail

Green Bay 31 vs. Cowboys 13

October 8: Dallas' first trip to Green Bay since the 1967 Ice Bowl featured temperatures in the 60s. The forecast for the Cowboys was not so balmy. The Packers piled up more than 500 offensive yards and pulled away in the second half.

Don Majkowski threw for 313 yards and four TDs without an interception, directing a hot Green Bay attack. Steve Walsh, making his first start for the Cowboys, fared admirably if not as effectively. He went 18-for-29 with a TD pass to Michael Irvin on a day when the Dallas running game was bottled up.

GAME 6: The Last of the Winless

San Francisco 31 at Cowboys 14

October 15: Dallas became the last winless team in the NFL despite outgaining an opponent for the first time in the Jimmy Johnson era. The Cowboys' 330 yards compared to the 49ers' 318 did not matter much, however, because San Francisco was far better at finding the end zone.

Steve Wallace blocked a Dallas field goal attempt and Johnnie Jackson returned it 75 yards for a TD to break a 7–7 halftime stalemate.

Dallas re-tied it when RB Darryl Clack, making his first start, ran in from the 1-yard line later in the third quarter. But the 49ers scored 17 unanswered points in the final frame against the fading hosts. Steve Walsh led Dallas with 294 passing yards, but once again he received no support from the run (20 carries, 60 yards).

GAME 7: Chiefs Pull Away Early

Kansas City 36 vs. Cowboys 28

October 22: The Chiefs compiled more than 300 yards in the first half against their helpless visitors, who scored two fourth-quarter TDs to make the final score look much closer than the game was. Christian Okoye was a nightmare, running for 170 yards and two TDs on 33 carries, while Steve DeBerg hit all but five of his 22 throws.

Kansas City also got a special-teams score, blocking a punt out of the end zone for a safety, and former Cowboys QB Steve Pelluer even made a TD run while filling in for DeBerg in the second half. The highlights for Dallas were a 63-yard Paul Palmer TD run and a 97-yard kickoff return TD by James Dixon.

GAME 8: Slump Hits Season's Halfway Mark

Phoenix 19 at Cowboys 10

October 29: Dallas made it to the season's midway point without a win, although this time the Cowboys were in it until late. Derrick

Head coach Jimmy Johnson encourages his team from the sideline during a game on October 8, 1989, against the Green Bay Packers at Lambeau Field in Green Bay, Wisconsin. The Packers beat the Cowboys, 31–13. (Photo by Tony Tomsic/Getty Images)

Shepard, who caught a 37-yard pass from Steve Walsh to narrow Phoenix's lead to 16–10 in the fourth quarter, fumbled a punt in the final two minutes that led to a game-clinching Cardinals field goal.

It was the third turnover of the game for the Cowboys. Steve Walsh threw two interceptions on a 264-yard passing day. Former Dallas QB Gary Hogeboom directed St. Louis to the win. He did so largely by handing off to Earl Ferrell and Tony Jordan, as the Cardinals gained 158 rushing yards to the Cowboys' 45.

GAME 9: Finally, a Win!

Cowboys 13 at Washington 3

November 5: Jimmy Johnson claimed his first victory as an NFL head coach and had no trouble pinpointing the difference between this game and his previous eight losses. The Cowboys were not penalized and did not commit a turnover against a Redskins team favored by more than two TDs.

Paul Palmer rushed for 110 yards on 18 carries and scored the game's only TD. His two-yard run culminated a five-play, 60-yard march late in the third quarter that broke a 3–3 tie. The drive's big play was a third-down draw to Palmer that went for 47 yards.

Doug Williams passed for 296 yards for the Redskins, but it took him 52 pass attempts to do it, and his two interceptions were costly. Cowboys QB Steve Walsh completed only 10-of-30 passes for 147 yards, but Palmer and the Dallas defense put him in the rare position of having only to minimize mistakes, which the Cowboys did expertly.

GAME 10: Aikman's Record Means Little

Phoenix 24 vs. Cowboys 20

November 12: Rookie Troy Aikman returned to the lineup after breaking his finger more than a month earlier and set an NFL rookie record with 379 passing yards. However, the QB would have traded every one of those yards for a win, which eluded his Cowboys against the winning Cardinals.

Phoenix's scores came on big plays—a 53-yard interception return by Tim McDonald and two Tom Tupa-to-Ernie Jones bombs covering 38 and 72 yards. The long one came with just 58 seconds remaining, spoiling what looked like a second consecutive Dallas victory in the making. Aikman connected with James Dixon six times for 203 yards, including a 75-yard score that had given the Cowboys the lead with less than two minutes remaining. Aikman went 21-of-40 with two TDs and two interceptions.

GAME 11: The One That Got Away

Miami 17 at Cowboys 14

November 19: For the second straight week, an opponent rallied to steal a win from a Dallas team desperate for a second one. The Cowboys led 14–3 in the second quarter on TDs by Broderick Sargent and Daryl Johnston, but the

The Trade

Cowboys Hit the Jackpot in 18-Player Deal with Minnesota

After losing to the Packers on October 8, 1989, the Cowboys (3–13 the year before) were 0–5. They couldn't stop anybody, allowing at least 27 points in each of the five games, and rookie quarterback Troy Aikman was tossed around like a rag doll on the backfield. Cowboys head coach Jimmy Johnson knew that the team needed to make a change—one of Texas-sized proportions.

Dallas needed warm bodies on defense and high draft picks to replenish the team's talent pool. Fortunately for the Cowboys, they had a prime commodity to trade: Herschel Walker, the locomotive halfback who had rushed for 1,514 yards in his breakout season of 1988.

When the Cowboys put the word out that Walker was available, teams became giddy with excitement. Cleveland offered two first-round picks, three-second round selections, and a player. Vikings GM Mike Lynn told Johnson that he could do better, and boy did he ever!

On October 12, the largest trade in NFL history was made. Below are the 18 players and draft picks involved.

In 1989, the Herschel Walker trade sent the star running back to Minnesota in a history-making move that involved 18 players and draft picks. (Photo by Jonathan Daniel/Allsport/Getty Images)

Vikings Received
- Herschel Walker (42 games, 2,264 rushing yards for Minnesota, left team in 1992)
- Dallas' 1990 third-round pick (tight end Mike Jones, who caught just two passes for Minnesota)
- San Diego's 1990 fifth-round pick (receiver Reggie Thornton, who didn't make the team)
- Dallas' 1990 tenth-round pick (receiver Reggie Thornton, who didn't make the team)
- Dallas' 1991 third-round pick (receiver Jake Reed, four 1,000-yard seasons with Minnesota)

Cowboys Received
- Cornerback Isaac Holt (starter for Cowboys, 1990–92)
- Linebacker Jesse Solomon (one year, no starts with Dallas)
- Linebacker David Howard (one year, no starts with Dallas)
- Defensive end Alex Stewart (soon released)
- Running back Darrin Nelson (soon traded)
- Minnesota's 1990 first-round pick (Dallas traded this pick and a third-round pick to Pittsburgh for a 1990 first-round pick, which they used to draft Emmitt Smith)
- Minnesota's 1990 second-round pick (receiver Alexander Wright, who made six starts with Dallas)
- Minnesota's 1990 sixth-round pick (traded to New Orleans)
- Minnesota's 1991 first-round pick, conditional (receiver Alvin Harper, a three-year starter and game-breaking threat for Dallas)
- Minnesota's 1990 second-round pick, conditional (linebacker Dixon Edwards, a three-year starter for Dallas)
- Minnesota's 1992 second-round pick, conditional (defensive back Darren Woodson, an 11-year starter and five-time Pro Bowler for Dallas)
- Minnesota's 1992 third-round pick, conditional (traded to New England)
- Minnesota's 1993 first-round pick, conditional (traded to Philadelphia)

The Cowboys not only benefited directly from the Vikings trade—particularly with Emmitt Smith, Alvin Harper, and Darren Woodson—but they dealt some of their acquired capital for more draft picks. They used two of those picks to draft future All-Pro cornerback Kevin Smith and future Pro Bowl defensive tackle Russell Maryland.

Both Minnesota and Dallas would be playoff mainstays through the 1995 season, but while the Vikings went 0–4 in the postseason, the Cowboys won three Super Bowls. Ironically, Dallas reacquired Herschel Walker in 1996—then defeated Minnesota in that year's playoffs.

Dolphins scored on a Hail Mary on the last play of the first half, got the winning TD on Sammie Smith's fourth-quarter run, and survived a last-second 53-yard field goal try by the Cowboys' Luis Zendejas.

The Hail Mary was the stinger. Time had expired on the first-half clock and the Cowboys were running for the locker room, but referee Jerry Markbreit said Dolphins QB Dan Marino had called a timeout with :01 remaining. Marino then heaved a bomb that Andre Brown caught at the peak of his jump amid three defenders at the 1-yard line, then Brown crossed the goal line for the improbable TD. Troy Aikman threw for 261 yards and a TD, plus 71 rushing yards, but his team lost despite compiling 428 offensive yards.

GAME 12: Dallas Blanked and Miffed

Philadelphia 27 at Cowboys 0

November 23: After the game, Cowboys coach Jimmy Johnson accused the Eagles of putting monetary bounties on the heads of two of his players—kicker Luis Zendejas and QB Troy Aikman. The Eagles, denying the charge, didn't knock either of those players out of the game, though they did put a hit on Zendejas on his only kickoff.

Philadelphia's most crushing blows came elsewhere—all over the field, in fact. The Eagles held the Cowboys to 191 total yards and a 9-of-25 pass completion rate in a game that was one-sided from start to finish. They intercepted

Aikman three times, and Randall Cunningham threw two TD passes to Cris Carter.

GAME 13: Rams Rally in Shootout

L.A. Rams 35 at Cowboys 31

December 3: Jim Everett rallied the Rams with two TD passes in the final four minutes as his team overcame a 31–21 deficit at Texas Stadium. For much of the day, despite Everett and the Rams' 400-yard offensive onslaught, it looked as though the Cowboys had their second win in the bag.

Troy Aikman matched Everett with four TD tosses, including three straight in the second half that turned a 21–10 shortfall into a 10-point cushion. The Dallas QB hit four different receivers in the end zone on a day when most of his completions covered ground in small chunks. Aikman, who threw one interception, also led the Cowboys with 57 rushing yards.

However, Everett's 341 passing yards and late charge proved to be the difference. The Cowboys had one last chance but ran out of time after driving to the L.A. 13-yard line.

GAME 14: Not a Snowball's Chance

Philadelphia 20 vs. Cowboys 10

December 10: With snowballs flying at Veterans Stadium, the Eagles were too much for the Cowboys, even on a day when Dallas played turnover-free football until the game's final minute. Philly held Dallas to less than 200 total yards and took a 14–0 lead in the second quarter en route to a defensive-minded win over its reeling rival.

For the second straight game, Troy Aikman led the Cowboys in both passing (152 yards and a fourth-quarter TD to Daryl Johnston) and running (six carries, 60 yards). The latter, however, was not a positive sign for a Dallas team in need of a consistent rushing attack. Cris Carter's two second-quarter TD receptions were all the offense the Eagles needed.

GAME 15: Another Whitewashing
N.Y. Giants 15 vs. Cowboys 0

December 16: Dallas was shut out for the third time in Jimmy Johnson's debut year as coach—more than the team's total (two) in 29 seasons under Tom Landry. They also set dubious club distinctions for most losses in a season, fewest first downs in a game (seven), and fewest total yards in a game (108) in one of the most inept efforts in the team's history.

The Giants managed just three field goals in the first half, but it was clear they would provide more than enough cushion on this day. When Ottis Anderson ran for a third-quarter TD to highlight his 91-yard rushing game, the win was way out of reach. Dallas did not have a runner gain more than 15 yards in the game.

GAME 16: A Merciful Ending
Green Bay 20 at Cowboys 10

December 24: On Christmas Eve, it didn't take three wise men to declare the end of the season a blessing for the Cowboys. Their 1–15 debut with Jimmy Johnson at the helm and Troy Aikman under center ended badly when second-half miscues allowed the Packers to pull away from a 10–10 tie.

The Cowboys knotted the score when Jack Del Rio returned a third-quarter fumble 57 yards for a TD. However, the Packers drove for the go-ahead score—a five-yard pass from Don Majkowski to Ed West—and jumped on two turnovers to seal the win. First, Daryl Johnston coughed up a fumble that led to a Packers drive of nearly nine minutes for an insurance field goal. Any hopes for a Cowboys comeback died when Aikman threw his fourth interception of the game.

1990

TEAM ON THE RISE

Smith, Johnson Earn Big Honors in Turnaround

Rebuilding the Cowboys did not take so long after all. They improved by six games in 1990, going 7–9 and beginning to look like a contender again. Running back Emmitt Smith was named NFL Offensive Rookie of the Year, and Jimmy Johnson garnered Coach of the Year accolades as a new decade dawned with an emerging power.

Smith rushed for 937 yards and 11 TDs, while Troy Aikman threw for 11 scores. The Cowboys won four straight games in November and December, but back-to-back road losses to finish the season kept them from a .500 record and possibly reaching the playoffs.

Still, all signs were pointing toward a winner, and Cowboys fans would not have to wait much longer.

GAME 1: Dallas Puts '89 Behind

Cowboys 17 vs. San Diego 14

September 9: The Cowboys needed just one game to match their 1989 victory total. They scored 10 unanswered points in the fourth quarter to post their first home win in almost two calendar years. Trailing 14–7 at halftime, Dallas held San Diego to just two first downs in the second half.

The Cowboys, who had opened the game's scoring on a pass from Troy Aikman to Dennis McKinnon, pulled to within 14–10 on a Ken Willis field goal. Following an unsuccessful fake punt attempt by the Chargers near midfield with less than six minutes to play, Aikman directed Dallas to the winning TD—his own one-yard plunge. The Cowboys held the Chargers to 212 yards, with just 70 of those yards coming after halftime.

GAME 2: Back to Reality

N.Y. Giants 28 at Cowboys 7

September 16: One week after their encouraging opening win, the Cowboys were reminded how far they had to climb in the NFC East. The Giants simply lined up and beat them, running for 161 yards while holding Dallas to 20 yards on the ground in a game decided in the trenches.

The Cowboys' only score came on a thrilling 90-yard kickoff return by Alexander Wright in the second quarter. Their offense was shut out by New York, while Phil Simms directed a crisp Giants attack with a 16-of-21 passing day.

GAME 3: Redskins Gain Revenge

Washington 19 vs. Cowboys 15

September 23: Washington, the only team Dallas beat in 1989, was fortunate it did not happen again on this day. The Cowboys out-gained the Redskins at RFK Stadium, but key mistakes prevented them from pulling ahead of the hosts in this one.

Troy Aikman was sacked eight times and threw two interceptions. The first of those picks was returned 18 yards by Darrell Green for a fourth-quarter TD that stretched the Redskins' lead to 19–6. After rookie Emmitt Smith scored the only Dallas TD of the day, a second Aikman misfire kept the Cowboys from a chance at a late rally.

GAME 4: New Route, Same Result

N.Y. Giants 31 vs. Cowboys 17

September 30: New York dumped Dallas for the second time in three weeks. The Giants ran over the Cowboys in the first win; this time, they took to the air. Phil Simms was 16-of-22 and threw three TD passes without an interception. His scoring strikes to Mark Ingram and Bob Mrosko provided a 17–3 halftime cushion.

Troy Aikman was 21-for-26 for 233 yards and a TD, but once again the Cowboys could not run on the Giants. They carried 20 times for just 51 yards.

GAME 5: Dallas Doubles '89 Win Total

Cowboys 14 vs. Tampa Bay 10

October 7: It took just five weeks for Dallas to accomplish what it failed to do in all of 1989— win a second game. The Cowboys did so on the legs of rookie RB Emmitt Smith, who posted his first 100-yard rushing game. Smith carried 23 times for 121 yards and the winning TD, a 14-yard run in the fourth quarter.

A 12-yard pass from Troy Aikman to Jay Novacek had given the Cowboys the early lead, but a Tampa Bay field goal and a 58-yard third-quarter TD pass from Vinny Testaverde to Gary Anderson put the Buccaneers in front entering the last frame. That's when Smith capped his best day yet, and back-to-back sacks by Jimmie Jones and Tony Tolbert squashed Tampa Bay's comeback hopes.

Emmitt Smith (No. 22) carries the ball during a game against the New York Jets on November 4, 1990. The Jets defeated the Cowboys 24–9. (Photo by Rick Stewart /Allsport, Getty Images)

GAME 6: Century Mark No Honor
Phoenix 20 vs. Cowboys 3

October 14: Dallas reached a new low in Phoenix, gaining only 100 offensive yards, eclipsing a 108-yard debacle in New York the previous December as the worst showing in franchise history. The Cowboys ran for 66 yards against the Cardinals but netted just 34 through the air with the help of four QB sacks.

The Cardinals had two individuals account for more yardage than the entire Dallas team. Johnny Johnson ran for 120 yards and a score, and Timm Rosenbach passed for 171. Troy Aikman was just 9-of-25 with two interceptions.

GAME 7: Bucs Serve as Winning Tonic
Cowboys 17 at Tampa Bay 13

October 21: Coming off the worst offensive outing in their history, the Cowboys were fortunate enough to run into a team it seemed they could beat at any time. Thanks to five Tampa Bay turnovers, Dallas overcame another shaky offensive day to pull out a fourth-quarter win, its eighth straight victory over the Buccaneers and second in three weeks.

The Cowboys took their first lead of the game with 23 seconds remaining on a 28-yard pass from Troy Aikman to Michael Irvin. Earlier, Irvin had caught his first regular-season pass in more than a year. The receiver had missed the last 10 games of 1989 and the first four of 1990 because of a knee injury, but he came up big on the 80-yard winning drive.

GAME 8: Turnabout Favors Eagles
Philadelphia 21 at Cowboys 20

October 28: One week after winning on a TD pass in the game's final minute, Dallas lost via the same formula. Randall Cunningham lofted a 10-yard pass that Calvin Williams outjumped the Dallas defenders to grab with 44 seconds remaining, giving Philadelphia its eighth consecutive win over its Texas rival.

For the Cowboys, this one stung. They had overcome a 14–6 hole in the fourth quarter on a TD pass from Troy Aikman to Jay Novacek and a three-yard Emmitt Smith scamper. They had outgained the Eagles and made an offensive breakthrough with 23 first downs. Cunningham, though, came through in the clutch.

GAME 9: Mistakes Cost Dallas
N.Y. Jets 24 vs. Cowboys 9

November 4: Dallas held the Jets to a dreadful 8-of-25 passing rate and yielded only 15 first downs at the Meadowlands. However, that defensive excellence made little difference on the scoreboard. Terance Mathis returned a punt 98 yards for a New York TD, and the Jets took

All the Way With J.J.

Jimmy Johnson Takes College Success to the Pros

From Tom Landry to Jimmy Johnson, there could hardly have been a more dramatic change on the sidelines. Landry was the Christian virtue–touting, soft-spoken leader who built the Cowboys with class. Johnson was brash and bold, making many more enemies than friends while leading the Miami Hurricanes to a national title and a well-earned reputation for nasty, in-your-face, get-out-of-our-way football.

"Jimmy Johnson would be the first to tell you that he couldn't carry Tom Landry's water bucket," owner Jerry Jones shouted to a group of reporters after making the 1989 hire. Jones went on to insist Johnson could bring a 3–13 team back to the top, while comparing Landry to Vince Lombardi for his impact on the game.

It was a tumultuous time, but winning is a proven salve.

Johnson won just one of 16 games in his debut season but made a six-game improvement in 1990 and then began a run of three consecutive trips to the playoffs. That stretch included back-to-back

Head coach Jimmie Johnson (left) and team owner Jerry Jones stand on the field of Texas Stadium in 1990. (Photo by Allen Dean Steele/ Allsport, Getty Images)

Super Bowl victories in 1992 and '93, vindicating Jones for the faith he showed in the starch-haired man he once played football with at the University of Arkansas.

Johnson did it by following the blueprint he built at Miami. He wanted the Cowboys to be quicker and more aggressive on both sides of the ball. A handful of his former Hurricanes players, including receiver Michael Irvin, helped him do just that. And they did it with the swagger that had made Johnson's Miami squads the most feared in college football.

"The guys that are making plays in high school and the guys that are making plays in college invariably are the guys that make plays in professional football," Johnson noted, explaining his approach to bringing in big-time playmakers.[1]

In his final three years at the helm, Johnson's Cowboys won 75 percent of their regular-season games, going 36–12. They won a wild-card playoff game in 1991 and ran through the next two postseasons unscathed toward earning acclaim as the NFL's "Team of the '90s." His playoff record was 7–1 at the time he resigned thanks largely to differences that developed between coach and owner, two old college friends.

"Anyone who knows me knows I have to go 100 percent totally focused, totally into it, or else I'm not going to be as good as I need to be," Johnson told a group of reporters upon announcing his resignation.

Johnson returned to coaching with the Miami Dolphins in 1996, guiding the club through 1999 before taking a TV analyst job.

advantage of two Troy Aikman interceptions to win an ugly game.

Aikman completed 25-of-40 passes for 249 yards, but his two picks stopped potential scoring drives in New York territory. The Jets did not manage an offensive TD until two runs late in the fourth quarter, one of which was set up by Aikman's second interception. Three Ken Willis field goals accounted for all of the Cowboys' points.

GAME 10: Offense Sputters Again
San Francisco 24 at Cowboys 6

November 11: Two games, no touchdowns. Dallas continued to plod along, failing to reach the end zone for the second straight week. They made just nine first downs against the defending Super Bowl champion 49ers and settled for two Ken Willis field goals.

Meanwhile, San Francisco got a 12-catch game from Jerry Rice and a 27-for-37, 290-yard passing performance from Joe Montana for a runaway win at Texas Stadium. Rice's dozen receptions tied a career high and covered 147 yards. Counting playoff games, the 49ers won for the 17th consecutive time.

GAME 11: Dallas Ends Slump

Cowboys 24 at L.A. Rams 21

November 18: Reaching the end zone for the first time in three games, Dallas decided to repeat the feat again and again. Michael Irvin caught two first-half TD passes sandwiched around a Tommie Agee scoring grab, as Troy Aikman and the Cowboys ended a three-game losing streak and a two-week end-zone drought.

Aikman threw for 303 yards and the three first-half scores. The final one covered 61 yards to Irvin and provided a 21–14 halftime lead. Cleveland Gary ran for three TDs for the Rams, the last of which tied the game at 21 in the third quarter. But Gary's fumble in the fourth kept L.A. from taking the lead deep in Dallas territory, and the Cowboys won it on a 23-yard Ken Willis field goal. Emmitt Smith caught four passes for 117 yards.

GAME 12: Aikman Stars on Thanksgiving

Cowboys 27 vs. Washington 17

November 22: Dallas trailed 17–10 in the third quarter, but Emmitt Smith tied it on a one-yard run, Ken Willis gave the Cowboys the lead on a 41-yard field goal, and Smith raced 48 yards for an insurance TD. The two scores highlighted a

23-carry, 132-yard game for Smith. Dallas stuffed the Redskins on the ground, holding them to 36 yards on 15 carries.

Troy Aikman directed two fourth-quarter scoring drives to break a 17–17 tie, leading the Cowboys to their first back-to-back wins since 1987. He was 7-of-8 for 107 yards in the final frame and 20-for-31 for 222 yards in the game.

GAME 13: Dallas Roars Back

Cowboys 17 vs. New Orleans 13

December 2: Trailing 10–0 at halftime, Troy Aikman and the Cowboys became the team that couldn't miss. Aikman went a perfect 11-for-11 in the second half and engineered three scoring drives to defeat former teammate Steve Walsh and the Saints.

Emmitt Smith started the comeback with a one-yard run on an 85-yard rushing day. After a 50-yard Morten Andersen field goal gave the Saints a 13–7 lead, Aikman hit Daryl Johnston for a five-yard TD to give the Cowboys the lead, and Ken Willis tacked on a 47-yard field goal for good measure. Aikman threw for 148 second-half yards. Walsh, directing the Saints, went 18-of-27 for 177 yards.

GAME 14: Win Streak Reaches Four

Cowboys 41 vs. Phoenix 10

December 16: With no drama at all, Dallas extended its winning streak to four games for the first time since 1985 and evened its record at 7–7. Emmitt Smith ran for 103 yards and a club record–tying four TDs.

Troy Aikman went 12-of-18 through the air and was able to rest for most of the fourth quarter. And James Washington, with two interceptions, led a Cowboys defense that picked off Timm Rosenbach three times and held the Cardinals to 49 rushing yards.

GAME 15: Aikman Lost in Setback
Philadelphia 17 vs. Cowboys 3

December 23: Troy Aikman suffered a season-ending shoulder injury in the first quarter, and the Cowboys suffered their ninth straight loss to Philadelphia. No one was saying which was more painful.

Without their QB, the Dallas offense stalled. Babe Laufenberg replaced Aikman and threw four interceptions—two to Eric Allen. Allen returned one of them 35 yards for a fourth-quarter TD that extended a 10–3 halftime lead and put away the Cowboys.

GAME 16: Season Ends…Eventually
Atlanta 26 vs. Cowboys 7

December 30: Even after Dallas lost back-to-back games to finish the season 7–9, the Cowboys were alive for the playoffs for more than 24 hours—that is until the Saints beat the Rams in the Monday night game.

Babe Laufenberg, who replaced injured QB Troy Aikman the previous week, finally steered the Cowboys to the end zone. He did so, however, after the Falcons had taken a 26–0 lead in the fourth quarter. Laufenberg's 27-yard TD pass to Jay Novacek could not make up for two interceptions. Deion Sanders returned one of those picks 61 yards for a TD. Atlanta also scored on a 76-yard Keith Jones kick return and got 155 yards on 21 carries from Mike Rozier.

1991

BIG THREE LEAD PLAYOFF REVIVAL

Aikman, Smith, Irvin Become a Star Trio

The 1991 season saw the Cowboys return to the playoffs for the first time since 1985, and their 11–5 record was the squad's best since 1983. Even more important, Troy Aikman, Emmitt Smith, and Michael Irvin emerged as the Big Three, a triumvirate poised to carry Dallas to the top of pro football in the years to come.

Smith and Irvin became the first teammates to lead the NFL in rushing yardage and receiving yardage in the same season. Smith ran for 1,563, and Irvin set a franchise record with 93 catches for 1,523 yards. Aikman threw more TDs than interceptions for the first time and made his Pro Bowl debut (one of four Dallas offensive players to make the Pro Bowl in 1991), despite losing four games to injury.

A five-game winning streak to close the season propelled the Cowboys to a wild-card berth in the playoffs where they knocked off Chicago before falling at Detroit. Thanks in large part to a Herschel Walker trade that allowed Dallas to stockpile draft choices, no team in the league was loading up on young talent like the Cowboys.

GAME 1: Dallas Controls Clock, Game

Cowboys 26 at Cleveland 14

September 1: The Cowboys took Browns fans out of the game by hoarding the ball for 38-plus minutes. Emmitt Smith carried 32 times for 112 yards, Michael Irvin caught nine passes for 123 yards, and Troy Aikman threw for 274 yards and two TDs in a dominant—and turnover-free—offensive display.

Aikman completed both TD tosses in the second quarter when Dallas pulled away on a 17–0 surge. The Cowboys defense held the Browns to 32 rushing yards on 14 carries. No Cleveland player ran for more than 13 yards.

GAME 2: Redskins Claim Shootout

Washington 33 at Cowboys 31

September 9: It had been nearly 20 years since this rivalry saw this much offense—a combined 681 yards. While Dallas held a slight edge in that category, it was Washington that pulled away in the fourth quarter to win a Monday night track meet.

Each team had a 100-yard rusher: Emmitt Smith (112) for the Cowboys, and Earnest Byner (101) for the Redskins. Each team had a clutch kicker: Chip Lohmiller (hit field goals from 53, 52, 46, and 46 yards) and Ken Willis (making a 50-plus yarder for the second straight week). Troy Aikman threw three TD passes for the Cowboys, but counterpart Mark Rypien directed two fourth-quarter scoring drives that gave Washington the only commanding lead of the game, 33–24.

GAME 3: A New Offensive Low

Philadelphia 24 at Cowboys 0

September 15: Under a new coaching staff (Rich Kotite having replaced Buddy Ryan) and with Jim McMahon filling in at QB for the injured Randall Cunningham, the Eagles still produced a familiar result. They used stifling defense to post their eighth successive win over the Cowboys.

One week after totaling 349 yards against the Redskins, Dallas limped to 90 against Philadelphia, a record low for the franchise. The Cowboys managed only eight first downs while yielding 11 sacks and committing four turnovers. Troy Aikman threw three interceptions, and Emmitt Smith ran for 44 yards. The rest of the team combined to rush for one yard. McMahon tossed two TD passes for the Eagles.

GAME 4: Smith Sparks Revival

Cowboys 17 at Phoenix 9

September 22: Emmitt Smith was not going to let the Cowboys struggle this time. One week after being blanked by the Eagles, Dallas rode two first-quarter TD runs by its star back to a win in Arizona. Smith crossed the goal line from 60 and 12 yards before the game was 15 minutes old, and the Cowboys' defense took over from there.

While Smith finished with a career-high 182 yards on 23 carries, the Cardinals could not find the end zone at all against a defense that stiffened up near the goal line. Their points came on three short Greg Davis field goals.

GAME 5: Dallas Drives Past Champs

Cowboys 21 vs. N.Y. Giants 16

September 29: It took a late 84-yard drive to knock off the defending Super Bowl champs, and that only made the win more impressive. Troy Aikman hit Michael Irvin with the 23-yard game-winning TD with 2:13 remaining, and one minute later, Issiac Holt made an interception in the end zone to clinch the Cowboys' first win over the Giants since 1987.

Emmitt Smith's second-quarter TD run and Ray Horton's 20-yard fumble return for a score in the third gave Dallas a 14–3 lead. However, the Giants surged to a 16–14 cushion with 5½ minutes to play before Aikman engineered the impressive winning drive. Both QBs had big

days—Aikman went 20-of-27 for 277 yards, while Jeff Hostetler was 28-for-34 for 368 yards.

GAME 6: Power Football Prevails

Cowboys 20 at Green Bay 17

October 6: Dallas ran 76 plays to Green Bay's 49, using Emmitt Smith's legs to own the clock and Troy Aikman's arm to keep the chains moving at Lambeau Field. Smith carried 32 times for 122 yards, and Aikman completed 31-of-41 passes for 287 yards, and a TD in the Cowboys' second turnover-free performance of the year.

A late Packers score made the final score close, but Dallas held leads of 14–0 and 20–10. Ray Horton gave the Cowboys their opening score on a 65-yard return of a Blair Kiel interception. Green Bay got a special-teams TD when Charles Wilson returned the second-half kickoff 82 yards.

GAME 7: Fourth-Quarter Surge Decisive

Cowboys 35 vs. Cincinnati 23

October 13: Dallas won its fourth consecutive game thanks to a big fourth quarter and some usually quiet performers. Ricky Blake ran for a 30-yard TD on his first NFL carry in the second quarter, and the Cowboys' defense came up big after entering the final quarter trailing 23–21.

The Cowboys made two interceptions and recovered a fumble in the last 15 minutes. Emmitt Smith ran for the go-ahead TD, and Dixon Edwards then returned an interception 36 yards to stretch the lead late. Troy Aikman, like Cincinnati's Boomer Esiason, threw two interceptions. But Aikman also tossed a TD pass to Jay Novacek and hit 14-of-22 passes for 276 yards. Harold Green ran for 124 for the Bengals.

GAME 8: Dallas Rusty After Week Off

Detroit 34 vs. Cowboys 10

October 27: The bye week was no friend to Dallas. Neither were the Lions. Detroit pounced on four turnovers while committing none of its own, running away from the Cowboys despite gaining only half as many yards in the game.

The Lions scored on William White's 55-yard return of a blocked field goal and Ray Crockett's 96-yard interception return. It was the second of two picks thrown by Troy Aikman, whose 331 passing yards produced two 100-yard receiving efforts—Jay Novacek's 10 catches for 131 yards, and Michael Irvin's eight grabs for 143.

GAME 9: A Second-Half Uprising

Cowboys 27 vs. Phoenix 7

November 3: Dallas kicked off the second half of the schedule with a sharp second half. After a lethargic first 30 minutes that produced a 10–7 lead and inspired a halftime tirade by Coach Jimmy Johnson, the Cowboys rode two Emmitt Smith TD runs and a crisp all-around performance in the final two quarters to a runaway victory.

Robert Williams blocked a Phoenix punt that set up the Cowboys' first second-half score and ignited the barrage. Dallas held the Cardinals to three first downs after halftime while producing 15 of its own. Smith ran for just 62 yards in the game but reached the end zone three times.

GAME 10: Outrun and Outshot

Houston 26 vs. Cowboys 23 (OT)

November 10: Houston's run-and-shoot offense exploded for 583 yards, but it was an improbable offensive miscue by Dallas that put the Oilers over the top. Emmitt Smith's first fumble all year (more than 200 touches) came in overtime, preventing the Cowboys from trying a winning field goal and leading to Al Del Greco's winning 23-yard kick.

Statistically, the Oilers deserved the win. Warren Moon completed 41-of-56 passes for 432 yards, moving Houston's offense seemingly at will after Dallas opened the scoring on an 18-yard blocked punt return by Robert Williams. The Cowboys trailed 23–16 late when the Oilers muffed a punt, Dallas recovered at the Houston 10, and Troy Aikman found Michael Irvin for a TD on the next play to force overtime.

Smith had run a draw play inside the Houston 20—easily in Ken Willis' field-goal

Emmitt Smith (No. 22) evades the Cleveland Browns defense during the September 1, 1991, game at Municipal Stadium in Cleveland, Ohio. (Photo by Focus on Sport/Getty Images)

range—when the ball popped free and the Oilers recovered. Moon then marched his team 80 yards for the winning field goal.

GAME 11: Johnson Rips Refs

N.Y. Giants 22 vs. Cowboys 9

November 17: Jimmy Johnson called it the worst-officiated game he'd ever seen. The Cowboys coach apparently decided it was worth being fined for such comments after a game in which his team lost a controversial fumble, was flagged for penalties at inopportune times, and failed to reach the end zone.

The fumble came from Emmitt Smith, who dropped a pass from Troy Aikman and stopped when the ball hit the ground, thinking it was an incompletion. Instead, both the referee and replay official declared it a Giants fumble recovery. It led to one of three Matt Bahr field goals and was one of several calls Johnson disputed. The Cowboys also got three field goals, but the Giants supplemented theirs with a Rodney Hampton scoring plunge and a Jeff Hostetler TD toss to Mark Ingram. Emmitt Smith ran for 97 Dallas yards.

GAME 12: Redskins' Run Halted

Cowboys 24 at Washington 21

November 24: Dallas ruined Washington's bid for a perfect season despite playing without a few key starters and losing QB Troy Aikman on the first series of the second half. Steve Beuerlein took over after Aikman injured his knee. The QBs combined to go 20-for-32 for 313 yards and two TD passes.

Emmitt Smith carried 34 times for 132 yards and scored on a 32-yard second-quarter TD dash. Alvin Harper then caught a 34-yard TD pass from Aikman, and Beuerlein's 24-yard strike to Michael Irvin in the fourth quarter gave the Cowboys a 21–7 cushion. They led 24–14 before a late Redskins score set the final margin. The Dallas defense held Washington to just 50 rushing yards.

GAME 13: Beuerlein Wins First Start

Cowboys 20 vs. Pittsburgh 10

November 28: Steve Beuerlein leaned on Emmitt Smith and Michael Irvin to lead Dallas to a convincing win over the Steelers in his first Cowboys start. He handed to Smith 32 times, resulting in 109 yards and a TD. The former Notre Dame standout also completed nine passes to Irvin for 157 yards and a 66-yard score.

With Troy Aikman nursing a sprained knee, Beuerlein went 14-for-25 for 217 yards without throwing an interception. Meanwhile, the Cowboys' defense limited Pittsburgh to 199 total yards. Dallas led 10–0 at halftime and did not allow the Steelers to reach the end zone until the fourth quarter.

Man with the Golden Arm

Landry Saw Enough: Aikman Would Lead Dallas to Glory

Tom Landry never coached Troy Aikman, but he was responsible for bringing him to Dallas. In December 1988, Aikman's UCLA Bruins practiced at Texas Stadium in preparation for the Cotton Bowl. Landry, in his final weeks as Cowboys coach, attended the practice to see if Aikman was worthy of Dallas's No. 1 overall pick in the upcoming NFL Draft.

Recalled Cowboys personnel director Gil Brandt, "After the practice, I said, 'Coach, do you want to come back tomorrow to look at him again?' He said, 'No, I've seen enough. He's our choice.'"[1]

What Landry saw was one of the greatest arms in the history of professional football. Not only could Aikman rifle the pigskin, he could lay it on a receiver's fingertips from 40 yards away. Moreover, coaches raved about his incredibly quick release.

With Landry's dismissal in February 1989 and Aikman's arrival in April, a new chapter began in Cowboys football. The first page, however, read like a horror story. The Cowboys finished at 1–15 in 1989, with Aikman suffering mental and physical anguish, including a concussion and a broken finger.

But the baptism by fire toughened up the golden boy. Aikman, receiver Michael Irvin, and rookie running back Emmitt Smith took the 'Boys to the verge of the playoffs in 1990. With the arrival of Norv Turner as offensive coordinator in 1991, Aikman began to flourish, earning a Pro Bowl berth and leading Dallas to the postseason.

From then on, there was no stopping him. Troy threw for 3,445 yards in 1992 and led Dallas to victory in the Super Bowl. His 273 yards and four touchdown passes against

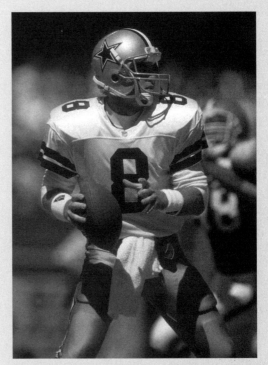

Quarterback Troy Aikman drops back to pass against the Cleveland Browns during the September 1, 1991, game at Cleveland Municipal Stadium in Cleveland, Ohio. (Photo by Focus on Sport/Getty Images)

Buffalo earned him the game's MVP Award. Aikman marched the Cowboys to victory in Super Bowls XXVIII and XXX, and he ran his string of Pro Bowl invitations to six in 1996.

In the 1990s, Aikman notched 94 regular-season victories, more than any NFL quarterback in any decade. Few could match his leadership and toughness: He stood strong in the pocket despite suffering 10 concussions during his career. Upon his retirement following the 2000 season, Aikman held dozens of Cowboys records, including career completions (2,898), passing yards (32,942), touchdowns (165), and completion percentage (61.5).

"I feel Troy is one of the best things to ever happen to the Cowboys," said Roger Staubach. "He probably threw the football as well as anyone ever in the NFL." Most important, Staubach said, "he always produced when the guys needed him the most."[2]

GAME 14: New Blood Emerges

Cowboys 23 vs. New Orleans 14

December 8: Daryl Johnston and Tommie Agee scored TDs for the first time all season, the former to open the scoring and the latter to close it. In between, Emmitt Smith rushed for 112 yards, and Steve Beuerlein hit Michael Irvin five times for 101 as Dallas won for the third straight week.

Perhaps most important for the Cowboys, kicker Ken Willis broke out of a slump to boot field goals of 50, 41, and 40 yards. The last of those erased New Orleans' only lead, 14–13 in the fourth quarter. Smith became the first back to run for 100 yards against the 1991 Saints before being helped off the field with a knee injury in the fourth quarter.

GAME 15: Dallas Ends Eagles' Streaks

Cowboys 25 at Philadelphia 13

December 15: Dallas snapped a string of eight consecutive losses to Philadelphia and halted the Eagles' six-game winning streak with this game. Ferocious defense made the difference in the Cowboys' first victory in Philadelphia since 1986. The win also clinched Dallas' first playoff trip since 1985.

Neither team topped 240 yards in this defensive struggle. However, the Cowboys notched the game's only two takeaways on interceptions of Jeff Kemp. They also sacked Kemp seven times and scored twice on special teams. First, Manny Hendrix tallied a first-quarter safety when the Eagles flubbed a kickoff return. Then, in the final quarter, Kelvin Martin returned a punt 85 yards for a TD to give Dallas the lead for keeps, 15–10.

GAME 16: Smith Claims Rushing Title

Cowboys 31 vs. Atlanta 27

December 22: Dallas had nothing on the line, but Atlanta needed a win to claim the NFC West title and earn a home playoff game. It was the Cowboys, however, who entered the post-season on a roll, winning for the fifth consecutive time. Emmitt Smith scored the winning TD in the fourth quarter, and his 160 yards on 32 carries made him the first player in Cowboys history to win an NFL rushing title. With 1,563 yards, he edged Detroit's Barry Sanders by 15 yards.

Smith's running and Alexander Wright's club-record 102-yard kickoff return sparked Dallas to a 24–14 lead in the second quarter. Atlanta scored 13 straight points, taking the lead on Chris Miller's third TD pass, but Smith scored his second TD of the day to send his team into the playoffs with momentum.

GAME 17: Defense Carries Dallas

Cowboys 17 at Chicago 13

December 29: Dallas was not content simply to make its first playoff showing in six years. The Cowboys recovered a Jim Harbaugh fumble on an early sack, turned it into a field goal, and intercepted Harbaugh twice on the way to upsetting the Bears at Soldier Field. Emmitt Smith carried 26 times for 105 yards and a TD for a Dallas attack that played conservative, turnover-free football.

The Cowboys dominated on defense. In addition to the three takeaways, they allowed Chicago just three points total on three treks inside the Dallas 10-yard line. While the Cowboys got TDs on an early Smith run and a Steve Beuerlein pass to Jay Novacek in the third quarter, the Bears did not find the end zone until late in the final quarter.

GAME 18: Streak, Season End

Detroit 38 vs. Cowboys 6

January 5, 1992: A run of six straight victories came to a screeching halt in Detroit where Dallas got away from its formula of ball protection and defense. The Cowboys lost two fumbles, threw two interceptions, and allowed the Lions to amass 421 offensive yards in a humbling divisional playoff loss.

Detroit got a late TD from star running back Barry Sanders, but it was QB Erik Kramer who did most of the damage. Kramer completed 29-of-38 passes for 341 yards and three TDs without an interception. Troy Aikman returned from a knee injury for Dallas, but both Aikman and Steve Beuerlein each threw an interception. Emmitt Smith carried 15 times for 80 yards.

SUPER STARS

Cowboys Return to the Top, Claim Third Championship

Fans of America's Team could call their team the best in the land for the first time since the 1977 season. The Cowboys won a franchise-record 13 games, played before sellout crowds in every one of their starts, and rolled through the playoffs with three double-figure victories to claim their third Super Bowl championship.

Emmitt Smith, Troy Aikman, and Michael Irvin led the way. Smith became the first player since Eric Dickerson in 1983 and '84 to win back-to-back rushing titles, running for 1,713 yards and 18 scores. Aikman threw for 3,445 yards and 23 scores, while Irvin made 78 catches for 1,396 yards. Those three were among six players from the Dallas offense named to the Pro Bowl.

Pro Bowl nods were fine, but this club entered the season knowing it was capable of more. It delivered in dominant style, outscoring opponents by more than 10 points per game while ranking second in the NFL in scoring offense and fifth in scoring defense.

The Cowboys were young, talented, hungry, and already the best team in the NFL. It was a frightening combination for opponents.

GAME 1: Another First for Smith

Cowboys 23 vs. Washington 10

September 7: Emmitt Smith became the first back ever to post four consecutive 100-yard rushing games against the Redskins, going for 140 on 27 carries in an impressive opening win for Dallas. The Cowboys dominated the first half, took a 23–7 advantage on Kelvin Martin's 79-yard punt return in the third quarter, and cruised past the defending Super Bowl champs.

Troy Aikman threw two interceptions against one TD pass—to Alvin Harper—but Smith's running and a stout defensive effort were more than enough. Charles Haley, in his first game with the Cowboys, recorded a sack and helped Dallas pressure QB Mark Rypien throughout the game.

GAME 2: Too Close for Comfort

Cowboys 34 at N.Y. Giants 28

September 13: As dominant as ever for most of the game, Dallas had to survive a furious New York comeback before escaping with its first win since 1987 at Giants Stadium. The Cowboys led 34–0 in the third quarter but nearly fell victim to what would have been the greatest comeback in NFL history. The Giants had the ball late, down by six, but Dallas forced a punt and ran out the clock.

Robert Williams' TD on a blocked punt and two Troy Aikman TD passes helped the Cowboys reach their insurmountable edge. Emmitt Smith also ran for a score, and Lin Elliott booted two first-half field goals. Phil Simms threw three second-half TD passes to bring the Giants almost all the way back from the grave.

GAME 3: Unbeaten but Exposed

Cowboys 31 vs. Phoenix 20

September 20: There was a lot to like about a 3–0 start, but Dallas had plenty to work on as it entered its bye week so early in the year. The Cowboys allowed Chris Chandler to pass for 383 yards in a game they could have put away much earlier.

Emmitt Smith carried 26 times for 112 yards and a TD; Troy Aikman threw for 263 yards and three scores, completing two-thirds of his tosses without an interception; and Michael

Irvin was at his game-breaking best, catching TD passes of 87, 41, and 4 yards on a 210-yard receiving day. Phoenix never led despite gaining 438 offensive yards.

GAME 4: Eagles Unstoppable
Philadelphia 31 vs. Cowboys 7

October 5: An anticipated matchup with the Eagles flew south in a hurry for the Dallas Cowboys, who coughed up the football four times in the first three quarters. The result, against a strong foe like Philadelphia, was predictable. The Eagles broke a 7–7 tie with 24 unanswered points, and Herschel Walker ran for two TDs against his former club.

Troy Aikman threw for 256 yards and a seven-yard first-quarter TD to Kelvin Martin, but his three interceptions doomed the Cowboys to a day of watching the Eagles pull away. They led 10–7 at halftime before Walker's scores put the game out of reach.

GAME 5: Dallas Sets Defensive Mark
Cowboys 27 vs. Seattle 0

October 11: One week after their first loss, the Cowboys were leaving nothing to chance against Seattle. They held the Seahawks to 62 yards in the best defensive effort in club history. The previous record was 63 yards against Green Bay in 1965.

The Dallas defense outscored the Seattle offense, getting a 15-yard interception-return

TD from Ray Horton in the third quarter. Offensively, Emmitt Smith rushed for 78 yards and two TDs, while Troy Aikman was an efficient 15-of-23. Two Lin Elliott field goals helped the Cowboys to a 20–0 halftime lead.

GAME 6: All Alone in First
Cowboys 17 vs. Kansas City 10

October 18: Dallas shut out the Chiefs in the second half to take over sole possession of first place in the NFC East, thanks in part to Philadelphia's loss to Washington. It marked the first time since the Tom Landry era that the Cowboys stood all alone in first place.

To get there, they had to overcome 11 penalties—eight on the offensive side of the ball. Daryl Johnston and Emmitt Smith ran for two-yard TDs in the first half for a 14–3 lead, and the defense took over from there. Barry Word scored for the Chiefs to make it 14–10 at halftime, but the Dallas defense swarmed after the break. Smith ran for 95 yards—four more than Kansas City produced on the ground.

GAME 7: Dallas Displays Wares for 91K
Cowboys 28 at L.A. Raiders 13

October 25: The largest crowd ever to watch a Cowboys game—91,505 at the Los Angeles Memorial Coliseum—saw Emmitt Smith trample the Raiders. Smith rushed for 152 yards and three TDs, and his 167 total yards from scrimmage were two more than L.A. churned out as a team.

The game was a testament to the Dallas defense, which harassed the Raiders into 8-of-26 passing. L.A. led 13–7 on a TD pass from Todd Marinovich to Willie Gault early in the third quarter, but Dallas scored the game's last 21 points on Smith's last two TD runs and a Troy Aikman bootleg from the 3-yard line.

GAME 8: Eagles Can't Stop Smith
Cowboys 20 vs. Philadelphia 10

November 1: The Eagles had gone a remarkable 53 consecutive regular-season games without allowing a 100-yard rusher. They failed to extend it, by a country mile, against Emmitt Smith, who carried 30 times for 163 yards in a big Dallas win that avenged a 24-point dismantling at the hands of Philadelphia early in the season.

Cornerback Kevin Smith returns an interception against the San Francisco 49ers in the 1992 NFC Championship Game on January 17, 1993, at Candlestick Park in San Francisco, California. The Cowboys defeated the 49ers 30–20. (Photo by Louis Raynor/NFL Photos/Getty Images)

Two early field-goal misses by the Cowboys' Lin Elliott kept the Eagles in the game for a while. But they gained only 190 yards against a physical Dallas defense, never sustaining either a ground or aerial attack. The Cowboys amassed more than double that total. Troy Aikman hit Kelvin Martin and Daryl Johnston with TD passes, and Elliott did make two field goals.

GAME 9: Revenge Tastes Sweet

Cowboys 37 at Detroit 3

November 8: One week after avenging an earlier drubbing at the hands of the Eagles, the Cowboys made amends for a one-sided loss in the previous year's NFC playoffs. In their first meeting with Detroit since that 38–6 setback, they put an even bigger beating on the Lions before more than 74,000 fans at the Pontiac Silverdome.

Jimmy Johnson dismissed revenge as a motivating factor, but his players sure performed like they had something to prove. They gained almost 400 yards of offense while holding Detroit to 201 and keeping the Lions out of the end zone. Emmitt Smith ran for three TDs, Lin Elliott kicked three field goals, and Troy Aikman hit Michael Irvin with a 15-yard TD pass in the rout. Irvin was benched for the first series and fined by the club for missing the team flight the day before the game.

GAME 10: Rams Score Big Upset

L.A. Rams 27 at Cowboys 23

November 15: The Cowboys entered the game with the NFL's top-ranked defense and exited scratching their helmets. The Rams, losers of 12 straight road games, snapped the Cowboys' 11-game Texas Stadium winning streak by racking up 367 yards against that vaunted defense.

Jimmy Johnson coached Cleveland Gary in college, but on this day his Cowboys were unable to stop the former Miami star from gaining 154 total yards and scoring twice. The Rams led 21–13 at halftime and kept the Dallas offense out of the end zone in the second half. The only Cowboys TD after the break came on Kelvin Martin's breathtaking 74-yard punt return, but two fourth-quarter field goals by Tony Zendejas put the Rams over the top.

GAME 11: Chandler No Factor This Time

Cowboys 16 at Phoenix 10

November 22: Two months earlier, Chris Chandler had burned Dallas for 383 passing yards. This time, the Cowboys knocked him out of the game on a first-quarter hit, and the Cardinals' offense withered with Timm Rosenbach under center. Phoenix made a mere nine first downs in the game.

It wasn't the best offensive showing for the Cowboys either, but it was good enough. Troy Aikman threw TD passes to Jay Novacek and Alvin Harper. Although Emmitt Smith rushed

Super Bowl XXVII: Buffalo Blitz

After Long Absence, Dallas Returns to the Top in Dominant Fashion

It had been too long. Far too long, as far as Dallas fans were concerned. The last time their team played in the Super Bowl, 14 years earlier, the winning player's share was $18,000, compared to the $36,000 it had doubled to by Super Bowl XXVII. The halftime performance in the Cowboys' Super Bowl XIII loss to the Steelers was a "Carnival Salute to the Caribbean," featuring various little-known bands. This time, Michael Jackson belted out "Billy Jean" and "Black or White."

It was a game originally scheduled for Arizona, but a controversy over the state's delay in recognizing Dr. Martin Luther King Day as a holiday prompted the NFL to move it to the Rose Bowl in Pasadena. The Cowboys and Bills could have played this game on the moon, and it wouldn't have mattered. Buffalo was out of its league.

The Bills fell in the Super Bowl to an NFC East power for the third straight year. They put up strong fights against the Giants and Redskins, but the Cowboys were overwhelming in a 52–17 rout that set a record for most combined points. Dallas nearly broke the 49ers' record of 55 points in a Super Bowl game, but a showboating Leon Lett had the ball knocked out of his hand by Don Beebe as the Cowboys defender was about to lumber across the goal line on a late fumble return in the game's most memorable, and comical, play.

Linebacker Ken Norton Jr. (No. 51) of the Dallas Cowboys returns a fumble by quarterback Frank Reich of the Buffalo Bills for a touchdown in the fourth quarter of Super Bowl XXVII at the Rose Bowl on January 31, 1994 in Pasadena, California. The Cowboys defeated the Bills 52–17. (Photo by Gin Ellis/NFL Photos/Getty Images)

By then, the outcome had long been decided. And Lett could leave the game satisfied with his two forced fumbles, one recovery, and a sack. It was part of a dominant defensive effort that forced the Bills into a Super Bowl–record nine turnovers and scored TDs on fumble returns by Ken Norton Jr. and Jimmie Jones. Buffalo fumbled eight times, losing five, while QBs Jim Kelly and Frank Reich were intercepted twice each.

"I felt like we had the best football team," Dallas coach Jimmy Johnson said. "When you turn the ball over as many times as they did, you'll have trouble. Sometimes it snowballs."[1]

This one got out of hand early. Thurman Thomas gave the Bills a 7–0 lead on a two-yard TD run, but the Cowboys scored 31 of the game's next 34 points. Troy Aikman hit Michael Irvin on second-quarter TD passes of 19 and 18 yards, just 18 seconds apart, for a 28–10 halftime lead. By the time Jackson took the halftime stage, he ought to have worked "Beat It" into the set list.

Aikman earned MVP honors on the strength of a 22-for-30, 273-yard, four-TD passing performance. Emmitt Smith carried 22 times for 108 yards and a score.

---

for a ho-hum 84 yards, he caught 12 passes for 64 yards on a day when Dallas erased an early 7–0 deficit with 16 consecutive points.

GAME 12: A Thanksgiving Feast
Cowboys 30 vs. N.Y. Giants 3

November 26: Thanksgiving was no holiday for the Giants, who were thoroughly cooked in the second half. Dallas led just 9–3 after a first-half battle of field goals, but Emmitt Smith scored two long third-quarter TDs as the Cowboys poured it on after the intermission.

Smith gained more than half of his 120 rushing yards on a 68-yard scoring dash, and he also caught a 26-yard TD pass from Troy Aikman. The QB also hit Alvin Harper for a score on a 19-for-29 passing day. Third-string

QB Kent Graham directed the anemic Giants offense for most of the afternoon.

GAME 13: Rallying into the Playoffs
Cowboys 31 at Denver 27

December 6: Troy Aikman directed Dallas 77 yards for the winning TD—an Emmitt Smith run with 2:47 remaining—to avoid losing a game the Cowboys once led 14–0. An interception by Kenneth Gant on Denver's last drive then secured the victory, which clinched a playoff berth for Dallas.

The Broncos gave up back-to-back TD passes from Aikman to Michael Irvin in the game's first seven minutes. Tommy Maddox, however, responded with two quick scoring strikes of his own. Dallas led 24–13 in the third quarter before Denver took its first lead on Maddox's third TD pass and a trick-play, 81-yard option pass from Arthur Marshall to fellow wide receiver Cedric Tillman. The Broncos outgained the Cowboys by 50 yards but were ultimately doomed by five turnovers, including four interceptions.

GAME 14: Division Clincher Fumbled Away

Washington 20 vs. Cowboys 17

December 13: Trying to avoid a safety after recovering teammate Troy Aikman's fumble in the end zone, Emmitt Smith tossed the ball forward as he was being tackled, and Danny Copeland gladly grabbed the gift for the Redskins' winning TD. It capped Washington's comeback from a 17–7 halftime deficit and highlighted a fourth quarter in which the Cowboys coughed up the ball three times on as many possessions.

Dallas outran and outpassed Washington, and the Cowboys appeared to be on the verge of clinching the NFC East title before fumbling away the game. Smith ran for 99 yards, while Aikman threw for 245 and two scores. Yet the Redskins won despite gaining just 246 yards.

GAME 15: A Return to the Top

Cowboys 41 at Atlanta 17

December 21: Dallas wrapped up its first NFC East title since 1985 with a dominant win in the team's first trip to the Georgia Dome. Troy Aikman completed 18-of-21 passes for 239 yards and three TDs, while Emmitt Smith ran for 174 yards and two scores.

The Cowboys pounced on three Falcon fumbles to ease their path to the crown. Two of those came early in the second half and led directly to TDs as Dallas, leading 20–10 at the break, pulled away in front of a national *Monday Night Football* TV audience.

GAME 16: Dallas Wins Lucky 13th

Cowboys 27 vs. Chicago 14

December 27: Four final-quarter turnovers was no way to march into the playoffs, but the Cowboys overcame the miscues and held on to win a season finale with little meaning. Emmitt Smith won his second consecutive NFL rushing title with a 131-yard game, breaking Tony Dorsett's club record with 1,713 yards for the season.

Dallas led 27–0 before its fourth-quarter turnover barrage. Chris Zorich returned a fumble 42 yards for the Bears' final TD, but it was too little and too late. The Cowboys held the Bears to 28 rushing yards and 92 total yards in the game, completing a 13–3 campaign.

GAME 17: Rivals Run Over

Cowboys 34 vs. Philadelphia 10

January 10, 1993: The rubber match of a three-game series with Philadelphia was a blowout, just like the first two. And for the second straight time, it was Dallas doing the dominating. Emmitt Smith ran for 115 yards and a TD, Troy Aikman threw for 200 yards and two scores, and the Cowboys' defense was relentless in dismissing a heated rival.

After an Eagles field goal opened the scoring, Dallas scored 34 consecutive points to turn its playoff opener into a rout. Philly gained just 178 yards from scrimmage and did not reach the end zone until the game's final minute.

GAME 18: Dallas Returns to Super Bowl

Cowboys 30 at San Francisco 20

January 17, 1993: This time, there was no "Catch" to bail out the 49ers with the NFC crown at stake. There was only Dallas hauling in its NFL-leading sixth trip to the Super Bowl, and the team's first trip there in 14 years.

Emmitt Smith, who ran for 114 yards and a TD, caught a 16-yard TD pass from Troy Aikman that stretched the Cowboys' lead to 23–14 early in the fourth quarter. When the 49ers threatened one of their patented comebacks on a five-yard scoring strike from Steve Young to Jerry Rice, Dallas answered with a TD hookup from Aikman to Kelvin Martin that put the game away.

Some called it a changing of the guard in the NFC. Aikman outplayed Young, albeit barely, in a battle between 300-yard passers. The Cowboys QB threw for 322 yards without an interception. And Smith, as usual, powered a Dallas running game that kept the 49ers' defense crowding the line of scrimmage. The teams were a mere one yard apart in offensive yardage (Dallas 416, San Francisco 415), but the 49ers committed four turnovers to the Cowboys' none.

1993

SUPER STREAK

Second Straight Title for Dallas, Third for Smith

Emmitt Smith became just the fourth man in NFL history to win three consecutive rushing titles. He was glad, however, when that distinction took a backseat to a greater team honor a few weeks later. That's because the Cowboys became only the fifth team to claim back-to-back Super Bowl victories when they again prolonged the misery of the Buffalo Bills.

Smith was selected as the NFL Player of the Year after rushing for 1,486 yards and the Super Bowl MVP after scoring two big second-half TDs to propel a comeback. He was one of many weapons on a Cowboys team that produced eight offensive Pro Bowl selections, including seven starters. They set an NFC record with 11 total honorees.

Dallas was dominant in winning the NFC East with a 12–4 record, one game better than the Giants. They fielded both the NFL's No. 2 offense and defense in the scoring column, a lethal combination for opponents. While Smith was chewing up yardage behind a mean, massive, and athletic line, Troy Aikman was completing more than 69 percent of his passes and Michael Irvin was catching 88 passes for 1,330 yards.

There was no reason to believe after the Super Bowl win that the Cowboys could be stopped any time soon. A coaching change and some off-field issues later, that was about to change, but the "Team of the Nineties" was not finished yet.

GAME 1: Turnabout for Redskins

Washington 35 vs. Cowboys 16

September 6: One year earlier, the defending Super Bowl champ Redskins were beaten by Dallas in the season opener. This time, the Cowboys were the defending champs who took a pummeling at the hands of their division rivals. Brian Mitchell carried 21 times for 116 yards and two TDs to lead the Redskins to victory at RFK Stadium.

Dallas opened its title defense by losing four fumbles and failing to rush for 100 yards. Not coincidentally, star runner Emmitt Smith was absent while in the midst of a contract holdout. Rookie Derrick Lassic led the rushing attack with 75 yards on 16 carries. Troy Aikman threw for 267 yards and two TDs in the losing cause.

GAME 2: Bills Avenge Super Bowl Loss

Buffalo 13 at Cowboys 10

September 12: It didn't count for nearly as much as their meeting 7½ months earlier, but Buffalo gained some measure of satisfaction in slipping past Dallas on a late Steve Christie field goal and a game-clinching interception by Matt Darby at the 1-yard line with 12 seconds remaining.

The Cowboys played without Emmitt Smith, still holding out over a contract dispute, for the second consecutive week. And for the second straight week, the Cowboys were doomed by four turnovers. Troy Aikman passed for 297 yards but was intercepted twice. Dallas got its only TD on a fourth-quarter run by Kevin Williams that tied the game at 10.

GAME 3: Smith, Winning Return

Cowboys 17 at Phoenix 10

September 19: Emmitt Smith returned from his contract holdout, but it was the Dallas defense that made the biggest statement in the club's first win since the Super Bowl. The Cowboys shut out the Cardinals for more than 2½ quarters in building a 17–0 edge before hanging on for the victory.

Smith saw his first action of the season midway through the third quarter. He carried eight times for 45 yards—15 less than rookie Derrick Lassic compiled on 14 carries. Troy Aikman completed 21-of-27 passes for 281 yards, more than the Cardinals gained from scrimmage. One of the very few things to go wrong for the Cowboys was the loss of defensive tackle Leon Lett to a broken ankle.

GAME 4: Dallas Pummels Green Bay
Cowboys 36 vs. Green Bay 14

October 3: Kicker Eddie Murray, with five field goals and three extra points, outscored Green Bay all by himself. His teammates weren't bad either as Dallas came off a bye week to rout the Packers at Texas Stadium.

Murray's kicks included a 50- and 48-yarder, and he also successfully bounced an onside kick that the Cowboys recovered in the first half. Emmitt Smith and Derrick Lassic ran for TDs, and Michael Irvin caught a 61-yard scoring strike from Troy Aikman, who passed for 317 yards with an 18-for-23 success rate.

GAME 5: Takeaways Fuel Victory
Cowboys 27 at Indianapolis 3

October 10: Emmitt Smith topped the century mark for the first time in the season and Dallas pounced on five Colts turnovers to pull away at the Hoosier Dome. Though Indy managed nearly as many yards and had the game's top rusher in Roosevelt Potts (18 carries for 113 yards), the Colts' miscues kept this from being a tight game.

Smith, in his third game back from a contract holdout, carried 25 times for 104 yards and a 20-yard first-quarter TD run. Troy Aikman hit 21-of-28 passes for 245 yards and a TD to Daryl Johnston. Tight end Jay Novacek also ran for a score.

GAME 6: Dallas Wins 49er Shootout
Cowboys 26 vs. San Francisco 17

October 17: San Francisco racked up more than 400 yards of offense, but it was the Cowboys who had the winning combination in this battle of NFL heavyweights. Troy Aikman and Michael Irvin hooked up 12 times—a career-high in receptions for Irvin—for 168 yards and the winning TD late in the third quarter.

The 49ers had grabbed a 17–16 lead on a TD pass from Steve Young to Brent Jones with 2:32 remaining in the third quarter. However, the Cowboys turned a San Francisco fumble into the winning score, a 36-yard Irvin reception, and added an Eddie Murray field goal late. Aikman made only nine completions to players not named Michael Irvin, and Emmitt Smith powered the running attack with 92 yards.

GAME 7: Smith All the Way Back
Cowboys 23 at Philadelphia 10

October 31: Emmitt Smith running with the ball was a scary sight for the Eagles. Smith sitting out the first two games of the year became a distant memory for the Cowboys on this rainy Halloween as Smith broke Tony Dorsett's single-game team rushing record with 237 yards on 30 carries. Dallas never trailed, but

Eddie Murray (No. 3) kicks a field goal against the San Francisco 49ers at Texas Stadium in the 1993 NFC Championship Game on January 23, 1994, in Irving, Texas. The Cowboys defeated the 49ers 38–21. (Photo by James Smith/NFL Photos/Getty Images)

it took Smith's 62-yard final-quarter scoring burst to put Philadelphia away.

Neither team netted even 100 passing yards in the rain. It came down to the run, where Smith gave the Cowboys a huge advantage. His rushing total was nine yards more than the Eagles' total offensive production and 31 yards better than Dorsett's previous club record, also set against Philadelphia.

GAME 8: Vaulting into First
Cowboys 31 vs. N.Y. Giants 9

November 7: After back-to-back losses to start the season, few would have pegged the Cowboys for sole possession of first place in the NFC East at the midway point. Yet that's precisely what they earned by knocking off the Giants behind Emmitt Smith's 117 rushing yards and two TDs.

Troy Aikman was also off to a splendid day, having completed 11-of-13 passes for 162 yards and two long scores to Alvin Harper when a hamstring injury sidelined him. The Cowboys leaned on Smith even more after that, and their star runner came through.

GAME 9: Kosar Keeps Streak Alive
Cowboys 20 vs. Phoenix 15

November 14: Bernie Kosar made his Dallas debut while Troy Aikman continued to nurse a hamstring injury, and the Cowboys posted their first seven-game winning streak in a decade. Kosar wasn't brilliant, but he didn't have to be. He managed the game well, connected 13-of-21 passes for 199 yards, hit Jay Novacek for a TD that gave his team a 17–0 bulge, and did not throw an interception.

The backup QB did cost his team a safety when he was called for intentional grounding in the end zone, but that came late. The Dallas defense held Phoenix to 51 yards on the ground, recovered two fumbles, and intercepted Chris Chandler once.

GAME 10: Falcons Halt Streak
Atlanta 27 vs. Cowboys 14

November 21: Troy Aikman remained out with a hamstring injury, and Emmitt Smith carried just one time before leaving the game with a thigh bruise. By the end, all of the Cowboys were hurting after watching their seven-game winning streak buried under Atlanta's 400-yard offensive barrage.

Bernie Kosar quarterbacked Dallas admirably for the second straight week, throwing two TD passes without an interception and directing a turnover-free attack. Without Smith, though, the Cowboys were unable to establish a running game. Falcons QB Bobby Hebert lit up the Georgia Dome for 315 passing yards and three TDs—two to Mike Pritchard and a 70-yard bomb to cornerback-turned-receiver Deion Sanders.

GAME 11: The Slide Heard 'Round the World

Miami 16 at Cowboys 14

November 25: Dallas should have been celebrating a Thanksgiving Day win. Instead, they suffered what would become one of the most replayed blunders in sports history. In this game, Leon Lett slid across an icy Texas Stadium field into what would have been a dead ball after the Cowboys blocked a late Miami field-goal try. But Lett's inexplicable gaffe allowed the Dolphins to recover a suddenly live ball and ride Pete Stoyanovich's 19-yard chip shot to an improbable victory.

"I don't think I've ever seen one end like that," said veteran Miami coach Don Shula after his 9–2 team used three second-half field goals to overcome a 14–7 halftime deficit. Troy Aikman returned from a hamstring injury to QB the Cowboys in snowy, icy conditions. Dallas gained only 293 yards but took the lead on two Kevin Williams TDs—a pass reception and a 64-yard punt return.

GAME 12: Back in the Win Column

Cowboys 23 vs. Philadelphia 17

December 6: Eleven days to ponder back-to-back losses and the crazy circumstances surrounding the prior loss left Dallas eager to suit up again. The Cowboys looked ready for vengeance while racing to a 16–0 lead, then they held on against their rivals from Philadelphia.

Emmitt Smith carried 23 times for 172 yards, and his 57-yard dash set up the fourth-quarter TD that kept the Eagles at bay. Troy Aikman hooked up with Michael Irvin in the end zone to open the scoring, and three Eddie Murray field goals gave Dallas its 16-point margin. Dallas held Philly to just 59 rushing yards.

GAME 13: Big Scores in "Homer Dome"

Cowboys 37 at Minnesota 20

December 12: The Metrodome, known for high-scoring baseball games, became the site of an offensive clinic by the Cowboys in this NFL romp. Dallas scored on seven of its first eight possessions and got big games from its brightest stars.

Emmitt Smith ran for 104 yards and a TD, Michael Irvin caught eight passes for 125 yards and a score, and Troy Aikman went 19-for-29 for 208 yards without an interception. About the only negative was the Cowboys' pass defense, which yielded a 20-for-25 completion rate, but Kevin Smith did account for the game's only takeaway on an interception of Jim McMahon.

GAME 14: Comedy of Errors Goes to Dallas

Cowboys 28 at N.Y. Jets 7

December 18: The Cowboys made five of the game's nine turnovers but somehow managed to

Super Bowl XXVIII: Back-To-Back Bills Beatings

Cowboys Cruise Again as Buffalo Drops Fourth Straight Title Game

Buffalo players wondered aloud, after losing the previous year's Super Bowl to Dallas, whether they would be remembered like Minnesota and Denver among history's big-game losers. On January 30, 1994, they got their answer. Thanks to a Cowboys team intent on becoming a dynasty, the Bills would be remembered as the club whose Super Bowl misery exceeded even that of the Vikings and Broncos.

Dallas defended its championship, 30–13, thanks to a second-half rampage that made Buffalo the only team in history to lose four Super Bowls consecutively. Minnesota and Denver were also four-time Super Bowl losers, but neither lost more than two games successively. The rematch of the previous year's combatants was also a Super Bowl first, and the Bills did fare a little better this time around.

Still, the Cowboys overcame a 13–6 halftime deficit with 24 unanswered points to match the Steelers and 49ers with their fourth championship. Emmitt Smith won MVP honors, running for 132 yards and two second-half TDs to power the comeback, while Troy Aikman completed 19-of-27 passes for 207 yards at the Georgia Dome.

The key play, as was so often the case with these Cowboys, was provided by the defense. Less than a minute into the second half, Leon Lett stripped the ball from Bills star Thurman Thomas. James Washington recovered and raced 46 yards for a TD that tied the score at 13.

Smith then took the game into his own hands. He carried seven times for 61 yards on a drive that covered 64 yards on eight plays, scoring from 15 yards out to give Dallas the lead for good. His second TD was set up by Washington's fourth-quarter interception of Jim Kelly. A safety who started just once during the regular season, Washington also made 11 tackles.

Jim Kelly of the Buffalo Bills is on his back, looking up at the man responsible, Jim Jeffcoat of the Dallas Cowboys, at Super Bowl XXVIII in Atlanta, Georgia, on January 30, 1994. (Photo by Al Messerschmidt/Getty Images)

"I wish there was some way they could have given co-awards," Smith said of his MVP accolade, "so James Washington could have gotten something."[1]

Thomas, after being held to 37 yards on 16 carries, accepted the brunt of the blame for the Bills. His fumble, he said, cost his team the game. Kelly completed a Super Bowl–record 31 passes—no TDs, though—and became the first QB in history to attempt at least 50 passes in two Super Bowls. It was a pale distinction, to be sure.

After the game, both Dallas coach Jimmy Johnson and owner Jerry Jones celebrated their status as just the fifth team in history to win back-to-back Super Bowl titles. They were a dynasty in the making, with one exception. The two men didn't know at the time that their differences would come to a head, making this the last game for Johnson at the helm. He resigned two months later, eschewing the chance to shoot for an unprecedented third straight crown.

comfortably win a contest that sealed another playoff appearance. Michael Irvin caught Troy Aikman TD passes in the second and third quarters, and Kevin Smith returned an interception 32 yards for a score that gave Dallas a 21–0 lead entering the fourth frame.

Still, this was not a game the Cowboys felt much like celebrating. Aikman threw for 252 yards and misfired on only six of his 27 passes, but three of those miscues wound up in enemy hands. Eric Thomas made two picks for the Jets.

carried 21 times for 153 yards and a TD as Dallas impressively avenged that opening setback.

The Dallas defense also showed a night-and-day turnaround from late summer, keeping a Washington team that scored five TDs in the opener out of the Texas Stadium end zones. And Kevin Williams gave the special teams a highlight, returning a punt 62 yards for a TD. Troy Aikman hit 16-of-20 passes and led Dallas to 38 straight points after the Redskins opened the scoring on a field goal.

GAME 15: Not This Time, Redskins
Cowboys 38 vs. Washington 3

December 26: This was a vastly different Cowboys team than the one that defended its Super Bowl title with a loss to the Redskins at the beginning of the season. Most obviously, this group had the services of Emmitt Smith, who

GAME 16: NFC East Decided in OT
Cowboys 16 at N.Y. Giants 13 (OT)

January 2, 1994: The battle for the NFC East crown came down to the last game of the season and then some. A defensive war this win required more than 10 extra minutes to decide, with Dallas claiming the title—and a first-round postseason bye—on Eddie Murray's 41-yard overtime field goal.

For much of the game, the Cowboys looked like they might just cruise at the Meadowlands. They led 13–0 at halftime on a five-yard TD pass from Troy Aikman to Emmitt Smith and two Murray field goals. Smith ran for 109 of his 168 yards in the first two quarters, separating his shoulder just before halftime.

But the second half was all Giants. A muffed punt by Kevin Williams set up the first New York TD, and two short David Treadwell field goals—the second with 10 ticks remaining—sent the game into overtime. The Giants got the ball first but were forced to punt. Smith then accounted for 41 yards on a 52-yard drive that led to the winning boot.

GAME 17: Not Pretty, But Effective

Cowboys 27 vs. Green Bay 17

January 16, 1994: After back-to-back games hitting 80 percent of his passes, Troy Aikman was picked off twice. After a stout defensive effort against the Giants, the Cowboys allowed Brett Favre to pass for 331 yards. And after another terrific regular season, Emmitt Smith gained only 60 yards on 13 carries while recovering from a separated shoulder. No, it was not a great Dallas effort.

However, it was good enough to build a 24–3 lead and hold on against the Packers, setting up another NFC title showdown with San Francisco. Aikman threw three TD passes, and Michael Irvin caught nine balls for 126 yards and a score. While the Dallas defense bent, it also bailed itself out with four takeaways.

GAME 18: One More Time

Cowboys 38 vs. San Francisco 21

January 23, 1994: Against some foes, a 17-point win might not count as a blowout. Against the mighty 49ers, it was precisely that. Facing San Francisco in the NFC title game for the fifth time, the Cowboys earned their sixth Super Bowl trip in convincing fashion. They blazed to a 28–7 halftime cushion behind Troy Aikman and Emmitt Smith, then they made it stand up with stellar defense after Aikman left the game with a concussion.

Aikman spent the night at a hospital after taking a knee to the helmet early in the third quarter. Before that, he threw two TD passes (one to Smith) and completed 14-of-18 throws for 177 yards. Bernie Kosar replaced him and threw a second-half TD pass to Alvin Harper. Steve Young threw for one TD and ran for another for San Francisco, which suffered its most lopsided loss in five years under Coach George Seifert.

Emmitt Smith ran for a score in addition to his TD reception. He was both the top runner (23 carries for 88 yards) and top receiver (seven catches for 85) in the game.

1994

SUDDEN SPEED BUMP

Change at the Helm Causes Slight Setback

After winning back-to-back Super Bowls, Jimmy Johnson should have been on top of the coaching world. Instead, he found himself in the middle of a bitter feud with team owner Jerry Jones and out of a job. Johnson's resignation opened the door for Barry Switzer, another successful college coach with University of Arkansas ties to Jones.

The 1994 season suffered for the change, though most clubs would have loved the troubles that Dallas considered part of a 12–4 season with another 11-member Pro Bowl contingent. They played a preseason game before 112,376 fans in Mexico City, relished 1,484 rushing yards and 21 ground TDs from Emmitt Smith, and enjoyed Michael Irvin's 79 receptions for 1,241 yards.

When it came right down to it, though, Switzer was unable to carry the Super Bowl run to a third straight season as San Francisco delivered an NFC title game blow that sent the Cowboys home earlier than expected.

They did not stay down for long, however.

GAME 1: Switzer Wins Debut
Cowboys 26 at Pittsburgh 9

September 4: With a new coach at their helm, the two-time defending Super Bowl champs looked as dominant as ever. Barry Switzer savored his first NFL victory, which was built on a swarming defensive display.

Dallas sacked QB Neil O'Donnell nine times and held the Steelers to 126 total yards. Emmitt Smith powered a clock-chewing offensive attack with 171 yards on 31 carries. Troy Aikman racked up 245 passing yards, most of them (139) on eight completions to Michael Irvin. Chris Boniol kicked four field goals in his Dallas debut.

GAME 2: Oilers Nearly Pull Upset
Cowboys 20 vs. Houston 17

September 11: Barry Switzer's home opener as Dallas coach nearly turned disastrous against a two-TD underdog. The Oilers looked every bit the Cowboys' equal, save for a few key miscues that allowed Dallas to escape. The biggest gaffe came in the last minute of the first half when Houston, thinking it had made a first down in the shadow of its own goal posts, threw a third-down pass instead of running out the clock. It fell incomplete, leaving the Cowboys time for a go-ahead field goal.

Those three points proved to be the difference. Troy Aikman's third-quarter TD pass to Alvin Harper stretched the margin to 20–10, and a fourth-quarter Houston TD was not enough. The Oilers' 339 yards were just one less than Dallas managed, but two interceptions and eight penalties hurt their upset bid.

GAME 3: Sanders Outduels Smith
Detroit 20 at Cowboys 17 (OT)

September 19: A battle between the two best backs in the NFC, if not the NFL, favored Detroit's elusive Barry Sanders on this day. Sanders exploded for 194 yards on 40 carries in his team's OT win at Texas Stadium, while Emmitt Smith's 29 totes for 143 yards and a game-tying fourth-quarter TD were not enough to save the Cowboys.

In the end, mistakes hurt Dallas as much as the team's inability to contain Sanders or prevent QB Scott Mitchell from taking his club to a 17–7 lead on TD passes in the second and third quarters. While the Lions protected the football, the Cowboys lost three fumbles and would have lost earlier if not for Leon Lett's two blocked field goals. He could not get his mitts on a third one, however, when Jason Hanson ended the marathon on a 44-yarder with 32 seconds left in overtime.

Alvin Harper makes a catch during the game against the Philadelphia Eagles on December 4, 1994, at Veterans Stadium in Philadelphia, Pennsylvania. (Photo by Mitchell Layton/Getty Images)

GAME 4: Redskins Fall Quickly

Cowboys 34 at Washington 7

October 2: Three turnovers on their first four possessions, all in their own territory, doomed the Redskins to a 31–0 halftime hole. They never got much better against a Dallas team that simply had to show up. Emmitt Smith ran for the first two TDs before leaving with a second-quarter hamstring injury and left tackle Mark Tuinei was sidelined by a back injury in the first quarter, but the Cowboys had more than enough firepower.

Troy Aikman hit 20-of-28 passes with a TD toss to Jay Novacek. The Redskins lost three fumbles and got a dismal 11-of-30 passing performance from rookie Heath Shuler in his debut as their starter.

GAME 5: Another Easy One

Cowboys 38 vs. Arizona 3

October 9: For the second straight week, an opponent crumbled before the Cowboys' eyes. Arizona threw five interceptions, had more turnovers than first downs in the first half, was flagged for 10 penalties, and fell to Dallas for the eighth consecutive time. It was Buddy Ryan's most lopsided loss as an NFL head coach, too.

Emmitt Smith played sparingly after running for two early TDs. Troy Aikman threw two TD passes, and Kevin Williams added insult to injury with an 87-yard kickoff return following the Cardinals' only score of the day.

GAME 6: Defense Makes Statement

Cowboys 24 vs. Philadelphia 13

October 16: Dallas defenders took it personally when they heard talk that their big efforts to this point had come against inferior competition. They turned in their best performance of the year against the Eagles, intercepting and sacking Randall Cunningham four times apiece.

In all, the Cowboys took advantage of five turnovers. They scored 24 consecutive points after giving up an early TD, enjoying two TD passes from Troy Aikman and 106 rushing yards from Emmitt Smith—his first 100-yard day since injuring his hamstring two weeks earlier.

GAME 7: Cards Make a Game of It

Cowboys 28 at Arizona 21

October 23: Two weeks earlier at Texas Stadium, Arizona didn't have a chance. On their home field this time, the Cardinals made a valiant upset bid before having their chances spoiled by backup QB Rodney Peete.

In the first quarter, Troy Aikman threw a TD pass to Alvin Harper on his first play after taking a Wilber Marshall helmet to the chin, then exited the game. Peete, who took over when Aikman suffered a concussion, led Dallas to two fourth-quarter TDs that erased a 21–14 deficit. First, his second TD pass of the day to Michael Irvin covered 65 yards when an Arizona defender tried to strip the ball instead of making a tackle. The winning TD, a six-yard run by Emmitt Smith, came with 5:13 to go. Peete went 12-for-19 in his clutch relief performance.

GAME 8: Winless Bengals Show Fight

Cowboys 23 at Cincinnati 20

October 30: A quarterback making his first NFL start for a team that had yet to win a game nearly knocked off the two-time defending Super Bowl champs. Dallas needed a Chris Boniol field goal with five minutes remaining to survive what would have been among the most crushing defeats in franchise history.

Jeff Blake was the Bengals' surprising catalyst, throwing for 247 yards and two TDs to Darnay Scott that gave Cincinnati a 14–0 lead 16 minutes into the game. Those bombs covered 67 and 55 yards. Troy Aikman fired TD passes to Michael Irvin and Alvin Harper in the second quarter to slice the Bengals' lead to 17–14 at halftime. The second half was a battle of defense and field goals, with Boniol connecting three times to save the Cowboys.

GAME 9: Dallas Rolls to Sixth Straight Win

Cowboys 38 vs. N.Y. Giants 10

November 7: Alvin Harper's first-quarter TD reception from Troy Aikman started the Cowboys toward an impressive win over the Giants, but it was his knee injury late in the first half that dominated the postgame conversation. Dallas feared it might be season-ending, though it turned out to be less serious than initially thought.

As for the game, the Giants never mounted a serious threat. Emmitt Smith rambled for 163 yards and two TDs, Aikman threw just five incomplete passes in 24 attempts and ran for a score, and Michael Irvin caught seven balls for 118 yards. Dallas led 35–3 after three quarters.

GAME 10: A Bad Omen?

San Francisco 21 vs. Cowboys 14

November 13: The largest crowd ever to watch a 49ers game in Candlestick Park, along with the top two teams in the NFC, gave this game a playoff atmosphere from start to finish. Dallas, however, did not deliver a playoff-caliber performance in front of the more than 69,000 screaming patrons.

Three Troy Aikman interceptions spelled defeat for a Cowboys team that played well enough defensively to win and outgained the 49ers by 100 yards. Emmitt Smith ran for the game's first and last TDs, but in between Steve Young made more impact plays than anyone on the Cowboys. The San Francisco QB ran for one TD and threw for two others, including a 57-yarder to Jerry Rice. Most significantly, Young and the 49ers protected the football, while Aikman coughed it up on a day when he threw for 339 yards.

GAME 11: Garrett Pressed into Action

Cowboys 31 vs. Washington 7

November 20: A costly win for the Cowboys became an opportunity for Ivy Leaguer Jason Garrett. The former Princeton QB took over

Switch to Switzer: Familiar Formula, Different Direction

Before the Fall, Barry Switzer Brings Cowboys Another Super Bowl

Give Jerry Jones this much: When something works, he's not going to change it. Hiring a former Arkansas teammate and successful college coach, Jimmy Johnson, earned the Cowboys owner two Super Bowl titles in the 1990s. So after a falling-out with Johnson left him in search of a replacement, Jones went right back to the formula.

Barry Switzer had preceded Jones and Johnson as an Arkansas player but returned as an assistant coach for the Razorbacks during Jones' tenure. He, too, had taken college football by storm, winning three national titles at Oklahoma. And so, with great gusto, he took a Dallas podium in 1994 and shouted: "We got a job to do, and we gonna do it, baby!"[1]

Switzer, the son of an Arkansas bootlegger, told friends and reporters he felt like he had just won the lottery. Having left the college ranks amid scandal for allowing his Sooners program to trample the NCAA rule book for years, he had landed a job with a team coming off back-to-back Super Bowl victories—one blessed with some of the best talent in football. It showed immediately.

The Cowboys went 12–4 in Switzer's NFL debut, but a heartbreaking loss to San Francisco in the NFC title game left them short of the Super Bowl. They duplicated that regular-season mark in 1995, then swept through the playoffs and earned their third Super Bowl ring in four years with a satisfying 27–17 win over their longtime rivals from Pittsburgh. Switzer was, once again, on top of the football world.

However, just as his success came with a price in the college ranks, his dream job began turning nightmarish in Dallas. Unlike Johnson, a boss who demanded respect and accountability

Head coach Barry Switzer watches his players during the October 29, 1995, game against the Atlanta Falcons at the Georiga Dome in Atlanta, Georiga. The Cowboys won the game 28–13. (Photo by Getty Images)

from his players, Switzer gave his players seemingly unlimited leeway to enjoy their fame and fortune as they pleased. If Johnson was overbearing, Switzer was the opposite. It might have been a change the Cowboys needed to add another championship to their résumé, but it had consequences in the long term. Off-field troubles began overshadowing the team's success.

"The players actually ran that team at that point," explained safety Brock Marion, who played for both Johnson and Switzer. "We had a figurehead who was Barry Switzer."[2]

The team's downfall came swiftly thereafter. The Cowboys slipped to 10–6 in 1996, making the playoffs but losing to Carolina in the divisional round. The following summer, during training camp, Switzer was arrested on a gun charge after a loaded .38-caliber pistol was found in his carry-on baggage at the Dallas airport. That season, the Cowboys dropped their last five games to finish 6–10, and Switzer—like Johnson before him—was forced out.

after Troy Aikman sprained his left knee early in the game and backup Rodney Peete sprained his right thumb late.

It didn't matter who was under center against the Redskins, who committed five turnovers against the Cowboys—Dallas still bounced back from the previous week's loss. Emmitt Smith ran for two TDs, and Kevin Williams returned a punt 83 yards for another. Garrett attempted just five passes, completing one, but he was suddenly the man on the spot.

GAME 12: Garrett Smashing in Debut

Cowboys 42 vs. Green Bay 31

November 24: Worries? What worries? Those who feared Dallas might collapse with a third-stringer under center had their fears alleviated in a Thanksgiving shootout. With the nation watching as it digested its turkey, Jason Garrett threw for 311 yards and two TDs in his first NFL start to defeat Brett Favre and the Packers.

Garrett got plenty of help. Emmitt Smith carried 32 times for 133 yards and two TDs, and the Dallas defense held Green Bay to 29 rushing yards. But when he needed to make big plays, Garrett did just that. He hit Alvin Harper and Michael Irvin for long TDs to help Dallas overcome an early 17–3 deficit. Those strikes bookended a crucial run of 26 successive Cowboys points in the second half. Favre threw four TD passes.

GAME 13: An Early Clincher

Cowboys 31 at Philadelphia 19

December 4: Dallas earned the luxury of playing its final three games with the knowledge it had already wrapped up the NFC East title by grabbing an early lead in Philadelphia and holding off the Eagles. It gave them a four-game cushion in the standings over a Philly team that absorbed five sacks on its home field.

Emmitt Smith's short TD runs gave the Cowboys leads of 14–3 in the first half and 21–6 in the second. Eagles QB Randall Cunningham threw for 327 yards and two TDs despite relentless Dallas pressure, but he also fired an interception that Darren Woodson returned 94 yards for a score. Rodney Peete returned from a thumb injury to complete 10-of-17 passes for the Cowboys, including a TD pass to Michael Irvin.

GAME 14: Inches Short

Cleveland 19 at Cowboys 14

December 10: Jay Novacek gained 5½ yards on the Cowboys' last play of the game, but he needed six. The tight end slipped after catching a Troy Aikman pass, and Eric Turner fell on him just short of the goal line as time expired on a defensive war between two top teams at Texas Stadium.

On the scoreboard, it was four Matt Stover field goals that made the difference for the Browns. In reality, it was four turnovers that prevented Dallas from building on an early 7–0 lead or coming all the way back from a 16–7 deficit. Emmitt Smith ran for 112 yards and scored two TDs for the Cowboys. Troy Aikman returned for the first time since suffering a knee injury on November 20 and was intercepted twice.

GAME 15: Smith Injured Again

Cowboys 24 at New Orleans 16

December 19: An early season hamstring injury did not pose a great problem for Emmitt Smith. This time, the Cowboys were a bit more concerned after watching their star runner leave the game after running for 74 yards and a TD that gave his team a 17–6 third-quarter lead at the Superdome.

Fortunately for Dallas, its playoff spot had long been clinched, and a first-round bye was on the way. And in this game, the Cowboys didn't need much from their offense, with the defense scoring two TDs. Tony Tolbert and Darrin Smith returned interceptions to the end zone. Those were the most damaging of Jim Everett's three picks. Troy Aikman completed 21-of-28 passes but was intercepted twice.

GAME 16: A Ho-Hum Finale

N.Y. Giants 15 vs. Cowboys 10

December 24: With Emmitt Smith sitting out to recover from a hamstring injury and several other starters resting for the playoffs, the Cowboys dropped their regular-season finale but reached their goal of adding no one new to the injury report. Dallas did not reach 100 net yards either running or passing.

Blair Thomas, with 63 yards and a TD, was the Cowboys' leading rusher. The Giants took the lead for good at 12–10 when Dallas QB Rodney Peete fumbled the ball out of the end zone for a safety in the third quarter.

GAME 17: Packers, NFL Record Fall
Cowboys 35 vs. Green Bay 9

January 8, 1995: Troy Aikman connected with Alvin Harper on a 94-yard TD pass, the longest in NFL playoff history, to send the Cowboys on their way to another date with the 49ers with the NFC title at stake. But that was not the only history made on this day.

Harper, Michael Irvin, and Jay Novacek became just the second trio of teammates in NFL playoff history to amass 100-plus receiving yards apiece. They were the primary targets in Troy Aikman's 23-of-30, 337-yard passing demonstration.

Emmitt Smith reinjured a hamstring that had kept him out of the regular-season finale, but he vowed to play at San Francisco. Against the Packers, who yielded 450 yards of offense, Blair Thomas came in and rushed for 70 yards on 23 carries in Smith's absence.

GAME 18: Title Run Ends
San Francisco 38 vs. Cowboys 28

January 15, 1995: There would be no third straight trip to the Super Bowl for Dallas. An old nemesis made certain of that.

After falling to the Cowboys in each of the last two NFC title games, the 49ers took aim at a fifth Super Bowl title by jumping on mistakes at Candlestick Park. Dallas committed five turnovers, including three in the game's first five minutes. Those mistakes contributed to a 21–0 San Francisco start, and the Cowboys never recovered.

Troy Aikman threw for 380 yards and two TDs to Michael Irvin, whose 12 catches for 192 yards helped Dallas make a game of it. But Aikman's three interceptions were huge, particularly the one Eric Davis returned 44 yards for a TD to open the scoring. It was one of two picks for Davis.

Emmitt Smith showed no ill effects from a hamstring injury when he ran for two Dallas TDs late in the game. Dallas outgained San Francisco by 157 yards, but turnovers and nine penalties for 98 yards were telling.

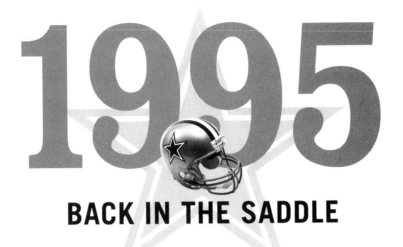

1995

BACK IN THE SADDLE

Cowboys Celebrate Third Championship in Four Years

The Dallas Cowboys knew how to celebrate. Perhaps too much so, according to their critics. Indeed, off-the-field problems became exposed in the mid-1990s, and the team's third Super Bowl title in four years came with concerns about the various costs that accompanied the club's swagger. It further separated NFL fans into two factions—those who loved the Cowboys, and those who loathed them.

History, however, could not be denied. The Cowboys became the first team ever to claim three Super Bowls in a four-year stretch, as Barry Switzer earned his first championship as head coach.

Switzer guided the team to its second straight 12–4 mark and NFC East title, and Emmitt Smith won his fourth career NFL rushing crown with a franchise-record 1,773 yards. This time, Dallas carried its momentum right through the playoffs, too.

Third-ranked in scoring offense and scoring defense during the regular season, the Cowboys won all three playoff games by 10 or more points while winning the fifth Super Bowl title in their history.

GAME 1: A Near-Perfect Start
Cowboys 35 at N.Y. Giants 0

September 4: The only downer in Dallas' season opener was the sight of cornerback Kevin Smith leaving New York on crutches after injuring his Achilles tendon. The rest of the night's pain was absorbed by the Giants, who gave up 232 rushing yards while gaining just 65 of their own.

Emmitt Smith got off to a blazing start with 21 carries for 163 yards and four TDs. Troy Aikman completed 15-of-20 passes, and Michael Irvin caught seven balls for 109 yards and a TD. Kevin Smith suffered his injury while covering a deep pass in the second quarter.

GAME 2: Another 30-Point Game
Cowboys 31 vs. Denver 21

September 10: For the second straight week, Dallas topped 30 points and never trailed in a systematic dismantling of an opponent. This time, it was the Broncos who succumbed to the 100-yard rushing of Emmitt Smith and a sturdy Dallas defense.

Smith ran 26 times for 114 yards and a score. Troy Aikman hit Daryl Johnston with a TD pass and also ran for a score in the second quarter to give the Cowboys a 14–0 advantage. Aikman also threw a TD pass to Jay Novacek, and Charles Haley powered the defense with two sacks.

GAME 3: Smith Settles Game in OT
Cowboys 23 at Minnesota 17 (OT)

September 17: After two relatively easy wins to start the season, the Cowboys had to work for this one. Emmitt Smith capped a 150-yard rushing day with a 31-yard scoring sprint in overtime that kept his team's record perfect.

Warren Moon fired two TD passes for the Vikings, including an eight-yarder to Cris Carter that, after the PAT, tied the game with 30 seconds remaining in regulation. But Smith, who had given the Cowboys a 17–10 lead on his first scoring run early in the fourth quarter, negated the need for a field-goal attempt by breaking free for the winner.

Troy Aikman completed 24-of-38 passes for 246 yards and a 19-yard TD pass to Michael Irvin. With the game on the line, Aikman went 9-of-11 in the fourth quarter and overtime.

GAME 4: Smith Keeps Churning
Cowboys 34 vs. Arizona 20

September 24: Emmitt Smith topped the century mark for the fourth time in as many weeks, and the Cowboys rode the effort to their fourth straight win. Smith covered 116 yards on 21 carries before leaving with a bruised left elbow, while the Cardinals nursed the bruises of never having gotten within 10 points after giving up two first-quarter TDs.

Dave Krieg threw for 324 yards and two scores for Arizona, but his three interceptions aided a Cowboys team that did not necessarily need the help. Troy Aikman passed for 251 yards, while Michael Irvin enjoyed another 100-yard receiving game.

GAME 5: Dallas Feels a Sting
Washington 27 vs. Cowboys 23

October 1: A loss to a bitter rival was bad enough. But Dallas also suffered the pain of injury as QB Troy Aikman went out with a calf strain early in the game and did not return. That was not the only trouble for Dallas. The defense gave up 121 rushing yards to Terry Allen and was burned by Gus Frerotte for two TD passes.

Emmitt Smith (95 yards) failed to run for 100 for the first time this season and also coughed up a key fumble. Washington scored 24 straight points to turn a 10–3 deficit into a 27–10 lead, and backup QB Wade Wilson could not bring the Cowboys all the way back.

GAME 6: Aikman, Dallas Back
Cowboys 34 vs. Green Bay 24

October 8: Lucky Packers. They were there when, for the first time in history, Troy Aikman threw for 300 yards, Emmitt Smith ran for 100, and Michael Irvin caught passes for 100 in the same game. That combination helped Dallas recover quickly from its first loss of the year.

Smith's first of two TDs gave the Cowboys a 17–3 halftime lead. Aikman then opened the third quarter by hitting Irvin with a 48-yard bomb for a score, and the Packers were in too deep of a hole to recover. Smith ran for 106 yards, Irvin caught eight passes for 150, and Aikman finished 24-for-31 for 316 yards and two TDs. Brett Favre threw for 295 yards for Green Bay.

GAME 7: Unusual Formula
Cowboys 23 at San Diego 9

October 15: The Cowboys, for the first time all year, won a game in which Emmitt Smith failed to run for 100 yards. It was made much easier thanks to Chargers QB Gale Gilbert, who set up Dallas with three interceptions and a fumble on his first four possessions. Gilbert was making just his fourth NFL start.

It was San Diego's defense that made the game's first scoring play, sacking Troy Aikman in the end zone for a 2–0 lead. After that, it was all Cowboys. The takeaways negated the need for a big-yardage offensive day. Smith ran for two short TDs, Daryl Johnston plunged in for another, and Aikman threw for 222 yards.

GAME 8: Sanders Arrives in Another Win

Cowboys 28 at Atlanta 13

October 29: Deion Sanders made his season debut, playing both ways for the Cowboys and sparking them to a comeback victory over his former team. Atlanta jumped to a 10–0 lead, but Emmitt Smith shredded the Falcons' defense for 167 rushing yards and 30 receiving yards, while Michael Irvin caught 10 passes for 135.

Sanders was a rock at cornerback, making life miserable for Atlanta QB Jeff George and catching a pass on offense. Second-quarter TDs by Smith and Jay Novacek gave Dallas a 14–10 halftime edge, and Irvin's 43-yard TD grab from Aikman helped the Cowboys accelerate in the second half.

GAME 9: Irvin Ties Record in Romp

Cowboys 34 vs. Philadelphia 12

November 6: Michael Irvin matched an NFL record with his seventh consecutive 100-yard receiving game as Dallas improved to 8–1. As usual, the Cowboys receiver had loads of help. Emmitt Smith ran for 158 yards and two TDs, and Troy Aikman threw for 202 yards. Irvin caught eight Aikman throws for 115 yards and a TD.

It was the Cowboys' seventh straight win over the Eagles. Former Cowboys QB Rodney Peete, starting for Philly, contributed to his team's struggles with two interceptions. Larry Brown returned one 20 yards to the end zone.

GAME 10: Another Loss to San Fran

San Francisco 38 at Cowboys 20

November 12: Dallas lost for the third time in a calendar year—364 days, to be exact—to the 49ers, and once again turnovers were largely to blame. The Cowboys threw three interceptions and lost a fumble, while San Francisco did not turn the ball over in delivering Dallas its second loss of the year.

The 49ers put the clamps on Michael Irvin, snapping his seven-game string of 100-yard receiving contests and scoring on his first-quarter fumble when Merton Hanks recovered the ball and raced 38 yards for a TD. Emmitt Smith ran for 100 yards, but by the time he reached the end zone, the 49ers had raced to a 24–0 lead thanks to the early takeaways. Troy Aikman suffered a bruised knee in the first half, and Wade Wilson could not engineer a comeback in relief.

GAME 11: Back to Basics

Cowboys 34 at Oakland 21

November 19: Following its second loss of the year, Dallas went back to what always works.

Emmitt Smith battered the Raiders for 110 yards and three TDs on the ground, and Troy Aikman hooked up with Michael Irvin seven times for 109 yards and a score.

Oakland fell behind 14–0 early and could never recover. The Raiders rolled to 449 total yards on the passing of Vince Evans and Jeff Hostetler, but three interceptions prevented them from making a game of it. Aikman, coming back from a knee injury the previous week, was accurate on 19-of-24 passes for 227 yards.

Wide receiver Michael Irvin (No. 88) gets open behind Green Bay Packers cornerback Craig Newsome (No. 21) during the NFC Championship Game, a 38–27 Cowboys victory on January 14, 1996, at Texas Stadium in Irving, Texas. (Photo by Al Messerschmidt/Getty Images)

GAME 12: Painful Victory

Cowboys 24 vs. Kansas City 12

November 23: Emmitt Smith went down, untouched, with a knee injury in the third quarter while defensive line staple Ray Donaldson broke his ankle in a costly victory over AFC power Kansas City. It was just the second loss of the season for the Chiefs, who were held to 73 rushing yards in the game and kept out of the end zone until the third quarter by an aggressive Dallas defense.

Smith played long enough to get the Cowboys going. His 15-yard TD run and Michael Irvin's 33-yard TD pass from Troy Aikman produced a 14–0 first-quarter lead. Irvin made 11 grabs for 121 yards, and Aikman was a cool 21-for-29 with two TD tosses and no interceptions. The Chiefs were down 21–6 before scoring their first TD.

GAME 13: Redskins Sweep Series

Washington 24 at Cowboys 17

December 3: It was just the fourth win of the year for the Redskins and their first on the road. Two of those four wins came against the Cowboys, though, and that provided no small level of satisfaction for their players and fans.

Emmitt Smith, back on the field after injuring his knee the previous week, fumbled twice—losing one—and fell short of the 100-yard mark with 91 on 21 runs. Washington scored the first 17 points of the second half to turn a 10–7 half-time deficit into a win. Terry Allen outdueled

Smith with 98 yards and two scores for the Redskins. Michael Irvin scored a late TD for Dallas, gaining more than 100 receiving yards for an NFL record 11th time in one year.

GAME 14: Chilling Loss

Philadelphia 20 vs. Cowboys 17

December 10: The wind-chill factor was minus-7 degrees at Veterans Stadium, but Dallas felt even colder than that after squandering a 17–3 lead and handing the Eagles a victory when a late gamble backfired. Facing fourth-and-1 at their own 29 with two minutes to play in a 17–17 game, the Cowboys decided to try for a first down, and Emmitt Smith was stopped short. That set up Gary Anderson's winning 42-yard field goal.

Coach Barry Switzer, who made the risky call, described his team as "shattered." The Cowboys led by 14 on TDs by Emmitt Smith (108 rushing yards) and Larry Brown (a 65-yard interception return), but former Cowboys QB Rodney Peete led the Eagles' charge. Peete hit 20-of-29 passes, and Ricky Watters carried 33 times for 112 yards and a TD.

GAME 15: Kicking a Slump

Cowboys 21 vs. N.Y. Giants 20

December 17: Dallas was seconds away from a third consecutive loss when Chris Boniol came through with the first game-winning kick of his NFL career. Troy Aikman marched the

Super Bowl XXX: Dynasty Determined
Third Championship in Four Years Lifts Dallas Among All-Time Elite

The most qualified person to comment on whether the Cowboys' third Super Bowl title in four years made them a dynasty might have been the coach whose former team they defeated for that crown. Chuck Noll directed the Pittsburgh Steelers to four championships in the 1970s, including two Super Bowl wins over the Cowboys, and was well aware of the fact no team had ever crammed three crowns into a four-year stretch until this 1990s Dallas crew came along.

"They are a great, great team," Noll told *The Sporting News* after watching the Cowboys send the Steelers to their first-ever Super Bowl loss, 27–17. "People think it's easy to do what they have done. It's not, or more would have done it."[1]

The teams battling at Sun Devil Stadium on January 28, 1996, were familiar with the Super Bowl's bright lights, even if their coaches were not. Bill Cowher, who had taken over for Noll at the Pittsburgh helm four years earlier, and second-year Cowboys head coach Barry Switzer were there for the first time. The victory was sweet redemption for Switzer, who had replaced Jimmy Johnson after the latter had coached Dallas to back-to-back championships in '92 and '93. His

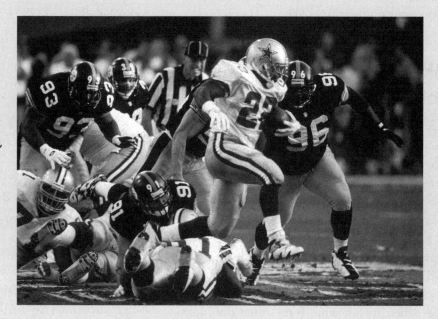

Running back Emmitt Smith (No. 22) carries the ball against the Pittsburgh Steelers during Super Bowl XXX on January 28, 1996, at Sun Devil Stadium in Tempe, Arizona. The Cowboys won 27–17. (Photo by Focus on Sport/ Getty Images)

Cowboys had been viewed by many as an out-of-control collection of overpaid megastars concerned more about contracts and wild parties than in playing as a team.

Before 76,347 fans and an estimated 94 million TV viewers, Switzer's team came together quickly. The Cowboys took a 13–0 lead early in the second quarter and never trailed. The Steelers staged an inspired comeback bid after falling behind 20–7, but Larry Brown's two second-half interceptions thwarted their chances and earned the cornerback MVP honors.

"We did it our way, baby!" Switzer shouted after the game to Jerry Jones, the owner who had forced out Johnson two years earlier. "We did it! We did it!"[2]

Their way was a winning blend of running, passing, and defense. Emmitt Smith ran for two second-half TDs, including the game's final score with 3:43 remaining after the Steelers had pulled within 20–17. Troy Aikman completed 15-of-23 passes for 209 yards and an early TD to tight end Jay Novacek. And the Cowboys intercepted shaky Steelers QB Neil O'Donnell three times—all in the second half.

Aikman directed a turnover-free Dallas attack to join Terry Bradshaw and Joe Montana as the only QBs ever to win at least three Super Bowls.

Cowboys 58 yards to the Giants' 17-yard line with five seconds remaining, and Boniol split the uprights from 35 yards to settle the outcome.

Boniol was the story for the Cowboys, kicking five field goals on a day when the end zone proved hard to reach. Emmitt Smith rushed for 103 yards and the only Dallas TD, lifting his team to an 18–17 lead in the fourth quarter. However, the Cowboys defense was unable to corral Rodney Hampton (34 carries for 187 yards), and the Giants reclaimed the lead on Brad Daluiso's second short field goal of the second half.

GAME 16: Grand Finale
Cowboys 37 at Arizona 13

December 25: NFC East champ Dallas secured home-field advantage throughout the playoffs and celebrated another Emmitt Smith rushing title in a one-sided Christmas night finale. Smith ran for his NFL-record 25th TD of the season.

Troy Aikman passed for 350 yards and two TDs, while Kevin Williams stole the receiving spotlight from Michael Irvin with nine catches for 203 yards and both aerial scores. The Cardinals managed only 12 first downs and did not reach the end zone on offense. Aeneas Williams returned an interception 48 yards for the Cardinals' only TD.

GAME 17: Birds Grounded
Cowboys 30 vs. Philadelphia 11

January 7, 1996: Dallas was hot in the coldest game ever played at Texas Stadium. The kickoff temperature was 26 degrees, with a wind chill of 2. The Cowboys heated up the turf with Troy Aikman's 17-of-24 passing, Emmitt Smith's 99 rushing yards, and Kevin Williams' six receptions for 124 yards.

Deion Sanders made an impact on both sides of scrimmage, starting a run of 27 consecutive Cowboys points when he scored on a 21-yard reverse and intercepted a Randall Cunningham pass. Smith and Michael Irvin also scored TDs, and Chris Boniol booted a 51-yard field goal.

GAME 18: New Foe Can't Slow Super Charge
Cowboys 38 vs. Green Bay 27

January 14, 1996: It was downright strange seeing the Cowboys play someone other than San Francisco with a Super Bowl berth at stake. Their road to the big game, though, was quite familiar.

Dallas took an early lead on back-to-back first-quarter TD hookups from Troy Aikman to Michael Irvin. Emmitt Smith and his offensive line then pounded the upset-minded Packers. Smith ran 35 times for 150 yards and three TDs in the game.

Green Bay recovered from the early onslaught, as Brett Favre threw first-half TD passes to Robert Brooks (a 73-yarder) and Keith Jackson to tie the score at 17–17. His second TD toss to Brooks gave the Packers a 27–24 lead entering the fourth quarter.

However, Smith had the final word. He bulled in from the 5 for the winning TD and added an insurance 16-yarder down the stretch. Favre threw for 307 yards and three scores but was intercepted twice. Aikman and the Cowboys did not commit a turnover in booking their return trip to the Super Bowl.

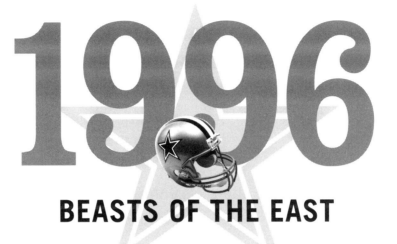

1996

BEASTS OF THE EAST

Dallas Becomes First to Win Five Straight NFC East Titles

The "Team of the Nineties" claimed its fifth consecutive NFC East championship in 1996, an unprecedented feat in the powerful division. The Cowboys did it with a 10–6 mark, crafted despite the turbulence of drug charges and dissent, which speaks to the remarkable talent level that helped the club to three Super Bowl wins.

On the field, Dallas was not its usual self. In particular, the offense struggled in part because Michael Irvin was suspended early in the year. Without his presence downfield, foes could key in on Emmitt Smith, and the four-time rushing champ saw his production slip to a "mere" 1,204 yards. If only all backs could have such down seasons!

These were not the same Cowboys by the time they lost a 26–17 playoff decision to the Carolina Panthers after a wild-card win over Minnesota. That win would be the club's last in a playoff game until 2009.

GAME 1: Shorthanded Dallas Falters

Chicago 22 vs. Cowboys 6

September 2: Playing the game without Michael Irvin (suspended after pleading no contest to a drug charge) and finishing it without Emmitt Smith (neck and back injuries), Dallas was a shadow of its usual self. The Cowboys failed to score a TD for the first time in 70 games while dropping their opener in Chicago.

Smith was taken off the field on a cart late in the game after carrying 18 times for 70 yards. Deion Sanders tried to pick up the slack for Irvin, catching nine passes for 87 yards, but Dallas could manage only two Chris Boniol field goals. Bears linebacker Bryan Cox recovered a fumble—one of four Cowboys turnovers—for a TD.

GAME 2: Goose Eggs for Giants

Cowboys 27 vs. N.Y. Giants 0

September 8: For the second straight September, the Cowboys posted a shutout of the Giants. Troy Aikman threw three TD passes, and the Dallas defense was dominant, giving up just 105 total yards while registering three sacks and two takeaways.

Deion Sanders, Emmitt Smith, and Kevin Williams all caught TD passes in the first half in the home opener at Texas Stadium. That was more than enough against a Giants team that mustered only seven first downs all day.

GAME 3: Off the Crossbar

Indianapolis 25 at Cowboys 24

September 15: Dallas squandered a 21–3 lead at Texas Stadium, then fell a few inches short of a victory when Chris Boniol's last-second, 57-yard field goal attempt bounced off the crossbar. The 18-point blown lead was the largest ever for the Cowboys at home.

Emmitt Smith topped 100 rushing yards for the first time this year. His TD run and Deion Sanders' 22-yard fumble return for a score gave the Cowboys their big lead in the second quarter. However, Jim Harbaugh rallied the Colts with two third-quarter TD passes. Boniol, who made a career-long 52-yarder but missed a 40-yarder with 2½ minutes to go, was accurate on his final boot but just short.

GAME 4: Going South Up North

Buffalo 10 vs. Cowboys 7

September 22: Troy Aikman threw three second-half interceptions, Emmitt Smith ran for just 25 yards on 15 carries, and Dallas looked like an NFL bottom-feeder in losing for the third time in four games. As a team, the Cowboys rushed for 32 yards, and they were blanked until Smith reached the end zone in the fourth quarter.

By then, a Thurman Thomas TD and a Steve Christie field goal had given the Bills a 10–0 lead against a Cowboys team that looked dazed and confused. Dallas gained 192 total yards.

GAME 5: Season-Saving Win
Cowboys 23 at Philadelphia 19

September 30: Sitting at 1–3 and trailing 10–0 at Philadelphia, Dallas faced the prospect of a lost season before the calendar even turned to October. Then Troy Aikman threw a TD pass to Eric Bjornson, Emmitt Smith ran for a score, Chris Boniol kicked two field goals, and a 20–10 halftime lead turned into a key victory.

It was defense that turned the tide. After looking beatable early, the Cowboys took advantage of five Philly turnovers—three fumbles and interceptions by both Ty Detmer and Rodney Peete. Smith rushed for 92 yards.

GAME 6: Irvin Returns, Defense Wins
Cowboys 17 vs. Arizona 3

October 13: Michael Irvin suited up after missing the first five games under a drug suspension, and he was the Cowboys' top receiver with five catches for 51 yards. Emmitt Smith ran for 112 yards and both Dallas TDs, but it was defense that determined the outcome.

The Cowboys held Arizona to 58 rushing yards and sacked QB Kent Graham three times. They also intercepted him once and kept the Cardinals from crossing midfield on their last four possessions.

GAME 7: Late Bomb Averts Loss
Cowboys 32 vs. Atlanta 28

October 20: Troy Aikman's 60-yard TD pass to Kelvin Martin with 1:42 remaining saved the Cowboys from an upset loss against winless Atlanta. The Falcons used their run-and-shoot attack to fluster Dallas for much of the day, taking leads of 25–17 and 28–25 in the second half behind five Morten Andersen field goals.

Aikman, however, got one more chance in the late going. Starting at his own 7-yard line with 2:46 on the clock, he needed only a minute to find Martin over the middle and watch his teammate race for the winning score. Emmitt Smith ran for just 50 yards but two TDs. Bobby Hebert hit 25-of-40 passes for 272 yards and a TD for the Falcons.

GAME 8: Irvin Erupts Against Dolphins
Cowboys 29 at Miami 10

October 27: Michael Irvin returned to Miami, where he played college ball, and put a Hurricane-sized whipping on the Dolphins. He caught 12 passes for 186 yards and a TD, helping Troy Aikman to a 363-yard passing day.

The Cowboys trailed 10–9 at halftime after managing just three field goals, but Aikman threw three unanswered TD tosses in the second half.

Aikman hit 33-of-41 throws without an interception. The Cowboys picked off Dan Marino once and recovered two Dolphins fumbles.

GAME 9: Eagles Stop Streak
Philadelphia 31 at Cowboys 21

November 3: Having seemingly righted their course with four straight wins, the Cowboys were reminded that NFL success can be fleeting. Against the visiting Eagles, two Troy Aikman

Wide receiver Jerry Rice (No. 80) of the San Francisco 49ers faces former teammate Deion Sanders (No. 21) during their 20–17 loss to the Dallas Cowboys on November 10, 1996, at 3Com Park in San Francisco, California. (Photo by Otto Greule Jr./Getty Images)

interceptions and a shaky defense that allowed Ricky Watters to gain 116 rushing yards led to their demise.

Emmitt Smith ran for 114 yards and two TDs for Dallas. His second score, followed by a successful two-point conversion, tied the game 21–21 in the final quarter. However, Gary Anderson kicked a 30-yard field goal, then James Willis intercepted Aikman in the end zone, ran to the 10, and tossed a lateral to Troy Vincent, who raced the remaining 90 yards to put the game on ice.

GAME 10: Memorable Rematch

Cowboys 20 at San Francisco 17 (OT)

November 10: There's usually something special about a Cowboys-49ers game, and this one tasted especially sweet for Dallas. After spotting the hosts a 10–0 lead, the Cowboys clamped down on defense, tied the game on a late TD, and won it when Chris Boniol booted a 29-yard field goal 6:17 into overtime. It was the first time Dallas led.

Troy Aikman ran for a second-quarter TD, and Boniol tied the game in the fourth on a 26-yard kick. Terry Kirby's seven-yard TD run—the 49ers' first points since the opening quarter—put San Fran back on top, but Aikman found Eric Bjornson from the 6-yard line with 2:45 remaining to force overtime. The Cowboys needed just one possession to win it. Aikman went 5-for-5 on the march, and Emmitt Smith's 16-yard burst made the field goal a chip shot.

GAME 11: Getting Their Kicks

Cowboys 21 vs. Green Bay 6

November 18: In one of the most dominant performances in NFL history by a team that failed to reach the end zone, Chris Boniol matched an NFL record with seven field goals as Dallas showed Green Bay it was not ready to give up its NFC stronghold. Two 45-yarders were among his five first-half three-pointers, and the Packers trailed 18–0 in the second half before finally getting on the board.

"It wasn't like they were a bunch of chip shots," said Boniol, whose final kick was his shortest at 28 yards. The Cowboys kept Green Bay to less than 100 rushing yards and 200 passing yards in this Monday night game. Troy Aikman threw for 206 yards for Dallas.

GAME 12: Scoring Troubles Persist

N.Y. Giants 20 vs. Cowboys 6

November 24: This time, no TDs meant no chance. Unlike the previous week, when the Cowboys won on seven field goals, their inability to reach the end zone—as it usually does—resulted in a one-sided loss. It marked the first time in six years Dallas went without a TD in back-to-back games.

The Giants' offense failed to cross the goal line until the fourth quarter, but Tito Wooten returned a fumble recovery 54 yards for a TD that produced a 13–3 Giants halftime lead. Dallas rushed for just 33 yards against a physical New York defense. Emmitt Smith gained only 18 on 11 carries.

The Playmaker

Michael Irvin Walked the Walk as Troy Aikman's Favorite Target

When Michael Irvin arrived in Dallas in 1988, his license plate read "PLYMKR"—as in *playmaker*. Pretty brash stuff for a rookie, but that was Irvin. He wore fur coats and jewelry and talked up a storm on the field. When he caught a pass downfield, he indicated with his arm, emphatically, that it was a first down.

Irvin talked the talk, and he walked the walk…right into the Hall of Fame.

The 15th of 17 siblings, Irvin helped University of Miami coach Jimmy Johnson win the 1987 national championship. The team was known for its showboating. But when Irvin routinely pointed to the sky after scoring a touchdown, he did so to honor his father, who had died when Michael was 17.

While fans wondered how the hot-dogging receiver would fare under coach Tom Landry, Irvin responded by earning a starting job and averaging 20.4 yards per catch as a rookie. With the emergence of Troy Aikman as a star in 1991, the Cowboys and Irvin began to flourish. That year, Michael caught 93 passes for an NFL-high 1,523 yards, earning his first of five consecutive Pro Bowl invitations.

Despite all the bling, Irvin was a warrior who fought defensive backs for position. He fearlessly skied for catches in the middle of the field, knowing that safeties would make him pay the price. Irvin ran sharp routes, and Aikman often connected with him on perfect timing passes. Troy often expressed his fondness for Michael, his favorite target for 11 years.

From 1991–98, Irvin recorded seven 1,000-yard seasons. In 1995, he amassed 11 100-yard

Michael Irvin (No. 88) during the game against the Phoenix Cardinals at Sun Devil Stadium on November 22, 1992, in Tempe, Arizona. The Cowboys defeated the Cardinals 16–10. (Photo by Rogers Photo Archive/Getty Images)

games, setting an NFL record. On September 20, 1992, he burned the Phoenix Cardinals for 210 receiving yards and three touchdowns. In Super Bowl XXVII, he caught two touchdown passes in the span of 18 seconds.

Irvin was named to the NFL All-Decade Team for the 1990s, and he achieved the goals he set early in his career: to become the greatest receiver in team history and make the Ring of Honor. In his 12-year NFL career, played exclusively with the Cowboys, Michael obliterated team records with 750 receptions and 11,904 yards.

Irvin's large appetites frequently got him into trouble. During and after his career, he was arrested multiple times for drug possession. His 2007 Hall of Fame induction sparked controversy, but his speech in Canton—a heartfelt expression of love for friends and family and repentance for his sins—brought football fans to tears. He said about raising his two sons, "I say, 'God, I have my struggles and I made some bad decisions, but whatever you do, whatever you do, don't let me mess this up.'"

GAME 13: Smith Bounces Back

Cowboys 21 vs. Washington 10

November 28: Emmitt Smith followed one of the worst games of his career with a sensational one. His second-quarter TD run ended the Cowboys' string of nine straight quarters without crossing the goal line, and it was the first of his three TDs in the Thanksgiving Day game. He carried 29 times for 155 yards.

While the Cowboys were controlling the day on the ground, Redskins QB Gus Frerotte was throwing two interceptions. Dallas ran for 201 yards and held Washington to 46 yards on 16 carries.

GAME 14: Overcoming Adversity

Cowboys 10 at Arizona 6

December 8: Dallas' third drug-related suspension of the year—this one concerning defensive tackle Leon Lett—left the Cowboys short-handed on the front seven. Yet one would not have known it by the way Dallas kept the Cardinals out of the end zone.

Arizona failed to score after two first-half field goals had them up 6–0 at the break. Troy Aikman hit Michael Irvin from 50 yards for the game-winning TD in the third quarter, and Chris Boniol added a field goal in the fourth. Irvin was a one-man machine in an otherwise defensive game, catching eight passes for 198 yards.

GAME 15: Fifth Straight Eastern Title

Cowboys 12 vs. New England 6

December 15: After the Cowboys' 1–3 start and their up-and-down attack, few might have pegged the Cowboys for a fifth consecutive NFC East title. Yet that's exactly what they earned thanks again to stout defense in a TD-less win over the Patriots.

Chris Boniol kicked four field goals as the Cowboys won for the second time without the benefit of a TD. Adam Vinatieri had given New England a 6–0 edge on two first-quarter field goals, but that was all the Patriots could manage against an opportunistic Dallas squad. Drew Bledsoe was intercepted three times, twice by Darren Woodson.

GAME 16: RFK Finale a Scrimmage

Washington 37 vs. Cowboys 10

December 22: With nothing to play for, Dallas rested its starters in the last game played at RFK Stadium. The Redskins made the most of the opportunity, drubbing a group made up largely of reserves.

Troy Aikman and Emmitt Smith did not play for the Cowboys. Jason Garrett and Wade Wilson divided the QB duties. Terry Allen ran for three TDs, and Gus Frerotte threw for 346 yards for Washington.

GAME 17: Wild-Card Rout

Cowboys 40 vs. Minnesota 15

December 28: For a team not used to playing in the wild-card round, Dallas sure looked like it knew what it was doing. George Teague returned an interception 29 yards for a TD, and the offense came to life after struggling in the regular season.

Emmitt Smith amassed 116 yards on just 17 carries and scored twice, Michael Irvin caught eight passes for 103 yards, and Troy Aikman guided an efficient attack that put the Vikings in a huge hole from which they never emerged. Dallas led 30–0 at halftime.

GAME 18: End of the Road

Carolina 26 vs. Cowboys 17

January 5, 1997: Dallas failed to reach the NFC title game for the first time since 1991, ending a season that brought scrutiny, scandal, and suspensions. It also saw inept offense for much of the year, and Troy Aikman's three interceptions in this divisional playoff game continued the trend.

Aikman's two-yard TD toss to Daryl Johnston in the second quarter was the only time the Cowboys crossed the goal line. They also scored on a second-quarter safety and got three Chris Boniol field goals, but Josh Casey kicked four for Carolina, which took a 17–11 halftime lead and never trailed thereafter.

1997

STRUGGLES COST SWITZER

Cowboys Miss Playoffs for First Time Since 1990

The Big Three were still producing. Emmitt Smith topped 1,000 rushing yards, Michael Irvin caught 75 balls for 1,180 yards and eclipsed 10,000 yards for his career, and Troy Aikman remained one of the most respected signal-callers in the game.

But the Cowboys were not themselves, going 6–10 in 1997 and ending a five-year run of playoff appearances. Some offered, by way of an explanation, that Coach Barry Switzer had lost the locker room—the players, not the coaches, were now running the show. Others pointed to a lack of motivation among veterans who had already won three championship rings.

For any number of reasons, Dallas finished the year and the Switzer era with five successive losses.

GAME 1: Hot August Start

Cowboys 37 at Pittsburgh 7

August 31: Trying to put the turmoil of 1996 behind, Dallas routed Pittsburgh in a rare August opener. It was simply no contest. Troy Aikman threw for four TDs, including two to Michael Irvin. The club's top receiver covered 153 yards on seven receptions.

The Cowboys registered three sacks and two takeaways while keeping the Steelers off the scoreboard until the fourth quarter before a stunned Three Rivers Stadium crowd of 60,000-plus. By then, it was 37–0. Aikman threw for 295 yards.

GAME 1: Finally, Cardinals Celebrate

Arizona 25 vs. Cowboys 22 (OT)

September 7: Kevin Butler's winning field goal in overtime clanged off the upright, but it was hardly the most damage done to the yellow post. Seconds later, fans swarmed from the stands to pull down the structures after Arizona snapped a run of 13 consecutive losses to the Cowboys.

From the Dallas perspective, it never should have come to that. The Cowboys held a 22–7 third-quarter lead on five Richie Cunningham field goals and a four-yard fumble return by Chad Hennings. Arizona, though, got two late TD passes from Kent Graham and a two-point conversion toss from Graham to Rob Moore to force overtime. Emmitt Smith rushed for 132

yards for the Cowboys, who committed 12 penalties for 115 yards.

GAME 3: Eagles Botch One

Cowboys 21 vs. Philadelphia 20

September 15: Chris Boniol, automatic from short range, was all set to boot his former team with a 22-yard field goal with four seconds remaining. However, Eagles holder Tom Hutton dropped the snap, costing Boniol the chance and Philadelphia the game.

It was a game the Eagles led 20–9 in the final quarter, but Richie Cunningham kicked his fourth and fifth field goals for Dallas, and Troy Aikman gave the Cowboys a late lead on a 14-yard pass to Anthony Miller. The Eagles got 106 rushing yards from Ricky Watters, recovered two fumbles, and led most statistical categories. But they hurt their own cause with 13 penalties for 107 yards. Dallas was flagged just three times.

GAME 4: Defense Comes Through

Cowboys 27 vs. Chicago 3

September 28: An anemic offensive showing was not enough to keep Dallas down against the reeling Bears. Deion Sanders returned a punt 83 yards for a TD and Troy Aikman tossed two TD passes on an otherwise nondescript day to keep Chicago winless.

Dallas gained only 180 yards, its worst output in six years. While Raymont Harris ran for 120 yards for the Bears, the Cowboys' Emmitt Smith managed just 43 of his team's 56-yard total on the ground. Two turnovers and eight penalties helped keep Chicago from scoring after an early field goal put them up 3–0.

GAME 5: Dallas Self-Destructs

N.Y. Giants 20 vs. Cowboys 17

October 5: Key turnovers, 11 penalties for 119 yards, and a failure to finish drives were by far the biggest culprits in the Cowboys' loss at Giants Stadium. As a result, the Giants won despite gaining only 57 rushing yards and 166 total yards.

Troy Aikman threw for 317 yards and Emmitt Smith ran for 91 as Dallas dwarfed New York's yardage total and controlled the clock for more than two-thirds of the game. None of it mattered on the scoreboard, where the Giants' Tito Wooten made a dent with a 61-yard third quarter interception return that gave his team the lead for keeps.

GAME 6: No Luck in D.C.

Washington 21 vs. Cowboys 16

October 13: Their first trip to Jack Kent Cooke Stadium resulted in no change of fortune for the Cowboys. They fell into a 21–3 hole and could not emerge to avoid falling behind the first-place Redskins in the NFC East.

Each team recorded three sacks, less than 300 offensive yards, and a turnover. The difference was the goal-line nose of Stephen Davis, who scored two TDs for the Redskins and ran for a game-high 94 yards. Troy Aikman and Michael Irvin hooked up on a final-quarter TD pass to make it a one-score game, but the Cowboys failed to score on a late drive that started in Washington territory.

GAME 7: Walker Goes Deep, Beats Jags

Cowboys 26 vs. Jacksonville 22

October 19: He was an older and wiser Herschel Walker than the one who started his NFL career with the Cowboys and gained them a bevy of talent when he was traded to Minnesota. Back with Dallas now, Walker showed his knack for the big play and breakaway speed were still there.

Walker broke free for a 64-yard winning TD after catching a Troy Aikman pass midway through the fourth quarter. It capped a game in which the Cowboys bounced back from consecutive losses with 24 first downs, 337 yards of offense, and no turnovers. Aikman threw for 262 yards and two TDs, reviving Dallas after the Jaguars had erased a 19–7 deficit in the second half.

GAME 8: Dizzying Loss

Philadelphia 13 vs. Cowboys 12

October 26: Troy Aikman sustained the fifth concussion of his career in the first quarter and

Dallas played without four injured regulars, but the crushing blow came with 45 seconds left in the game. That's when Rodney Peete threw an eight-yard TD pass to unheralded tight end Chad Lewis to deflate the Cowboys.

Emmitt Smith topped 100 rushing yards for the second time of the season with 126 on 25 carries, and Wade Wilson went 11-for-16 in relief of Aikman, who was sacked twice and hit hard in the first quarter. The winning pass was

the only TD of the game. Richie Cunningham kicked four field goals for Dallas.

GAME 9: End Zone Still Elusive
San Francisco 17 vs. Cowboys 10

November 2: For the fifth time in as many road games, the Cowboys fell. And finding a reason was again not difficult—Dallas scored just three

Wide receiver Michael Irvin catches a touchdown pass as defensive backs Marcus Robertson and Darryll Lewis of the Tennessee Oilers try to stop him during the November 27, 1997, game at Texas Stadium in Irving, Texas. The Oilers won 27–14. (Photo by Getty Images)

offensive TDs in those setbacks, including one in San Francisco.

Michael Irvin's five-yard TD grab from Troy Aikman in the first quarter gave Dallas a 7–0 lead, but the 49ers held the visitors to a field goal after that. Meanwhile, Garrison Hearst dashed for 104 yards for San Francisco and a TD, and William Floyd bulled in for the winning TD early in the final quarter. Aikman threw for 218 yards but also had two interceptions.

GAME 10: Defense Swarms Cardinals

Cowboys 24 vs. Arizona 6

November 9: Dallas avenged its first loss in 13 meetings with the Cardinals in dominant form, sacking Arizona QBs nine times and finally ending their offensive woes, too. Troy Aikman went 15-for-22 with a TD to Herschel Walker, while Emmitt Smith and Sherman Williams each ran for score.

Eight different receivers caught passes for the Cowboys, while it was all the Cardinals could do to get a pass launched. Tony Tolbert and Shante Carver made two sacks apiece.

GAME 11: Comeback a Success

Cowboys 17 vs. Washington 14

November 16: Winning back-to-back games for the first time since September took some doing. Washington led 14–6 in the fourth quarter, but Troy Aikman hit Michael Irvin on a six-yard TD pass and Vinson Smith on the tying two-point conversion, then Richie Cunningham won it on a 42-yard field goal with four seconds remaining.

Dallas celebrated, and with good reason. They prevailed in a turnover-free game, got 99 rushing yards from Emmitt Smith, and watched Irvin carve up the secondary for 91 yards on seven catches. Cunningham kicked three field goals in the victory.

GAME 12: Packers End Drought vs. Dallas

Green Bay 45 vs. Cowboys 17

November 23: Green Bay had been thwarted eight straight times by the Cowboys, the prior seven at Texas Stadium. Finally getting a shot at Dallas before those loud, hearty Lambeau Field cheeseheads, the Packers took full advantage.

In a game that featured rushing, passing, interception-return and fumble-return TDs, along with plenty of cold and wind, Green Bay blew the Cowboys out of the park. Dorsey Levens ran for 190 yards and a TD, Brett Favre fired four TD passes, and the Packers ran up more than 400 total yards. Deion Sanders' 50-yard interception return in the second quarter produced the only Dallas TD until Emmitt Smith's run in the fourth made it a game at 24–17. However, Green Bay tacked on three more TDs to pull away.

Neon Deion
Deion Sanders Brought the Spectacular to Big D

He was Tom Landry's worst nightmare. Deion Sanders seemed to violate every code in the old-school football handbook. He wore bandanas and diamond-studded gold chains. He high-stepped into the end zone before breaking into a touchdown dance. He went by "Neon Deion" and "Prime Time," cut two hip-hop albums, and had an ego the size of Texas.

"I'm going to give the kids something to dream about," he once said about himself. As for personal appetites, he said, "I don't think of buying a home, I think of owning 50,000-square-foot mansions."[1]

Although he talked the talk, Sanders walked the walk. In fact, he walked it faster than virtually everybody. The NFL Network once ranked Deion as the fourth fastest player in NFL history, with a 40-yard dash time in the 4.20s. His blinding speed made him one of the best cornerbacks and kick returners in NFL history, as well as a burner for four major-league baseball teams.

A two-time consensus All-American at Florida State, Sanders led the nation in punt return average in 1988. He believed he could play professional baseball and football, and he did, suiting up for both the New York Yankees and Atlanta Falcons in 1989. He played nine seasons with the Yankees, Braves, Reds, and Giants, tallying a .263 batting average and 186 stolen bases. In the 1992 World Series, he rapped .533 for Atlanta.

After earning three Pro Bowl invitations with the Falcons and the NFL Defensive Player of the Year Award with San Francisco in 1994, Dallas won the "Deion Sweepstakes" in 1995,

Cornerback Deion Sanders (No. 21) runs with the ball in a game against the San Francisco 49ers on November 2, 1997, in San Francisco, California. (Photo by Glenn James/NFL, Getty Images)

making the free agent the highest paid defensive player in the league ($35 million for seven years). Sanders missed half of 1995 with an injury, but he made a big impact for the Cowboys upon his return, including a 47-yard reception in the Super Bowl.

Sanders' speed allowed him to stick with every receiver in the league, and he often got to the ball first (53 career interceptions). In his five seasons with Dallas, he intercepted 14 passes and earned AP first-team All-Pro honors from 1996 to 1998. Deion could break open a game at cornerback, receiver, kick returner, and punt returner. In 1996, he became the first two-way starter in the NFL since Chuck Bednarik, who had retired in 1962. For the Cowboys in '98, Sanders returned two punts for touchdowns.

Love him or hate him, he definitely gave kids something to dream about.

GAME 13: Dallas Coughs One Up

Tennessee 27 at Cowboys 14

November 27: Three Troy Aikman interceptions and two lost fumbles handed Tennessee a rather easy Thanksgiving Day win, as a nation watched the "Team of the Ninties" move to the brink of postseason elimination. The miscues allowed the Oilers to win a game in which they passed for only 81 yards.

Four of the five Dallas turnovers came in the first half, allowing Tennessee to build a 24–7 lead at the break. Aikman threw for 356 yards and two TDs, but the picks had a greater impact on the outcome. The Cowboys also could not stop a barrage of five- and six-yard gains by Eddie George, who carried 34 times for 110 yards.

GAME 14: Panthers Prevail

Carolina 23 at Cowboys 13

December 8: More than 63,000 turned out at Texas Stadium, and by the time the game was over, it was clear the Dallas fans were supporting a team on its last leg. Fred Lane battered the Cowboys for 138 rushing yards, Kerry Collins threw two TD passes, and the Panthers yielded a mere 78 rushing yards to all but eliminate Dallas from playoff contention.

Troy Aikman's 52-yard fourth-quarter TD pass to Michael Irvin cut the Panthers' lead to 20–13 and gave the Dallas fans a glimmer of hope. But Carolina added a late chip-shot field goal to clinch a game in which it never trailed.

GAME 15: Over and Out

Cincinnati 31 vs. Cowboys 24

December 14: What had been clear for weeks became official at Cinergy Field—the Cowboys' dominant run was over. They were eliminated from playoff contention for the first time since 1990, though they could hang their helmets on a furious fourth-quarter comeback attempt.

The Bengals led 31–10 before Troy Aikman completed late scoring strikes to David LaFleur. The Cowboys got the ball back twice more but could not score again. Boomer Esiason threw for 269 yards and two scores for the Bengals, who got 127 rushing yards from Corey Dillon. Michael Irvin and Anthony Miller caught nine balls each for Dallas.

GAME 16: Lackluster Finale

N.Y. Giants 20 at Cowboys 7

December 21: There were as many empty seats at Texas Stadium as full ones as the end neared, and speculation ran rampant that Barry Switzer's coaching office would soon be vacated, too. With the way the Cowboys played out the string, losing for the fifth straight time, change seemed the logical solution.

Just 184 total yards, three turnovers, and nine penalties seemed a fitting way to close a frustrating year in which the offense never put it together. The Dallas defense finally kept a foe from producing a 100-yard rusher, but the Giants did not need one. They opened a 20–0 halftime lead and sacked Cowboys QBs four times. Emmitt Smith scored the lone Dallas TD.

1998

GAILEY BRINGS 'EM BACK

First-Year Coach Sparks Return to Postseason

The 1998 season was a big one for Chan Gailey and Emmitt Smith. The former left his job as Steelers offensive coordinator to take over a Cowboys team that had won three Super Bowls in the 1990s. He turned a 6–10 club from the previous year into a 10–6 operation, winning the NFC East title in the process.

Smith surpassed Tony Dorsett as the Cowboys' career rushing leader, enjoying a resurgent year with 1,332 yards on the ground. With help from the likes of Troy Aikman, Deion Sanders, and Michael Irvin, Gailey and Smith put Dallas back in the postseason where their fans had been accustomed to seeing them.

Three straight losses in November and December had those fans sweating at 8–6, but wins over division rivals Philadelphia and Washington closed Gailey's first regular season as an NFL head coach.

GAME 1: Big Debut for Gailey

Cowboys 38 vs. Arizona 10

September 6: Totaling 444 yards and its highest point total in nearly four years, Dallas made a winner of Chan Gailey in his debut as head coach. Troy Aikman ran for two TDs and threw for two more, Emmitt Smith rushed for 124 yards, and Michael Irvin caught nine passes for 119.

The defense was impressive, too. The Cowboys limited the Cardinals to 45 rushing yards and hounded Jake Plummer into a 14-of-33 passing day. Aikman, meanwhile, was 22-of-32 for 256 yards.

GAME 2: Collared in Colorado

Denver 42 vs. Cowboys 23

September 13: Troy Aikman broke his left collarbone and the Cowboys had their feel-good start smashed at Mile High Stadium. The Broncos rolled up 515 offensive yards and got 191 rushing yards and three TDs from Terrell Davis in a game they never trailed.

Jason Garrett relieved the injured Aikman and completed 14-of-19 passes for 113 yards. John Elway passed for 268 and two scores for Denver, while Davis ran virtually untouched for first-quarter TDs of 63 and 59 yards to start the rout.

GAME 3: Prime Time Performance

Cowboys 31 at N.Y. Giants 7

September 21: Deion "Prime Time" Sanders put on a *Monday Night Football* show for the ages, returning an early punt 59 yards for a TD and a late interception 71 yards for a score to single-handedly outscore the Giants. Sanders also caught a 55-yard pass from Jason Garrett, who started for the injured Troy Aikman.

Garrett gave Dallas the lead for good on an 80-yard second-quarter TD pass to Billy Davis. The Cowboys' defense took over from there. In addition to the interception-return score, they picked off two other passes, recovered a fumble, and sacked the Giants four times.

GAME 4: Offense Anemic in Loss

Oakland 13 at Cowboys 12

September 27: Jason Garrett lost for the first time in four games as a starter, throwing two crushing second-half interceptions against the Raiders. The first came with the Cowboys at the Oakland 7-yard line in the third quarter. The second squandered a potential tying field-goal attempt with Dallas at the Raider 43, down 13–10 in the last two minutes.

Those miscues, however, were not the only trouble for Garrett and the offense. The Cowboys rushed for just 68 yards and lost a fumble. Defensively, they allowed Napoleon Kaufman to run for 116 yards and did not register a takeaway, but Oakland never trailed. The final margin was set when the Raiders gave up an intentional safety in the final seconds.

GAME 5: Another Gaudy Win
Cowboys 31 at Washington 10

October 4: Dallas continued turning its victories into blowouts, routing an opponent for the third time. This one put the Cowboys all alone atop the NFC East. Jason Garrett fired only three incompletions in 17 pass attempts, and Dallas had two 100-yard rushers in the same game for the first time in more than 20 years.

Emmitt Smith ran for 120 yards and a TD, while Chris Warren needed only 14 carries to compile 104 yards and two scores, thanks to a 49-yard burst against the struggling 'Skins. Washington QB Trent Green absorbed four sacks and was intercepted by Deion Sanders.

GAME 6: Panthers Finally Tamed
Cowboys 27 vs. Carolina 20

October 11: The Cowboys beat the Panthers for the first time thanks to big days from Jason Garrett, Emmitt Smith, Michael Irvin, and Ernie Mills. Garrett threw for 287 yards and two scores, hitting Irvin six times for 146 yards and Mills five times for 110. Smith carried 21 times for 112 yards and a TD.

Yet even with those big performances, the Cowboys did not put away the Panthers until a desperation heave on the final play fell incomplete. Steve Beuerlein threw for 286 yards and three TDs—two to Raghib "Rocket" Ismail that gave Carolina an early 14–3 lead. Garrett then directed the Cowboys to 24 straight points.

GAME 7: Offense Grounded
Chicago 13 vs. Cowboys 12

October 18: As was the case in another 13–12 loss three weeks earlier, mistakes killed the Cowboys. That time, it was interceptions. This time, it was a 2-for-14 conversion rate on third down and 11 penalties for 92 yards. Jeff Jaeger kicked the winning field goal, a 29-yarder, with 11 seconds remaining.

Dallas self-destructed inside Bears territory, capitalizing on just one of its deep drives with a David LaFleur TD run for a 12–7 third-quarter lead. But just 236 yards of offense, coupled with the Cowboys' penalty penchant, determined their fate at Soldier Field. The Bears also failed to reach 300 offensive yards.

GAME 8: Rested and Ready
Cowboys 34 at Philadelphia 0

November 2: With Troy Aikman back under center, the Cowboys roared out of their bye week to devour the Eagles at Veterans Stadium. Aikman threw for a modest 171 yards but directed a turnover-free attack and got the support of Emmitt Smith's 101 rushing yards. A dominant defense helped, too.

Dallas shut out an opponent for the first time in more than two years. Deion Sanders and Darren Woodson intercepted Bobby Hoying passes, and the Cowboys registered three sacks. The Eagles were flagged 11 times in their second shutout loss of the season.

Head coach Chan Gailey looks on during the October 4, 1998, game against the Washington Redskins at Jack Kent Cooke Stadium. The Cowboys defeated the Redskins 31–10. (Photo by Getty Images)

GAME 9: Smith Gains Record
Cowboys 16 vs. N.Y. Giants 6

November 8: Emmitt Smith rushed for 163 yards to surpass Tony Dorsett as the Cowboys' career rushing leader. Dallas needed that kind of effort from its franchise back on a day when Troy Aikman played the final three quarters with a sliced index finger on his throwing hand.

Dismal weather fit the game perfectly as the clubs bumbled to five field goals through three quarters. The Cowboys led 9–6 entering the fourth, when Aikman hit Eric Bjornson from the 2-yard line for the game's only TD. Gary Brown rushed for 119 yards on just 15 carries to lead the Giants in a game that served as evidence that the NFC East was not what it once was.

GAME 10: Dallas Holds On
Cowboys 35 at Arizona 28

November 15: A 28–0 lead, as it turned out, was no rout for the Cowboys. Instead, they clung for dear life before finally holding off a late charge by the Cardinals. Emmitt Smith rushed for 118 yards and three TDs, the final one giving his team a 35–14 lead in the third quarter. But Jake Plummer capped a 465-yard passing day with two more scoring strikes, and Dallas barely escaped with its third straight win when Arizona ran out of time in Cowboys territory.

Plummer went 31-for-56 while throwing for three TDs and the second-highest passing yardage total ever against Dallas. On the other side, Troy Aikman was an efficient 14-of-18 for 208 yards and one TD as the Cowboys relied largely on the ground game.

GAME 11: Overcoming Obstacles
Cowboys 30 vs. Seattle 22

November 22: Dallas was its own worst enemy, racking up 15 penalties for 129 yards. Countering those miscues, though, were 465 yards of offense—enough to overcome the ugliness and post a fourth consecutive victory. Troy Aikman threw for 296 yards, connecting with 10 different receivers, and two TDs.

Aikman's biggest miscue, an interception, was returned 25 yards for a TD by 300-pounder Sam Adams in the second quarter as Seattle took its only lead, 16–14. A Richie Cunningham field goal put the Cowboys up 17–16 at the half, and fourth-quarter TDs by Billy Davis and Chris Warren stretched the lead to 30–16.

GAME 12: Moss Makes Mark
Minnesota 46 at Cowboys 36

November 26: This Thanksgiving Day game was fun to watch, unless you were a defensive coordinator...or perhaps a Dallas fan. Randall Cunningham threw four TD passes—three long ones to Randy Moss—and never let his Vikings fall behind despite a career-high 455-yard passing day from Troy Aikman. The Cowboys gave up more points than they had since allowing 50 to Cincinnati in 1985.

Troy's Protectors

There Were Five Big Reasons Aikman's Jersey Stayed So Clean

Troy Aikman was sacked a mere 28 times in 30 regular-season games during 1994 and '95, enjoying more time in the pocket than any other QB of his era. Between 1991 and '95, Emmitt Smith led the NFL in rushing four times on his way to the league's career yardage mark. Would Aikman and Smith have been terrific players on other teams? Certainly. Would they have been all-time greats had they not played for the Cowboys, behind one of history's most dominant offensive lines? Fortunately for them, it's a question no one can answer definitively.

Aikman and Smith benefited from a luxury few players at their positions have ever enjoyed to their extent. Guards Nate Newton and Larry Allen, tackles Erik Williams and Mark Tuinei, and center Mark Stepnoski combined to earn 30 Pro Bowl honors in the 1990s. They were hulking, strong, mean, and athletic. They pummeled defensive linemen to create gaping holes on running plays and used every technique and trick—legal and otherwise—to keep pass rushers away from Aikman. Columnist Skip Bayless called them, over a stretch of four years, the "biggest, baddest offensive line in NFL history."[1]

The best of them all may have been Allen. The quiet 320-pounder who once sprinted 50 yards to chase down and tackle Saints linebacker Darion Conner from behind was named to a staggering 10 Pro Bowls. Seven of those honors came consecutively beginning in 1995, a feat every bit as impressive as the 700 pounds he once bench-pressed.

Williams, considered the best right tackle of his day, brought his 6'6", 324-pound frame to the Pro Bowl four times in the 1990s and was a unanimous All-Pro first-teamer in '93. Newton was the most quotable and affable of the bunch, unless you were an opposing

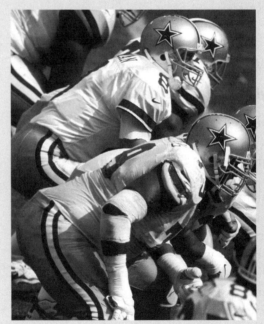

Quarterback Troy Aikman was protected by one of the league's most respected offensive lines.
(Photo by Al Messerschmidt/Getty Images)

lineman. In between his radio gigs and locker-room pranks, he made six Pro Bowls and two All-Pro squads while powering three Super Bowl winners in a four-year span.

Perhaps the best thing the Cowboys had going for them up front was chemistry. In an age when clubs were always looking for the quick fix, the core group stayed together for the better part of the mid- to late-1990s, giving Aikman, Smith, and the rest of the Dallas offense a unique comfort zone in executing their game plan.

"Like most quarterbacks, if you can get to him then you can disrupt things," Giants defensive lineman Keith Hamilton once said of Aikman. "But he has that great offensive line, and he usually barely gets touched."[2]

Between 1992 and '95, the Cowboys ranked second in the NFL in total offense three times and finished third the other year. Literally and figuratively, their big men were front and center.

Moss was unstoppable. The big, speedy, and athletic receiver caught scoring strikes of 51, 56, and 56 yards. They were his only catches of the day. Cris Carter caught seven balls for 135 yards and one TD for the Vikings, while Michael Irvin gave the Cowboys 10 grabs for 137 yards. Despite Aikman's 34-of-57 performance, Dallas could not catch the Vikings.

Emmitt Smith's third-quarter TD whittled what had been a 21–6 disadvantage down to 24–19, but Minnesota kept pouring it on. Smith added two more TD runs in the fourth quarter, but neither brought his team within single digits.

GAME 13: Offense Lays Egg

New Orleans 22 vs. Cowboys 3

December 6: One week after topping 500 offensive yards in a high-scoring loss to Minnesota, Dallas set a dubious franchise record with a grand total of eight rushing yards—yes, eight—at the Superdome. Emmitt Smith carried 15 times for six yards in the game as the Cowboys' top ground gainer. "We stunk," Smith said.

It was a notch in the belt of the New Orleans front seven and a sign of the work to be done for Dallas. The Cowboys led 3–2 after one quarter (Troy Aikman gave up a safety on an intentional grounding penalty), but Kerry Collins threw two TD passes in the second stanza and the Saints were never challenged.

GAME 14: Dallas Drops Third Straight

Kansas City 20 vs. Cowboys 17

December 13: Unable to get its ground game in gear, Dallas lost its third straight game and once again put off clinching a playoff spot for another week. The Cowboys ran for 51 yards—43 more than their previous week's output, but it wasn't enough to make their offense a serious postseason threat.

The Chiefs broke open a 3–3 game when Bam Morris and Rich Gannon ran for third-quarter TDs. Troy Aikman fired two fourth-quarter TD passes for the Cowboys but could never pull his team back to even on the scoreboard. Morris ran for 137 yards, while Dallas committed the game's only two turnovers.

GAME 15: East Is Theirs Again

Cowboys 13 vs. Philadelphia 9

December 20: The offense was still plodding and the defense trying to adjust without an injured Deion Sanders, but Dallas was back on top in the NFC East. The Cowboys earned the division title with a win over a three-win Eagles team that typified a down year in the once-proud division.

It did not take much on a soggy day at Texas Stadium. Emmitt Smith carried 25 times for 110 yards, his first 100-yard rushing day in more than a month. The Cowboys gained just 248 total yards to Philadelphia's 356, but the Eagles could not find the end zone while Eric Bjornson ran for a seven-yard Dallas TD in the first quarter.

GAME 16: A Fine Finisher

Cowboys 23 vs. Washington 7

December 27: It meant nothing to their playoff scenario, but the Cowboys' victory in the regular-season finale was their most impressive performance in more than a month. They took control on two second-quarter TD runs by Emmitt Smith and stopped a Redskins team that had won six of its previous eight games.

Coach Chan Gailey rested many of his regulars in the second half. Troy Aikman attempted just 15 passes, completing 10, and Sherman Williams came off the bench to run for 90 yards on 23 carries.

GAME 17: Early Exit

Arizona 20 at Cowboys 7

January 2, 1999: The third time was no charm for Dallas. The Cowboys were unable to make it a three-game sweep of the Cardinals in one season, their wild-card loss at Texas Stadium coming largely on the pain of self-inflicted wounds.

Troy Aikman threw three interceptions, Richie Cunningham missed an early field goal, and Emmitt Smith was unable to pick up short yardage on a fourth-down play as Dallas was shut out for three quarters. By the time Aikman hooked up with Billy Davis on a six-yard fourth-quarter TD pass, the Cardinals had put 20 points on the board.

Adrian Murrell broke a 74-yard run against the Cowboys and caught a 12-yard TD pass in the first quarter that sent Arizona on its way.

1999

BEST DECADE CLOSES

Cowboys Finish 1990s Modestly at 8–8

The NFL's most accomplished team during the 1990s finished the decade with an 8–8 season, but it was not without fanfare. Michael Irvin made his 750th and final reception. Emmitt Smith became the NFL's all-time playoff rushing leader thanks to the Cowboys' unlikely wild-card berth at .500. And Troy Aikman became the winningest QB in a decade in NFL history, gathering 90 victories as a starter in the 1990s.

Still, owner Jerry Jones wanted a champion, meaning Chan Gailey had coached his final game with the Cowboys when they fell to Minnesota in the playoffs. After opening the year with three straight wins, Gailey's 1999 team failed to claim back-to-back games again. He was fired as head coach two days after the season finale.

GAME 1: Rocket Launch

Cowboys 41 at Washington 35 (OT)

September 12: Raghib "Rocket" Ismail capped his Cowboys debut by catching a Troy Aikman pass and taking it 76 yards for an overtime TD. It completed the largest Dallas comeback in history, as Washington led 35–14 with 11 minutes remaining after scoring 32 consecutive points.

If that was an eruption by the Redskins, the Cowboys' finish was pure fireworks. Emmitt Smith got it started on a short TD run. Then, as the Dallas defense stiffened, Aikman hit Michael Irvin with back-to-back TD passes from 37 and 12 yards. The three fourth-quarter TD drives covered 70, 66, and 90 yards.

Ismail, who finished with eight catches, broke open down the middle on a play-action pass in OT. It was the same play on which he dropped a sure TD in the first quarter. The teams combined for 1,045 offensive yards in the wild opener. The QBs, Aikman and Brad Johnson, each passed for 350-plus yards, and each team had a 109-yard rusher (Smith and Stephen Davis).

GAME 2: Defense Turns It On

Cowboys 24 vs. Atlanta 7

September 20: Emmitt Smith rushed for 109 yards for the second straight game, and a defense that yielded more than 500 yards in a wild opening win dominated the Falcons. Dallas

recorded four sacks, intercepted three passes, and recovered a fumble.

Smith scored twice in leading the Cowboys to a 17–0 third-quarter lead. Troy Aikman passed for just 109 yards, but it was more than enough. The Cowboys started one scoring drive on the Atlanta 10 thanks to a turnover, and Greg Ellis returned an interception 87 yards for the final score.

GAME 3: Playoffs Remembered

Cowboys 35 vs. Arizona 7

October 3: Having been eliminated from the 1998 playoffs by the Cardinals, the Cowboys were delighted to unleash some defensive fury on their rivals. They forced five turnovers, two of which became TDs—one on a 32-yard interception return by George Teague, and another on a 98-yard fumble return by Greg Ellis.

That would have been enough "offense" for the win, but Troy Aikman added two TD passes, plus Rocket Ismail caught four balls for 104 yards and a score. Teague's pick came on Jake Plummer's first pass of the game.

GAME 4: Eagles' Dagger Stings

Philadelphia 13 vs. Cowboys 10

October 10: Dallas' first 3–0 start in four years came to a stunning end when the Eagles, on a route they called the "Dagger," got a 28-yard TD pass from Doug Pederson to Charles

Johnson with 1:07 to play. It completed their comeback from a 10–0 halftime deficit against a Cowboys team that was kicking itself for not putting the game away much sooner.

The opportunities were there, but three turnovers—including two Troy Aikman interceptions—hurt every bit as much as the fateful pass play. Emmitt Smith rushed for 114 yards for the Cowboys, and Duce Staley had 110 for the Eagles. The game was stopped for 20 minutes in the first quarter as Cowboys receiver Michael Irvin was taken to the hospital with a spine injury.

GAME 5: Déjà Vu
N.Y. Giants 13 vs. Cowboys 10

October 18: For the second straight week, and by the same frustrating score, the Cowboys surrendered just before the final gun. This time it was the Giants who got a 21-yard field goal from Brad Daluiso with five seconds remaining.

Tiki Barber was the main culprit. His 85-yard punt return in the fourth quarter gave New York a 10–3 lead in a defensive war. Dallas came back to tie it on a two-yard run by Emmitt Smith, but Barber caught a 56-yard pass from Kent Graham to set up the decisive kick. The Cowboys were held to 24 rushing yards on 25 carries. Aikman threw for 266.

GAME 6: Redskins Humbled
Cowboys 38 vs. Washington 20

October 24: Deion Sanders heard all week about certain Redskins players who were predicting they would burn him. Instead, Sanders returned a punt 70 yards for a TD, allowing the Cowboys to recover from back-to-back losses with an impressive win at Texas Stadium.

Dallas snared a 17–0 lead early in the second quarter and weathered two Washington flurries to hold on. The Sanders score was the clincher. Troy Aikman went 20-of-32 for 244 yards and two TDs.

GAME 7: Halloween Nightmare
Indianapolis 34 vs. Cowboys 24

October 31: Halloween in Indianapolis saw Dallas do a poor job of impersonating its championship-caliber teams. Instead, the Cowboys handed the Colts a treat in the form of blown opportunities, blown coverages, and a blown 10–0 lead.

Peyton Manning rallied Indy from that deficit by throwing for 313 yards and a TD. Edgerrin James ran for 117 yards and caught seven passes for 92 more, including a 54-yarder. Emmitt Smith rushed for two Dallas scores and Troy Aikman was a blistering 19-of-24 passing, but the Cowboys yielded 419 total yards to the up-and-coming Colts.

Linebacker Bill Romanowski (No. 53) of the Denver Broncos in action against wide receiver Billy Davis (No. 87) of the Dallas Cowboys during the September 13, 1998, game at Mile High Stadium in Denver, Colorado. The Broncos defeated the Cowboys 42–23. (Photo by Getty Images)

GAME 8: Mediocre at Midseason
Minnesota 27 vs. Cowboys 17

November 8: Emmitt Smith broke a bone in his hand, Troy Aikman suffered his sixth career concussion, and Dallas reached the midway point of the season at 4–4, a disappointing mark considering its 3–0 start. With Aikman in the game and Smith running for two second-quarter TDs, the Cowboys took a 17–0 lead.

After Smith went out in the second quarter and Aikman in the third, it was all Minnesota. The Cowboys gained just 41 yards after halftime as Jeff George threw for three Vikings TDs—two to Randy Moss and one to Cris Carter. That tandem combined for 15 receptions and 207 receiving yards.

GAME 9: Backups Bump Pack
Cowboys 27 vs. Green Bay 13

November 14: The Cowboys played without at least one of their Big Three—Emmitt Smith, Michael Irvin, and Troy Aikman—for the first time in more than a decade. Yet somehow they won handily.

Jason Garrett threw TD passes to David LaFleur and Rocket Ismail, and Chris Warren ran for 85 yards in place of the injured stars. Amid questions about their shorthanded attack, the Cowboys amassed a 20–3 lead thanks to dominant defense before the Packers found the end zone in the fourth quarter.

GAME 10: Road Woes Persist
Arizona 13 vs. Cowboys 9

November 21: The Cardinals gained just 207 total yards and committed the game's only two turnovers, yet they still managed to send Dallas to its fifth consecutive road loss. Arizona recovered from an early TD pass from Jason Garrett to David LaFleur to take a 13–7 lead in this battle of injury-depleted clubs.

A late safety gave the Cowboys a chance in the final two minutes. Deion Sanders returned the ensuing kick 31 yards to give his team great field position, but Garrett could not steer his club to the end zone. Emmitt Smith totaled 127 rushing yards in his return from a broken hand.

GAME 11: Marino Hangs Five
Cowboys 20 vs. Miami 0

November 25: Troy Aikman returned to QB the Cowboys, but it was his prominent counterpart who played the biggest role in the outcome. Dan Marino threw five interceptions in a turkey of a Thanksgiving Day outing.

Dexter Coakley returned one of his two picks 46 yards for the game's first points in the third quarter. Deion Sanders also snared two of Marino's throws as the leading passer in NFL history completed just 15 passes to his teammates in 36 attempts. Aikman got 65 of his 232 passing yards on one play, a scoring strike to Rocket Ismail that extended the margin to 17–0 in the fourth quarter. Emmitt Smith carried 31 times for 103 yards.

Team of the Nineties
Three Super Bowl Titles Gave Dallas Decade Dominance

Three NFL teams won more regular-season games than the Cowboys during the 1990s. None can make a legitimate claim to "Team of the Nineties" status. That belongs to Dallas alone.

Three Super Bowl victories in one decade will do that. The Cowboys reached four NFC title games and won six division championships. In each case, San Francisco managed one more than Dallas during the decade. The 49ers, though, made only one Super Bowl compared to the Cowboys' trio, and Dallas won all three. Like San Francisco, Buffalo and Kansas City earned more regular-season victories during the '90s, but the Bills dropped two Super Bowls to the Cowboys (four overall) and the Chiefs never made the big game.

With their victory in Super Bowl XXX there was no denying that the Cowboys were the "Team of the Nineties." (Photo by Otto Greule Jr. /Allsport, Getty Images)

Hindsight, of course, makes it easy to crown Dallas king of the '90s. In this case, its dynasty was one that opponents could see coming like a hurricane gaining strength over tropical waters even before the first of the Cowboys' championships that decade.

Sports Illustrated ran a story in its 1992 NFL preview edition headlined, "The Team of The '90s?" It was about Jimmy Johnson's up-and-coming Cowboys, speculating that the pieces were in place for a franchise stocked with young talent to race to the top and stay there.

"We're young and we're hungry, and we're developing an attitude," defensive coordinator Dave Wannstedt said in the article.[1]

Fortunately for the Cowboys, there was no *Sports Illustrated* "cover jinx" attached to this piece. This time, the publication was prophetic, pointing out that a young, franchise running back and a "keynote" running back were constants in all previous "teams of the decade." That season, Troy Aikman and Emmitt Smith—along with receiver Michael Irvin and an aggressive young defense—began a dominant run that produced three Super Bowl titles in four years.

Two of those teams that won more regular-season games in the decade were merely speed bumps along the way. Dallas (101–59 in 1990s regular-season games) beat San Francisco (113–47) in the NFC title game and Buffalo (103–57) in the Super Bowl in both '92 and '93. The 49ers avenged the conference title loss the following year, but Dallas returned to the top in '95.

The Cowboys returned to the playoffs three times in the decade's final four years, though their Super Bowl run was complete. And no team came close to stealing their rule of the '90s.

Five Dallas standouts—Irvin, Smith, Deion Sanders, Larry Allen, and Mark Stepnoski—were among the Pro Football Hall of Fame's All-Decade Team for the 1990s. It could hardly have been written any better.

GAME 12: Offense Crumbles

New England 13 vs. Cowboys 6

December 5: For the fourth time in 1999, Dallas gave up just 13 points and lost a football game. It was the Cowboys' sixth consecutive road loss, and the offense—or lack thereof—was again primarily responsible. Only late in the game did the Cowboys top 200 total yards.

New England broke open a 6–3 halftime lead on Terry Allen's short fourth-quarter TD run. Emmitt Smith rushed for 75 yards, but his Cowboys teammates combined for minus-12 yards on running plays, and the Patriots yielded only short completions to Troy Aikman. Dallas made only 12 first downs all day.

GAME 13: Home Sweet Home
Cowboys 20 vs. Philadelphia 10

December 12: Dallas won for the sixth time in as many home games behind Troy Aikman's 242-yard passing day. With Emmitt Smith leaving the game early with a groin injury and Michael Irvin still out, Aikman spread the ball to eight different receivers. His eight-yard TD pass to David LaFleur in the third quarter made it a 20–3 game.

Chris Warren ran for 92 yards and a TD after Smith went out. Dallas sacked Eagles QBs three times, intercepted Donovan McNabb once, and recovered two fumbles.

Game 14: Jets End Home Streak
N.Y. Jets 22 at Cowboys 21

December 19: John Hall's 37-yard field goal in the fourth quarter sent Dallas to its first loss of the year at Texas Stadium. Actually, the boot was simply the final blow. Others were self-inflicted in the form of eight penalties for 92 yards and two Troy Aikman interceptions.

A pass interference call in the end zone set up one Jets TD. A tripping call in the fourth quarter forced the Cowboys to punt, leading to New York's winning drive. Emmitt Smith ran for 110 yards and caught a TD pass, while receiver Rocket Ismail and tight end Eric Bjornson ran for scores. Curtis Martin rushed for 113 yards and Ray Lucas threw two scoring strikes for the Jets.

GAME 15: Bourbon Street Blues
New Orleans 31 vs. Cowboys 24

December 24: Just when it appeared Dallas might finally win a road game, the Saints marched to two fourth-quarter TDs to overcome a 24–17 deficit to deliver the Cowboys' seventh straight loss away from home. The winning score came with 10 minutes to go, when Fred Weary picked up an Emmitt Smith fumble and raced 58 yards for a TD.

It was hardly the Cowboys' first big mistake in the Big Easy. Troy Aikman threw two interceptions, and his penalty-prone team committed 11 infractions, costing 86 yards. Smith ran for 110 yards and a TD. Aikman tossed two TD passes, and seven of his 23 completions went to rookie Jason Tucker, covering 128 yards.

GAME 16: Dallas Slips into Playoffs
Cowboys 26 vs. N.Y. Giants 18

January 2, 2000: For Cowboy fans, the good news was that Dallas capped a 7–1 home slate and secured a playoff berth in the last game of the season, an impressive win over the Giants. But the bad news was that Texas Stadium would not be the site of that postseason game. That concern, however, could wait a week.

On this day, Emmitt Smith rushed for 122 yards, Jason Tucker caught a 90-yard TD strike, Troy Aikman threw for 282 yards and two TDs, and the Cowboys did not commit a turnover. Defensively, Dallas gave up just 72 rushing yards, and many of Kerry Collins' 316 passing yards came after his team fell into a 16–0 hole. Tucker's long reception stretched it to 23–3 after three quarters.

GAME 17: Quick Trip

Minnesota 27 vs. Cowboys 10

January 9, 2000: Having lost their last seven games away from home, there was no reason to believe the Cowboys would find a welcome mat outside the Metrodome. And the Vikings made sure Dallas did not become the first NFL team to win a game after entering the playoffs with a record of .500 or worse.

The Cowboys showed how they got to such a mark by committing the game's only three turnovers and allowing Robert Smith to ramble for 140 yards on 28 carries. That was it, really. An Eddie Murray field goal and Emmitt Smith's five-yard TD run gave them a fleeting 10–3 lead early, but the Vikings rolled to 24 unanswered points thereafter.

Rocket Ismail caught eight passes for 163 yards, accounting for well more than half of Troy Aikman's 286-yard passing total. Jeff George threw three TD passes for the Vikings.

Y2K PRECAUTIONS

Longtime Assistant Campo Promoted to Head Coach

Dave Campo had been a Cowboys assistant for 11 years, spanning three Super Bowl titles, and he served as defensive coordinator during the 1995 championship run. In January 2000, he was promoted to head coach, becoming just the fifth one in club history.

Campo's job was a large one—turn the "Team of the Nineties" into a contender in the millennium. And his first season, in 2000, did not give a great indication about whether that might be possible.

Thirty-somethings Emmitt Smith and Troy Aikman gave him their all. The former rushed for 1,203 yards, but the latter played only 11 games. Both offense and defense struggled during a 5–11 campaign in which Dallas won only once each in September, November, and December.

GAME 1: Campo Opens with Thud
Philadelphia 41 at Cowboys 14

September 3: No one panicked when Dallas suffered through a winless preseason under new head coach Dave Campo. When the failures stretched to a game that matched a 1964 club record for the worst loss in a home opener, concern grew. After all, this one counted.

The Cowboys recorded 93 penalty yards—26 more than they gained on the ground and seven less than they gained through the air. They fell behind 24–0 in the first half and did not reach the end zone until the fourth quarter, at which time they trailed 41–6. Eagles running back Duce Staley, with 201 rushing and 61 receiving yards, outgained the Cowboys by 95 yards himself. Dallas QB Troy Aikman left with a concussion.

GAME 2: Road Slump Hits Nine
Arizona 32 vs. Cowboys 31

September 10: Dallas surrendered a 31–23 fourth-quarter lead to suffer its ninth consecutive road loss. It was the first for rookie Coach Dave Campo, but it was a frustrating way to squander what looked like an initial victory. Cary Blanchard kicked a 51-yard field goal and Jake Plummer drove the Cardinals 85 yards for the winning TD, hitting David Boston for 63 yards and Frank Sanders from the 17 for the score.

Randall Cunningham, playing for Troy Aikman (concussion), matched Plummer's 243 passing yards and threw for three Cowboys TDs. However, he threw four consecutive incomplete passes to end the game, unable to drive Dallas into range for a potential winning field-goal try.

GAME 3: Finally, a Road Win
Cowboys 27 at Washington 21

September 18: Dave Campo's first victory as Dallas head coach came in the most unlikely place—somewhere not named Texas Stadium. For the first time in 10 tries since the 1999 season opener, the Cowboys won a road game and celebrated before a record crowd of 84,000-plus at FedEx Field.

A double-digit underdog despite entering the game with a string of five straight wins over Washington, Dallas ran for 153 yards, made several big plays and, instead of fading with the game on the line, scored twice in the fourth quarter to keep its lead. Randall Cunningham threw for two TDs, including a 76-yarder to Chris Warren. Emmitt Smith ran for 83 yards and a TD, and the defense sacked Washington three times.

GAME 4: Aikman Returns to Boos
San Francisco 41 at Cowboys 24

September 24: Some at Texas Stadium were booing their team. Others were clearly letting Troy Aikman hear it. One week after backup QB Randall Cunningham directed Dallas to its first win, Aikman returned in a dud against the previously winless 49ers.

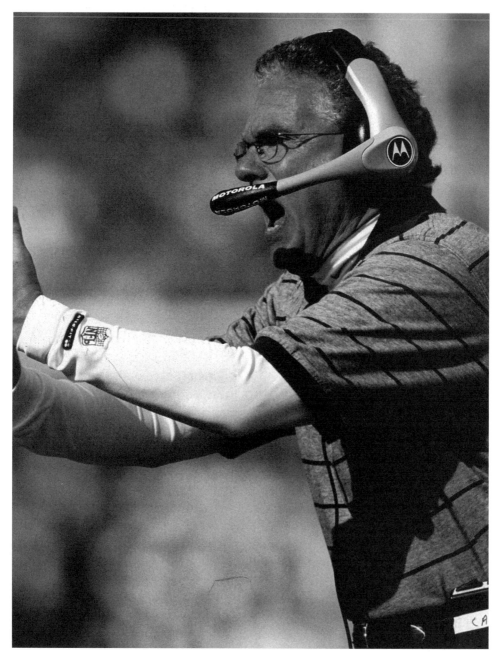

Head coach Dave Campo yells instructions during the December 3, 2000, game against the Tampa Bay Buccaneers in Tampa Bay, Florida. (Photo by Al Messerschmidt/Getty Images)

There was plenty of blame to go around. The defense allowed a 200-yard rusher for the second time in four weeks, as Charlie Garner went for 201 and a TD. The Cowboys were unable to spring Emmitt Smith, who gained just 31 yards. And yes, Aikman was not at his best in throwing for 197 yards and a TD with one interception—one of three Dallas turnovers. San Francisco's Jeff Garcia threw two TD passes apiece to Jerry Rice and Terrell Owens.

GAME 5: Back to Basics
Cowboys 16 at Carolina 13 (OT)

October 1: After not winning a road game in nine straight tries, Dallas made it two straight when rookie Tim Seder kicked a 24-yard field goal on the first OT possession. Seder got a second chance after missing a potential winner from 45 yards with one minute left in regulation time, his first miss in seven career attempts.

Though Seder ended the defensive battle, it was a return to simple fundamental football that gave him the chance. Emmitt Smith carried 24 times for 132 yards, 13 more than the Panthers totaled on the ground. The defense also recovered two Tim Biakabutuka fumbles and scored on a first-quarter safety.

GAME 6: Low Five for Aikman
N.Y. Giants 19 vs. Cowboys 14

October 15: Considering Troy Aikman tied a club record by throwing five interceptions, it was somewhat remarkable his team had a chance to win late. However, his desperation pass on the final play caromed off two players before falling to the turf to finish a 22-for-42 afternoon at Giants Stadium.

Aikman's third-quarter scoring pass to Robert Thomas gave the Cowboys a 10–7 lead, and Emmitt Smith's short TD run provided a 14–13 margin late in the third. But an Aikman interception set up the Giants for the winning TD in the fourth quarter from Ron Dayne, who ran for 108 yards. Each team committed nine penalties.

GAME 7: Putting It All Together
Cowboys 48 vs. Arizona 7

October 22: Looking like the Cowboys of old, Dallas won its first home game of the Dave Campo era and had a sellout crowd at Texas Stadium cheering on several counts. Troy Aikman threw two TD passes, Emmitt Smith scampered for 112 yards and a score, and the defense intercepted Jake Plummer three times.

It was the Cowboys' 11th consecutive regular-season win over the Cardinals, and it was never close after Wane McGarity returned a first-quarter punt 59 yards for a TD and a 14–0 lead. Only a late Michael Pittman TD run against defensive reserves kept the Cardinals from being shut out.

GAME 8: Jags Break Free in OT
Jacksonville 23 at Cowboys 17 (OT)

October 29: Alvis Whitted got loose for a 37-yard TD after catching a short pass from Mark

Magic Man

Emmitt Smith Made Defenders Disappear En Route to NFL Rushing Record

Football fans must wonder how Emmitt Smith and not one of history's other great backs became the all-time NFL rushing leader. Was he fast? Not especially; he ran the 40-yard dash in a sluggish 4.7 seconds. Big? Come on; he was 5'9". Powerful? Certainly, but he was not in the class of Jerome Bettis, and he was listed at a modest 216 pounds.

Without much of an explanation, his teammates early in his career simply called him "Magic Man." Smith had the Houdini-like ability to run through holes that seemingly didn't exist and then escape from the tacklers' grasps.

"He has a knack for hitting a hole at the right time," Cowboys fullback Daryl Johnston explained. "Sometimes it's a quick move, sometimes he'll cut back. Every game you see one move that's better than the last time."[1]

The magic began at Escambia High School in Florida, where Smith rushed for an unbelievable 8,804 yards. "For four years we did three things, and won two state championships doing them," said Escambia head coach Dwight Thomas. "Hand the ball to Emmitt, pitch the ball to Emmitt, throw the ball to Emmitt."[2]

Smith rushed for 3,928 yards at the University of Florida and an NFL-record 18,355 yards, including 17,162 in 13 years with the Cowboys (1990–2002). All told in prep, college, and pro football, Emmitt amassed 31,087 yards—the equivalent of 17.7 miles.

Emmitt Smith (top) leaps over a pile of defenders to score a touchdown on November 13, 1994, against the San Francisco 49ers at Candlestick Park in San Francisco, California. (Photo by Tony Tomsic/Getty Images)

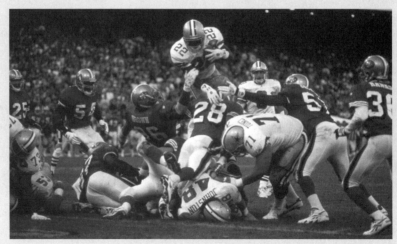

With the Cowboys, Smith had all the advantages: a mountain-moving offensive line, an explosive passing attack that softened the run defense, and Pro Bowl fullback Daryl Johnston laying blocks for him for 10 years. Emmitt's numbers were off the charts. From 1991–95, he topped 1,400 yards each year and led the NFL in rushing four times. He enjoyed his greatest season of all in 1995, when he rang up a career-high 1,773 rushing yards and an NFL record-setting 25 rushing touchdowns.

Amazingly durable and dependable, Smith set NFL records for rushing attempts (4,142) and consecutive 1,000-yard seasons (11). He established league marks with 164 rushing touchdowns and 78 100-yard rushing games.

A list of Smith's awards and honors could fill a book. Highlights include NFL MVP honors in 1993, eight Pro Bowl selections, three Super Bowl rings, and the MVP Award for Super Bowl XXVIII, when he rushed for 132 yards and two touchdowns against Buffalo.

Smith was inducted into the Cowboys Ring of Honor in 2005 and the Pro Football Hall of Fame in 2010.

Brunell to defeat Dallas in overtime. It capped a 20-for-24 three-TD passing day for Brunell, who outperformed the Cowboys' Randall Cunningham after the latter took over for an injured Troy Aikman.

Aikman suffered a back injury after absorbing a hard early tackle. The Jaguars turned Cunningham's interception and fumble into points, scoring all 17 of theirs in the second half for a 17–7 advantage. Cunningham led Dallas to a tying TD in the fourth quarter, finishing the drive on a run of his own from the 1-yard line. Each team had a 100-yard rusher—Fred Taylor for Jacksonville and Emmitt Smith for Dallas—but it was the Jaguars who made the clinching big play to end a five-game losing streak.

GAME 9: Another Marathon Loss
Philadelphia 16 vs. Cowboys 13 (OT)

November 5: Eagles fans were getting anxious, to say the least, with their team trailing 10–0 to backup QB Randall Cunningham and the Cowboys in the fourth quarter. Some even headed for the exits. But they missed another Dallas collapse for a second straight overtime loss.

A fumble by Dallas fullback Robert Thomas set up David Akers for the winning kick, which gave Philly its only lead of the game. The Cowboys had swiped the ball from the Eagles on a Barron Wortham interception of Donovan McNabb earlier in the extra session. It should never have come to that, as far as Dallas was concerned.

Emmitt Smith's seven-yard TD run provided a 7–0 halftime lead, and second-half field goals from Tim Seder made it 10–0 and 13–10. Smith rushed for 134 yards. The Cowboys, though, tripped themselves with 12 penalties.

GAME 10: Aikman, Seder Shine
Cowboys 23 vs. Cincinnati 6

November 12: Troy Aikman's back was in pain, but his right arm felt just fine. Aikman returned from an injury to throw for 308 yards. His 35-yard TD pass to James McKnight in the opening quarter gave Dallas the lead for good.

It was perhaps the most memorable game of Tim Seder's career. In the second half, the rookie kicker booted three field goals and ran for a one-yard TD on a fake to help his team pull away. Dallas sacked Akili Smith three times and held him to 68 passing yards on a 10-of-25 completion rate.

GAME 11: Ravens Blank Dallas
Baltimore 27 vs. Cowboys 0

November 19: One of the best defenses seen in the NFL in recent years dominated Dallas in this one. The Ravens intercepted Troy Aikman three times and held the Cowboys to 192 total yards, including just 55 on the ground, in sending them to their first regular-season shutout in 152 games.

Dallas crossed the Baltimore 40-yard line only three times. Two of those drives ended with interceptions; the other ended with a missed field goal. With 187 rushing yards and 20 receiving yards, Jamal Lewis outgained the Cowboys all by himself. Trent Dilfer delivered long TD passes to Qadry Ismail and Shannon Sharpe.

GAME 12: Ailments Grow Worse
Minnesota 27 at Cowboys 15

November 23: Emmitt Smith ran for 100 yards on just 12 carries in a Thanksgiving Day game against the Vikings. After he left the game in the third quarter with concussion-like symptoms—joining six other Dallas starters who had been sidelined in recent weeks—there was little hope of stopping the inevitable.

Randy Moss caught two third-quarter TD passes from Daunte Culpepper as Minnesota broke open a one-point halftime margin. Moss racked up 144 yards on seven receptions, and Culpepper was a cool 15-of-22. Troy Aikman threw for 276 yards for the Cowboys, who lost despite totaling 404 offensive yards.

GAME 13: Dallas Drubbed Again
Tampa Bay 27 vs. Cowboys 7

December 3: Dallas became the first team in NFL history to allow three opposing rushers 200-yard games in one season. This time it was Warrick Dunn darting through gaping holes for 210 yards and two TDs on just 22 attempts—an average of 9.5 yards per carry.

While Dunn was taking off with the ball on TD scampers of 70 and 4 yards, the Cowboys were simply dropping it. They fumbled four times, losing three, and also coughed up a Troy Aikman interception. Their only score came on a four-yard third-quarter run by Emmitt Smith, but Dunn and the Bucs had 20 points on the board by then.

GAME 14: One to Count On
Cowboys 32 vs. Washington 13

December 10: No matter how bad things got for the Cowboys in this and recent seasons, they could usually count on one thing—beating Washington. They did so for the seventh consecutive time, the longest streak for either team in the long rivalry, ending a three-game slide in the process.

Dallas smashed the 'Skins for 242 rushing yards, including Emmitt Smith's 150 on 23 carries, and got four Tim Seder field goals. Troy Aikman left the game after absorbing a big first-half hit from LaVar Arrington, but Anthony Wright took over and completed a turnover-free attack by the Cowboys. Dallas sacked Jeff George five times and gave up just 79 rushing yards.

GAME 15: Wright Game in Debut
N.Y. Giants 17 at Cowboys 13

December 17: Second-year QB Anthony Wright made his first NFL start against one of the best teams in the league, directing the Cowboys to a surprising 13–0 halftime lead before things fell apart. Wright's lone interception led to a Giants TD that sparked a 17-point second-half outburst, and a ferocious New York pass rush sacked the newcomer five times.

Wright, playing for an injured Troy Aikman, finished 13-of-25 for 119 yards. The conservative game plan netted only 145 total yards for the Cowboys, but a short run by Emmitt Smith and two Tim Seder field goals gave them the edge at the break. For the Giants, who got TDs from Tiki Barber and Amani Toomer, it was a matter of being patient and jumping on Dallas mistakes.

GAME 16: Blanked Again
Tennessee 31 vs. Cowboys 0

December 25: A Dallas team that once went 151 consecutive games without being shut out was whitewashed for the second time in six starts. It was a cold Christmas in Nashville and one of the most frigid feelings in franchise history for the visitors, who gained six first downs and 95 total yards while committing five turnovers.

Despite that performance, the Cowboys trailed just 7–0 at halftime, but Steve McNair's 15-of-19 first-half completion rate set an ominous tone. The Titans scored on both fumble and interception returns in the second half en route to their 13th win of the year. Dallas QB Anthony Wright was 5-for-20 with two interceptions.

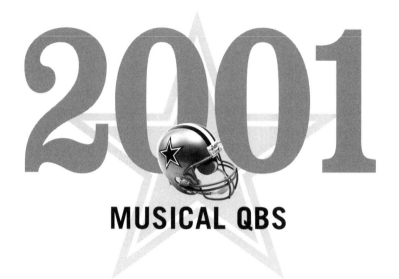

MUSICAL QBS

Without Aikman, Cowboys Spin a Revolving Door

Troy Aikman's retirement announcement in April 2001 started a new chapter in Cowboys history. Some thought the Quincy Carter era had begun. As it turned out, Carter was the first of four QBs to start for Dallas in 2001. None fared particularly well, and their struggles contributed to a second straight 5–11 season.

Anthony Wright, Clint Stoerner, and Ryan Leaf followed Carter under center, but none could spark the offense from doldrums that had Dallas finishing 31st among 32 teams in scoring offense. The bright light of that attack was again Emmitt Smith, who notched his 11th consecutive 1,000-yard season and moved into second place on the all-time NFL rushing chart.

GAME 1: Too Much Bucs Defense

Tampa Bay 10 at Cowboys 6

September 9: Expected to be one of the top defensive teams in the NFL, Tampa Bay kept Dallas out of the end zone and intercepted QB Quincy Carter in the last two minutes to erase the Cowboys' last hopes. Dallas made just eight first downs and 127 total yards.

Carter, the team's new QB, went just 9-of-19, passing for 34 yards and throwing two picks. His longest completion covered 11 yards. Brad Johnson threw for 195 yards for Tampa Bay and scored the game's only TD on a fourth-quarter keeper.

GAME 2: After Break, a Second Loss

San Diego 32 at Cowboys 21

September 23: Football outcomes seemed a bit less important after the events of September 11, but that didn't keep the Cowboys from lamenting their second loss after the league took a week off following the terrorist attacks on America. Doug Flutie passed for 348 yards and two TDs against a soft Dallas defense.

With Quincy Carter nursing a thumb injury he suffered in practice, Anthony Wright had an erratic day under center with three TD passes and three interceptions. San Diego took a 17–0 lead, saw Dallas pull within 20–14 at halftime, and widened the margin in the second half.

GAME 3: Not Even Close

Philadelphia 40 vs. Cowboys 18

September 30: Dave Campo's coaching job was looking more precarious by the week. On this afternoon, his Cowboys committed five turnovers and were unable to slow the Eagles, surrendering 26 points in the second quarter alone.

Donovan McNabb threw for three TDs and the Eagles got six more points when Damon Moore returned a Cowboys fumble 10 yards to the end zone in that big second stanza. It was one of four lost fumbles by Dallas. Anthony Wright started at QB for the second straight game and went 7-of-23 before he was pulled.

GAME 4: Slump Reaches Six

Oakland 28 vs. Cowboys 21

October 7: The Raiders overcame a late charge, sending the Cowboys to their fourth loss of the season and sixth straight dating to 2000. Dallas played some of its best football of the year in trying to rally from 14–0 and 28–7 deficits, but the Raiders had too much firepower.

Rich Gannon threw for 209 yards and a TD, and Tyrone Wheatley ran for two Oakland scores. Anthony Wright enjoyed his most productive day at QB, throwing for two TDs without an interception while completing 14-of-22 passes. Kicker Tim Seder scored a third-quarter Dallas TD on a fake field goal.

Quincy Carter heads downfield against the San Francisco 49ers during the December 30, 2001, game at Texas Stadium in Irving, Texas. The Cowboys won 27–21. (Photo by Ronald Martinez/ Getty Images)

GAME 5: First Victim: Redskins, Of Course

Cowboys 9 vs. Washington 7

October 15: The sight of the Redskins on the schedule could make the Cowboys smile even in the darkest of times. It was far from pretty, but Dallas snapped a six-game losing streak by beating Washington for the eighth straight time, riding three Tim Seder field goals and strong defense.

Washington took a 7–3 fourth-quarter lead on a TD pass from Tony Banks to Michael Westbrook, but Seder connected twice thereafter, winning the game on a 26-yarder on the final play. John Nix forced a Stephen Davis fumble that Greg Ellis recovered with 2:40 to go to set up the winning drive. Anthony Wright directed the Cowboys 59 yards for the victorious boot.

Emmitt Smith rushed for a season-high 107 yards while his defensive teammates held the Redskins to 226 total yards. Dallas gained nearly that many on the ground (211).

GAME 6: Unknown QB Leads Cowboys

Cowboys 17 vs. Arizona 3

October 28: Texas native Clint Stoerner, an undrafted second-year QB, gave the Cowboys their first back-to-back wins in more than two years. Replacing the injured Anthony Wright as the third Dallas starter of the year, he didn't need to do anything special thanks to support from defense and the ground game.

Stoerner ran for a six-yard TD to break a 3–3 tie in the third quarter. He was 9-of-19 passing for 93 yards and added 23 rushing yards on seven carries. Dexter Coakley then returned an interception 10 yards for a clinching score. It was one of four Cowboys takeaways and one of two interceptions of Jake Plummer.

GAME 7: Third Straight Not to Be

N.Y. Giants 27 vs. Cowboys 24 (OT)

November 4: Enter another QB. One week after guiding the Cowboys to victory, Clint Stoerner was pulled late in the game for the newly signed Ryan Leaf. Stoerner's four interceptions helped Dallas squander leads of 17–0 and 24–7, as the Giants rallied for 20 unanswered points in the second half and overtime.

Leaf, a former second-overall draft choice who flopped in San Diego, took over late in regulation time but could not rescue the Cowboys from the collapse. Kerry Collins threw two of his three TDs in the second half to lead the Giants back, and Morten Andersen kicked the winning OT field goal from 42 yards. Dallas scored twice on interception returns—Mario Edwards' 71-yarder and Dexter Coakley's second in as many weeks.

GAME 8: Record Road Loss

Atlanta 20 vs. Cowboys 13

November 11: Dallas tied a club record by falling on the road for the ninth consecutive time. Ryan Leaf, the team's fourth starting QB

The Maverick: Jerry Jones
Cowboys' Hands-On Owner Dares to Dream...and Do

Who is the tall dark stranger there? Maverick is his name,
Riding the trail to who-knows-where, luck is his companion, gambling is his game.
—George Thorogood, "Maverick"

Jerry Jones has been called a maverick, and the hat certainly fits. It was a huge gamble firing living legend Tom Landry, the only coach who had ever patrolled the Cowboys sideline, and bringing in former college teammate Jimmy Johnson after purchasing the team in 1989. Jones had co-captained Arkansas to an 11–0 record in 1964, playing guard and never had football far from his mind even while making a fortune in the oil industry.

"If this doesn't work," Jones once said, "I'd be known as the idiot who wanted to coach so bad he blew it all. So this has to work."[1]

It worked, all right. Most of what Jones touches works, and the Cowboys were no exception. Since he bought the team and named himself general manager, Jones has presided over three of the franchise's five Super Bowl championships—all in a four-year span of the 1990s. Dallas has also captured eight NFC East titles under his watch, including five consecutively, beginning in 1992.

Along the way, Jones has made countless friends and more than a few enemies. His oft-overbearing on-field presence has been questioned, as has his building of a $1.15 billion palace of a stadium during a nationwide recession. Not all of his coaching hires—see Chan Gailey and Dave Campo—have been productive or popular. His falling-out with Bill Parcells

Jerry Jones is the bigger-than-life owner of the Dallas Cowboys. (Photo by Paul Jasienski/Getty Images)

caused his biggest-name hire to flee, and his 2010 extension of Wade Phillips' tenure was greeted with mixed reaction among fans. He sometimes says the wrong thing at precisely the wrong time.

Though it all, Jones refuses to flinch. With every success comes a group of people wanting to knock you down, he figures. So he takes the criticism and stashes it alongside his numerous civic, financial, and entrepreneurial awards. Heck, Barbara Walters chose this guy as one of "America's 10 Most Interesting People" in 1994. What could possibly be wrong?

"I am very aware that we have the visibility that we have," said Jones, who married college sweetheart and former Arkansas beauty pageant winner Gene Jones more than 40 years ago and has three children. "With all of that goes a lot of criticism. Not just a teaspoonful, but a large amount of criticism. It's structured that way."[2]

A maverick would not have it any other way.

in eight games, was sacked three times, intercepted once, and held to 114 passing yards.

Still, Dallas built a 13–7 halftime lead on a ground attack powered by Troy Hambrick, who finished with a career-high 127 yards on 20 carries. Then came a familiar second-half collapse. The Falcons scored all 13 second-half points, getting a game-high 148 rushing yards from Maurice Smith. Atlanta prevailed despite getting just seven completions from QBs Michael Vick and Doug Johnson.

GAME 9: No Mercy From Eagles

Philadelphia 36 at Cowboys 3

November 18: The Eagles kicked the Cowboys while they were down and enjoyed every minute of it. Dallas' most one-sided defeat since 1988 featured 10 Cowboys penalties for 81 yards, four Cowboys turnovers, and two defensive TDs by Philadelphia. In fact, the Eagles scored just one offensive TD all day—the game's opening score.

Ryan Leaf threw two interceptions and was unable to stop Jeremiah Trotter or William Hampton from returning them across the goal line. Duce Staley powered the Eagles' running attack with 102 yards.

GAME 10: Inspired Rally Falls Short

Denver 26 at Cowboys 24

November 22: Fans had every reason to exit Texas Stadium with their heads down after three-plus quarters in which Denver dominated, building a 26–3 lead. Those who stayed nearly witnessed a miracle as three fourth-quarter TDs put a scare into the Broncos before they secured their victory by recovering a final Cowboys onside kick.

Ryan Leaf led two TD drives that Troy Hambrick capped with one-yard TD runs. In between, Reggie Swinton returned a punt 65 yards for a Dallas score. Leaf overcame his early struggles to complete half of his 32 passes for 193 yards. The Broncos held Dallas to 27 rushing yards, got 118 of their own from Mike Anderson, and rode four field goals by Jason Elam.

GAME 11: Slump Busters

Cowboys 20 at Washington 14

December 2: For the second time in as many meetings, the Redskins were the cure for an ailing Dallas team. It was the ninth consecutive Cowboys win over their NFC East rivals, easily a record in a series dating to 1960.

Considering the state of this Dallas team, Washington had to be thinking this was its chance. The Cowboys entered the game having lost nine straight on the road, but Emmitt Smith ran for 102 yards and a TD and Quincy Carter threw a 64-yard TD pass to Rocket Ismail in his first game since an early season surgery to repair a hamstring injury. The TD toss highlighted a run of 13 straight Cowboys points to pull away from a 7–7 tie in the fourth quarter. Dallas rushed for 215 yards.

GAME 12: Carter Delivers Comeback

Cowboys 20 vs. N.Y. Giants 13

December 9: After going more than two years without back-to-back wins, Dallas did it twice in the same season. Quincy Carter and Rocket Ismail hooked up 10 times for 118 yards, and the Cowboys pounced on two turnovers in a game New York led 13–3 in the second quarter.

Carter, scrambling nimbly to avoid the rush and hitting 17-of-26 passes for 194 yards, directed two second-half scoring drives that produced the win. Emmitt Smith ran for the tying TD in the third quarter, and Carter connected with Jackie Harris for the winning TD in the fourth.

GAME 13: Chilly Setback

Seattle 29 vs. Cowboys 3

December 16: The icy rain of Seattle helped stall a Dallas team coming off two straight wins. So did a Quincy Carter interception that Ike Charlton returned for a Seahawks TD and a plodding Cowboys offense that gained only 10 first downs and 218 total yards.

Dallas committed all six of the game's penalties and its only turnover. Seattle's Ricky Watters ran for 104 yards and a TD. The Seahawks also got a safety from their defense, which by itself produced three times as many points as the Cowboys.

GAME 14: Bound for Last

Arizona 17 vs. Cowboys 10

December 23: Beating the Cardinals was the only chance for the Cowboys to avoid a rare last-place finish in the NFC East, but it was not to be. Quincy Carter was intercepted twice, and Dallas botched the snaps on two field-goal attempts against Arizona.

The Cardinals scored all their points in the second quarter, beginning with Ronald McKinnon's 24-yard TD return of a Carter interception. Carter responded with a 45-yard TD strike to Reggie Swinton for a 10–7 edge, but there were few Dallas highlights after that. The Cowboys made 21 first downs to the Cardinals' 11 and outgained Arizona by more than 100 yards, but their three turnovers cost them the game. Emmitt Smith amassed 128 yards on the ground.

GAME 15: All Is Not Lost

Cowboys 27 vs. San Francisco 21

December 30: For the first time all season, Dallas had one of its four QBs pass for 200 yards. Quincy Carter completed 15-of-25 attempts for 241 yards and two TDs and ran for a score in his best career game—and the best for the Cowboys all year. Emmitt Smith rushed for 126 yards, and Joey Galloway caught six passes for 146 yards and a TD.

The Dallas defense shone, too, holding the 49ers to 56 rushing yards. San Francisco led 14–10 at halftime, but Carter's one-yard scoring run and his 47-yard TD strike to Galloway—both in the third quarter—put the game in the Cowboys' control. Jon Hilbert made it a 20–10 lead in the fourth with his second field goal. Carter led a turnover-free attack.

GAME 16: Smith Sets Record

Detroit 15 vs. Cowboys 10

January 6, 2002: Emmitt Smith set an NFL record by reaching 1,000 rushing yards for the 11th straight season, but the Cowboys otherwise finished the season with a whimper. Smith carried 18 times for 77 yards and the game's first TD, but Detroit outgained the visitors by more than 100 yards to close the Pontiac Silverdome with a victory.

Jon Hilbert's field goal gave Dallas a 10–9 lead in the fourth quarter, but Ty Detmer threw a 16-yard pass to Johnnie Morton for the winning TD. Detmer passed for 242 yards and two TDs for the Lions, who won for just the second time all season.

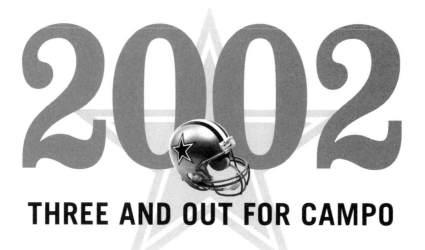

THREE AND OUT FOR CAMPO

Third Consecutive 5–11 Season Highlighted by Smith's Record

Emmitt Smith became the NFL's career rushing king in 2002, but his surpassing of Walter Payton was not nearly enough to save Dave Campo's head coaching job after a third straight 5–11 campaign. That's because, although Smith was still productive and his run to the record had kept fans interested, the club was in need of young talent to step up in support. There had been few signs of such during Campo's three seasons.

For the second straight year, the Cowboys finished second-to-last in scoring offense. Over the last 10 games, they scored seven points or less five times. Chad Hutchinson and Quincy Carter were clearly not the QBs of the present or the future. A retooled defense was showing some progress, but Dallas went searching for a big-time head coach, ultimately landing the "Big Tuna"—Bill Parcells—before 2003.

GAME 1: Milestone Start for Texans

Houston 19 vs. Cowboys 10

September 8: Nearly 70,000 screaming fans at Reliant Stadium witnessed a stunning opener for the stadium and their new franchise as the Texans became the first expansion club in 41 years to win its debut. For the Cowboys in the state they once ruled, it might have been a new low.

David Carr overcame six Dallas sacks to throw two TD passes. One got Houston off to a 10–0 lead, and the other, a 65-yarder to Corey Bradford in the fourth quarter, broke the tie and put the Texans up for good. They added a late safety, too. The teams combined for almost 200 penalty yards on 20 flags. Quincy Carter went just 13-of-30 in the passing department for the Cowboys.

GAME 2: Defense Rises Up

Cowboys 21 vs. Tennessee 13

September 15: It was fitting that Dexter Coakley's 52-yard interception return for a third-quarter TD gave the Cowboys the lead for keeps because it was defense that lifted them to their first win. They kept the Titans out of the end zone for the final three quarters while sacking QB Steve McNair three times.

Quincy Carter bounced back from an awful opener in Houston to pass for 240 yards and two TDs without a turnover. After Coakley's big play gave the Cowboys a 14–10 edge, Carter delivered a 38-yard TD pass to Joey Galloway

to stretch the margin. Greg Ellis sacked McNair twice.

GAME 3: Another Eagle Beating

Philadelphia 44 vs. Cowboys 13

September 22: Coach Dave Campo said the Eagles were the type of team his Cowboys were trying to become. These days, there was a considerable gap between the two. Canyon might be a better description.

Dallas QB Quincy Carter fired two interceptions and lost a fumble while his good friend Donovan McNabb threw for 287 yards and three TDs and ran for another score. In five straight losses to the Eagles, the Cowboys had been outscored by 116 points. McNabb was also the game's leading rusher with 67 yards. Dallas scored its lone TD on a breathtaking 100-yard kickoff return by Reggie Swinton in the first quarter.

GAME 4: Cundiff Kicks Rams

Cowboys 13 at St. Louis 10

September 29: It ranked among Dave Campo's greatest wins as Cowboys coach, and it was not secured until rookie Billy Cundiff's 48-yard field goal tumbled over the crossbar on the game's final play, sending a Rams team thought to be a Super Bowl favorite to its fourth consecutive loss. Cundiff's teammates tackled him, ran screaming all over the Rams' indoor home, and congratulated Quincy Carter on his signature win.

The QB led the winning nine-play drive in the final 1:27 without a timeout, topped 200 passing yards for the third straight week, completed 26-of-36 throws, and rushed for 26 yards. He completed passes to nine different teammates. The Cowboys intercepted two Rams QBs and held St. Louis to 93 rushing yards.

GAME 5: Dallas Misfires

N.Y. Giants 21 at Cowboys 17

October 6: Kerry Collins threw three TD passes, including the game-winner in the fourth quarter, while Quincy Carter overthrew a wide-open Antonio Bryant on a play that would have put the Cowboys back on top late in the game. Those were the most glaring differences between these two NFC East rivals at Texas Stadium.

Carter hit Bryant for a five-yard score to give Dallas a 17–14 lead early in the fourth. After Collins and Marcellus Rivers hooked up for the Giants' final score, however, Carter missed badly with no defenders near Bryant downfield. It was one of 19 incomplete passes for Carter on a 42-attempt, 262-yard day. New York won despite committing the game's only two turnovers.

GAME 6: Happy Birthday for Carter

Cowboys 14 vs. Carolina 13

October 13: On his 25th birthday, Quincy Carter gave the Cowboys a surprise celebration. Trailing 13–0 with less than four minutes to go, Carter threw an 80-yard TD pass to Joey Galloway that bounced off a safety's helmet and a highlight-reel 24-yarder to Antonio Bryant, who made a breathtaking juggling grab with 56 seconds to go, to send Texas Stadium into a frenzy.

It was the kind of excitement that had been lacking from the Cowboys for the better part of a few seasons and more than three quarters in this game. The Panthers jumped on top on a TD pass from Rodney Peete to Brad Hoover and two second-half field goals. After 56 minutes, the Cowboys had accomplished nothing on the scoreboard and little aside.

Then lightning struck. Carter completed less than half of his passes but finished with 225 yards—his fifth consecutive 200-yard game. Dallas made nine penalties, but Carolina softened the blow with 14 of its own that cost 106 yards.

GAME 7: Desert Downer

Arizona 9 vs. Cowboys 6 (OT)

October 20: Dallas followed its most thrilling finish with an epic flop. Quincy Carter threw four interceptions and still the Cowboys could have prevailed if not for a botched PAT, Billy Cundiff's missed 49-yard field-goal try in the closing seconds, or the redemption of Arizona kicker Bill Gramatica in overtime.

Gramática missed twice in the fourth quarter but split the uprights from 40 yards in OT for the win. Carter's miscues were the most glaring of many troubles for Dallas, though his 78-yard

TD pass to Antonio Bryant in the third quarter would have given his team a lead if not for a dropped snap on the extra-point try. Two of Carter's picks came from inside the red zone deep in Cardinals territory.

GAME 8: Smith NFL Rushing King
Seattle 17 at Cowboys 14

October 27: An otherwise nondescript home loss to Seattle will forever have a place in Dallas football lore. That's because Emmitt Smith broke Walter Payton's NFL career rushing record, and he did so on his first 100-yard game of the season.

Smith carried 24 times for 109 yards and a score. Fittingly, he shook off tackles on an 11-yard gain—the kind of run Smith virtually patented in Dallas—in the final quarter to eclipse Payton's 16,726 career yards. Payton's widow Connie delivered a recorded postgame video message to Smith, and a banner was lowered honoring the achievement as tears filled Smith's eyes.

It might have been a near-perfect day for Cowboys fans if not for Ryan Lindell's 20-yard field goal with 25 seconds remaining. The kick clinched defeat for Dallas, which gave QB Chad Hutchinson his first NFL start. He went 12-of-24 for 145 yards and a TD.

GAME 9: Booted Again
Detroit 9 vs. Cowboys 7

November 3: Losing on late field goals was nothing new to Dallas. This time, it was Jason Hanson who kicked a 43-yarder with 48 seconds remaining as a struggling Lions team topped the Cowboys for the second straight season. In reality, though, Dallas' struggles had more to do with a team kicking itself.

Cowboys QB Chad Hutchinson was sacked five times, and his offense put the ball on the ground three times—losing two—while crossing the goal line just once. Detroit won despite gaining just eight first downs and 148 total yards. Hanson's three field goals produced all the points the Lions needed.

GAME 10: Hutchinson Struggles
Indianapolis 20 vs. Cowboys 3

November 17: Dallas continued its quest to see if Chad Hutchinson might emerge as a legitimate NFL starting QB, but such promise wasn't evident on this day. The former baseball standout hit 11-of-23 passes for just 131 yards and, for the second consecutive weeks, hit the turf five times on sacks.

The result was a TD-less attack at the RCA Dome that paled in comparison to Peyton Manning's 252-yard, two-score performance. Emmitt Smith shared ball-carrying duties with Troy Hambrick, but they combined for only 64 yards on 15 totes. Edgerrin James rushed for 106 for Indianapolis.

GAME 11: Offense Equals Win

Cowboys 21 vs. Jacksonville 19

November 24: Chad Hutchinson earned his first NFL victory in his fourth start, completing 16-of-24 passes for 301 yards and two TDs to Joey Galloway as Dallas halted a four-game losing streak. Galloway was easily his top target, catching seven balls for 144 yards.

After Galloway's 43-yard first-quarter scoring catch, the Cowboys never trailed. Hutchinson had some low points, fumbling for an early Jaguars safety and throwing two interceptions. But he also showed poise in leading Dallas to 405 total yards, including 73 rushing yards and a TD from Emmitt Smith. Fred Taylor ran for 100 yards for Jacksonville.

GAME 12: Redskin-Ready

Cowboys 27 vs. Washington 20

November 28: Not even Steve Spurrier could stop "The Streak" on this day. The first-year

Running back Emmitt Smith reaches the all-time rushing record in a 14–17 loss to the Seattle Seahawks on October 27, 2002. Smith surpassed Walter Payton's record of 16,726 rushing yards. (Photo by James D. Smith/NFL, Getty Images)

Redskins coach became the latest to fall to the Cowboys, who secured their 10th consecutive victory over their rivals. Emmitt Smith led the charge to double-digits, rambling for 144 yards on 23 carries.

Chad Hutchinson led Dallas back from a 20–10 second-half deficit with a big assist from his defense. Roy Williams returned one of Danny Wuerffel's three interceptions five yards for a TD that started the comeback. Hutchinson then threw his second TD pass, a 41-yarder to Joey Galloway, to put his team on top for good. Hutchinson engineered a turnover-free attack, while Washington coughed up the ball four times.

GAME 13: Cowboy Collapse
San Francisco 31 at Cowboys 27

December 8: Squandering a 10-point lead in the final seven minutes was no way for Dallas to try saving its coach's job. Dave Campo's hot seat grew warmer after Jeff Garcia fired two TD passes in that span, including an eight-yarder to Terrell Owens with 12 seconds remaining, to complete the winning surge and a 401-yard offensive day for the 49ers. Garcia threw three scoring strikes.

Emmitt Smith ran for two scores for the Cowboys. Woody Dantzler's 84-yard kickoff return and Smith's second TD run gave Dallas a 27–17 lead with those last seven minutes remaining, but that was all Garcia and the 49ers needed. Chad Hutchinson was intercepted twice in the loss.

GAME 14: Swamped and Swarmed
N.Y. Giants 37 vs. Cowboys 7

December 15: If Jimmy Hoffa's body was indeed buried under Giants Stadium, as urban legend held, it might have turned the other way for this game. The Cowboys stunk up the place, losing three turnovers and rolling over against a New York team that scored the game's first 37 points.

Ron Dayne and Tiki Barber combined for 161 rushing yards and three TDs on 30 carries, including a 60-yard dash by the latter. Cowboys QB Chad Hutchinson threw two interceptions and lost a fumble that Kenny Holmes returned 50 yards for a TD.

GAME 15: Phaltering Again
Philadelphia 27 at Cowboys 3

December 21: Six consecutive victories over the Cowboys produced only one close call for the Eagles, and this was not the one. Philadelphia held Dallas to nine first downs and 146 total yards, keeping the home team out of the end zone and not allowing them to convert a third down all day.

Shawn Barber returned a Chad Hutchinson interception 80 yards for a TD. That was more yardage than the Cowboys netted either rushing (68) or passing (78). Dallas put the ball on the Texas Stadium turf a whopping six times, losing two.

Schramm's-Giving Tradition

Visionary GM Saw Thanksgiving Football as a Path to Popularity

The Detroit Lions have been hosting Thanksgiving Day football, off and on, since the 1930s. NFL commissioner Pete Rozelle extended an offer to the other 15 teams in 1966, and 14 of them said "thanks but no thanks." The lone exception: Dallas Cowboys GM Tex Schramm.

Schramm saw things others missed. Most GMs might have considered placement in the NFL Eastern Division a death sentence with the Eagles, Giants, and Redskins as regular rivals. Schramm practically insisted on such placement for Dallas, seeing the chance to play before East Coast, big-city crowds as a way to increase his team's exposure and popularity.

So while the rest of the NFL sized up home Thanksgiving games as potentially risky attendance propositions or an infringement on family time for players and staff members, Schramm saw the chance for national-TV audiences and the growing of a fan base.

The Cowboys were granted that 1966 Thanksgiving Day game, a 26–14 win over the Cleveland Browns, and since then have hosted a game every Turkey Day except '75 and '77. Before ESPN and cable sports news provided national exposure for every team in the league, these games were

Thanks to Tex Schramm, most of us spend Thanksgiving with the Cowboys. (Photo by Wesley Hitt/Getty Images)

keys to the Cowboys' growth as "America's Team" just as Schramm had hoped. Holiday weekend sandlot and backyard games across the country had countless youngsters pretending to throw like Roger Staubach or catch like Bob Hayes.

Watching the Lions and Cowboys playing Thanksgiving football—usually in front of sellout crowds—has become something of a national pastime, as much an annual tradition as that post-dinner nap on a couch or recliner. Thanksgiving Day has also produced some of the great performances in Dallas history.

There were breakout games by backup QBs Clint Longley and Jason Garrett, leading the Cowboys to improbable wins 20 years apart. There was Leon Lett sliding across the icy turf to touch a blocked kick in a 1993 blunder. There was Tony Romo emerging with five scoring strikes in 2006, and Craig Morton rallying Dallas to a 1969 tie with the 49ers.

Schramm, the team's GM from its 1960 inception until 1989, made countless contributions to the Cowboys and several to the NFL, as well. He chaired the competition committee, was instrumental in bringing about instant replay, and embraced innovation like few other front-office men. He was inducted in the Pro Football Hall of Fame in 1991 and died in 2003 at age 83. Cowboys fans around the world owe Schramm a debt of gratitude every Thanksgiving Day when their team takes the field, proudly wearing home jerseys.

GAME 16: Final Humiliation
Washington 20 vs. Cowboys 14

December 29: Down as they were, the Cowboys could usually count on beating Washington but no longer. In what everyone from D.C. to Dallas was certain was Dave Campo's last game as Cowboys coach, the Redskins finally ended their series-long 10-game losing streak.

Redskins coach Steve Spurrier, who was promised a game ball from owner Daniel Snyder as soon as he ended the misery against Dallas, gladly accepted. His team never trailed in a game that contained nine turnovers and a defensive TD from each team. LaVar Arrington recovered a fumble for a Redskins score, and Roy Williams returned an interception 85 yards for the Cowboys. The Dallas offense did not reach the end zone until Chad Hutchinson threw a late TD pass to Antonio Bryant.

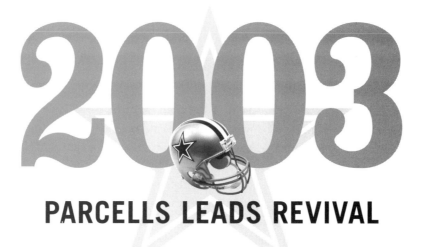

2003

PARCELLS LEADS REVIVAL

From the Ashes, It's 10 Wins and a Playoff Trip

The most famous coach since Tom Landry to guide the Cowboys was hired days after the 2002 season, and Bill Parcells got right to work. The team released NFL career rushing leader Emmitt Smith before Parcells' debut on the Dallas sideline, so it was a new-direction offense he took to battle in 2003.

Parcells' firing of Smith paid immediate dividends. The New York Giants' two-time Super Bowl winner won five of his first six games with Quincy Carter calling signals and Troy Hambrick carrying the rushing load.

Of course, Parcells made his name with defense, and that's where the Cowboys showed the greatest improvement. Their aggressive scheme yielded just 16.2 points per contest, second in the NFL, and kept Dallas in nearly every game on the way to 10 wins—double their total from each of the last three seasons—and a wild-card playoff berth, the club's first post-season trip since 1999.

GAME 1: Frustrating Debut

Atlanta 27 at Cowboys 13

September 7: Dallas gained more than 400 yards in the anticipated debut of Bill Parcells as head coach, but mistakes turned the effort into a two-TD loss at Texas Stadium. Big penalties, dropped passes, turnovers, and missed kicks were among them.

Aveion Cason broke a 63-yard TD run and Quincy Carter, in his return as starting QB, threw for 268 yards and a score, but he also gave up an interception and a fumble, and the defense could not keep Atlanta from seizing control in the fourth quarter. Doug Johnson threw for two Falcons TDs. Joey Galloway caught seven balls for 139 yards and a 49-yard score from Carter.

GAME 2: Cundiff Record Gets Win

Cowboys 35 at N.Y. Giants 32 (OT)

September 15: Billy Cundiff tied an NFL record with seven field goals in a game, and the Cowboys needed every one of them. A booming 52-yarder on the final play of regulation time and a 25-yarder in OT gave Bill Parcells his first win as Dallas coach, on the field of his former team, on ABC's *Monday Night Football*.

"One of the wildest ones I've ever been involved in," said Parcells, whose team blew a 15-point fourth-quarter lead before rallying to force OT. Kerry Collins tossed three TD passes for the Giants, and Quincy Carter passed for 321 Cowboys yards and ran for a score. For the second straight week, Dallas topped 400 yards of offense. But its top weapon was Cundiff's instep, which made good on all seven attempts.

GAME 3: "Home-Field" Advantage

Cowboys 17 at N.Y. Jets 6

September 28: Playing at Giants Stadium, his old stomping grounds, for the second time in as many games, new Cowboys coach Bill Parcells was feeling right at home. And just like old times, any victory was a good one. Troy Hambrick ran for a career-high 127 yards, and Parcells got a Gatorade shower after his second win.

Hambrick's 31-yard TD run and a TD pass from Quincy Carter to Antonio Bryant gave the Cowboys a comfortable 14–3 second-quarter lead against the winless Jets. The defense took it from there. New York ran for just 66 yards, lost two fumbles, and failed to crack the end zone despite a 21-for-29 passing effort from Vinny Testaverde.

GAME 4: Early Milestone

Cowboys 24 vs. Arizona 7

October 5: Sure it was just four games into the season. But when Bill Parcells' first home win as Dallas coach put his club in first place in the NFC East, fans and players alike had another reason to start feeling good again. Quincy Carter completed 20-of-31 throws for 277 yards and two TDs, and the Cowboys held Arizona to 32 rushing yards.

It was a dominant defensive performance at Texas Stadium. Dallas recorded two safeties, something it hadn't done in 31 years, along with three sacks and two interceptions. Terry Glenn caught a 51-yard TD pass from Carter in the opening quarter to start the Cowboys toward the win.

GAME 5: Statement Win

Cowboys 23 vs. Philadelphia 21

October 12: All of a sudden, everything changed. As refreshing as three earlier wins were to Cowboys fans, the team's hot start under Bill Parcells took on a whole new meaning when a six-game string of misery against the Eagles came to an end.

It did so with big plays early and late. Philadelphia tried to deflate the Cowboys early with an opening onside kick. Randal Williams returned it 37 yards for a score. With 1:11 remaining, Billy Cundiff capped a third field goal with a 37-yarder that provided the winning margin. And with the Eagles near midfield and driving for a last-second win, Dexter Coakley forced a Donovan McNabb fumble that La'Roi Glover recovered to spark a Texas Stadium celebration.

It was a defensive scrum, as expected. The Cowboys held McNabb to an 11-of-26 passing rate and the Eagles to 232 total yards. Troy Hambrick's one-yard TD run in the third quarter gave Dallas a 17–7 lead, but Duce Staley and Correll Buckhalter found the end zone as Philadelphia took a 21–20 lead.

GAME 6: A Rare Rout

Cowboys 38 at Detroit 7

October 19: These were not yesterday's Cowboys, who needed just six games to match their win total of the previous three seasons. After back-to-back seasons of falling to the lowly Lions, Dallas visited Ford Field and took care of business, shutting out the Detroit offense, grabbing four turnovers, and getting three TD passes and an 18-for-25 performance from Quincy Carter.

The Lions' only points came on a 67-yard fumble return by Dré Bly to open the scoring. Thereafter, the Cowboys protected the football and sprung Terry Glenn three times for TD receptions. They came from 20, 19, and eight yards—all in the first half. Detroit was limited to 157 total yards.

GAME 7: Champs Too Much

Tampa Bay 16 vs. Cowboys 0

October 26: The Buccaneers showcased their championship defense in stopping Dallas' four-game winning streak. The defending Super Bowl champs held the Cowboys to 60 rushing yards, sacked Quincy Carter four times, and intercepted him twice in a whitewashing at Raymond James Stadium.

Three Martin Gramatica field goals and a TD pass from Brad Johnson to Keyshawn Johnson provided more than enough points for Tampa Bay, which also got 113 rushing yards from Michael Pittman. Dallas made nine first downs, and top rusher Troy Hambrick managed just 25 yards on 11 carries.

GAME 8: Defense Rises

Cowboys 21 vs. Washington 14

November 2: Dallas was rapidly gaining notice as a defensive force. The Cowboys overcame four turnovers and two apparent TDs that were nullified by penalties to handle the Redskins for the 11th time in 12 meetings. They did it with four sacks and by holding Washington to 213 total yards.

Offensively, a 400-yard day would have normally produced more points, but turnovers and penalties stung. Troy Hambrick carried 21 times for 100 yards and two TDs—short runs in the second and third quarters—that turned a 6–0 shortfall into a 14–6 lead. Quincy Carter then widened the gap with a 19-yard TD pass to Terry Glenn.

GAME 9: The Bills Stop Here

Cowboys 10 vs. Buffalo 6

November 9: Dallas entered the game ranked No. 1 in the NFL in defense, and they lived up to that billing. The Cowboys held the Bills to two second-quarter field goals and 185 yards of offense while recovering two fumbles in another defensive gem.

The game's only TD came on a two-yard pass from Quincy Carter to tight end Dan Campbell in the first quarter. As it turned out, it was all the Cowboys needed. Carter threw for just 116 yards, and the running game was not much better at 122 yards, but Dallas was proving that defense wins. And no one was doing it better.

GAME 10: Blanked Again

New England 12 vs. Cowboys 0

November 16: Sometimes, defense is not enough. Dallas was shut out for the second time in four weeks as its rugged defense got no help from an offense that coughed up three Quincy Carter interceptions.

The Cowboys' top-ranked defense was again stingy, holding New England to 65 rushing yards. Antowain Smith scored the game's only TD on a two-yard run in the second quarter for a 10–0 lead. It wound up being an insurmountable margin against a team that had produced one TD in two games. Dallas also hurt itself with 10 penalties for 78 yards.

GAME 11: Offense at Last

Cowboys 24 vs. Carolina 20

November 23: Dallas finally put it all together in a game Bill Parcells described as "pivotal." The coach grew emotional after the win. The

Head coach Bill Parcells (center) of the Dallas Cowboys has a cooler of ice water dumped on him by running back Richie Anderson (No. 20) and quarterback Quincy Carter (No. 17) in the 19–3 win over the New York Giants at Texas Stadium in Irving, Texas, on December 21, 2003. (Photo by James D. Smith/NFL, Getty Images)

Cowboys unleashed their usual stout defense, holding running machine Stephen Davis to 59 yards and Jake Delhomme to 9-of-24 passing. And for the first time in a month, their offense showed up, too.

Quincy Carter threw for 254 yards and two TDs in a game Dallas didn't trail despite never building a lead of more than seven points. It was a big game, Parcells said, because the Panthers entered 8–2 and with one of the most feared pass rushes in the NFL. They sacked Carter just once, and an interception was the Cowboys' lone turnover. Aveion Cason ran for the winning score in the third quarter, breaking a 17–17 tie.

GAME 12: Holiday Headaches
Miami 40 at Cowboys 21

November 27: "Embarrassing" was uttered by several in the Dallas locker room, including Coach Bill Parcells. In a nationally televised Thanksgiving Day game, the Cowboys took a trip back in time and interrupted their promising season with a blowout loss in which everything fell apart.

Their killer defense was torched for 365 yards, including Ricky Williams' 104 on the ground. An offense that looked resurgent the previous week stumbled under the direction of Quincy Carter, who threw three interceptions and lost a fumble that was returned 34 yards for a TD by Jason Taylor. Dallas turned it over five times. Jay Fiedler and Chris Chambers hooked up for three Miami TD passes.

GAME 13: Back to Earth
Philadelphia 36 vs. Cowboys 10

December 7: The defense that had been dominating the NFL yielded more than 400 yards, while the offense that had struggled for much of the year did so again. The result was a second straight loss—the Cowboys' third straight on the road—and a feeling that what once looked like an NFL feel-good story was going to be a battle to reach the playoffs.

Quincy Carter was sacked three times, intercepted twice, had a shotgun snap zip past him for a safety, and threw for just 93 yards. The Eagles had much better success, getting three TD passes from Donovan McNabb and 115 rushing yards on just 13 carries from Correll Buckhalter. The result was Philadelphia's eighth consecutive victory.

GAME 14: A Snowball's Chance
Cowboys 27 at Washington 0

December 14: Redskins fans threw snowballs and some even reached the end zone, which was more than their team could manage. Dallas dialed up a stifling defensive effort to secure its first winning season since 1998 and first shutout since 1999.

Troy Hambrick rushed for a career-high 189 yards, and Terence Newman tied a club record with three interceptions. It was the Cowboys' 12th win in the last 13 meetings with the Redskins, who made this one easy with six turnovers. Four were interceptions thrown

"Big Tuna" Makes a Splash

Bill Parcells Wasn't Looking to Make Friends; He Came to Win

The Cowboys went from no success to no excuses when they brought in Bill Parcells after three consecutive 5–11 seasons. Owner Jerry Jones knew Parcells was unlikely to be embraced by each of his players, or even a majority of them. His demand for excellence could rub people the wrong way. Those were the kinds of people Parcells had no use for.

Receiver Keyshawn Johnson, one player Parcells could tolerate (at least most of the time), recounted an incident in 2004 training camp during which one Cowboys hopeful left and never came back. "We had a guy quit…because he just wanted to get away from Bill Parcells," Johnson recalled. "Told Bill he couldn't do it anymore. I think Bill told him to go ahead. 'Adios, amigos!'"[1]

No one in the Cowboys' camp could question Parcells' credentials. After three dismal seasons under Dave Campo, Jones had lured a man who had taken the New York Giants to two Super Bowl titles, the New England Patriots to a Super Bowl appearance, and the New York Jets to a 12–4 season. He left the game for three years, but said he was starting to get bored and was feeling those old competitive fires—the ones that made Parcells one of the most driven and demanding bosses in America.

"I'm not really in the excuse business," Parcells said after his first of four seasons with the Cowboys. "We have this expression, 'Don't tell me about the pain, just show me the baby.' You know, let's get the job done here. Don't tell me about the process."[2]

Bill Parcels spent four seasons at the helm of the Dallas Cowboys. He is pictured here during the 21–20 loss to the Seattle Seahawks in the NFC Wild Card playoff game at Qwest Field in Seattle, Washington, on January 6, 2007. (Photo by Kirby Lee/NFL, Getty Images)

The process of making Dallas a winner was a quick one. With Parcells giving the club instant respectability and a top-flight coaching staff, those three straight 5–11 seasons became a distant memory during a 10–6 run in 2003. In typical Parcells fashion, the Cowboys did it with defense, finishing No. 1 in the NFL in pass defense and total defense and No. 2 in scoring defense. They reached the playoffs for the first time since 1999, falling to Carolina.

By Parcells' standards, though, the job went unfinished in Dallas. The Cowboys slipped to 6–10 in his second season, and he completed his four-year, $17 million contract with back-to-back 9–7 campaigns, falling again in the first round of the 1996 playoffs. Consistency was not a staple during his Texas tenure. Four different QBs led his four Dallas teams in passing, and a shaky relationship with star receiver Terrell Owens was never a secret.

Parcells stepped down when his contract expired, returned to the broadcast booth, and took a front-office job with the Miami Dolphins in December 2007. His nickname, "Big Tuna," goes back to his days as a Giants assistant coach. At times while in Dallas, Jones called him something far more telling.

"Boss."

during a 6-for-26, 56-yard passing game by a rattled Tim Hasselbeck. Dallas notched six QB sacks.

GAME 15: Playoff Return
Cowboys 19 vs. N.Y. Giants 3

December 21: Three consecutive 5–11 seasons gave no indication that Dallas was on the verge of anything big. Then along came Bill Parcells. In his first year since being hired to clean up the mess, the Big Tuna coached the Cowboys to their first playoff appearance since 1999, clinched on the strength of an impressive win against his old team.

His defense sacked the Giants five times and held them to 54 rushing yards. Their only points came on a first-quarter field goal. Dallas QB Quincy Carter went 17-of-25 for 240 yards. His 36-yard first-quarter pass to Jason Witten accounted for the game's lone TD.

GAME 16: No Momentum
New Orleans 13 vs. Cowboys 7

December 28: Dallas stumbled into the playoffs with a sloppy loss in its regular-season finale. Quincy Carter threw three interceptions. Coach Bill Parcells also lamented missed tackles, key penalties, and dropped passes against a Saints team that won despite gaining just 58 rushing yards.

Carter hit Richie Anderson from the 3-yard line for a 7–3 lead in the second quarter, but a 76-yard pass from Aaron Brooks to Donté Stallworth later in the stanza proved to be the winner. Carter threw a late interception with his team driving deep in New Orleans territory, preventing any chance of pulling out a win. Anderson caught 10 passes in the loss.

GAME 17: Carolina Blues

Carolina 29 vs. Cowboys 10

January 3, 2004: Dallas was happy to be back in the playoffs, if not so thrilled about the length of the stay. Stephen Davis ran for 104 yards as the Panthers avenged a regular-season loss in which their running game was corralled. This time, with more at stake, they powered to a 26–3 lead and were never seriously challenged.

Carolina put on a clinic, playing penalty-free and turnover-free football. Jake Delhomme threw for 273 yards and a TD to Steve Smith, who was one of two Panthers to rack up 100-plus receiving yards. Defensively, Carolina sacked Quincy Carter three times and intercepted him once. It was not until the fourth quarter that Carter ran for the only Cowboys TD.

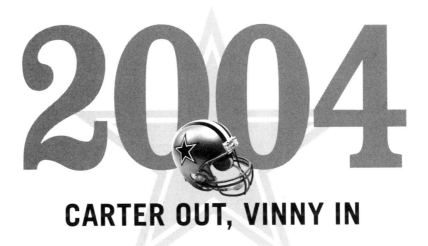

CARTER OUT, VINNY IN

Veteran QB Can't Get Cowboys to Promised Land

The Quincy Carter experiment ended when the QB was released before the 2004 season. Coach Bill Parcells opted for a proven veteran in Vinny Testaverde, and the results were mixed at best. Testaverde, 41, completed 60 percent of his passes and threw for 17 TDs, but he also delivered 20 interceptions.

Between offensive inconsistency and a defense that slipped down the NFL rankings from second to 27th in points allowed, the Cowboys' decline to a last-place tie in the NFC East at 6–10 occurred every bit as quickly as their previous year's ascent.

Two offensive bright spots were running back Julius Jones and receiver Keyshawn Johnson. Jones, in just eight games, led the team with 819 rushing yards, while the dealt-for Johnson (from Tampa Bay) caught 70 passes in his first year in Dallas.

GAME 1: Culpepper Owns Opener

Minnesota 35 vs. Cowboys 17

September 12: Daunte Culpepper fired five TD passes, the most Dallas had allowed in a game since 1969, in an opening rout at the Metrodome. He threw just six incompletions in 23 pass attempts. Randy Moss caught two scoring strikes and even completed a 37-yard pass. It was that kind of day for the Cowboys.

Vinny Testaverde debuted as Dallas QB and threw 50 passes, completing 29 for 355 yards. Like Culpepper, he did not throw an interception but managed just one TD pass in a game that featured 842 yards of offense. Also debuting for the Cowboys, Keyshawn Johnson caught nine passes for 111 yards, while Antonio Bryant snared eight for 112. Nine penalties and two lost fumbles hurt the Cowboys.

GAME 2: Defense Rises

Cowboys 19 vs. Cleveland 12

September 19: Dallas held Cleveland to 202 yards, picked off three passes, and kept the Browns out of the end zone to win its home opener. The Cowboys also overcame 11 penalties for 120 yards in the kind of defensive effort to which they had grown accustomed.

Vinny Testaverde topped 300 passing yards for the second time in as many games, but he also threw his first three interceptions in a Cowboys uniform. His one-yard TD pass to Jeff Robinson opened the scoring and gave his team the lead for good. Eddie George ran for his first Dallas TD in the third quarter. Dallas coaxed a miserable 8-for-27 passing performance from Cleveland's Jeff Garcia.

GAME 3: Monday Night Victory

Cowboys 21 at Washington 18

September 27: More than 90,000 fans at FedEx Field and a Monday night national TV audience saw a revamped Dallas club take every shot the Redskins delivered. In the end, the Cowboys were the ones standing, survivors of a game in which they ran for just 50 yards and were outgained by almost 100.

Despite the numbers, they never trailed. Eddie George bulled in from the 1-yard line in the opening quarter, and Vinny Testaverde hit tight end Jason Witten for a 10-yard score that produced a 14–3 lead in the third. Every time Washington inched close, Dallas answered. Its most spectacular response saw Richie Anderson take a handoff and throw a 26-yard halfback-option pass that Terry Glenn caught with a diving effort in the end zone. That gave the Cowboys a 21–10 lead and helped them weather Mark Brunell's 325-yard two-TD passing night.

GAME 4: Tiki Torches Dallas

N.Y. Giants 26 at Cowboys 10

October 10: Tiki Barber ran for 122 yards and a TD and added another 76 yards in receptions to lead the Giants past former coach Bill

Parcells. A TD pass from Vinny Testaverde to Keyshawn Johnson helped the Cowboys to a 10–3 second-quarter lead, but New York scored the game's final 23 points against the mistake-prone hosts.

Dallas was flagged 11 times, failed to gain a first down while going for it on fourth-and-1 in its own territory, and committed two turnovers. All that, along with the inability to slow Barber, proved too much to overcome. Eddie George and Richie Anderson combined to rush for 131 yards on 24 carries for the Cowboys.

GAME 5: Game Slips Away

Pittsburgh 24 at Cowboys 20

October 17: Vinny Testaverde lost the football, and Dallas lost the game. Testaverde's late fumble was returned to the Cowboys 24-yard line by Kimo von Oelhoffen, setting up the winning TD run by Jerome Bettis with 30 seconds remaining and capping the Steelers' fourth-quarter comeback from a 20–10 hole.

QB Ben Roethlisberger drove Pittsburgh to victory from those depths. He completed a sizzling 21-of-25 passes for two TDs, including a seven-yarder to Jerame Tuman that started the final-quarter rally. Testaverde threw for 284 yards and a TD to Keyshawn Johnson, and his desperation heave bounced off Johnson's hands on the final play. Terry Glenn caught seven passes for 140 yards for Dallas.

GAME 6: Where's the D?

Green Bay 41 vs. Cowboys 20

October 24: One year after shooting to the top of the NFL defensive rankings, the Dallas defense was shooting itself in the foot. Green Bay blistered the Cowboys for 480 yards of offense, led by Ahman Green's 163 rushing yards, in a blowout at Lambeau Field.

Green raced to the end zone from one and 90 yards as his team pulled away, grabbing leads of 20–6 at halftime and 41–13 after three quarters. Brett Favre was 23-of-29 for 258 yards and two scores for the winners. Vinny Testaverde threw for 308 yards while trying to keep the Cowboys in the game. His top target was tight end Jason Witten, who made eight catches for 112 yards and a TD.

GAME 7: George Comes Through

Cowboys 31 vs. Detroit 21

October 31: Looking to generate a steady running attack, Dallas turned to Eddie George and was rewarded. The first-year Cowboy ran 31 times for 99 yards, both season highs, and Keyshawn Johnson made two TD receptions to help end a three-game slump.

Vinny Testaverde had a roller-coaster day at QB for the Cowboys, giving the game an erratic feel. He threw three interceptions, one of which Dré Bly returned 55 yards for a TD that gave Detroit a second-quarter lead. But Testaverde also threw three TD passes, including a 26-yarder to Johnson in response to Bly's play.

Testaverde also ran for a third-quarter TD that gave the Cowboys the lead for good at 21–14.

GAME 8: Bengals Ride Dallas Bumbles

Cincinnati 26 vs. Cowboys 3

November 7: Vinny Testaverde threw three interceptions for the second straight game and also lost a fumble, helping to hand Cincinnati a comfortable victory at Paul Brown Stadium. Dallas committed all five turnovers in the game, setting up one Bengals score after another.

Shayne Graham kicked four field goals and Carson Palmer had a hand in both Cincinnati TDs, running for one and throwing a 76-yard pass to Matt Schobel for the other. The Cowboys got only a 24-yard field goal from Billy Cundiff.

Quarterback Vinny Testaverde (No. 16) passes against defensive tackle Brandon Noble (No. 75) and the Washington Redskins during the game on December 26, 2004, at Texas Stadium in Irving, Texas. The Cowboys won 13–10. (Photo by Ronald Martinez/Getty Images)

GAME 9: Record Flight for Eagles
Philadelphia 49 at Cowboys 21

November 15: The Dallas defense reached new lows before a national Monday night TV audience and 64,000 fans at Texas Stadium. Donovan McNabb threw four TD passes, three to Terrell Owens, as the Eagles embarrassed the Cowboys.

The visitors scored four TDs in the second stanza, a feat that had never been accomplished in any single quarter against the Cowboys. Those scores made it a 35–14 game at halftime and sent the TV crew to its "blowout material." McNabb threw for 345 of his team's 485 total yards. Vinny Testaverde and Jason Witten hooked up for two Cowboys scores.

GAME 10: Slide Prompts Change
Baltimore 30 vs. Cowboys 10

November 21: Yet another one-sided loss had Dallas thinking about its future. Rookie QB Drew Henson replaced Vinny Testaverde in the second half and completed all six of his passes, while fellow rookie Julius Jones carried 30 times for 81 yards.

None of it made a difference to the Ravens, who overcame a 3–0 halftime shortfall on two Kyle Boller TD passes in the third quarter en route to 30 second-half points. Their final TD was set up when Henson fumbled his first snap. However, the QB recovered for a promising finish.

GAME 11: Role Reversal
Cowboys 21 vs. Chicago 7

November 25: Dallas gave QB Drew Henson his first NFL start for Thanksgiving. Then coach Bill Parcells called on 41-year-old Vinny Testaverde in the second half to provide needed relief and a victory that snapped the Cowboys' three-game losing streak.

Henson struggled in his anticipated debut. The rookie went just 4-for-12 with an interception in the first half, but the Dallas defense kept it a 7–7 game. Testaverde, who was under center to start the second half, hit Darian Barnes for the go-ahead TD in the third quarter and finished 9-of-14 on the day. Julius Jones powered the victory, carrying 33 times for 150 yards and two TDs. The Bears were held to 140 total yards.

GAME 12: Seattle Shootout
Cowboys 43 at Seattle 39

December 6: Dallas scored two TDs in the final 1:45 to win a wild one against the Seahawks. Julius Jones ran for 198 yards on 30 carries in a take-charge performance, scoring his third TD on a 17-yard dash with 32 seconds left to shock Seattle and 68,000-plus fans at Qwest Field.

It was a frenzied game throughout. Dallas took a 29–14 lead early in the second half, but Matt Hasselbeck steered the Seahawks to 25 consecutive points in the third and fourth quarters en route to a 414-yard three-TD passing

Tight End Tradition
Dallas Has Never Been Shy About Throwing to the Big Men

"**U**se the tight end! Use the tight end! He's always open! Why don't we ever throw to the tight end?" Such phrases form a familiar refrain for armchair coaches and QBs across the country. For many coaches, tight ends are an afterthought in the passing game, existing to block defenders and little else. That has rarely been the case in the history of the Dallas Cowboys, thanks to star-power tight ends like Billy Joe Dupree, Doug Cosbie, Jay Novacek, and Jason Witten.

Between them, that foursome made 17 Pro Bowl appearances in Cowboys uniforms, continually raising the bar at their position.

Dupree began the Texas tradition, serving as Roger Staubach's go-to man when all downfield options were covered and doubling as a top blocker. The first-round draftee in 1973 never missed a game in his 11 seasons, a streak spanning 181 outings, including playoffs. He caught 41 career TD passes and was long considered the best tight end in franchise history.

Tight end Jason Witten (No. 82) scores a touchdown as Philadelphia Eagles cornerback Lito Sheppard (No. 26) tries to knock him out of bounds on Monday, November 15, 2004, at Texas Stadium in Irving, Texas. (Photo by Drew Hallowell/NFL, Getty Images)

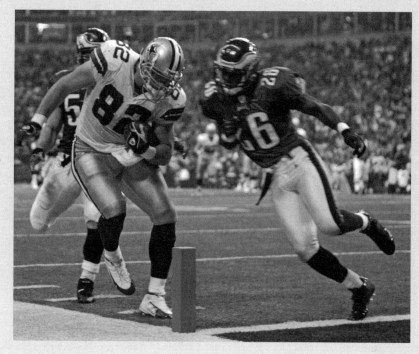

Cosbie was for Danny White what Dupree was for Staubach. A third-round pick who did not start until his fourth season, Cosbie was also a sure-handed target and sturdy blocker. He caught at least 60 passes in 1984 and '85 and eclipsed Dupree's club record for tight ends with 3,728 receiving yards.

That number was dwarfed once Novacek came around in the 1990s, though not all of his numbers came with the Cowboys. A sixth-rounder in '85 who never got a chance to star with the Cardinals, he arrived in Dallas in '90 and was an immediate factor in Jimmy Johnson's offensive scheme. He became a favorite target for Troy Aikman, made five consecutive five Pro Bowls, and helped the team to three Super Bowl titles.

If Dupree, Cosbie, and Novacek helped set the bar for Cowboys tight ends, Witten has cleared it like a champion high jumper in the early rounds of a track meet.

"Jason has a combination of Doug Cosbie, Billy Joe Dupree, and Jay Novacek put together," Dupree said. "Each one of those guys has specific talents. He's a lot larger than Jay, bulk-wise. Maybe a little better blocker than Jay.

"He also has quick feet and most people, defenders, don't really understand he may be a little quicker and faster than what they anticipate. Jason Witten is the best tight end who's played here."[1]

Witten began his Tennessee career as a defensive end but switched to tight end as a freshman and proved to be one of the best in college football. A third-rounder in 2003, he caught 35 passes as a rookie and grabbed 87 the next year, setting a club record for tight ends, leading all NFC players at the position, and earning the first of his six consecutive Pro Bowl honors.

Witten registered one of the best receiving seasons by a Cowboys player at any position in 2007. His 96 receptions for 1,145 yards and seven TDs were all club records for a tight end. He topped 90 catches again in 2009, bringing his team-record totals at his position to more than 500 receptions for nearly 6,000 yards.

day. With less than two minutes remaining, it was 39–29.

However, Vinny Testaverde hit Keyshawn Johnson with a 34-yard TD pass, Jason Witten recovered a perfect onside kick from Billy Cundiff, and Testaverde drove the team into position for Jones' winning score. The Cowboys won despite surrendering 507 total yards. Dallas gained 405 and a thrilling win.

GAME 13: Dallas Self-Destructs

New Orleans 27 at Cowboys 13

December 12: It wasn't Deuce McAllister's two TDs or Aaron Brooks' big plays so much that beat Dallas at Texas Stadium. It was largely the Cowboys themselves. They gained Coach Bill Parcells' wrath in committing 11 penalties and four turnovers in a game in which they were held to three points over the final three quarters.

New Orleans overcame a 10–0 deficit to win for just the fifth time. Parcells promised changes after his team threw two interceptions—one by receiver Keyshawn Johnson—and lost two fumbles. Vinny Testaverde completed just 14-of-35 passes.

GAME 14: Finally, a Fight

Philadelphia 12 vs. Cowboys 7

December 19: Dallas lost, to be sure. For the first time in its last six setbacks, though, it was not by a double-digit margin. And it came against a powerful Eagles team that improved to 13–1 in overcoming one of the Cowboys' better efforts of the year.

A second-quarter TD pass from Vinny Testaverde to Keyshawn Johnson gave Dallas a 7–6 lead it maintained into the final quarter when Donovan McNabb and the Eagles finally snatched away victory and secured home-field advantage through the playoffs. McNabb made the key plays in a 64-yard drive that Dorsey Levens capped with a two-yard TD run with less than two minutes remaining. Testaverde then threw his second interception while trying to engineer a winning drive.

GAME 15: Rally Downs Redskins

Cowboys 13 vs. Washington 10

December 26: Vinny Testaverde fired a 39-yard TD pass to Patrick Crayton with 30 seconds remaining to produce what had become the usual result—a Dallas victory over Washington. It was the 14th win in the last 15 meetings with the Redskins, although this one was more difficult than most.

Neither team found the end zone until Patrick Ramsey gave Washington a 10–6 fourth-quarter lead on a five-yard pass to Robert Royal. The Cowboys' winning drive featured a Testaverde-to-Crayton gain of 15 yards on fourth-and-10 from their own 25. Dallas limited Washington to 233 yards, made three takeaways, and benefited from eight Redskins penalties.

GAME 16: Season in a Nutshell

N.Y. Giants 28 vs. Cowboys 24

January 2, 2005: New York's winning drive featured some of the big reasons Dallas trudged through a disappointing year. Eli Manning took the Giants 66 yards in six plays, with Tiki Barber scoring the decisive TD with 11 seconds remaining. Poor defense and a 15-yard roughing-the-passer penalty contributed as the Cowboys again hurt themselves.

Dallas got 149 rushing yards and a TD from Julius Jones, and the team led 16–7 entering the fourth quarter. Two Manning TD passes gave the Giants a 21–16 lead, but Jones scored from the 1-yard line and Jason Witten added a two-point conversion. It was not enough to save Dallas from its 10th loss to end a season that started with high hopes.

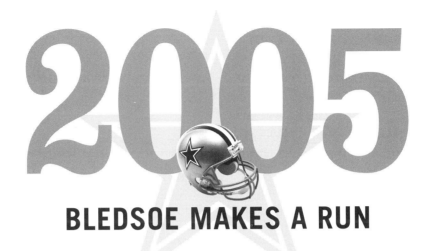

BLEDSOE MAKES A RUN

Dallas Falls Just Short of Playoffs Under Another QB

One good veteran QB deserves another. At least that was Bill Parcells' philosophy in turning from Vinny Testaverde to Drew Bledsoe in 2005. Bledsoe, 33, had been around long enough to surpass 40,000 career passing yards in his Cowboys debut.

Dallas won that game and went on to claim eight more with Bledsoe under center. Its 9–7 record was not quite enough for a playoff berth though, as both the Giants and Redskins finished ahead of the Cowboys in the NFC East.

While Bledsoe was throwing 23 TD passes and hitting 60 percent of his throws, Julius Jones was rushing for 993 yards and rookie sensation DeMarcus Ware was matching Greg Ellis with eight sacks.

GAME 1: Bledsoe Shines in Debut

Cowboys 28 at San Diego 24

September 11: It took one game for Drew Bledsoe's addition to pay dividends. The new Dallas QB threw three TD passes, including the winner to Keyshawn Johnson with 3:06 remaining, to down the Chargers. Bledsoe, the former Patriots and Bills QB, completed 18-of-24 throws for 226 yards without an interception.

San Diego got two TD passes from Drew Brees to Keenan McCardell, and the Chargers marched to the Cowboys' 7-yard line in the last minute. However, Dallas stopped them four times from there. The Cowboys intercepted Brees twice in the victory and held LaDainian Tomlinson to 72 rushing yards. Julius Jones led the Cowboys with 93.

GAME 2: Redskins Rally

Washington 14 at Cowboys 13

September 19: Four minutes can ruin a perfectly good day. After shutting out the Redskins for 56 minutes, seemingly en route to their 15th victory in 16 games against Washington, the Cowboys surrendered two late TD passes from Mark Brunell to Santana Moss in a stunning home defeat.

The scores covered 39 and 70 yards and came on the same play, with Moss splitting the defense downfield. In between, the Cowboys had a chance to run out the clock but had an apparent first down negated by a holding penalty. Dallas had built a 13–0 edge on a 70-yard TD toss of its own from Drew Bledsoe to Terry Glenn along with two Jose Cortez field goals.

GAME 3: Conquering California

Cowboys 34 at San Francisco 31

September 25: Dallas overcame a 24–12 halftime deficit, fighting among some of its own players on the sideline, and the second of three early season trips to California to pull out a win on Drew Bledsoe's 14-yard TD pass to Keyshawn Johnson with 1:51 remaining. Bledsoe threw for 363 yards and two scores and was also intercepted twice.

After the game, Coach Bill Parcells did not want to discuss why star guard Larry Allen shoved kicker Jose Cortez in the face. He preferred to laud his club for overcoming a 31–19 deficit entering the fourth quarter on Julius Jones' second TD run and Bledsoe's clutch pass to Johnson. Dallas compiled 443 yards of offense, including 137 receiving yards from Terry Glenn. For the 49ers, Tim Rattay threw three TDs and two picks.

GAME 4: Raider Duo Comes Up Big

Oakland 19 vs. Cowboys 13

October 2: LaMont Jordan ran for 126 yards and Randy Moss caught four passes for 123, giving the Raiders a one-two punch Dallas could not match. The Cowboys never led, though they might have had a chance if not for key penalties and a Drew Bledsoe interception.

Bledsoe hit Patrick Crayton with a late pass that the latter turned into a 63-yard TD to make it a 16–13 game. After a Sebastian Janikowski field goal, Bledsoe marched Dallas to the Oakland 5-yard line in the final minutes but threw a fourth-down incompletion that sealed the outcome. If poorly timed penalties hurt the Cowboys, the Raiders won despite drawing 13 flags for 85 yards.

GAME 5: Eagles Grounded

Cowboys 33 vs. Philadelphia 10

October 9: Drew Bledsoe threw for 289 yards and three TDs, including two early ones to Terry Glenn, that started Dallas on its way to an impressive rout of the rival Eagles. The Cowboys racked up 456 yards of offense, held Philadelphia to 129, and kept the Eagles' offense out of the end zone in one of their most complete showings in some time.

Bledsoe completed 24-of-35 passes without an interception. Jose Cortez kicked four field goals. The defense recorded four sacks and allowed just 19 rushing yards. The Eagles got their only TD on an 80-yard fumble return by Sheldon Brown in the third quarter. By then, the Cowboys had amassed a 30–3 lead.

GAME 6: Cortez Kicks Giants

Cowboys 16 vs. N.Y. Giants 13 (OT)

October 16: José Cortez's third field goal came less than four minutes into overtime, covering 45 yards and lifting Dallas into first place in the NFC East. The kick rescued a game that seemed to be slipping away when Eli Manning hit Jeremy Shockey for a 24-yard TD with 19 seconds left in regulation time.

It was not nearly as impressive as the previous week's win over Philadelphia, though. Each team gave up four turnovers. The Cowboys held the Giants to 11 first downs while gaining 25 of their own, but Dallas settled for two short Cortez kicks in the fourth quarter instead of TDs that could have put the Giants away. Drew Bledsoe threw for 312 yards and a TD to Jason Witten.

GAME 7: Seahawks Steal One

Seattle 13 vs. Cowboys 10

October 23: A cold, dreary day in the Great Northwest turned far more dismal for Dallas when the Seahawks charged from a 10–3 fourth-quarter deficit and won on Josh Brown's 50-yard field goal as time expired. Thanks to the NFL schedule-maker, it was the Cowboys' fourth West Coast trip in the first seven games of the season.

They appeared to be well on their way to winning it, too, on Keyshawn Johnson's first-quarter TD catch and José Cortez's 21-yard field goal in the fourth. Even after Seattle QB

Running back Julius Jones carries the ball against the Carolina Panthers at Bank of America Stadium in Charlotte, North Carolina, on December 24, 2005. Carolina defeated Dallas 24–20. (Photo by Allen Kee/NFL, Getty Images)

Matt Hasselbeck led an 81-yard drive that tied the game on a one-yard Ryan Hannam run with 40 seconds to go, the Cowboys had the ball for a chance to win or go to overtime. Instead, Drew Bledsoe was intercepted by Jordan Babineaux, whose return to the Cowboys' 32 set up the winning kick.

GAME 8: Midway Might
Cowboys 34 vs. Arizona 13

October 30: Dallas reached the middle of its 2005 schedule set to enter a bye week and made sure it didn't have a loss to dwell on during the down time. Rookie Marion Barber had a breakout game with 27 carries for 127 yards and two TDs, and Drew Bledsoe completed 19-of-24 passes for 220 yards and a score in a runaway.

Barber's TDs came in the first half, from 28 and 10 yards, staking the Cowboys to a 24–10 lead. The defense had as much to do with it, holding the Cardinals to 213 yards and 12 first downs in the game and scoring on a 58-yard Anthony Henry runback of a Josh McCown interception in the fourth quarter.

GAME 9: Thriller at the Vet
Cowboys 21 at Philadelphia 20

November 14: Dallas stamped itself a factor in the NFC East with a dazzling, dramatic win— its first at Veterans Stadium since 1998. The Cowboys scored two TDs in the final 3:04, the game-winner coming on a 46-yard Roy Williams interception return, then celebrated after a 60-yard field-goal try from David Akers missed as time expired.

It was an unlikely outcome in a game the Eagles dominated most of the way. They outgained Dallas by more than 100 yards and built a 21–13 edge in first downs. They also led 20–7 with just more than three minutes remaining. After Drew Bledsoe hit Terry Glenn for a 20-yard Cowboys TD, Donovan McNabb failed to account for Williams on a sideline pass and was blocked trying to tackle the defender after throwing the interception. Bledsoe went 17-for-24, and Marion Barber ran for a Dallas score.

GAME 10: Winning Ugly
Cowboys 20 vs. Detroit 7

November 20: Dallas earned no style points in this one. Seventeen Detroit penalties helped the Cowboys along, but they failed to execute in most phases of the game and trudged to their seventh win. Marion Barber rushed for two TDs, and Julius Jones ran for 92 yards in a two-headed attack that helped the Cowboys possess the ball for more than 36 minutes.

The Lions gained just 226 yards—less than 100 more than they lost in penalties. The Cowboys' biggest highlight came on a kicking play. Billy Cundiff booted a club-record 56-yard field goal just before halftime.

Star Power: The Dallas Cowboys Cheerleaders

Texas' Finest Have Set the Standard for NFL Cheerleading Troupes

Even when the Cowboys slip near the bottom of the standings, they can always one-up their opponent on the sidelines. The Dallas Cowboys Cheerleaders, through good times and bad, keep smiles on the faces of their fans—men, women, and children alike.

Any discussion about the most recognizable uniform in sports ought to include the blue blouse, white vest, and white shorts of the Dallas Cowboys Cheerleaders, easily the most famous cheerleading squad in sports. The outfit, designed by Paula Van Waggoner of Dallas, has remained virtually unchanged since the group formed in 1972.

The DCC were the brainchild of Tex Schramm and Dee Brock. Brock had managed the team of high school girls and boys who led cheers for the Cowboys through the 1960s and through the 1971 Super Bowl championship season as the "CowBelles & Beaux." Schramm, the Cowboys general manager, recognized that football was fast becoming as much about entertainment as sport and realized the appeal that beautiful women would bring to the fan base.

The most recognizable cheerleading squad in professional sports, the Dallas Cowboys Cheerleaders are shown here performing at a game against the Indianapolis Colts at Texas Stadium on August 9, 2007, in Irving, Texas. (Photo by Tim Umphrey/Getty Images)

It was an idea he had tried before with little success when he hired professional models to roam the sidelines. This time, the goal was to bring in pretty women who were also athletic, able to dance, and perform routines for three hours on Sunday afternoons.

Texie Waterman, a local dance studio owner, helped pare down 60 auditioners to seven members of the inaugural Dallas Cowboys Cheerleaders, who stole the spotlight in 1972 as the first NFL group of its kind. Suzanne Mitchell, Shannon Baker Werthmann, Kelli Finglass, and others have carried on the tradition begun by Schramm and Brock, expanding the squad, its routines, and its reach as a world-famous entertainment ensemble.

In 1979, the Cheerleaders began an annual United Service Organization (USO) holiday visit to overseas troops that has lasted more than 30 years. In addition to their performances on game days, they do an extraordinary number of community and charity appearances year-round and have been the subject of two made-for-TV movies, the first starring Jane Seymour in 1979.

Fame came quickly to the group, and the competition for spots on the roster has never been tougher. A team that initially had 60 women trying out now typically draws more than 600 vying for 30-some positions. The tryouts have been recently televised as part of a CMT series, "Dallas Cowboys Cheerleaders: Making the Team."

It was not famous athletes, but the Dallas Cowboys Cheerleaders who stole the show at the 2009 Armed Forces Bowl football game in Fort Worth, Texas, jamming at a Guitar Hero Challenge preceding the game.

"Over the last few years, we've brought the best professional athletes to our troops stationed around the world," said event co-founder Greg Zinone. "Having the Dallas Cowboy Cheerleaders battle it out in Guitar Hero tops them all, and I'll bet the soldiers will back me up on that one."[1]

Somewhere, the late Schramm was smiling.

GAME 11: Crushing Thanksgiving
Denver 24 at Cowboys 21 (OT)

November 24: Ron Dayne ran, Jason Elam kicked, and the Cowboys lost in overtime, suffering a heartbreaking Thanksgiving Day fate in a game they never led. Elam's 24-yard OT winner was set up by Dayne's 55-yard burst as lightning struck quickly.

The teams traded TDs throughout regulation time, with Dallas answering each of Denver's scores. Drew Bledsoe had an interception returned 65 yards by Champ Bailey for the first points of the game, but Beldsoe rebounded to fire two TD passes and run for a score. Dayne gained 98 yards on seven carries and also scored a TD. Midway through the final quarter, Billy Cundiff missed a 34-yard field-goal attempt that would have given the Cowboys their first lead.

GAME 12: Dallas Drops Ball
N.Y. Giants 17 vs. Cowboys 10

December 4: Drew Bledsoe threw two interceptions, lost two fumbles, and was sacked twice as Dallas allowed the Giants to take command of the NFC East. There were other miscues, of course, including the defense's inability to stop Tiki Barber (115 rushing yards), but Bledsoe's mistakes were the most damaging.

Antonio Pierce returned one of the fumbles 12 yards for a third-quarter TD that gave the Giants a 17–10 lead. The Cowboys got a Billy Cundiff field goal and a Bledsoe-to-Terry Glenn TD pass thereafter but could not come all the way back against a defense that limited them to 206 yards.

GAME 13: Bledsoe Bounces Back
Cowboys 31 vs. Kansas City 28

December 11: Drew Bledsoe rebounded from one of his worst games with a 332-yard three-TD passing performance and some late-game heroics. His one-yard TD pass to tight end Dan Campbell with 22 seconds remaining gave Dallas a victory when the Chiefs' Lawrence Tynes missed a 41-yard field-goal try as time expired.

Trent Green (340 yards) and Larry Johnson (143) of the Chiefs were the wide-open game's top passer and rusher, respectively. But Bledsoe made the biggest plays when they mattered most. Trailing 14–3 early, he hit Terry Glenn for a 71-yard TD and Jason Witten for a 26-yarder to give Dallas a 17–14 halftime lead. Glenn also ran for a third-quarter TD, but Green's 47-yard pass to Eddie Kennison put the Chiefs in front 28–24 with less than four minutes to go.

GAME 14: Rare Redskins Sweep
Washington 35 vs. Cowboys 7

December 18: There was no drama this time as the Redskins earned their first two-game season sweep of Dallas in a decade. The team the Cowboys once dominated held them to 216 yards, took advantage of four turnovers, and kept Dallas off the scoreboard until building a 35–0 lead in the fourth quarter.

Mark Brunell threw four TD passes and Clinton Portis rushed for 112 yards in the triumph, which cost the Cowboys control of their playoff destiny. Drew Bledsoe was sacked seven times by the Redskins, and Dallas was flagged for nine penalties.

GAME 15: Jones Powers Victory
Cowboys 24 at Carolina 20

December 24: Julius Jones ran for 194 yards and two TDs to carry Dallas to a win that kept its playoff hopes alive, but a yellow flag was every bit as crucial. Stopped on a late drive, the

Cowboys grimaced when Billy Cundiff missed a potential tying field-goal try from 33 yards. Then they celebrated as Carolina was penalized for running into Cundiff, giving the Cowboys a first down. Dallas capitalized with 22 seconds left when Drew Bledsoe threw the winning TD pass to Terry Glenn, who made a spectacular juggling grab in the end zone.

Jones gave Dallas a 17–13 lead on a 43-yard scamper in the fourth quarter, but Jake Delhomme and Ricky Proehl hooked up from 35 yards to put the Panthers back on top in the fourth. Delhomme threw for 260 yards and two scores, while the Cowboys did their damage on the ground. Jones carried 34 times.

GAME 16: Out with a Whimper
St. Louis 20 at Cowboys 10

January 1, 2006: Dallas had its playoff hopes dashed before the game when Washington beat Philadelphia. The Cowboys then dashed two of their own hopes, failing in a bid for 10 victories and falling seven yards short in their quest to get Julius Jones to the 1,000-yard rushing mark.

Jones gained only 35 yards on 15 carries. St. Louis limited Dallas to 57 rushing yards as a team. Drew Bledsoe threw for 242 yards and a TD for the Cowboys, but four turnovers and 10 penalties did in Dallas. The Rams gained only 253 total yards, but they never coughed up the football and broke a 10–10 tie with 10 fourth-quarter points.

2006

ROMO IGNITES PLAYOFF RETURN

Third-Year QB Has Many Ups, One Big Down in Parcells' Last Year

Bill Parcells, after the 2005 campaign, signed a contract extension with the Cowboys. He wound up serving just one of those two extra seasons, leading Dallas back to the playoffs in 2006 before announcing his resignation. Fortunately for the Cowboys, they found a franchise QB in his final slate.

Tony Romo had not attempted a pass in his first two NFL seasons, but he took over in Week 7 after Drew Bledsoe had gone 3–3 to start the year. Romo, an unheralded former Eastern Illinois QB, won six of his 10 starts to rally the high-scoring Cowboys to a second-place divisional finish and wild-card playoff appearance.

That playoff game was lost when Romo dropped a snap on what would have been a winning chip-shot field goal. It turned out to be the last of

Parcells on the Dallas sideline but only the beginning for the emerging QB.

GAME 1: Quick Start Deceiving
Jacksonville 24 vs. Cowboys 17

September 10: Dallas scored on its first two possessions for a 10–0 lead but surrendered the next 24 points to falter in its season opener. Three Drew Bledsoe interceptions, nine penalties (including one that negated an apparent TD), and generally soft pass defense allowed the Jaguars to take command.

Byron Leftwich ran for one score and threw for another on a 23-for-34 day to lead Jacksonville. Bledsoe, meanwhile, completed less than half of his 33 attempts. Julius Jones and Terrell Owens scored Cowboys TDs.

GAME 2: 'Skins Swarmed
Cowboys 27 vs. Washington 10

September 17: Dallas controlled a hard-hitting game between bitter rivals that featured 20 penalties for 207 yards. Most of the flags went against the Redskins, who absorbed six sacks against QB Mark Brunell and fell at Texas Stadium.

Drew Bledsoe threw for 237 yards and two TDs, while Julius Jones added 94 yards on the ground. Washington mustered just 245 yards of offense, but a 100-yard kickoff return by Rock Cartwright before halftime allowed the visitors

to stay close until Bledsoe connected with Terry Glenn on a 40-yard score in the fourth quarter.

GAME 3: Bye-Bye Titans
Cowboys 45 at Tennessee 14

October 1: Raring to go after a freakishly early bye week, Dallas blew away Tennessee behind 122 rushing yards from Julius Jones and dominant defense. The Titans gained only 229 yards and were hounded into three turnovers, including a Vince Young interception that Bradie James returned 15 yards for a score.

It was the Cowboys' highest point total under Bill Parcells. They scored 31 in the second half and punted just once in the game. Jones, Marion Barber, and Tyson Thompson ran for scores, while Drew Bledsoe and Terry Glenn hooked up for two through the air. Dallas rushed for 217 yards as a team.

GAME 4: Eagles Torment Dallas
Philadelphia 38 vs. Cowboys 24

October 8: The Eagles pounced on five turnovers and sacked Dallas QB Drew Bledsoe seven times using a swarming take-no-prisoners defense. Still, the Cowboys were somehow six yards away from a potential tying TD in the final minute. Instead of finding a receiver in the end zone, though, Bledsoe found Lito Sheppard, who returned the interception 102 yards to set the final score.

The Cowboys also got a defensive TD on a 69-yard fumble return by DeMarcus Ware that helped them build a 21–17 halftime lead. But Donovan McNabb did them in, passing for 354 yards and two long second-half TDs to lead Philadelphia to victory. Julius Jones rushed for 100 yards in the loss, but Bledsoe threw three interceptions without a TD while running for his life.

GAME 5: T.O. Grabs Three for TDs
Cowboys 34 vs. Houston 6

October 15: Terrell Owens, in his second game back after breaking his finger and then being rushed to a hospital for what was termed an "accidental overdose," finally garnered headlines for his receiving abilities again. He caught three TD passes in a game Dallas dominated on both sides of scrimmage.

Julius Jones ran for 106 yards, Drew Bledsoe directed a turnover-free offense, and the Cowboys limited the Texans to 34 rushing yards while keeping them out of the end zone. Owens snared two Bledsoe throws in the end zone in the third quarter and another from Tony Romo in the fourth. It was Romo's first career TD toss.

GAME 6: Change in the Air
N.Y. Giants 36 at Cowboys 22

October 23: Drew Bledsoe took snaps in the first half; Tony Romo took them in the second. Neither got the job done, but speculation was building that Romo was about ready to take control of the Cowboys' offense. The third-year

QB completed 14-of-25 passes for 227 yards and two TDs, but he had one of his three interceptions returned 96 yards for a score.

The Giants, at times, looked as though their defense had 12 or 13 men. They made six sacks, forced four turnovers, and pulled away after the break, turning a 12–7 halftime lead into a 26–7 rout with two third-quarter TDs. Tiki Barber rushed for 114 yards.

GAME 7: Romo Arrives
Cowboys 35 at Carolina 14

October 29: The QB of the future became the QB of the present. Tony Romo impressed in his first NFL start, hitting 24-of-36 passes for 270 yards and a score and scrambling for another 18 yards to lead Dallas to a night win at Bank of America Stadium.

Romo wasn't perfect or even polished. He threw an early interception that led to a score that gave Carolina a 14–0 lead. However, the game's remaining 35 points came from a Romo-led offense, including a three-yard TD pass to Jason Witten, two Marion Barber scoring scampers, and one from Julius Jones, who ran for 92 yards. The Cowboys amassed 414 total yards, more than double Carolina's total.

GAME 8: Blocked and Booted
Washington 22 vs. Cowboys 19

November 5: Three balls were kicked in the game's final 31 seconds. The only one that split the uprights gave the Redskins a you've-got-to-be-kidding-me victory over the shell-shocked Cowboys at FedEx Field.

With :31 on the clock in a tie game, Washington's Nick Novak missed from 49 yards. Four plays later, QB Tony Romo had put Dallas in position to win on a 35-yard attempt by Mike Vanderjagt. But the Redskins' Troy Vincent shot through the line to block the boot, teammate Sean Taylor scooped it up, and time ran out as Taylor was halted at the Dallas 44. However, Cowboys lineman Kyle Kosier was flagged for face-mask penalties on the play, giving the Redskins 15 more yards and one final untimed down. Novak delivered the deciding kick from 47 yards.

Aside from the zany finish, Dallas could point to dropped balls or its 11 penalties for 153 yards as reasons for the heartbreaking loss. Romo was solid in his second start, going 24-of-36 for 284 yards and two TDs while directing a turnover-free attack.

GAME 9: New Half, New Life
Cowboys 27 at Arizona 10

November 12: Tony Romo threw for a career-high 308 yards and two TDs, and the Cowboys protected the football for the second straight game in dismantling the Cardinals on the road.

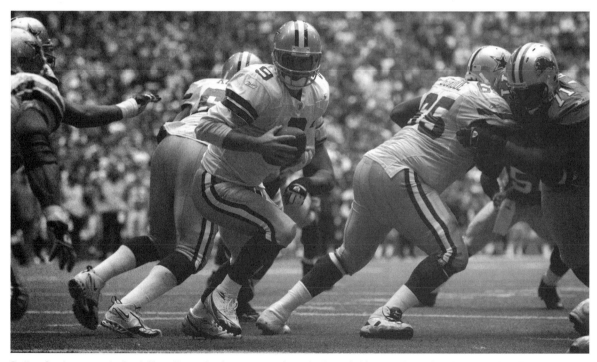

Dallas Cowboys quarterback Tony Romo in the game against the Detroit Lions at Texas Stadium in Irving, Texas, on December 31, 2006. The Lions defeated the Cowboys 39–31. (Photo by Jim Redman/NFL, Getty Images)

Romo was not sacked and had time in the pocket to complete 20 of his 29 throws in an efficient outing. Patrick Crayton and Terrell Owens each grabbed five passes, including a TD. Marion Barber and Julius Jones combined to carry 28 times for 110 yards. The Cowboys intercepted Matt Leinart twice and kept the Cardinals out of the end zone until the fourth quarter, with the outcome long decided.

GAME 10: Colts Corralled in Bid for Perfection

Cowboys 21 vs. Indianapolis 14

November 19: It wasn't necessarily that Dallas handed the Colts their first loss of the season that made the Cowboys so giddy about this one. It was the way they did it. Dallas overcame a 14–7 shortage on two fourth-quarter TDs by Marion Barber, showing a poise it hoped would carry the club toward a run into contention.

The Cowboys became the first team all season to intercept Peyton Manning twice in a game. Kevin Burnett returned the second one 39 yards for a TD that tied the score at 7–7. Then Tony Romo and the Dallas offense got into the action. After falling behind by a TD, Romo led drives that culminated in Barber's short TD runs, and Manning failed to answer after driving the Colts inside the Dallas 10 in the final minutes. Romo rarely missed in a short-passing attack, going 19-of-23 for 226 yards with one interception.

GAME 11: Thanksgiving Feast

Cowboys 38 vs. Tampa Bay 10

November 23: Tony Romo threw five TD passes to lead Dallas to its second-biggest margin of victory ever on Thanksgiving Day. In just his fifth start, the QB connected with Terry Glenn and Marion Barber twice each and Terrell Owens for his final scoring strike, shredding a once-proud Buccaneers defense.

Romo completed 22-of-29 throws for 306 yards without an interception. He directed a 435-yard offensive outburst that included no turnovers. Owens caught eight balls for 107 yards, and Barber ran for 83. Tampa Bay scored first on a Mike Alstott run, but Dallas intercepted Bruce Gradkowski twice and held the Bucs to 10 first downs on the day.

GAME 12: New Signee Makes Good

Cowboys 23 at N.Y. Giants 20

December 3: Just-signed kicker Martin Gramatica was put on the spot early, and the little man came through. The former Tampa Bay specialist split the Giants Stadium uprights from 46 yards with one second remaining to give Dallas its fourth straight victory.

Gramatica also connected from 41 and 35 yards, helping a Cowboys offense that got two rushing TDs from Marion Barber and 257 passing yards from Tony Romo. Romo threw two interceptions, but his 42-yard catch-and-run to tight end Jason Witten set up the winning kick after the Giants had pulled even on a last-minute

TD pass from Eli Manning to Plaxico Burress. Manning threw two TD passes, but Romo improved to 5–1 as a starter.

GAME 13: Saints Douse Dallas

New Orleans 42 at Cowboys 17

December 10: The red-hot Cowboys were cooled—even frozen—by Drew Brees, Deuce McAllister, and the Saints in a game they were hoping might produce a fifth straight win. Instead, Brees threw for 384 yards and five TDs and McAllister ran for 111 yards in a lopsided affair at Texas Stadium.

Unable to stop the run or the pass, there was little Dallas could do to avoid its fate. Brees completed 26-of-38 passes to 10 different receivers, including Reggie Bush six times for 125 yards. His counterpart, Tony Romo, lost for just the second time in seven career starts. He went 16-of-33 with two interceptions and one TD, a 34-yarder to Terrell Owens.

GAME 14: Georgia Turnaround

Cowboys 38 at Atlanta 28

December 16: Tony Romo recovered from the worst start of his young career to hit 22-of-29 passes for 278 yards and two TDs to Terrell Owens. He directed Dallas to 352 yards of offense to claim a shootout. The Cowboys scored the game's final 17 points after trailing 28–21 in the third quarter.

DeMarcus Ware gave Dallas a defensive TD when he returned an interception 41 yards for

an early 14–0 bulge. Atlanta's second-half cushion was erased on two Marion Barber TD runs and a 48-yard Martin Gramatica field goal. The Cowboys overcame a dazzling performance from Michael Vick—the Falcons QB threw four TD passes and ran for a team-leading 56 yards.

GAME 15: Christmas Blues

Philadelphia 23 at Cowboys 7

December 25: Dallas knew it had likely blown its chance to win the NFC East after the Eagles made a Christmas Day visit to Texas Stadium and played the role of the Grinch. The green-helmeted visitors never trailed, holding the Cowboys to 201 offensive yards while taking advantage of three turnovers to pull even in the standings at 9–6.

Brian Westbrook carried 26 times for 122 yards for Philadelphia, which scored two TDs but really only needed David Akers' three field goals to win. Cowboys QB Tony Romo struggled. He threw two interceptions and missed on more than half of his 29 pass attempts. His 14-yard TD pass to Terrell Owens was all Dallas could manage.

GAME 16: Lamentable Loss

Detroit 39 at Cowboys 31

December 31: Coach Bill Parcells, even knowing the next step was to prepare his team for a return to the playoffs, called it a low point. Losing the regular-season finale to one of the

Overnight Sensation

Undrafted Quarterback Tony Romo Rode a Fast Track to Stardom

It was halftime of the Cowboys-Giants game on October 15, 2006, and Dallas head coach Bill Parcells was fed up with his team's anemic passing attack. Quarterback Drew Bledsoe would sit in the second half. It was time to make a change. It was time for Tony Romo.

In his first real NFL opportunity, Romo put the zip back in the Cowboys' passing game. Yes, he tossed three interceptions in a Cowboys loss; but in just 30 minutes of football, he threw for 227 yards and two touchdowns. Tony earned the start the next week against Carolina on NBC *Sunday Night Football* and completed 24-of-36 passes for 270 yards and a touchdown. He also ran for two first downs, completed a two-point conversion pass, and rallied Dallas from a 14–0 deficit to a 35–14 victory. A star was born.

In succeeding games, Romo continued to put up big passing numbers as well as Ws. In a rout of Tampa Bay on Thanksgiving, he completed 22-of-29 passes for 306 yards, with five touchdown passes, zero interceptions, and an off-the-charts passer rating of 148.9. From Turkey Day to the end of calendar year, his jersey became the NFL's No. 1 seller.

Fans today look at the celebrity-dating superstar and assume that he coasted to the top. Yet the small-town Wisconsin boy had to climb every rung of the ladder. A three-time Division I-AA All-American at Eastern Illinois, Romo went undrafted in 2003. But Dallas assistant coach Sean Payton liked the look of the passed-over QB. "You saw a quick release and you saw someone who could locate the ball in tight traffic," Payton said.[1]

Romo made the Cowboys' roster that summer and worked to become backup QB in

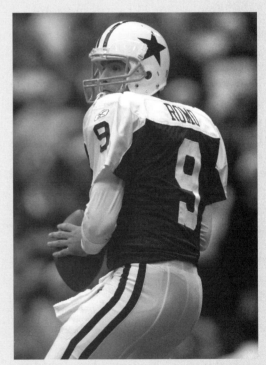

Quarterback Tony Romo drops back to pass against the Philadelphia Eagles on December 25, 2006, at Texas Stadium in Irving, Texas. (Photo by Ronald Martinez/Getty Images)

2005. In the 2006 exhibition season, he dazzled fans with his arm, mobility, and gunslinger mentality—a trait he picked up from his boyhood idol, Brett Favre. Romo performed so well in his 10 2006 starts that he (and not Favre) made the Pro Bowl.

Romo torched opposing defenses throughout the 2007 season, recording seven 300-yard games. He finished the year with 4,211 yards passing (third in the NFL) and 36 touchdown passes (second only to Tom Brady). In October 2007, just 12 months after his first NFL pass, the Cowboys signed him to a six-year, $67.5 million contract. While Romo's numbers dipped a bit in 2008 (3,448 yards in 13 games), he ventured into the new stadium in 2009 as the Cowboys' franchise quarterback and by season's end had delivered the team its first playoff win since 1996.

worst teams in the NFL certainly qualified as such.

The Lions (3–13) pounced on four Dallas turnovers and never trailed by more than one point in their upset win at Texas Stadium. The Cowboys lost three fumbles, allowed Jon Kitna to pass for 306 yards, and gave up the game's last nine points. Tony Romo went 23-of-32 for 321 yards with two TDs and an interception for Dallas. Terry Glenn and Terrell Owens each caught six passes for 100-plus yards, but the Cowboys' running game faltered, as did their defense.

GAME 17: Snap, Crackle, Drop

Seattle 21 vs. Cowboys 20

January 6, 2007: It's one of the most practiced plays in football, and it's supposed to be one of the most routine. The center snaps to the holder, who places the ball for the kick. Tony Romo was the middle man in that flowchart as Dallas lined up for a potential winning chip-shot field goal with 1:14 to play, but Romo dropped the snap and was tripped up at the 2-yard line while trying to save the play with a two-point conversion run. With that wild finish, the wild-card Cowboys were eliminated.

"I cost the Dallas Cowboys a playoff win," said Romo, who had an otherwise fine game with 17-of-29 passing, a TD pass to Patrick Crayton, and no interceptions. Romo directed an offense that got 112 rushing yards from Julius Jones and was helped by Miles Austin's 93-yard kickoff return in the second half. When the final minutes arrived, Romo had Dallas in great position for a go-ahead kick from extra-point range. Kicker Martin Gramatica never got the chance.

Matt Hasselbeck threw for 240 yards and two TDs for the Seahawks.

2007

LUCKY 13 IN PHILLIPS' DEBUT

Son of Bum Phillips Finds Big Success in "Big D"

Owner Jerry Jones turned from one defensive whiz to another when he hired Wade Phillips, son of longtime NFL coach Bum Phillips, as head coach before the 2007 slate. However, it was the offense that sparked a run to a franchise record-tying 13 victories and an NFC East crown.

Tony Romo, in his first full season as starting QB, helped both Jason Witten and Terrell Owens to 1,000-yard receiving seasons. The former caught 96 passes, shattering several single-season club records for tight ends, while Owens grabbed 81 balls for 1,355 yards. Only the undefeated Patriots scored more points than the Cowboys, who were led in rushing by Marion Barber's 975 yards and 10 scores.

Defensively, DeMarcus Ware racked up 14 sacks, and Greg Ellis was named NFL Comeback Player of the Year with 12½ sacks. A loss to the wild-card Giants continued the Cowboys' growing run of postseason hiccups, but Phillips seemed to have found an offensive support system for his defensive schemes.

GAME 1: Phillips Era Opens Loudly
Cowboys 45 vs. N.Y. Giants 35

September 9: Wade Phillips is a former line-backer known for his defensive mind. Still, his first game as head coach of the Cowboys featured a 478-yard offensive explosion as Dallas raced past the Giants in high-octane style.

Tony Romo threw for 345 yards and four TDs, Jason Witten caught six passes for 116 yards, Terrell Owens reached the end zone twice, and Julius Jones and Marion Barber combined for 131 yards on 27 carries. Giants receiver Plaxico Burress caught three TD passes, including a 60-yarder to open the scoring, but Dallas scored the next 17 points and never trailed again. The Giants got within 38–35 late, but a 51-yard scoring strike from Romo to Sam Hurd put the game away.

GAME 2: Defensive Gains
Cowboys 37 at Miami 20

September 16: The Dallas offense stayed hot, while the defense rebounded from a shaky opener to force five turnovers in an impressive road win. The Cowboys intercepted Trent Green four times, including two picks by Anthony Henry, as the Dolphins wilted after grabbing a 13–10 lead early in the second half.

Marion Barber carried 14 times for 89 yards and two Cowboys scores. Tony Romo had a sub-.500 passing game but threw scoring strikes to Terrell Owens and Tony Curtis while leading an offense that did not commit a turnover. Dallas pulled away despite being flagged 11 times for 101 penalty yards.

GAME 3: Happy Homecoming
Cowboys 34 at Chicago 10

September 23: Returning to the state where he played his college ball at Eastern Illinois, Tony Romo hit 22-of-35 passes for 329 yards and two TDs and sparked a sharp attack at Soldier Field. Dallas racked up 431 total yards, including Marion Barber's 102 on the ground, to overcome 100 yards in penalties.

Barber's 10-yard TD run broke a 10–10 tie before halftime and sent the Cowboys on their way. Bears QB Rex Grossman threw three interceptions, two into the hands of Anthony Henry. Terrell Owens was Romo's top target, making eight receptions for 145 yards. Barber and Jason Witten caught TD passes, too.

GAME 4: Early Romp Continues
Cowboys 35 vs. St. Louis 7

September 30: Dallas beat its fourth consecutive opponent by a double-digit margin by thoroughly outplaying another foe. Tony Romo threw for 339 yards and three second-half TDs and the Cowboys shut out the St. Louis offense, giving up their only points on Dante Hall's 85-yard punt return.

Romo was outstanding again. He completed 21-of-33 passes and also ran three times for 24 yards and a score. Patrick Crayton burned the Rams for seven receptions covering 184 yards, including third-quarter TD grabs from 59 and 37. The Cowboys held St. Louis to 187 total yards.

GAME 5: Folk's Foot a Winner
Cowboys 25 at Buffalo 24

October 8: Rookie Nick Folk coaxed a 53-yard field goal over the crossbar on the final play, capping a dizzying finish to give Dallas its fifth consecutive victory. The Cowboys prevailed somehow, despite five interceptions from Tony Romo, two of which were returned for TDs, and a 103-yard kick-return score from the Bills' Terrence McGee.

Romo's five picks tied a franchise record. He kept flinging it, though, hitting Patrick Crayton for a four-yard TD with 20 seconds remaining that sliced Buffalo's lead to 24–22. A two-point conversion attempt failed, but Folk punched an onside kick that the Cowboys' Tony Curtis recovered at the Buffalo 47. Two short gains gave Folk a chance for his fourth field goal of the game—the biggest of his career.

Despite his struggles, Romo topped 300 passing yards for the third straight week, and the Cowboys were off to their first 5–0 start since 1983.

GAME 6: Patriots Stay Perfect
New England 48 at Cowboys 27

October 14: An anticipated battle of 5–0 clubs went sour in a hurry for Dallas. Tom Brady threw two first-quarter TD passes and never let up, torching the Cowboys for five scoring strikes and 388 yards through the air.

Wes Welker made 11 catches for 124 yards and two TDs, Donté Stallworth snared seven balls for 136 yards and a score, and the Patriots amassed 448 total yards against a Dallas defense that had been among the NFL's best in recent weeks. Tony Romo hit Terrell Owens and Patrick Crayton for TDs that turned a 21–10 deficit into a 24–21 surplus early in the third, but the Cowboys managed only a field goal the rest of the way while Brady and the Patriots stayed hot and perfect. A dozen penalties for 100 yards also hurt Dallas.

GAME 7: Romo Sizzles
Cowboys 24 vs. Minnesota 14

October 21: Tony Romo's timing was perfect, even when it came to an injury. The Dallas QB bruised his right leg at just the right time—just before a bye week—and it didn't stop him from completing 31-of-39 passes for 277 yards and a TD to lift the Cowboys after their first loss of the year.

The play on which Romo was injured was a 50-yard fumble return by Cedric Griffin that gave Minnesota a 14–7 lead in the second quarter. A one-yard run by Marion Barber tied the game midway through the third, and Dallas

Wide receiver Terrell Owens makes a catch during the Thanksgiving game between the New York Jets and the Dallas Cowboys at Texas Stadium, Irving, Texas, on November 22, 2007. The Cowboys beat the Jets, 34–3. (Photo by Al Pereira/Getty Images)

grabbed the lead for good later in the quarter when Chris Canty blocked a field-goal try and Patrick Watkins returned it 68 yards for a TD. Barber rushed for 96 yards, and the Cowboys held the Vikings to 196 total yards.

GAME 8: T.O. Paints Philly Blue
Cowboys 38 at Philadelphia 17

November 4: After struggling in the previous year's trip to Philadelphia, Terrell Owens did a number on his former team this time. He caught 10 passes for 174 yards and a 45-yard TD grab from Tony Romo, shrugging off the boos and taunts to spark Dallas to a runaway triumph.

Tony Romo, in his first game since signing a lucrative six-year contract extension, hit 20-of-25 passes for 324 yards and three TDs. Marion Barber and Julius Jones totaled 29 totes for 113 yards and two scores in an offense that compiled 434 total yards. The Cowboys sacked Donovan McNabb three times and intercepted him twice.

GAME 9: Owens Stays Hot
Cowboys 31 at N.Y. Giants 20

November 11: Terrell Owens was gaining momentum, and the Cowboys were soaring right along with him. The star receiver enjoyed his second straight huge game, snaring six balls for 125 yards and two key TDs as Dallas strengthened its grasp in the NFC East.

Owens was responsible for half of Tony Romo's four TD passes. Romo went 20-for-28

for 247 yards. The game was tied 17–17 at half-time, but Owens' 25-yard score in the third quarter gave the Cowboys the lead for good, and his 50-yarder in the fourth put it away. Jeremy Shockey paced the Giants with 12 receptions for 129 yards and a TD, while Brandon Jacobs added 95 yards on the ground. New York fell to 6–3.

GAME 10: T.R. to T.O. Spells Victory
Cowboys 28 vs. Washington 23

November 18: Tony Romo and Terrell Owens hooked up four times for TDs covering four, 31, 46, and 52 yards. The two longest of those scores came in the fourth quarter as Dallas' dynamic duo outscored the Redskins all by themselves.

Romo went 22-for-32 for 293 yards and Owens finished with eight receptions for 173 in one of the most productive two-man showcases in club history. Tight end Jason Witten also caught eight Romo passes. The Redskins, who led 10–7 at halftime, also fielded a torrid tandem. Jason Campbell threw for 348 yards and Santana Moss made nine receptions for 121 yards, but Owens outshone them in the second half.

GAME 11: Historic Start
Cowboys 34 vs. N.Y. Jets 3

November 22: Dallas improved to 10–1 for the first time in franchise history against a Jets team that did not provide much of a speed bump. Marion Barber carried 18 times for 103 yards and a TD, and the Cowboys held New York to 180 total yards while keeping the visitors out of the end zone.

The Dallas defense pitched in on the scoreboard, too, when Terence Newman returned a Kellen Clemens interception 50 yards for a 21–0 lead in the second quarter. The Jets made only nine first downs in the game while giving up 21.

GAME 12: Beasts of the NFC
Cowboys 37 vs. Green Bay 27

November 29: A shot at regular-season NFC supremacy was on the line when these 10–1 teams squared off, and Dallas used the occasion to put on an offensive clinic. Tony Romo threw for 309 yards and four TDs and directed his team to 414 offensive yards and an early 27–10. Green Bay never climbed out of the hole.

Once again, Terrell Owens was Romo's go-to target. The receiver caught seven passes for 156 yards and a 10-yard TD that gave the Cowboys that 17-point cushion. Tight end Jason Witten added six receptions for 67 yards, and Patrick Crayton made two TD grabs. The Packers got 94 rushing yards from Ryan Grant. QB Aaron Rodgers threw for 201 yards but was sacked three times by Dallas, including twice by Greg Ellis.

GAME 13: Rally Clinches NFC East
Cowboys 28 at Detroit 27

December 9: On the verge of a stunning loss, Dallas scored 14 unanswered points in the fourth quarter to improve to 11–1 and wrap up the NFC East crown. Marion Barber ran one yard for a TD early in the fourth quarter to slice a 27–14 shortage to 27–21. Detroit's Jason Hanson missed a field goal to give the Cowboys life, and Tony Romo took advantage, firing a winning 16-yard TD pass to Jason Witten with 18 seconds remaining.

Romo threw for 302 yards and two scores. Witten and Marion Barber were his main men, combining for 25 receptions for 199 yards. Jon Kitna (248 passing yards), with help from runners Kevin Jones (92 yards, two TDs) and T.J. Duckett (60 yards, one TD), nearly engineered a major upset. Barber scored two rushing TDs and one through the air.

GAME 14: Romo, Dallas Struggle
Philadelphia 10 at Cowboys 6

December 16: Some were blaming Tony Romo's 13-for-36 passing performance on an injured thumb. Others were pointing to his love interest, singer and actress Jessica Simpson, who witnessed the subpar effort sporting a pink incarnation of Romo's No. 9 jersey. Whatever the reasons, Romo and the Cowboys were a shadow of themselves against the Eagles.

Romo threw three interceptions and failed to lead Dallas to the end zone. Philadelphia's

Son of a Bum

Coach Wade Phillips has Emerged from his Father's Ample Shadow

His father, the ever-quotable Bum Phillips, once insisted that "the Dallas Cowboys may be America's Team, but the Houston Oilers are Texas' team." Now that the Oilers are Tennessee's Titans and the Cowboys are coached by his son, Bum has changed his tune. And Wade Phillips, the man he raised and mentored, has come a long way toward establishing his own star in the NFL coaching ranks.

Wade Phillips is not the ham his father was, certainly. He provides neither bulletin-board fodder for opponents nor great column material for sports writers, other than the ones who have opined that he ought to be fired for his lack of postseason success. It was his father, not Wade, who said there are two kinds of coaches: "Them that's fired and them that's gonna be fired."[1]

Wade, a believer in the family creed that defense rules, quietly goes about the business of giving his teams a chance to win. Since he took over the Cowboys in 2007, they have done so 33 times against just 15 defeats. In 2009, Phillips guided them to their first playoff win in 13 years, a victory that may have sealed the extension he was granted after the following week's loss to Minnesota.

"When I was growing up, people thought bitching was coaching," Wade said. "But players eventually turn off the guys who yell and scream. My father once told me, 'Don't coach the way you were coached. Coach the way you are.' I don't believe in coaching by fear. I believe in coaching by teaching."[2]

The younger Phillips, a former University of Houston linebacker, began his coaching career

Head coach Wade Phillips looks on against the Detroit Lions on December 9, 2007, at Ford Field in Detroit, Michigan. The Cowboys won 28–27. (Photo by Chris McGrath/Getty Images)

as a graduate assistant at his alma mater and eventually was hired as the Oilers' linebacker coach by his father. They went to New Orleans together, and Wade took over as interim coach when Bum stepped down with four games remaining in 1985.

Wade then honed his already sharp mind for defense under the tutelage of another defensive legend, Buddy Ryan, as Philadelphia's defensive coordinator before landing head coaching jobs in Denver and Buffalo and another brief interim gig in Atlanta. His career record of 81–54 easily makes him the most successful coaching son of a former NFL coach.

Phillips replaced Bill Parcells at the Cowboys' helm in 2007, installed a 3-4 defense, and led the team to a 13–3 record, a four-game improvement over the previous year. However, a first-round loss to the Giants and a 9–7 backslide in 2008 left many Dallas fans clamoring for another change. Phillips added defensive coordinator duties to his head coaching role in '09 and after a midseason scare won the NFC East title on back-to-back, season-ending shutouts—a first in franchise history. The playoff victory over Philadelphia was Phillips' first as a head coach.

Cowboys fans—Bum Phillips among them—hope there are many more to come.

---

defense surrendered just 11 first downs. Donovan McNabb threw a one-yard TD pass to Reggie Brown in the second quarter, and it was all the offense the Eagles required.

GAME 15: T.O. Reaches Record Book

Cowboys 20 at Carolina 13

December 22: Terrell Owens set a club record with his 15th TD reception of the season, and Dallas matched a franchise mark with its 13th win of the year as Tony Romo made a quick comeback from his worst outing. The QB threw for 257 yards and a 10-yard TD to Owens in the first quarter. It sent the Cowboys toward a 14–0 lead from which the Panthers never recovered.

Marion Barber rushed for 110 yards and a score, and the Dallas defense sacked Matt Moore five times. The Panthers gained just 212 yards, 96 coming on two plays. Owens sprained his ankle in the win and left the stadium on crutches.

GAME 16: No Incentive, No Spark

Washington 27 vs. Cowboys 6

December 30: With home-field advantage through the NFC playoffs already in the bag, Dallas went into the tank. The Cowboys rested their regulars and managed only two Nick Folk field goals in a one-sided loss to the Redskins that, even for Washington fans, was hardly worth the price of admission.

Clinton Portis ran for 104 yards and two TDs and Todd Collins threw for 244 yards and a score to lead the Redskins. Dallas managed a single yard—yes, one yard—on 16 rushing attempts. The Cowboys gained 147 total yards.

GAME 17: Stunning Exit

N.Y. Giants 21 at Cowboys 17

January 13, 2008: A Giants team that twice fell by double-digit margins to Dallas in the regular season became the latest to send the Cowboys to a one-and-done exit from the NFC playoffs. Since the playoffs expanded to six teams per conference in 1990, the Cowboys became the first No. 1 NFC seed eliminated in the divisional round.

Mistakes and missed opportunities were largely to blame. Though Dallas outgained New York by more than 100 yards, it hurt itself with 11 penalties for 84 yards and did not take great advantage of its scoring chances. Eli Manning and Amani Toomer hooked up for two first-half Giants TDs covering 52 and four yards, but the Cowboys matched with a Marion Barber TD run and a five-yard TD pass from Tony Romo to Terrell Owens.

Barber rushed for 129 yards for Dallas, which took a 17–14 lead on Nick Folk's third-quarter field goal. However, the Cowboys failed to score again. Brandon Jacobs plunged for the one-yard winner in the fourth quarter. Romo's last-ditch effort to rescue his team ended with a fourth-down interceptions by R.W. McQuarters with nine seconds remaining. It sealed Dallas' fifth consecutive postseason loss.

SOPHOMORE JINX?

Phillips Misses Playoffs in Second Year at Helm

It's fair to say that the Dallas Cowboys were among the greatest disappointments of the 2008 NFL season. One year after winning 13 games and an NFC East title under first-year boss Wade Phillips, they slipped to 9–7 and a third-place showing, plus they missed out on the playoffs and were thrust into the conversation about coaching hot seats.

The offense that scored the second-most points in the NFL in 2007 slipped to 18th in that category. The defense, known as Phillips' calling card, finished 25th among 32 teams in yardage allowed. A minus-11 turnover ratio was 30th in the NFL, which created a recipe for disaster.

DeMarcus Ware was a bright spot as the fourth-year phenom recorded 20 QB sacks to lead the league and become the first NFL winner of the Butkus Award as top linebacker. The honor was formerly reserved for college players.

GAME 1: Dominant Opener

Cowboys 28 at Cleveland 10

September 7: Dallas waited a long time to ease the sting of a shocking 2007 playoff loss in a game that mattered. It was satisfying indeed as the Cowboys racked up 487 yards to the Browns' 205 in a season-opening dismantling of Cleveland.

The Cowboys made 30 first downs to the Browns' 11. Tony Romo threw for 320 yards and a TD to Terrell Owens, while Marion Barber ran for two scores. Dallas led 21–7 at the half and stretched it to 28–7 on a Felix Jones TD run in the third quarter.

GAME 2: Dallas Wins Wild One

Cowboys 41 vs. Philadelphia 37

September 15: The Eagles scored 24 points in the second quarter, including two TDs in a 14-second span, and still lost. The Cowboys gave up a fumble in the end zone for six Philadelphia points, drew 10 penalty flags, ran for just 68 yards, and still won.

It was a crazy day at Texas Stadium, to put it mildly. Felix Jones returned a kickoff 98 yards for a Dallas TD, while Philly got a defensive TD when Chris Gocong recovered the end-zone fumble. Tony Romo threw for 312 yards and three scores, including a 72-yarder to Terrell Owens, and Marion Barber powered in from the 1-yard line for the winning TD with 4½ minutes left in the game. That score produced the seventh and final lead change. Donovan McNabb threw for 281 yards and a score for the Eagles.

GAME 3: Lambeau Leap

Cowboys 27 at Green Bay 16

September 21: After five winless trips to Lambeau Field, Dallas earned its first-ever victory at one of football's most storied venues. The Cowboys ran right over that hallowed ground, rushing for 217 yards. Marion Barber carried 28 times for 142 yards and a score to highlight a 453-yard offensive day for the unbeaten visitors.

Tony Romo, who grew up a Packers fan, threw for 260 yards and a 52-yard TD pass to Miles Austin. The Cowboys sacked Aaron Rodgers five times, with Anthony Henry picking up two, and limited Green Bay to 84 rushing yards.

GAME 4: Redskins Spoil Start

Washington 26 at Cowboys 24

September 28: Clinton Portis became the first opposing back to top 100 yards against the 2008 Cowboys, going for 121 on 21 carries to power a Redskin upset at Texas Stadium. While Washington ground out 161 rushing yards, Dallas called 11 running plays for 44 yards—an inexplicable total considering the success of the running game in the first three contests.

Tony Romo threw for 300 yards and three TDs, including an 11-yarder to Miles Austin in the final two minutes to bring the Cowboys within two. They nearly recovered an onside kick for a chance to win, but the ball glanced off the fingers of Sam Hurd and out of bounds. Shaun Suisham kicked four field goals for the Redskins, including three consecutive boots in the second half after the score was tied at 17–17.

GAME 5: Dallas Keeps Cincy Winless

Cowboys 31 vs. Cincinnati 22

October 5: The winless Bengals made a bid to overcome a 17–0 deficit but could never quite get there. It took Tony Romo throwing TD tosses to Terrell Owens and Patrick Crayton in the final quarter to keep Cincinnati at bay each time the visitors moved within a point or two.

Romo threw three scoring strikes for the second straight week but amassed only 176 passing yards. Most of the Dallas damage came on the ground, with Felix Jones running for 96 yards and a score on just nine carries and Marion Barber toting 23 times for 84. The Bengals staged their comeback on a pair of second-half TD passes from Carson Palmer to T.J. Houshmandzadeh.

GAME 6: Not-So-Special Teams

Arizona 30 vs. Cowboys 24 (OT)

October 12: A frustrating loss for Dallas began and ended with historic firsts. Arizona's J.J. Arrington sprinted 93 yards to become the first foe ever to return the opening kickoff for a TD against the Cowboys. More than three hours later, the Cardinals became the first team ever to win an overtime game on a blocked punt, when Sean Morey smothered the kick right off the foot of Mat McBriar and Monty Beisel picked it up for the easy score. McBriar was trying for his 300th consecutive punt without having one blocked.

In between those gaffes, the Cowboys did some good things. Tony Romo threw for 321 yards and enjoyed his third consecutive three-TD game. His 70-yarder to Marion Barber and a 52-yard Nick Folk field goal allowed Dallas to overcome a 24–14 fourth-quarter shortage to force the extra session. The Cowboys amassed a 98-yard advantage in total offense, but it was the Cardinals who made history.

GAME 7: Dallas Stumbles Again

St. Louis 34 vs. Cowboys 14

October 19: A third loss in four games seemed inconceivable just a few weeks earlier when Dallas was playing like one of the best clubs in the NFL. Playing without QB Tony Romo (broken finger) against the Rams, the Cowboys looked nothing like a contender.

Veteran Brad Johnson filled in for Romo and threw three interceptions. Marion Barber gave Dallas 100 rushing yards and a score, but he was overshadowed by Rams speedster Steven Jackson, who went for 160 and three TDs. St. Louis played turnover-free football, while the Cowboys coughed up the ball four times.

DeMarcus Ware notched three of Dallas' five sacks against Rams QB Marc Bulger.

GAME 8: Defense Wins It

Cowboys 13 vs. Tampa Bay 9

October 26: With Tony Romo still sidelined by a broken finger and the offense still struggling, the Dallas defense took it upon itself to end a two-game slump. Never in club history had the Cowboys ever won a game with as few as 172 total yards—that is until this day against a similarly offensively challenged foe.

Roy Williams scored the game's only TD on a two-yard pass from Brad Johnson in the second quarter. Tampa Bay managed just three Matt Bryant field goals, while Nick Folk kicked two for the Cowboys. The Buccaneers moved to the Dallas 18-yard line in the final minute, but

Quarterback Donovan McNabb (No. 5) of the Philadelphia Eagles gets sacked by linebacker Greg Ellis (No. 98) at Lincoln Financial Field November 4, 2007, in Philadelphia, Pennsylvania. The Cowboys won 38–17. (Photo by Drew Hallowell/Getty Images)

they were stopped on fourth-and-5. Marion Barber ran for 71 yards, while the rest of the Cowboys produced minus-1 on the ground.

GAME 9: Giants Too Much

N.Y. Giants 35 vs. Cowboys 14

November 2: A loaded NFC East would not be ruled by the Cowboys this year—not after their convincing loss to a Giants club that improved to 8–1. Again playing without QB Tony Romo, Dallas staggered to 183 yards of offense and committed four turnovers, three on interceptions by Romo replacements Brad Johnson and Brooks Bollinger.

Eli Manning passes resulted in four TDs—three to his own players and one that was intercepted and returned for a score by Mike Jenkins. The pick produced the only Dallas points until the fourth quarter. Brandon Jacobs rushed for 117 yards for the Giants, who ran for 200 yards as a team.

GAME 10: Second-Half TD Sparks Win

Cowboys 14 at Washington 10

November 16: After three games off, Tony Romo and his pinkie finger were just what Dallas needed at Washington. The QB threw a 25-yard TD pass to Martellus Bennett in the fourth quarter to lift the Cowboys back into the NFC playoff picture.

Romo, who watched from the sidelines as Dallas lost two of three games, completed 19-of-

27 passes for 198 yards and was intercepted twice. However, there was no denying that his presence made a difference in the huddle and the attack. Marion Barber carried 24 times for 114 yards and a TD. Romo's TD pass was the only second-half scoring. Washington took an 7–0 lead but then struggled, finishing with 228 yards.

GAME 11: Romo Right on Target

Cowboys 35 vs. San Francisco 22

November 23: Tony Romo threw for 341 yards and TD passes to three different receivers as Texas Stadium celebrated his return, along with a big win over the 49ers. A 75-yard bomb to Terrell Owens in the second quarter overcame a 6–0 deficit and started the Cowboys on a run of 29 consecutive points to break open the game.

Owens had a huge day, catching seven balls for 213 yards and the score. Marion Barber totaled 109 yards—59 rushing and 50 on seven receptions. Patrick Crayton and Martellus Bennett also caught TD passes. Shaun Hill threw for 303 yards for the 49ers but was sacked four times and intercepted once.

GAME 12: That Magic 400 Mark

Cowboys 34 vs. Seattle 9

November 27: Dallas topped 400 total yards for the second time in four days while dispatching Seattle on Thanksgiving. It was a number the Cowboys reached twice in the first three games of the season but one they had failed to

Sack Man: DeMarcus Ware

"Big Softie" off the Field Becomes Fearsome on Sundays

His wife, former Air Force personnel worker Taniqua, calls him a "big softie." DeMarcus Ware wooed her at their Alabama high school and wrote poems to help win her love. Their lives were devastated by the stillbirth of a son, Omar, in 2006 and rejuvenated with the 2008 adoption of Marley, an infant daughter who means everything to the Wares. Not a day goes by, DeMarcus says, when he doesn't think of Omar and how no single breath should be taken for granted.

For NFL quarterbacks, the sight of Ware bearing down on them brings anything but "big softie" to mind. The Troy University product, drafted 11th overall in 2005, is perhaps the most frightening pass rusher in football—capable of changing any game or bruising any foe on a single play.

"He's brought back that combination of a rush linebacker and a drop linebacker in a 3-4 system," noted future Hall of Fame linebacker Derrick Brooks. "I think he's the epitome of what teams that play the 3-4 look for. He's one of the bright young players in our league right now."[1]

Ware's star shines largely because he can do it all. His combination of strength, agility, and quickness makes him a pass-rushing menace. In 2007 and '08, he tied an NFL record with a string of 10 consecutive games with at least one sack. Before sacks were an official NFL stat, however, Harvey Martin registered one in 11 straight games, so Ware still has his eye on bettering the all-time Cowboys mark.

Ware led the league with 20 sacks in 2008 and became the first NFL player to win the Butkus Award, given to the game's best linebacker. Prior to 2008, the award was reserved only for college players. In addition to his pass-rushing skills, he is an exceptional team player who can cover, tackle, and stop the run at a high level.

"He's just got tremendous effort," said Jon Gruden, who considered drafting Ware when his Buccaneers had the No. 5 pick in 2005.

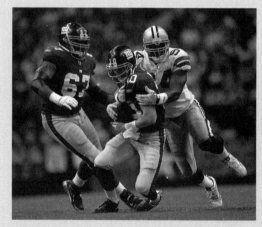

DeMarcus Ware (No. 94) sacks Eli Manning (No. 10) of the New York Giants on December 14, 2008, at Texas Stadium in Irving, Texas. The Cowboys defeated the Giants, 20–8. (Photo by G. Newman Lowrance/Getty Images)

"Forget about the sacks. The man is in on every play. He's got an arsenal of moves. I just love the way he plays. He's just got tremendous stamina."[2]

Ware already stands third on the Cowboys' career sack list, with 64½. Having signed a six-year contract extension while helping the 2009 team rank No. 2 in the NFL in total defense, he has a great chance to surpass Greg Ellis (77) and Jim Jeffcoat (94½) for the franchise's career sack record.

Not bad for a "big softie."

approach in the three-game absence of QB Tony Romo. The Dallas field general also enjoyed his second straight 300-yard three-TD passing game, throwing for 331 yards on a rate of 22-of-34.

Jason Witten (nine catches for 115 yards) and Terrell Owens (five for 98) caught scoring strikes for Dallas, which took a 14–0 first-quarter lead and was never threatened. Though the Seahawks got 287 passing yards from Matt Hasselbeck, the Cowboys' defense bore down when it had to, holding Seattle to three Olindo Mare field goals.

GAME 13: Dallas Relents at Pittsburgh

Pittsburgh 20 vs. Cowboys 13

December 7: It was there for the taking. Dallas held a 13–3 lead entering the fourth quarter and appeared to be on its way to a third straight victory—a win that could have stamped the Cowboys as a contender. In one quarter, however, it was gone.

Pittsburgh scored the last 17 points on a Jeff Reed field goal, a scoring pass from Ben Roethlisberger to Heath Miller, and a 25-yard interception return TD from Deshea Townsend. That crushing blow came with 1:40 on Tony Romo's third interception, capping a five-turnover day for the Cowboys. It was a defensive struggle from the outset, with each team managing one offensive TD and finishing below 100 net rushing yards and 200 net passing yards. But turnovers and the Steelers' late charge decided the outcome.

GAME 14: Sack Happy

Cowboys 20 vs. N.Y. Giants 8

December 14: The powerful Giants had no answer for the Dallas pass rush, falling under a swarm of star-helmeted defenders at Texas Stadium. The Cowboys sacked Eli Manning eight times while holding the Giants to 218 yards, keeping them from ever crossing the 10-yard line and sending them to just their third loss of the season.

DeMarcus Ware stopped Manning three times behind the line of scrimmage, powering the Cowboys' dominant defensive performance. Greg Ellis made 2½ sacks, and Terence Newman intercepted Manning twice. Tony Romo passed for two Dallas TDs, and Tashard Choice ran for another on a 91-yard rushing day.

GAME 15: Sad Farewell for Stadium

Baltimore 33 at Cowboys 24

December 20: Hollywood might have written a different ending to the final game at Texas Stadium. Instead of a triumphant win that put the Cowboys in playoff position, they coughed up a mistake-filled loss to the Ravens that assured just the opposite.

Ten penalties, 21 incompletions, two interceptions from Tony Romo, and a defense that allowed Baltimore two 100-yard rushers (Le'Ron McClain and Willis McGahee) and nearly 400 total yards doomed Dallas. Matt Stover's three field goals gave Baltimore a 9–7 halftime lead, and the Ravens' 24-point second half kept the Cowboys from reclaiming the lead.

Romo delivered fourth-quarter TD passes to Terrell Owens and Jason Witten, but each time the Ravens answered with a score of their own.

GAME 16: Mighty Collapse

Philadelphia 44 vs. Cowboys 6

December 28: Needing a victory to stay alive for the playoffs, Dallas instead had a meltdown, suffering its most lopsided loss in two decades— the most convincing under the ownership of Jerry Jones. The Eagles broke a 3–3 tie after one quarter with 41 consecutive points to eliminate the Cowboys from playoff contention and cause consternation that would last into the offseason.

The Eagles' Chris Clemons and Joselio Hanson returned fumbles for TDs of 73 and 96 yards, respectively, to open the second-half scoring and build on a 27–3 halftime lead. Those fumbles were two of the Cowboys' five turnovers in the game. Philadelphia outgained Dallas by just five offensive yards, but that was no consolation for the Cowboys. Donovan McNabb threw for two scores and ran for another.

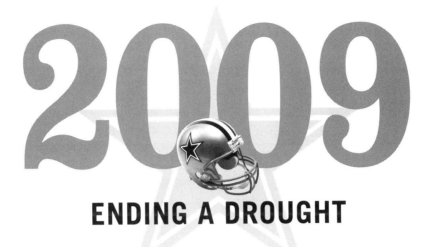

2009

ENDING A DROUGHT

Cowboys Get Back Into Postseason Win Column

Missing the playoffs, as they did the previous season, or bowing out in another postseason opener were not options that were going to qualify as any semblance of success for the talented 2009 Cowboys. They fell short of their ultimate goal, but the team did manage to exorcise a few demons with an inspired finish.

On the cusp of failure after beginning December with back-to-back losses, the Cowboys handed the Saints their first loss of the year and shut out the rival Redskins and Eagles in consecutive weeks to claim the NFC East at 11–5.

Playing the best defense in the NFL at season's end, Dallas then whipped Philadelphia for the second time in as many weeks to win its first playoff game since 1996. With Miles Austin emerging as a big-play threat for Tony

Romo as well as Marion Barber, Felix Jones, and Tashard Choice sharing the rushing load, Dallas gained the second-most yards in the NFL while its defense allowed the second-fewest points.

The road ended at Minnesota in the divisional playoff round, but it's a high bar the Cowboys will aim to hurdle as a new decade dawns.

GAME 1: For Openers, Romo 3–0

Cowboys 34 at Tampa Bay 21

September 13: The offseason release of Terrell Owens, Tony Romo's top end-zone target, did not stop Romo from winning his third season opener in as many tries. The Cowboys QB threw for 353 yards and hit three receivers for long TDs in a big-play barrage to bury the Buccaneers.

Romo threw for scores of 42 yards to Miles Austin, 66 to Roy Williams, and 80 to Patrick Crayton against a Tampa Bay defense susceptible to the home-run ball. The first of those TDs, which went to Austin, gave the Cowboys the lead for good at 13–7. Each team reached the 450-yard mark in total offense and neither committed a turnover, but Romo's impact plays made the difference.

GAME 2: Spectacular Opener Spoiled

N.Y. Giants 33 at Cowboys 31

September 20: The largest crowd ever to witness a regular-season NFL game—105,121 fans—jammed the new Cowboys Stadium. Most of the people were rooting for a team that stumbled in grand fashion on the grand stage. Four turnovers led to 24 Giants points, and New York got a 37-yard field goal from Lawrence Tynes as time expired to ruin Dallas' opening of a magnificent new home.

Tony Romo threw three interceptions, all of which led to TDs. One was returned 34 yards for a TD by Bruce Johnson, and nine seconds later Felix Jones fumbled away the ensuing kickoff to set up a New York field goal. Given the extra chances, Eli Manning shredded the Dallas defense for 330 yards and two TDs. His top targets, Mario Manningham and Steve Smith, caught 10 balls and one TD apiece. Marion Barber ran for 124 yards and Jones 96, and each scored once for the Cowboys.

GAME 3: Now It's Home

Cowboys 21 vs. Carolina 7

September 28: After six quarters in its new home, Dallas was wondering whether all the fuss over Cowboys Stadium was worth it, but the second half changed all that. The Cowboys recovered from a 7–0 halftime shortfall with 21 points to earn their first win in their sparking palace.

There was nothing fancy about it. The Cowboys took advantage of three Carolina turnovers, getting a 27-yard TD return from Terence Newman after he intercepted a Jake Delhomme pass, and amassed 449 yards of total offense. Tashard Choice raced for Dallas' lone offensive TD for a 10–7 lead in the third frame, Tony Romo threw for 255 yards, and Choice and Felix Jones combined for 176 on the ground.

GAME 4: Broncos Barge Past Dallas

Denver 17 vs. Cowboys 10

October 4: The Broncos completed a comeback from a 10–0 deficit on a 51-yard strike from Kyle Orton to Brandon Marshall in the last two minutes, keeping Dallas from taking back-to-back games for the first time. The winning TD left enough time for Tony Romo to take the Cowboys to the Denver 2 in the final seconds, but two straight pass plays failed from that range.

Orton completed 20-of-29 passes with second-half TDs to Knowshon Moreno and Marshall to carry his team to a fourth straight victory. Marion Barber had given Dallas a 10-point lead with his first-half TD plunge, but rushing yards were difficult to come by against the Broncos. Barber gained just 41 to lead the Cowboys. Romo threw for 255 yards for the second straight game.

GAME 5: Miles to Go

Cowboys 26 at Kansas City 20 (OT)

October 11: Dallas won a game and gained a star while weathering a scare at Kansas City. Miles Austin caught the winning 60-yard pass in overtime, capping a day on which he amassed a club-record 250 receiving yards on 10 receptions. After dropping two early passes that would have produced scores, the fourth-year pro reached the end zone twice while more than tripling his previous career high of three receptions in a game.

The Cowboys needed every one of Austin's catches against a Chiefs team that had yet to win a game. His first TD grab from Tony Romo covered 59 yards in the fourth quarter and gave Dallas its first lead of the game at 20–13. But Kansas City marched 74 yards to tie the game with 24 seconds remaining on a 16-yarder from Matt Cassel to Dwayne Bowe. Romo threw for 351 yards, but the Cowboys' two lost fumbles aided the Chiefs' upset bid.

GAME 6: Big Plays Burn Birds

Cowboys 37 vs. Atlanta 21

October 25: Tony Romo threw for 311 yards and three scores, while Miles Austin continued his coming-out party with six catches for 171 yards—two of those TDs—providing Dallas with its first back-to-back wins of the season. Romo hit 21-of-29 passes and added 31 rushing yards while directing an attack that gained 414 yards and scored 17 second-quarter points.

The Cowboys also rode a big day from their special teams. Nick Folk kicked three field goals, and Patrick Crayton returned a punt 73 yards for a score to go along with his five-yard TD grab. Dallas sacked Matt Ryan four times and intercepted him twice.

GAME 7: Spreading the Wealth
Cowboys 38 vs. Seattle 17

November 1: Ten Cowboys caught passes and six different players carried the ball in another impressive offensive performance. Tony Romo threw three TD passes with no single receiver gaining more than 61 yards. Marion Barber ran for a score and had a team-leading 53 rushing yards. It was one of those team-first days coaches love. Patrick Crayton also returned a punt 82 yards for a score that helped turn the game into a second-half rout. Seattle never led after kicking an early field goal, despite two TD tosses from Matt Hasselbeck.

GAME 8: A Whole New Team
Cowboys 20 at Philadelphia 16

November 8: Dallas considered Lincoln Financial Field a crime scene of sorts, at least on this visit. It was the site of the Cowboys' 38-point collapse 11 months earlier. The score, 44–6, was all one needed to mention to get their attention. Their ghosts were exorcised thanks to a 49-yard pass from Tony Romo to Miles Austin that broke a 13–13 fourth-quarter tie. It was

Austin's only reception of the game.

Romo completed 21-of-34 passes for 307 yards and never allowed his team to fall behind, where they had spent the entire game on their last trip to Philadelphia. Tashard Choice ran two yards for the game's first score, and Nick Folk kicked two field goals. Eagles QB Donovan McNabb threw two interceptions.

GAME 9: Four-Game Streak Ends
Green Bay 17 vs. Cowboys 7

November 15: The Cowboys' midseason dash hit a roadblock at Lambeau Field, where the Packers kept them out of the end zone until the fourth quarter. Truth be told, the visitors did just as much to keep themselves from scoring for most of the game.

Dallas committed three turnovers and gave up early on the running game, throwing 39 passes against 14 carries. Tony Romo completed 24 of those throws, but it wasn't until late in the game that he found Roy Williams for a score. By then, Packers QB Aaron Rodgers had run for one TD and passed for another for a 17–0 lead. The Green Bay defense sacked Romo five times, while Rodgers was dropped for four sacks.

GAME 10: Just Enough
Cowboys 7 vs. Washington 6

November 22: Back in 1970, Dallas earned a 6–2 decision over Cleveland. Football is a different game these days, but this one-point

Running back Marion Barber rushes upfield against the New Orleans Saints on December 19, 2009, at the Louisiana Superdome in New Orleans, Louisiana. (Photo by Al Messerschmidt/Getty Images)

win—the Cowboys' lowest-scoring victory since the aforementioned game—was a throwback. Tony Romo found Patrick Crayton from the 10-yard line for the winning TD with 2:42 left in the game. Anthony Spencer then intercepted Jason Campbell to preserve the win.

The Cowboys limited the Redskins to 78 rushing yards and held them to a pair of field goals. Romo completed only 15 passes all day, but seven of them came on the winning drive. Marion Barber led all rushers with 20 carries for 99 yards.

GAME 11: Offense Erupts

Cowboys 24 vs. Oakland 7

November 26: After back-to-back games with just one offensive TD, Dallas celebrated Thanksgiving with 494 yards of offense. The Cowboys broke loose in the first half for a 17–0 cushion and cruised past a Raiders team that entered with just three wins.

Big-yardage plays were the course of the day on this holiday. Felix Jones ripped off one of the first—a 46-yard run for the first TD of the game. Tony Romo passed for 309 yards and two TDs, while his top two targets, Miles Austin and Jason Witten, each covered 100-plus yards on receptions. Jones, Tashard Choice, and Marion Barber rushed for 60-plus yards apiece.

GAME 12: Dark December?

N.Y. Giants 31 vs. Cowboys 24

December 6: The Giants overcame a 17–14 second-half deficit with 17 points in a row, leaving Dallas fans wondering if this was the beginning of another December slide. Huge plays drove the surge. Brandon Jacobs turned an Eli Manning toss into a 74-yard TD pass, and Domenik Hixon returned a punt 79 yards for a score that pulled New York within one game of NFC East leaders Dallas and Philadelphia.

The Cowboys enjoyed one of their most prolific passing games. Tony Romo threw the ball a numbing 55 times, hitting 41 for 392 yards and three TDs without an interception. Jason Witten caught 14 balls for 156 yards, and Miles Austin made 10 grabs for 104 yards and a score. But the Giants overcame a 10–0 shortage for a 14–10 halftime lead before making their big second-half move.

GAME 13: Chargers Sharp in Texas

San Diego 20 at Cowboys 17

December 13: December continued to spell doom for Dallas, which lost back-to-back games to start a month that had troubled them in recent years. The Cowboys did not score their second TD until the final seconds against a Chargers team that made an impressive run to its 10th win of the year.

Philip Rivers went 21-of-32 for 272 yards and a TD, and San Diego never trailed after a one-yard TD run by LaDainian Tomlinson made it 7–3 in the first frame. Tony Romo threw for 249 yards and TDs to Miles Austin and Patrick Crayton. The former capped a 99-yard drive in the third quarter, but the latter came in the game's final seconds—too late against the high-powered Chargers. Nick Folk missed a field goal, and the Cowboys failed to score any points on a first-and-goal from the San Diego 4-yard line.

GAME 14: Superdome Statement

Cowboys 24 at New Orleans 17

December 19: As fate would have it, the Cowboys' make-or-break game came on the road against a Saints team making a bid for a perfect season. They used the occasion to play one of their best games in recent years, stamping themselves a legitimate contender in front of 70,000-plus fans at the Superdome and a national television audience.

Ending a December dive, Dallas shut down the Saints' top-ranked offense for three quarters while executing its own attack precisely and productively. Tony Romo outplayed MVP candidate Drew Brees, completing 22-of-34 passes for 312 yards and a TD to Miles Austin that gave the Cowboys a 7–0 lead. They made it 14–0 by the end of the opening quarter on a three-yard Marion Barber run and stretched it to 24–3 in the third on Barber's second score.

Romo and the Cowboys racked up 439 yards—topping high-flying New Orleans by more than 100—and did not commit a turnover. They sacked Brees (29-of-45 for 298) four times, intercepted him once, and recovered two New Orleans fumbles.

GAME 15: Downright Defensive

Cowboys 17 at Washington 0

December 27: Dallas clinched a playoff berth and recovered from consecutive losses to begin December, blanking the Redskins at FedEx Field. It was the Cowboys' first shutout in six seasons. That, too, came against Washington.

Sacking the Redskins four times, holding them to 43 rushing yards, and intercepting QB Jason Campbell were the defensive highlights. Offensively, the Cowboys lacked the fire they showed a week earlier in New Orleans, but they didn't need it. Marion Barber and Felix Jones combined for 121 rushing yards, and Tony Romo threw for 286 yards. His first-quarter TD pass to Roy Williams proved to be the game-winner.

GAME 16: New Decade, New Record

Cowboys 24 vs. Philadelphia 0

January 3, 2010: Dallas started 2010 by doing something unprecedented in franchise history—recording back-to-back shutouts. That they did so to culminate the 2009 regular season and beat the Eagles for NFC East supremacy made the second of those whitewashings even more special.

One Texas-Sized Home
Cowboys Stadium Sets New Standard in Sports

Jerry Jones, no stranger to controversy, surely pushed the limits with the planning, building, and 2009 unveiling of Cowboys Stadium. He compared it to the White House and Capitol building in stature, and its $1.15 billion price tag and local tax support in the midst of an economic recession rankled many who were dealing with issues such as job loss and putting dinner on the table.

Then again, pushing limits is what this palace was all about from the start. Its capacity can stretch to 110,000-plus with standing-room areas, the largest in the NFL. Its video board, the world's largest high-definition TV at 160 feet wide and 72 feet high, is a distraction to some, a wonder to others, and an obstruction to the occasional punter. Tennessee's A.J. Trapasso booted a punt off the bottom of it in a preseason game, prompting a rare NFL "do-over" that caused purists to cringe.

So many of the numbers are gaudy. The stadium itself covers 73 acres. The 660,000-square-foot retractable roof is one of the largest domed structures in the world. More than 105,000 fans, an

An arial photo of the new Cowboys Stadium. (Photo by AP Photo/Brandon Wade)

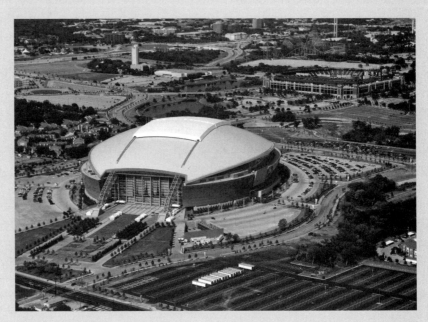

NFL regular-season record, attended the Cowboys' first game in their Taj Mahal on September 20, 2009. And a pizza—a very tasty pizza—goes for the jaw-dropping price of $60, though there are many more reasonably-priced options to be sure.

If everything's big in Texas, the state's biggest sports team might as well live in the most spectacular sports home.

"I could have built this for $850 million," Jones said. "And it would have been a fabulous place to play football. But this was such an opportunity for the 'wow' factor."[1]

Jones wanted one of the most recognizable buildings in the country, so he built it. Cowboys Stadium stands like a mecca with a sloping glass exterior in Arlington, giving fans of America's Team goosebumps as they approach. Even rival fans were star-struck during the grand opening.

"We compare [Jones] to [Yankees owner] George Steinbrenner," said Giants fan T.J. Churchill, who traveled from New Jersey to watch his team beat the Cowboys in the 2009 opener. "You get the money, you spend it. He sure can throw a party."[2]

Standing-room tickets started at $29 when the capacity was expanded for two crowds of 100,000-plus in the inaugural season. Seats began at $59 and climbed to $340 per ticket. Whether for parking or pizza, tickets or seat licenses, the dollars poured into the team's coffers by fans seemed worth it when the club treated them to their first playoff win since 1996—complete with all the comforts of home.

Instead of folding down the stretch, as they had in the recent past, the Cowboys raced into the playoffs having held the Eagles to 37 rushing yards while sacking Donovan McNabb four times. The offense contributed to the shutout by sustaining drives and keeping McNabb on the sidelines. Felix Jones and Marion Barber rushed for 91 yards apiece, with the former scoring on a 49-yard splash. Tony Romo threw for 311 yards, finding Jason Witten and Patrick Crayton for TDs.

GAME 17: Playoff Slump Ends
Cowboys 34 vs. Philadelphia 14

January 9, 2010: Facing Philly for the second time in as many weeks, or beating the Eagles for the third time in one season, could have seemed a daunting challenge. These Cowboys embraced the opportunity and won their first playoff game since 1996, treating 92,000-plus fans at Cowboys Stadium to a fourth consecutive clinic. It was the first postseason victory for Wade Phillips as a head coach.

Four different Cowboys scored TDs. Felix Jones did so on a 73-yard third-quarter sprint that highlighted his 148-yard rushing day. Tony Romo threw for 244 yards and two TDs and directed a 426-yard offensive attack. Although the defense gave up its first points in more than nine quarters, it also generated four sacks and four turnovers and held Philadelphia to 56 rushing yards.

GAME 18: Favre Cools Cowboys

Minnesota 34 vs. Cowboys 3

January 16, 2010: The Vikings' Brett Favre became the first 40-year-old QB ever to win an NFL playoff game, putting a chill on one of the hottest teams in football with four TD passes at the Metrodome. The first three went to Sidney Rice, and the fourth—on a fourth down in the last two minutes, no less—had Cowboys defender Keith Brooking calling the move "classless and disrespectful."

Since handing New Orleans its first loss almost a month earlier, the Cowboys had looked like one of the NFL's best. On this day, though, both their offense and defense failed. As Favre enjoyed one of his best postseason performances, Dallas QB Tony Romo was sacked six times, lost two fumbles, and threw an interception.

The Cowboys gained 118 yards in the opening quarter but added just 130 more over the final three frames.

NOTES

A Star is Born

1. "High Finance: Texas on Wall Street," *Time*, June 16, 1961
   http://www.time.com/time/magazine/article/0,9171,895393-6,00.html#ixzz0dYbyzAPE
2. "C.W. Murchison Jr. Dies in Texas at 63," *New York Times*, April 1, 1987.
   http://www.nytimes.com/1987/04/01/obituaries/cw-murchison-jr-dies-in-texas-at-63.html?pagewanted=1

Bigger Than Texas

1. Pro Football Hall of Fame induction speech.

"Chiseled from Granite"

1. Thiel, Art of the *Seattle Post-Intelligencer*. "Landry passed test of character," *Houston Chronicle*,
   February 20, 2000.

Mr. Cowboy

1. Carroll, Bob. *Football Legends of All-Time,* (Lincolnwood, IL: Publications International, 1997), p. 112.

Dandy Don

1. Cartwright, Gary. "Tony Romo Is the Greatest Cowboys Quarterback Since…" *Texas Monthly,*
   September 2008. http://www.texasmonthly.com/2008-09-01/feature2.php

Doomsday 'Backer

1. Lee Goddard, *Corpus Christi Caller-Times,* August 2, 2004
2. http://www.dallascowboys.com/history_roh_player.cfm?art=3

Bad, Bad Lee Roy Jordan

1. Lebreton, Gil. "Cowboys Are Only 13 Years Late in Honoring Lee Roy Jordan," *Chicago Tribune*,
   November 26, 1989.

Teacher Had a Vision

1. Renfro's recollection from his Hall of Fame induction speech.
2. Ibid.

World's Fastest Human

1. Monk, Cody. *Legends of the Dallas Cowboys* (Champaign, Ill.: Sports Publishing, LLC, 2004), p. 80.

Super Bowl V: The Blooper Bowl

1. Maule, Tex. "Eleven Big Mistakes," Sports Illustrated, Jan. 25, 1971.
   http://sportsillustrated.cnn.com/vault/article/magazine/MAG1084508/1/index.htm

Super Bowl VI: Champs at Last

1. Postgame interview. Video footage. http://www.youtube.com/watch?v=z4AXteskxP0
2. Ibid.

Milestone Man Hill is First to 1,000

1. Ivy League Black History, May 22, 2007. http://ivy50.com/blackHistory/story.aspx?sid=5/22/2007

Captain Comeback

1. Melody,Tom. *Akron Beacon Journal,* July 31, 1985.

Super Bowl X: Comeback Falls Short Against Steel Curtain

1. "Slipper didn't quite fit size, 21–17," *Dallas Morning News*, January 19, 1976,
   http://www.dallasnews.com/sharedcontent/dws/spt/football/cowboys/classic/superbowls/x/
2. Ibid.

Sunday was Doomsday for Dallas Foes

1. "Doomsday Defense Legends See Super Cowboys Run Possible," *USA Today*, January 11, 2010.
   http://www.usatoday.com/sports/football/nfl/cowboys/2010-01-10-cowboys-win- follow_N.htm

Super Bowl XII: Orange Crushed

1. "Doomsday in the Dome," *Sports Illustrated*, Jan. 23, 1978, http://sportsillustrated.cnn.com/football/features/superbowl/archives/12/

Super Bowl XIII: Loss to Steelers Smarts

1. Several sources, including ESPN.com, http://espn.go.com/page2/s/superbowlmoments50.html
2. "Dumb Like a F-O-X," *The Sporting News*, 1998 Super Bowl recaps.

Captain Crash

1. Harris, Cliff, and Charlie Waters. *Tales from the Dallas Cowboys* (Champaign, Ill.: Sports Publishing, LLC, 2003), p. viii.

Texas Stadium: A Heavenly View

1. Final-game announcement to crowd: Farewell to Texas Stadium tribute. http://www.farewelltotexasstadium.com/article.cfm?id=604A682F-AF6C-D2FD-83DB8FF459393828
2. Ibid.

America's Team

1. Annenberg School for Communication, Penn University, Alumni Spotlight: http://www.asc.upenn.edu/alumni/Bob-Ryan-and-Bill-Strong.aspx
2. "Cowboys' America's Team Mystique Doesn't Mean Much Here in the 'Hood," *St. Paul Pioneer Press*, January 10, 2010.
   http://www.twincities.com/ci_14162665?source=rss_viewed&nclick_check=1
3. ESPN.com, "The Great Debate: America's Team," http://espn.go.com/blog/nflnation/post/_/id/6329/the-great-debate-america-s-team

Dynamic Duo

1. Pearson, Drew. *Hail Mary: The Drew Pearson Story* (Denton, Texas: Rogers Publishing and Consulting, 2006), p. 254.

In Roger's Shadow: Danny White

1. Danny White's official Web site: http://www.dannywhite.com/bio.htm

The Manster

1. Cliff Harris and Charlie Waters, *Tales from the Dallas Cowboys Sidelines*, p. 107.
2. *Sports Illustrated*, http://sportsillustrated.cnn.com/vault/article/magazine/MAG1122764/4/
   index.htm

Touchdown, Tony Dorsett

1. "Dorsett Scores Big on His Day at Canton," *Pittsburgh Post-Gazette*, July 31, 1994.
2. "Dorsett, White to be inducted today into Hall of Fame," *Austin American-Statesman*, Saturday, July 30, 1994.

Herschel Walker: Locomotive on Spikes

1. "Herschel's in the Hall," University of Georgia, http://www.uga.edu/gm/300/FeatHerschel.html

Pickin' It: Everson Walls

1. *A Gift for Ron* As mentioned in this article from the Dallas Morning News
2. http://nflblog.dallasnews.com/archives/2009/11/book-review-gift-for-ron-by-ev.html

All the Way with J.J.

1. "How Johnson Built a Winner from Scratch," The Associated Press, January 17, 1993.
2. Jimmy Johnson press conference, March 29, 1994.

Man with the Golden Arm

1. Farmer, Sam. "Aikman's Journey Ends in Canton," *Los Angeles Times*, August 5, 2006.
2. Aron, Jaime, "Cowboys' Aikman did whatever it took," *The (Fredericksburg) Free Lance-Star*, August 5, 2006.

The Playmaker

1. Quote from Michael Irvin's Pro Football Hall of Fame induction speech.

Super Bowl XXVII: Buffalo Blitz

1. "Any Questions?" *Dallas Morning News*, February 1, 1993.
   http://www.dallasnews.com/sharedcontent/dws/spt/football/cowboys/classic/recordbook/
   yearbyyear/1992/020193bills.html

Super Bowl XXVIII: Back-To-Back Bills Beatings

1. "The Fumble!" *Sports Illustrated*, February 7, 1994. http://sportsillustrated.cnn.com/football/features/superbowl/archives/28/

Switch to Switzer: Familiar Formula, Different Direction

1. Video of Barry Switzer press conference, March 30, 1994.
2. "Top Five Reasons You Can't Blame Jerry Jones for the Demise of the Cowboys," ESPN, September 11, 2006.

Super Bowl XXX: Dynasty Determined

1. "Super Bowl 30: The Last of the Elites," *The Sporting News*, Feb. 5, 1996.
   http://www.sportingnews.com/archives/superbowl/30.html
2. "XXX-CELLENT," *Dallas Morning News*, Jan. 29, 1996. http://www.dallasnews.com/
   sharedcontent/dws/spt/football/cowboys/classic/superbowls/xxx/

Neon Deion

1. Both quotes from "Double-duty Deion," *Sport*, October 1996.

Troy's Protectors

1. ESPN.com, "Aikman was Lucky, and Good," http://sports.espn.go.com/espn/page2/story?page=bayless/060807

2. "If Giants Tweak Aikman, Cowboys Are Vulnerable," *New York Times*, December 16, 1995. http://www.nytimes.com/1995/12/16/sports/ pro-football-if-giants-tweak-aikman-cowboys- are-vulnerable.html?pagewanted=1

Team of the '90s

1. "The Team of The '90s?" *Sports Illustrated*, Sept. 7, 1992, http://sportsillustrated.cnn.com/vault/article/magazine/MAG1004192/2/index.htm

Magic Man

1. Shapiro, Leonard. *The Dallas Cowboys* (St. Martin's, 1993), p. 39.

2. *Sports Illustrated*, http://sportsillustrated.cnn.com/football/nfl/features/smith/timeline/

The Maverick: Jerry Jones

1. Ask Men, Jerry Jones Profile, 2009. http://www.askmen.com/celebs/men/ business_politics_60/72_jerry_jones.html

2. Dallasnews.com, "Jerry Jones Driven by Criticism of Dallas Cowboys," January 20, 2009, http://www.dallasnews.com/sharedcontent/dws/spt/football/cowboys/ stories/012109dnspocowlede.34972b9.html

"Big Tuna" Makes a Splash

1. 60 Minutes, "Bill Parcells: On the Couch," interview with Mike Wallace, October 3, 2004. http://www.cbsnews.com/stories/2003/08/28/60minutes/main570622.shtml

Tight End Tradition

1. Official Cowboys website: Top 50 All-Time Players http://www.dallascowboys.com/news/ news.cfm?id=A72865DC-0375-4C9D-74EBCAC479C5AE80

Star Power: The Dallas Cowboys Cheerleaders

1. Press release. PRWeb. Jan. 23, 2010. http://www.prweb.com/releases/2010/01/ prweb3502534.htm

Overnight Sensation

1. Fox,Ashley. "Boys find their man in Mr. Romo," *The Philadelphia Inquirer*, December 20, 2006.

Son of a Bum

1. Dallas Cowboys official site, "Like Father, Like Son," October 29, 2009. http://www.dallascowboys.com/news/news.cfm?id=A2A1943D-9DC0- 465A-FA1A498247610152

Sack Man: DeMarcus Ware

1. "Wade Calls Cowboys LB Ware 'Pretty Amazing,'" *The Associated Press*, October 31, 2008. http://cbs11tv.com/sports/DeMarcus.Ware.NFL.2.853423.html

2. Ibid.

One Texas-Sized Home

1. *New York Times*, July 16, 2009, http://www.nytimes.com/2009/07/17/sports/football/17cowboys.html

2. CBS News, September 21, 2009, http://www.cbsnews.com/stories/2009/09/21/sportsline/main5326868.shtml